MW01049834

TACOPEDIA

DÉBORAH HOLTZ
JUAN CARLOS MENA

5x15
10
F.C REAL
SAN LUCAS

PART 1
WHETTING YOUR APPETITE

PART 2
IT'S TACO TIME

PART 3
MEET THE FAMILY

FOREWORD

RENÉ REDZEPI

I'll never forget the first time I set off for Mexico many years ago. It was winter in Denmark, I was worn out from work, and I needed a beach.

As I sat there on the long plane ride over, I couldn't help but dread the fact that I was going to have to eat the food.

You see, in Europe it's virtually impossible to get a mouthful of authentic Mexican food. What we have here is a type of Tex-Mex, a tradition born in the U.S. that certainly has its rare pleasures. But imagine that variant being sent through a game of intercontinental telephone (Chinese whispers): what ends up here in Scandinavia is so far from its origins that it's downright sad. I foolishly thought it would be the same in Mexico.

"What the heck, you have your books and the beach," I reassured myself. "Just live off fruit."

We landed fairly late in Mérida, about 11:30 in the evening, and we were starving. I asked our host for something to eat. Stupid as I was, I requested pizza. He looked at me funny. I could almost hear him thinking "Stupid gringo."

We drove a good thirty minutes from the airport before stopping at a nondescript, over-lit restaurant. There was outdoor seating, all covered in plastic and soft drink logos. "This is it," he said as we pulled over. "We'll grab a bite here."

"Remember the beach, remember the beach," I repeated like a mantra to myself as we sat down, but within an instant I forgot those words.

Ice-cold beers arrived at our table in a flash, as our host signaled the kitchen to send us a round of tacos al pastor. As I stared down at the plate, the first thing I noticed was that the tortillas had a yellow hue to them that was so different from the white and dense variety I was used to finding in Denmark. The grilled pork was flaky and moist. There were fresh leaves of emerald-green cilantro sprinkled on top, as well as some thin slices of pineapple. On the side, a little condiment of sour orange juice with habanero. "Put seven drops of that on your pineapple," the host told me.

I did, and folded the taco together. It was already levels above what I had experienced in Europe—the aroma, the very look of it. But then I sunk my teeth in. Immediately I felt the tenderness, the rich umami character of the meat. And the tortilla! It was sweet and smoky, with a gentle chew to it, like a good sourdough bread. Suddenly the spice from the habaneros hit me, kept in check by the sweet, succulent pineapple.

That perfect bite made it a moment I'll always remember, sitting on those plastic chairs in the tropical heat.

WHY A TACOPEDIA?

DÉBORAH HOLTZ AND JUAN CARLOS MENA

Like any Mexican, the last stop before heading home from a party is to enjoy some good tacos.

One such night, I was left open-mouthed observing the expertise and coordination of the taco makers and everyone involved in the process of preparing a taco. At a taco outlet, everything functions with precision: the speed with which the taco maker slices the taco al pastor from the upright grill, or the steak or other filling he is cooking. The tortillas are shaped and heated to order, and the fresh salsas are placed on the table just as the customer arrives. Whatever time it is, the whole service works with a sense of rhythm and organization that contradicts the stereotypical ideas about Mexican apathy and inefficiency. I felt like I was observing a mechanism as reliable as a Swiss watch.

It occurred to me there must be something deeply rooted in our culture that makes tacos this culinary wonder loved by the whole world, that ensures the tortillas (our peerless contribution to the culinary universe) are perfectly cooked, that the salsas have just the right level of spice, and that the tacos are filled at five o'clock in the morning as if it were two in the afternoon, and served to people of all social classes. I realized that unlike any other dish, tacos are one of the most definitive traits of Mexican culture.

At that moment, the idea to pay tribute to the rich world of the taco was born: from recounting their remote history that is bound up with the corn that the Aztecs cultivated as their main food source, to explaining the different dishes in the words of those who prepare them, to the near-endless array of salsas that adorn them, and many other topics relating to this cuisine. In short, a portrait of an entire culture that revolves around this unique dish.

However, this was not a matter of producing an ordinary cookbook, but an encyclopedia. The project grew together with the desire to investigate and record every culinary detail and every local variant together with the perspectives of all those involved: taco makers, cooks, diners, the corn masa makers, et cetera.

Research, photographic documentation, editing, and design took four years. We allowed the book to shape itself organically, since throughout the process, we realized the need to include such things as the songs and the countless sayings relating to tacos, the chronicles of the astonished response of the Spanish Conquistadors when they discovered that the Mexicans eat tortillas, and even tweets on the theme.

Then there are the hundreds of utensils involved in their preparation, and the history of progress from handmade tortillas on a brazier to the invention of the individual metal tortilla-maker, and finally to the "Celorio" miniature production line that is, in a sense, our response to mass consumption, in every sense of the word. If at first we were unclear of the final product, as we assembled all the data in this handcrafted fashion, we could better focus on our goal. Having examined the sixteen types of tacos, for example, we asked: what was the opinion of the taco maker? Why all the different names? Which tacos are their best sellers?

Recipes had to be included, so with the help of leading taco makers and a wide range of sources, we selected those that every taco connoisseur should know.

The findings of our research led us to draw up a map illustrating the many and surprising taco varieties spread across the geography of Mexico: thus we mapped out the Tacography. It is our hope that after reading this book, you will seek to chart your own course through the world of the taco, and discover that all a good taco needs is the ability to roll up a good tortilla.

A-38-378

TACOS AND TAQUITOS

JORGE F. HERNANDEZ

Readers of this book be warned: a napkin will be required to catch the drooling that will inevitably occur when leafing through these pages. Their evocation of both the tacos and taco eateries, which have left their imprint on the Mexican national consciousness, may well inspire you to embark on your own personal chronicle of memorable tacos.

This tasty tome in your hands is, in fact, a full and expansive mural of the taco—a seemingly impossible endeavor precisely because of the ecumenical and widespread miracle of Mexican identity. Just like all of us are devotees of the Virgin of Guadalupe when it comes down to the line—yes, the atheists, too—we Mexicans also have a subtle appreciation of tacos: be it the reliable standby of steak tacos; the occasional daring *alambre*; the touristic excursion of a *gringa*; the sophistication of *suadero* tacos (a clandestine choice back in the day); the civic duty to combine intestines, stomach, and lungs in a single taco; the psychoanalytical minefield of an eyeball taco... And then there's the unfailing tradition of making the rounds at least once a month to taco stands so dear to us that they feel like they belong to us: be it the taco pilgrimage to Copacabana in Villa Coapa or the sentimental trip to Los Picudos, haven of reporters from the nearby *Proceso* offices.

There's the nighttime oasis of El Tizoncito and the memory of how they used to charge for tacos by counting the squares of paper each taco had been served in. And it's time to talk frankly about the whopping bets won in taco joints back then: that night when the *taquero* didn't believe how much I'd eaten and bet against me, and how, once the fifty tacos *al pastor* had been accounted for, my seven friends watched amazed as he paid our bill (I stank of marinated meat for weeks).

It seems that insane wagers of the sort are no more nowadays, despite the fact that taco culture doesn't usually change much from generation to generation. Even so, we've seen a vain parade of attempts to tint tacos with colors or even add different flavors that intend to start a Copernican revolution in the indisputable and privileged reign of pork chops with red salsa. We've witnessed the invention of cheese cracklings (going so far as to add cilantro and onion to its milky, Dalí-watch swoon), and inroads have also been made in the traditional menu by *costras* from the North, and all sorts of *volcanes*, as if the national geography changed with each taco generation. The thorough research undertaken by Alejandro Escalante and the tireless zeal of editors Déborah Holtz and Juan Carlos Mena take us on the adventure through *Tacopedia*, which goes back to the very beginnings of the tortilla, explaining that it is corn boiled in quicklime that becomes a flying saucer for every palate. Once the tortilla has been defined in all its shapes and sizes (from edible spoon to manna in the hand), we move on to another feat—perhaps the very essence of *Tacopedia*—with the chapter on the universe of the taco. While other cultures may explore outer space or delve into the enigmas of the deep sea, Mexicans are left to explore the everyday yet boundless territory of the taco: the changes in flavor from one meat to another, the topography (see pages 58–67) of the different cuts of beef, their exact locations (related perhaps to the particular flavor of each succulent marbled morsel), and the names of each flank, sirloin, chop and fillet, as if we were hiking through every plain, valley, hill, the uplands and wetlands of the land of our birth. In the world of tacos, there reigns, it seems, the erotic confusion of one roaming from thigh to breast, from hip to shoulder, falling in love with no less than the intestines, and puckering up for a kiss on the snout. The *Tacopedia* guides us through the different flavors of pork with a front and side profile in all its sweet-and-sour tang, then we move along to fish, lamb, and goat tacos, embarking on what could well be termed a galactic voyage through Mexican gastronomic culture, one that delves into every region and corner of the country.

Another smart move is the inclusion of the tacography (see pages 268–269), which appears in these pages so that the tropics don't get mixed up with the deserts, the mountains with the lagoons, or the valleys with the coast. There is no region or favorite haunt neglected in these tasty maps, which that should be required reading in all grade schools. With smart quotes and prose that goes down as quick as a taco, this book is erudition without pedantry. There's a linguistic tour from the origins and nature of the taco—be they from a flat griddle, a vertical grill, or a hole in the ground—to a lateral leap into the history and exploits of *birria* and head-meat tacos, then we sweat it out with basket tacos and *carnitas* (one of the most tender diminutives used in Mexico), followed by another trip through *chilorio*, *cochinita pibil*, all kinds of cooked meat, *tingas*, burritos, edible insects, *mixiotes*, and fish. The whole of Mexico is hungrily savored, with a clear explanation of the particular origin and even the preparation of each dish. The reader is wrapped up in something like the fervor felt when standing for the national anthem or hearing Moncayo's "Huapango," and feels a frenzied salivation, the nausea of a shipwreck survivor at the very idea of putting the book down for a few hours to satisfy the craving—then returning to the glorious page where *suadero* tacos, so often scorned at tables in past years, finally get their due. And we return to the guided tour of deep-fried tacos, *chimichangas*, and the long et cetera that each taco offers, with the precise address of the taco stands that will make it easier to move on to the next chapter. And indeed, in the next section, we find a parade of the dignified and lovable progeny of the taco family: enchiladas (so elegant and pampered), quesadillas (so gossipy that they spill it all as soon as they get warmed up), *tlayudas* (there to remind us that the family has deep ancestral roots). Then, wrapped up in the delirium of all these dear flavors, *Tacopedia* unleashes an indescribable explosion from an overflowing fountain—salsas, colors, flavors, preparations, tips, the whole shebang. The names read off like the notes in Casanova's little black book: *chilaca, pasilla, de arbol, jalapeño, habanero, piquín, chipotle*. Every explanation of each salsa is like a photo from a family gathering: "Taste buds enjoying the fiesta," reads the gossip column from the roof of the mouth at the arrival of fried green onions, tomatoes, cilantro, and chiles. Everything breaks into a dance in your mouth: it's salsa to the rhythm of saliva and satisfaction.

This book is a must for any reader willing to take up the challenge not to drool while reading, and carry on without wanting more than an eyeful of the eyeball tacos. Flipping pages like tortillas on a griddle, we come to a detailed tour of the derivatives of *the masa*: tamales and *chalupas*, *garnachas* and *panuchos*, *paseadas, picadas, pellizcadas*—a real picaresque piece! *Sopes*, *memelas*, *tlacoyos*, and the rest come under *antojitos* (providing a useful list of new nicknames we may need for our buddies), and then, an encyclopedic resource: the indispensable reference guide to all possible tamales, performing the unprecedented feat of breaking down tamales by region, as if taking a detailed X-ray of Mexico's soul. I firmly believe that *Tacopedia* is *the* gift for friends and family who've watched us stain their tablecloths or strut our stuff in greasy spoons of varying repute, because, in Mexico, at least, thou shalt not refuse thy neighbor a taco.

PANZA
CFE
TACOS
* PANZA * CORAZÓN
* LIBRO * MAZIZA
* TRIPA * NANA
* BOFE * UBRE
SURTIDO

TACOS

Bienvenidos
UERIA NUEV SAN FERNA

EVERYTHING FITS IN A TORTILLA

ALEJANDRO ESCALANTE

As Mexican as mariachi music, the taco is, without a doubt, Mexico's most popular food. Mexicans eat them so often that the expression *echarse un taco*, to grab a taco, is synonymous with eating. Tacos have, in fact, become so famous that they have crossed borders to become a symbol of Mexican cuisine. The taco, so commonplace and well-known, is hard to define, but we can start by saying that a taco is a maize tortilla wrapped around food. The tortilla is the vehicle, as well as a key element in itself. In its warm hospitality, it welcomes a vast array of stewed, grilled, fried meats, and other fillings, and on top, a tremendous variety of salsas and seasonings.

A taco, at its simplest, is a tortilla, filling, and salsa—the other holy trinity in Mexico—yet when these three elements are prepared with the proper care and ingredients, tacos can be raised to the status of haute cuisine. The nation's contrasts are also there to see, plain as day, in the taco. Tortilla in hand, you can make a taco with a pinch of salt or fillings of the simplest or most refined kind. Likewise, for salsas, which are so varied that they are an entire universe unto themselves and are thus assigned their own section in this book. In fact, the humble tortilla has an extraordinary capacity for adapting itself to fillings of every possible kind—meat, vegetables, fruit, cheese—and anything placed in a tortilla is, by definition, a taco.

Now, tacos are part of the wider world of *antojitos*. As such, they are just a kind of quick bite, an appetizer or a snack; but they can also be a meal in themselves. It's not unusual to see them served as the main course on tables across Mexico. From posh restaurants that serve international cuisine to taco restaurants that look like hamburger chains to metal shacks and street vendors—without forgetting the ubiquitous hole-in-the-wall, or the bikes and vans posted on strategic street corners—the shapes and sizes of places selling tacos are numerous. What's more, at important events like birthdays and weddings, the so-called *taquizas* come to the rescue, allowing the host to entertain guests with a wide range of fillings served up in pots, with tortillas ready for them to assemble their own tacos. We'll talk about homemade tacos later on, but in truth, the real taco—its essential flavor, its exoticism—is found outside, in the streets and in taco restaurants.

The inherent complexity of the different recipes means that many of them require long hours of preparation and are real specialties that should be made only by an expert. Instead of attempting to run through the long list of tacos, let's just say you can find almost any kind of taco out there on the street. You'll even come across new sorts that don't have names yet and, to top it off, you'll hear talk of morning tacos, daytime tacos, evening tacos, nighttime tacos—somehow all classified by some unwritten, ancestral code. At the end of the day, prestige aside, you never know exactly what's on your plate, which makes street tacos an unpredictable adventure—and not just a gastronomical, but a literal one, since some street vendors really like to live dangerously: like the taco stand perched on the sidewalk just feet from the eighteen-wheelers rumbling past, the gas tank placed a couple inches from the stove. And then there are the classic details: the plates wrapped in plastic bags, salt shakers that have acquired the patina of time through decades of use, napkins improvised from rough brown paper, and so many more. The street taco is personal and on the spot. It's made on demand—with this topping, with that, hold the

BY

1918

TACO
STANDS
IN
MEXICO CITY
WERE NO LONGER
CONSIDERED
INFORMAL

TRADE.

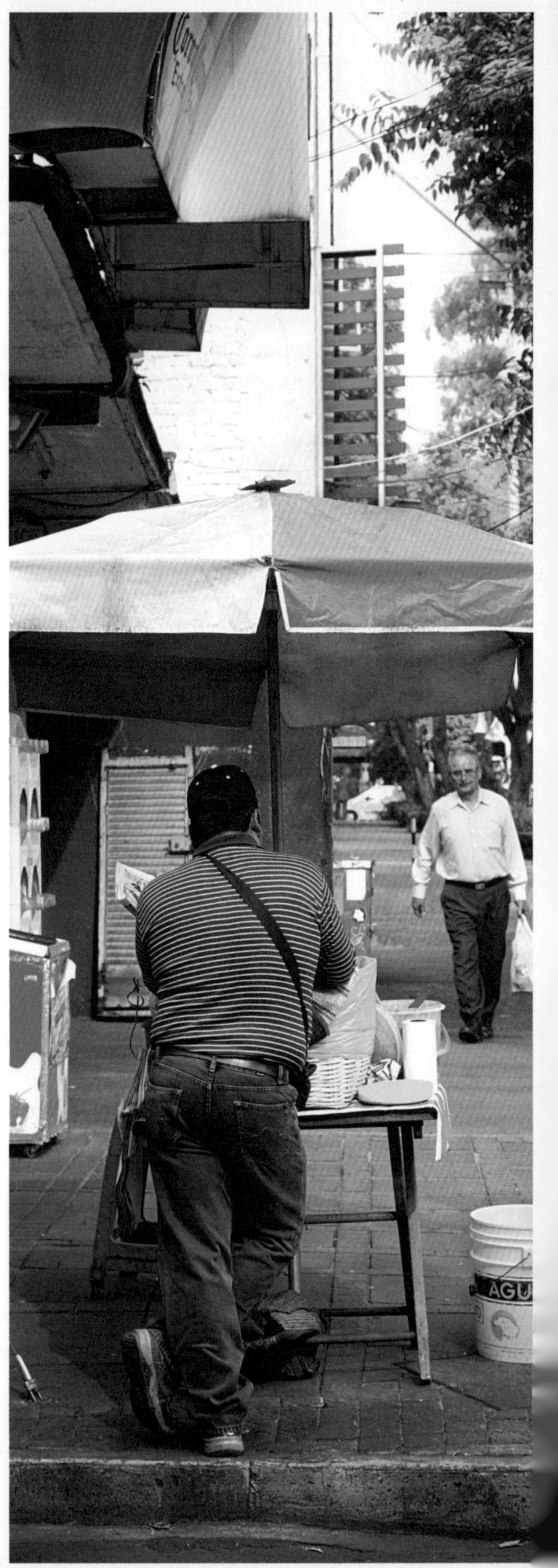

THE TACO
WAS INVENTED
BETWEEN
1000
AND
500 B.C.
AS
A KIND OF
EDIBLE
SPOON.

DURING
THE
PORFIRIO DÍAZ
REGIME
AT THE TURN
OF THE
20TH CENTURY,
TACOS
WERE SEEN
AS THE
FOOD
OF THE
POOR.

onion, extra salsa, just a little, or none at all. The *taquero*, or taco maker, has to be familiar with all the possibilities afforded by the range of ingredients on hand, and be able to judge by the patron's voice the personality a particular taco will assume. The *taquero* is, in his particular domain, a psychologist who interprets gestures and glances: the young lady and the well-dressed gentleman get two very different tacos, despite ordering the same thing. Being a *taquero* is something of a show, like being a bullfighter. From the get-go, there is a persona: you have to look like a *taquero* to stand out from the crowd, and have the voice and presence to go with it. *Taqueros* have ended up with a uniform of sorts—the apronand the cap. However, the rest is a sham. Mustache, military-style cap—these can be done without. Getting the lingo down is a must, though, together with the coordination and memory required to keep on top of all the orders: *doradito*, well-fried; *sin cebolla*, no onion; *pura maciza*, all lean meat; *sin verdura*, no greens; *con copia*, double tortilla; and *dos-tres*, not too much, not too little—all terms that a taco chef needs to know inside out to make it right.

Eating street tacos is a performance, and the interaction seasons the taco fillings, making for a blend of taste and circumstance. In these places you'll find, side by side or each to its own, the traditional and the picturesque, the humble and the decadent, the sordid and the rowdy, all the time aware that whatever you eat is "at your own risk." The list of ailments you could acquire eating at some less-than-hygienic places on the street is a long one. Moctezuma's revenge is not just for foreigners. Whenever it does happen, regret always comes too late, and the problem is not so much in the first fall—but in going back for more. In any case, what separates one taco stand from another is flavor, much more than quality or nutrition—hence the urban legend of dog meat tacos. To be sure, every Mexican suspects (almost entirely without foundation) having been served dog meat at least once. And while some unscrupulous places may use meat of the cheapest sort, and this has a bearing on product quality, in the end, it is the patron alone who decides exactly where and what to eat. In that sense, there's complete freedom. Street tacos are eaten with your plate in your lap, sitting on empty plastic paint buckets or wooden crates, or often just standing, preferably leaning against a wall or lamppost. For the average Mexican, tacos are just something to eat on the way to somewhere, as a snack—even if it ends up passing for lunch or supper. At taco stands, it's not unusual to see groups of people engaged in a kind of dance or ritual, with gestures and movements that reveal, to the trained eye, the quality of the tacos being served. Naturally, the number of people around a taco stand is itself a good indicator.

Tradition dictates that the taco connoisseur be accorded the proper deference: this individual becomes "the guide" or "the one who knows." This honor rewards wide-ranging knowledge of the field and commands awe and respect, since it implies experience: "I've been there before, and I had this, and this..." Such tales endow them with an aura of courage, like that once accorded to Aztec heroes. A taco might be greasy and it might be spicy, but it's always a gamble, and, with a bit of luck, a delicious surprise. It's a traditional morsel prepared on the spot, and eaten by hand in surroundings that radiate an air of constant celebration. Above all, we head to the taco stand with the knowledge that this—at long last—might be the one with that rare delicacy, or that sought-after, perfectly spicy salsa with the authentic, local flavor that no taco worthy of the name could do without.

PART
1

WHETTING YOUR APPETITE

THE MAIZE FESTIVAL, DIEGO RIVERA, 1923-1924, THE MINISTRY OF PUBLIC EDUCATION BUILDING. PHOTO: BOB SCHALKWIJK.

taco 1 m. Porción de alguna materia, como papel o tela, apretujada para rellenar un hueco o para *apretar el contenido de algo; como la que se mete para apretar la carga del *barreno, o la que se colocaba en las *armas de fuego entre la carga y el proyectil para que éste saliera con fuerza. **2** Trozo de madera u otro material semejante, corto y grueso, que se introduce en algún hueco o se emplea en cualquier uso. ≃ *Tarugo. ⊙ Pieza de madera o de plástico embutida en la pared para *clavar con seguridad en ella alguna cosa. **3** (Arg., Bol., Chi., Ec., Par., P. Rico, Perú, R. Dom., Ur.) **Tacón del calzado*. **4** Cada una de las piezas cónicas o puntiagudas que tienen en la suela algunos zapatos deportivos. **5** (Gran.) **Churro (que allí son rectos, cortos y gruesos)*. **6** Conjunto de hojas de papel o de billetes superpuestos en un solo bloque o unidos de forma que son fácilmente separables: 'Un taco de billetes de metro. Un taco de entradas para el teatro'. **7** *Palo o barra que se emplea para apretar el relleno de cualquier cosa; por ejemplo, para cargar las armas de fuego. ⇒ *Baqueta. **8** Palo que se emplea para jugar al *billar. ⇒ Espadilla, larga, mediacaña. ➤ Maza, suela, zapatilla. ➤ Taquera. ➤ Tiza. ➤ Entizar. **9** AGRÁF. *Palo aguzado con que se aprietan y aflojan las cuñas en la forma*. **10** **Lanza usada en el juego del *estafermo y en el de la *sortija*. **11** *Refrigerio que se toma entre las comidas*. ⇒ *Aperitivo. **12** Cada uno de los pedazos de cierto grosor en que se cortan algunos alimentos: Partió unos tacos de queso [o de jamón]'. **13** (Méj.) *Tortilla de maíz rellena de carne picada, queso, etc., que se toma como refrigerio*. **14** **Trago de vino*. **15** *Juguete consistente en un canuto en el cual se introducen con un palito dos tacos de papel o estopa que quedan perfectamente ajustados en el interior y dejando un espacio entre ambos: al empujar uno de ellos, sale despedido el otro por el aire comprimido. ≃ Tirabala, tiratacos, trabuco. ⇒ *Cerbatana. **16** (inf.; «Armar[se], Hacer[se]») Confusión o complicación que alguien causa con lo que dice o hace. ≃ Lío. **17** Maldición o palabrota. ≃ *Terno. **18** (pl.; inf.) Se emplea para expresar los años que tiene una persona: 'Ha cumplido treinta tacos'.

DEJAR HECHO [O HACER] UN TACO a alguien (inf.). *Confundirle o derrotarle en una discusión.

HACERSE [O ARMARSE] UN TACO alguien (inf.). *Aturdirse, *desconcertarse o *embarullarse.

tacómetro (del gr. «táchos», rapidez, y «metro»...

13. (MEX.) CORN TORTILLA STUFFED WITH CHOPPED MEAT, CHEESE, ETC., EATEN AS A SNACK OR LIGHT MEAL.

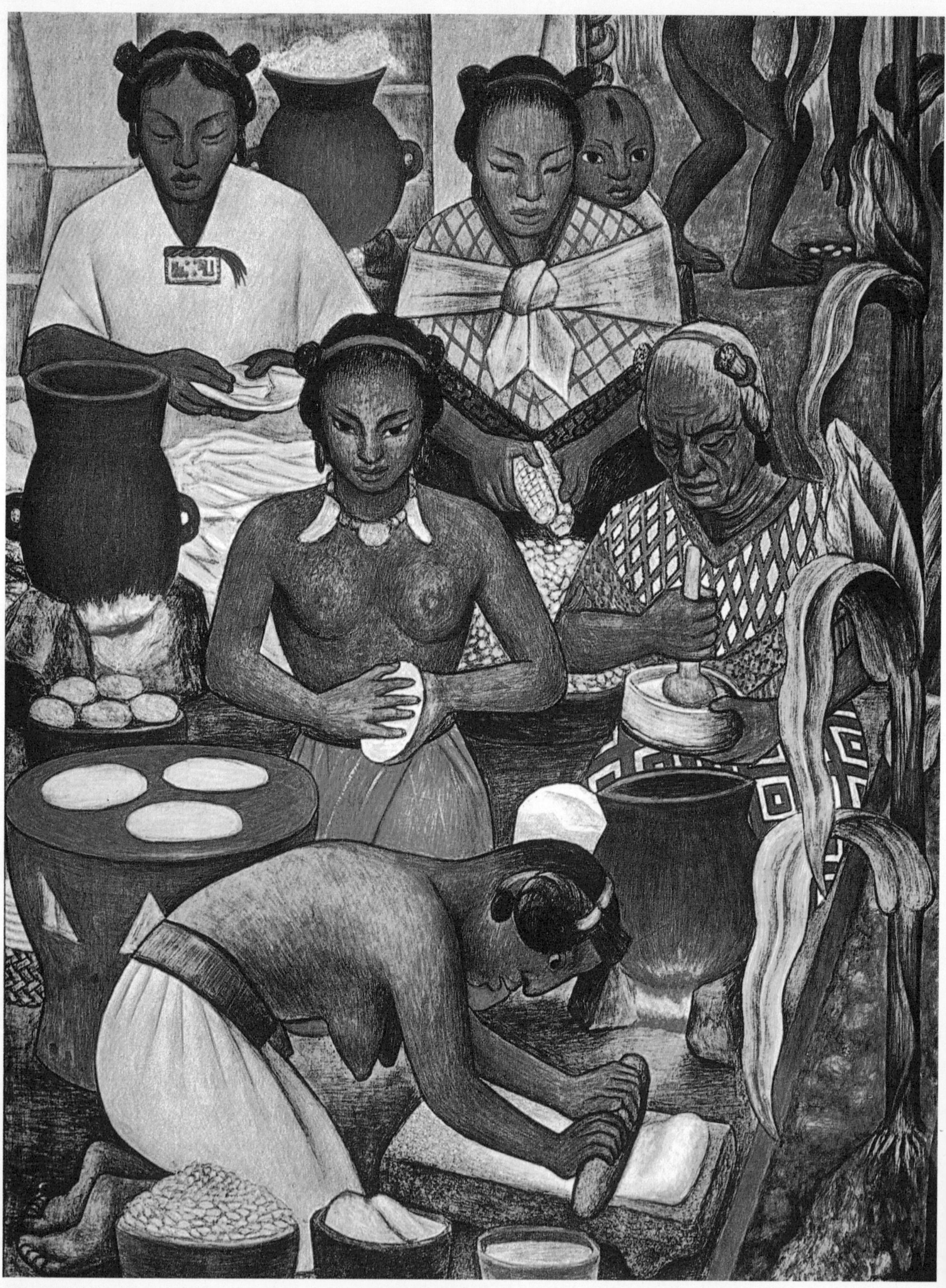

THE HISTORY OF THE HUASTECA CIVILIZATION, DIEGO RIVERA, NATIONAL PALACE, MEXICO CITY.

DIRECTLY FROM MEXICO, LOVELY AND BELOVED

The tortilla's virtues are well known; its history, somewhat less so. Let's start from the beginning with maize and follow the trail leading up to *masa de nixtamal,* the doughy base of tortillas, and thus, of tacos.

The ripened, dried corn we call maize did not always have the appearance it does today. To become our familiar maize, the plant underwent a long process of domestication. Five thousand-year-old paleobotanical remains found in the valley of Tehuacán, Puebla, have shed some light on the evolution of maize. The most widely accepted theory holds that maize came from another plant called *teocintle,* and it has been shown that both species crossbreed successfully.

Migration and trade among the ancient inhabitants of Mesoamerica gave rise to today's many varieties of maize, while also spreading maize throughout the Americas and providing sustenance to the native peoples, who venerated it on their altars. According to an ancient Mexican legend, the serpent god Quetzalcoatl convinced a black ant to reveal where the maize kernels were hidden. And that was how the god came upon the path leading to "the mountain of our sustenance" and then delivered the maize to our lips. So, we have the ants to thank.

"IN THE NARRATIVE, THE CREATOR DEITY, ACQUAINTED WITH THE BLACK ANT WHO KNEW WHERE 'OUR SUSTENANCE' WAS HIDDEN, PRETENDED TO COME UPON THE CREATURE BY CHANCE. HE PESTERED HIM WITH QUESTIONS UNTIL THE ANT GAVE IN AND GUIDED HIM TO TONACATEPETL, 'THE MOUNTAIN OF OUR SUSTENANCE.' HAVING ARRIVED THERE, QUETZALCOATL OBTAINED MAIZE FOR HUMANITY AND FOR THE GODS, WHO ALSO DESIRED THE SHELLED MAIZE ONCE THEY LEARNED OF QUETZALCOATL'S DISCOVERY. AFTERWARD, THE DEITY PLACED THE MAIZE ON THE LIPS OF THE FIRST HUMAN COUPLE, OXOMOCO AND CIPACTONAL, THE ANCIENT PROGENITORS AND FIRST CULTIVATORS OF MAIZE, SO THAT IN EATING IT—AS THE TEXT STATES—'THEY WOULD BECOME STRONG.'"

MIGUEL LEÓN-PORTILLA. *THE AZTEC IMAGE OF SELF AND SOCIETY*, TRANS. J. JORGE KLOR DE ALVA. SALT LAKE CITY: UNIVERSITY OF UTAH PRESS, PAGE 10.

The god of maize in the Aztec world was Cinteotl, or Centeotl, "the god of ripe corn," who, alongside his wife, Chicomecoatl, provided sustenance for humankind.

"THE FOURTH MONTH THEY CALLED 'UEI TOÇOZTLI.' ON THE FIRST DAY OF THIS MONTH THEY CELEBRATED A FEAST IN HONOR OF THE GOD NAMED CINTEOTL, WHOM THEY REGARDED AS GOD OF MAIZE [... AND] THE GODDESS WHOM THEY CALLED CHICOMECOATL [...] FOR THEY SAID THAT SHE WAS THE MAKER AND GIVER OF ALL THOSE THINGS WHICH ARE THE NECESSARIES OF LIFE, THAT THE PEOPLE MAY LIVE."

BERNARDINO DE SAHAGÚN. ***FLORENTINE CODEX: GENERAL HISTORY OF THE THINGS OF NEW SPAIN,*** BOOK 2: THE CEREMONIES, CHAPTER 4, TRANS. CHARLES E. DIBBLE AND ARTHUR J.O. ANDERSON. SANTA FE, NM: THE SCHOOL OF AMERICAN RESEARCH AND THE UNIVERSITY OF UTAH, 1963.

CHICOMECOATL AND CENTEOTL, THE AZTEC GODDESS AND GOD OF MAIZE.

The Zapotecs in the valley of Oaxaca honored Pitao Cozobi, the maize god who wore a headpiece made of corncobs; the Mayas revered Yum-Kaax, "the god of young corn"; and the Incas, Mama Sara, the "maize mother." After Columbus's voyage to the Caribbean in 1492, he famously brought ears of corn (among hundreds of other things) back to Europe, and that's how maize came to be known all over the world. It also explains why

AZTEC HARVEST CEREMONY, FLORENTINE CODEX, CA. 1540.

it's called "maize": the word comes from *mahís*, from Taino, a Caribbean language.

"AND ALSO SOME OF IT MAY BE MADE FROM MAIZE, WHICH IS A PLANT BEARING AN EAR LIKE AN EAR OF WHEAT, SOME OF WHICH I BROUGHT HOME, AND THERE IS NOW MUCH IN CASTILE."

CHRISTOPHER COLUMBUS. *THE FOUR VOYAGES OF COLUMBUS*, TRANS. CECIL JANE. NEW YORK: DOVER, 1988, PAGE 22.

In Náhuatl, maize is called *tlaolli*, a word also used for the dry kernels and for cereals and food in general. A dried ear of corn is called *centli*; the cob (the center, or heart of the maize), *olotl*; unripe corn, *xilotl*; and ripe corn, *élotl*. So, maize goes by many names in different languages, and names abound for each part of the plant, such as *totomoxtle*, the husk leaf around the cob, used to wrap tamales and other food.

Like rice, wheat, barley, and other cereal crops, maize can be stored over long periods and milled into flour. The meal ground from dried maize kernels is used for *mazamorra*, a traditional Andean drink with a gelatinous consistency (though otherwise like Mexican *atole*); and the fermented kernels for *chicha*, a low-alcohol beverage that was the wine of the Andean countries. Crushed kernels are used to make cornmeal dough, which once cooked can be considered a sort of bread and is the base of certain tamales in South America, like *hallacas* and *humitas*, which also have fresh corn kernels mixed in. The dried kernels can be used to prepare *pinole*, a treat eaten by Mexican children from ancient times up until

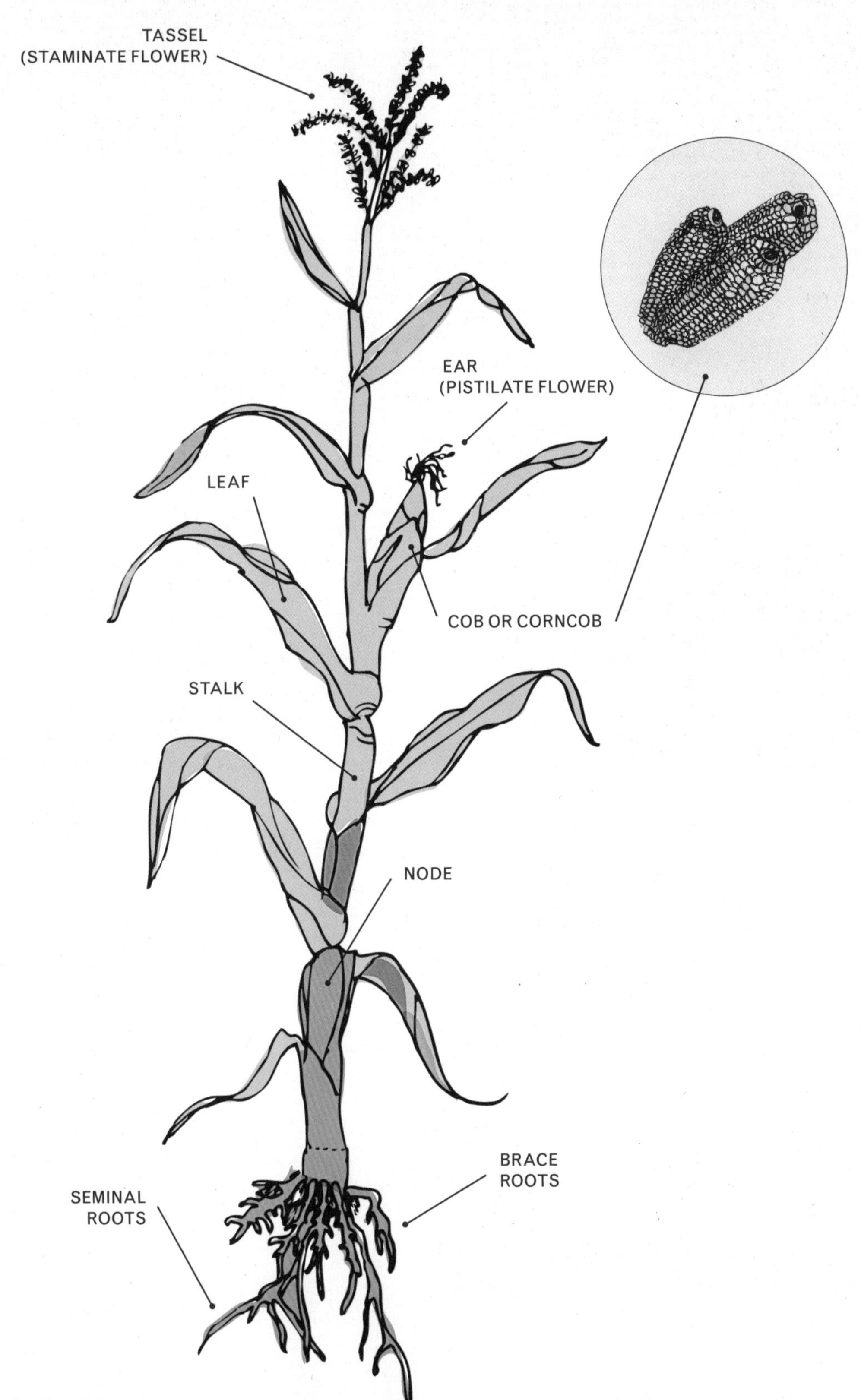
TASSEL
(STAMINATE FLOWER)
EAR
(PISTILATE FLOWER)
LEAF
COB OR CORNCOB
STALK
NODE
BRACE
ROOTS
SEMINAL
ROOTS

TLATELOLCO MARKET, *THE CEREAL AND MAIZE VENDORS*, DIEGO RIVERA, NATIONAL PALACE, MEXICO CITY.

the 1970s. And lastly, heating the kernels until they pop open (to produce our "popcorn" and the Peruvian equivalent, *cancha* or *canchita*) is another popular way to prepare the versatile product we know as maize.

However, this maize flour and cornmeal can't be used to make tortilla dough, because neither has the malleability or the cohesion to hold a shape when mixed with water, something that the Franciscan Bishop Diego de Landa lamented, no doubt homesick for bread back in his home country of Spain.

"THEY HAVE NOT LEARNED HOW TO MAKE FLOUR THAT CAN BE KNEADED LIKE WHEAT FLOUR, AND WHEN THEY DO MAKE IT AS ONE MAKES WHEAT BREAD, IT IS GOOD FOR NOTHING."

DIEGO DE LANDA. *YUCATÁN BEFORE AND AFTER THE CONQUEST*, TRANS. WILLIAM GATES. NEW YORK: DOVER, 1957.

One of the great contributions of Mesoamerican cultures to the rest of the world is the discovery of *nixtamal* (*textal* in Aztec), a process that transformed maize into a much more nourishing food—and deliciously edible, too. The first implement developed for the

NIXTAMAL

Without a doubt, the discovery, or rather the invention, of *nixtamal* was an event of great social and historical importance. Without *nixtamal*, we simply never would have known the great tortilla; and no tortilla means no tacos. Unfortunately, we will never know the hero, or more likely the heroine, of this tale. In fact, no one can say with any certainty when or where this breakthrough occurred or if it was indeed just a lucky accident. Nor does anyone know why this particular preparation of maize, having spread throughout Mesoamerica, never reached the Caribbean or made inroads in South America.

Here's how to make *nixtamal*: First, the maize is boiled in diluted lime. Once the kernels open, they are left to stand till nighttime. The water is changed, then each kernel is washed and scrubbed to get rid of the hull and the tip cap. Lastly, the kernels are ground into a smooth paste.

Masa de *nixtamal* is prepared the same in the humblest abode as it is in the biggest factory. It is a marvel that provides a direct link with ancient Mexican history—a recipe that hasn't changed in centuries.

Perhaps that's why it seems so mythical today.

LA MOLENDERA, DIEGO RIVERA, 1924.

NIXTAMAL DOUGH (MASA)

Ingredients
2 lbs (1 kg) maize*
3 tablespoons lime**

Preparation
1. Leave the lime to dissolve overnight in a pot with 12½ cups (3 litres) of water.
2. Remove any small stones or twigs from the maize, wash the maize thoroughly, then rinse well.
3. Place the pot with the dissolved lime and maize on the stove. Let the water boil until it yellows, and the hull (the skin of the kernel) peels and can be easily removed.
4. Remove pot from heat and let sit overnight.
5. The next morning, discard the *nejayote* (the water the kernels were cooked in); then change the water 2 or to 3 times to rinse the maize.
6. Strain, then patiently rub the kernels by hand to remove the hull and the tip cap, pinching the kernels one by one until all the maize has been cleaned.
7. With a little water, grind the kernels on a metate (a flat, rectangular mortar, also called a mealing stone) until you have a smooth, compact dough that is evenly mixed. Of course, this long and arduous process used to take up hours of a woman's day but can be skipped nowadays by having the maize ground at a *nixtamal* mill.

*Maize is dry, ripened corn. The dried kernels can be golden or white, and can be found in markets or specialty grocery stores.
**The lime in the recipe is the same as that used in construction. It is sold in some markets and hardware stores that sell construction supplies. Be sure to buy what's referred to as slaked lime (calcium hydroxide) and not burnt lime or quicklime (calcium oxide), which is also sold in hardware stores but which has no use for our purposes.

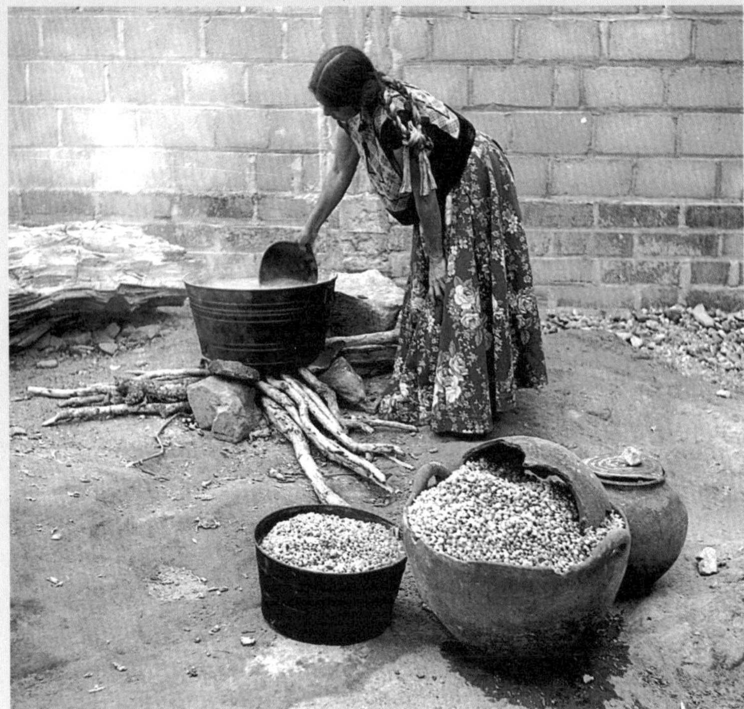

A MIXE WOMAN PREPARING *NIXTAMAL*. PHOTO: NACHO LÓPEZ / NATIONAL PHOTOGRAPHY ARCHIVE.

"THE INDIAN WOMEN PUT THE MAIZE TO SOAK THE NIGHT BEFORE IN LIME AND WATER, AND IN THE MORNING IT IS SOFT AND HALF COOKED, WITH THE HUSK AND NIB HAVING BEEN LOOSENED IN THE PROCESS."

DE LANDA. *YUCATAN BEFORE AND AFTER THE CONQUEST.*

WOMEN GRINDING MAIZE ON METATES. PHOTO: CASASOLA COLLECTION / NATIONAL PHOTOGRAPHY ARCHIVE.

"As to dried grains of maize, in many ways were the women none the less deluded. First, when they cooked it or set it in ashes—behold their folly: when they would place it in the olla with ashes, first of all they breathed upon it. It was held that in this way it would not take fright; thus, it would not fear the heat. [...]

Second, they deceived themselves in this way: if they saw or came upon dried grains of maize lying scattered on the ground, then they quickly gathered them up. They said: 'Our sustenance suffered: it lieth weeping. If we should not gather it up, it would accuse us before our lord. It would say: "O our lord, this vassal picked me not up when I lay scattered upon the ground. Punish him!" Or perhaps we should starve'."

Sahagún. Florentine Codex, Book 5: The Omens, Appendix, fourth chapter.

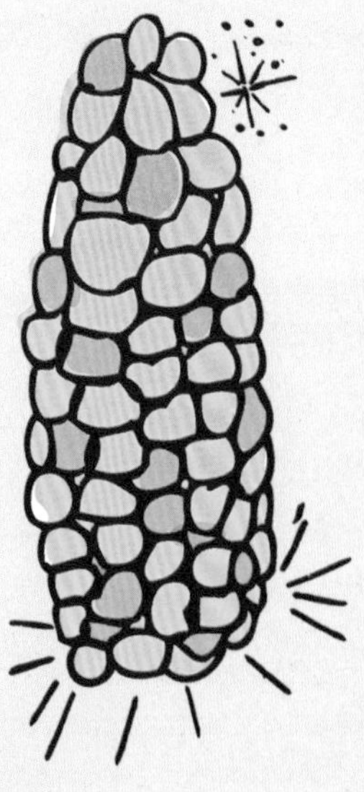

cultivation of maize was likely the *coa*, a wooden hoe that dates back to the origins of agriculture in the Americas and the domestication of maize. The metate is also one of the oldest instruments in the Americas and has been used to grind up all kinds of foods since the Stone Age.

"ABUNDANT EXAMPLES OF *METLAPILS* [GRINDERS], METATES, *MOLCAJETES* [THREE-LEGGED MORTAR AND PESTLE], *TEJOLOTES* [HANDHELD PESTLES], AND CUPS CARVED OUT OF VOLCANIC ROCK, SUCH AS BASALT AND ANDESITE, HAVE BEEN FOUND IN THE EARLIEST MESOAMERICAN SITES."

JANET LONG. "TECNOLOGÍA ALIMENTARIA PREHISPÁNICA," IN ***ESTUDIOS DE CULTURA NÁHUATL.*** MEXICO CITY: UNAM, INSTITUTO DE INVESTIGACIONES HISTÓRICAS, 2008, VOL. 39, PAGE 129.

So, the metate, or *métatl* in Aztec, was the tool used to prepare *nixtamal* dough. This piece of pre-Hispanic technology, which is still used today, is a rectangular three-legged slab carved from volcanic rock. It goes hand in hand with the *metlapil*, the oval-shaped roller used to grind the maize and a vast number of other ingredients to produce masa.

The traditional griddle dates from the Preclassic period (A.D. 2500–1000) and is called a comal, from the Aztec word *comalli*. It is a round clay pan placed above a fire on three stones, or *tenamaxtles*, to elevate it from the direct heat.

"THUS, THEIR FRAME AND SHAPE WERE GIVEN EXPRESSION BY OUR FIRST MOTHER AND OUR FIRST FATHER. THEIR FLESH WAS MERELY YELLOW EARS OF MAIZE AND WHITE EARS OF MAIZE. MERE FOOD WAS THE LEGS AND ARMS OF HUMANITY, OF OUR FIRST FATHERS. AND SO, THERE WERE FOUR WHO WERE MADE, AND MERE FOOD WAS THEIR FLESH."

POPOL VUH: THE SACRED BOOK OF THE MAYA, TRANS. ALLEN J. CHRISTENSON. NORMAN, OK: UNIVERSITY OF OKLAHOMA PRESS, PAGE 195.

The characteristics of corn masa are malleability and cohesion, indispensable qualities when preparing Mexican dishes like tortillas, tamales, and other fruits of the comal: *chalupas*, *sopes*, *gorditas*, *tlacoyos* (see page 275). According to pre-Hispanic myth, it was from maize dough that the gods modeled the first man.

"THEY PREPARE MANY KINDS OF BREAD, GOOD AND HEALTHFUL, EXCEPT THAT IT IS NOT GOOD TO EAT WHEN COLD."

DE LANDA. *YUCATÁN BEFORE AND AFTER THE CONQUEST.*

This divine intervention may not go beyond the realm of legend, but the ingenious invention of *nixtamal* dough, which in turn produced the tortilla, certainly had an enormous nutritional impact (see page 41). In principle, corn tortillas are no more than a thin disk of this corn masa cooked up on a hot griddle, and they need to stay hot to be good.

The average cooking time for a tortilla is less than a minute per side, and part of the charm of a tortilla lies in its distinct sides: a very thin layer, or *hollejo*, is considered the inside of the taco because it holds the filling; and the other, thicker side, which helps the tortilla keep its strength and its shape.

When the dough comes in contact with the heat of the comal, one side becomes firm, while the other retains its characteristic suppleness. Flipping the tortilla over, the steam is trapped inside, causing the uncooked side to expand. That's why the tortilla puffs up, the air separating the two sides, as Salvador Novo poetically describes it when speaking of the sobriety of the Nahuas:

"THE TORTILLA BULGES AS IF IT HAD COME ALIVE, AS IF IT WISHED TO FLY, TO ASCEND; AS IF EHÉCATL HAD BREATHED INTO IT. THIS IS THE TIME TO GENTLY LIFT IT FROM THE *COMALLI,* WHEN IT HAS, ON THE FLESH OF OUR FLESH, OF OUR SUSTENANCE, A SECOND, DELICATE EPIDERMIS."

SALVADOR NOVO. *COCINA MEXICANA: HISTORIA GASTRONÓMICA DE LA CIUDAD DE MÉXICO.* MEXICO CITY: PORRÚA, 2010, PAGE 6.

A fresh handmade corn tortilla, hot from the griddle, is a culinary marvel, as anyone who's ever eaten one knows. But quality aside, there have always been marked differences among tortillas, a distinction not lost on the chroniclers of old.

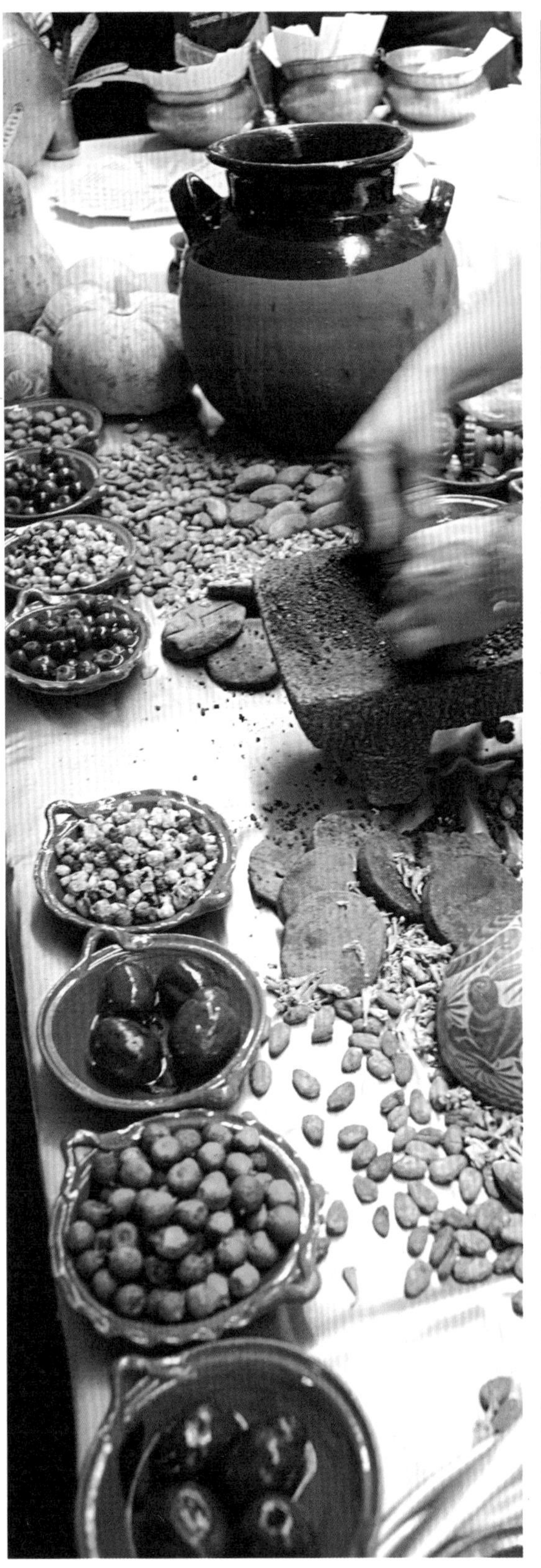

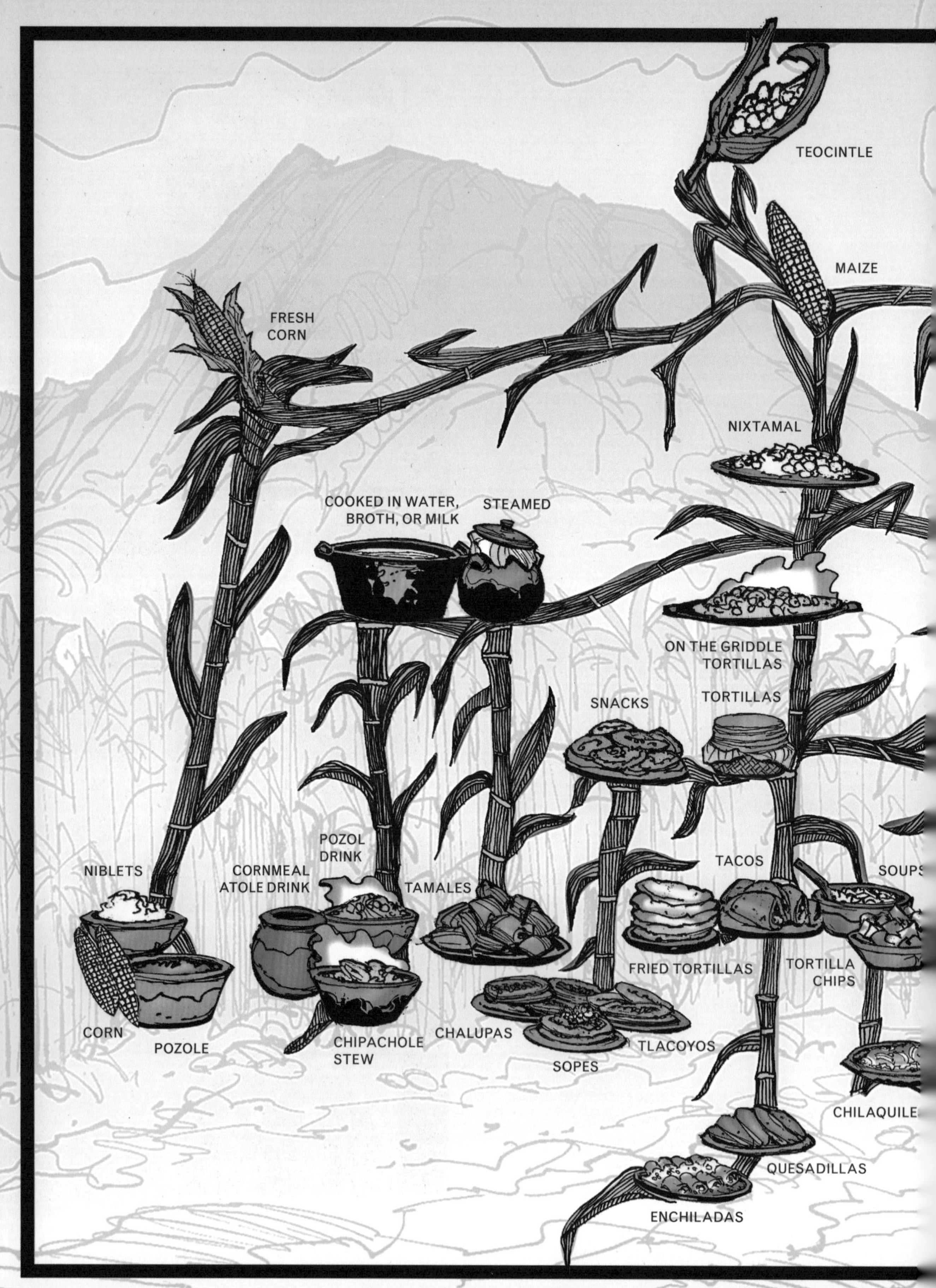
TEOCINTLE
MAIZE
FRESH CORN
NIXTAMAL
COOKED IN WATER, BROTH, OR MILK
STEAMED
ON THE GRIDDLE TORTILLAS
TORTILLAS
SNACKS
POZOL DRINK
NIBLETS
CORNMEAL ATOLE DRINK
TAMALES
TACOS
SOUPS
FRIED TORTILLAS
TORTILLA CHIPS
CORN
POZOLE
CHIPACHOLE STEW
CHALUPAS
SOPES
TLACOYOS
CHILAQUILE
QUESADILLAS
ENCHILADAS

FROM CORNFIELD TO MILL TO TACOS ON A GRILL

THE METATE, FROM THE SERIES LOTERÍA HUASTECA, ALEC DEMPSTER.

For people from the city, tortillas found in small towns and villages are a gastronomic experience because of their preparation: fresh ingredients that really taste of maize, with even a hint of charcoal.

"WHEN A WOMAN MADE TORTILLAS, IF HER TORTILLA DOUBLED OVER, THERE WAS ALSO A DELUSION OF THEIRS. SHE SAID: 'SOMEONE WHO NOW COMETH HATH KICKED IT OVER.' OR IF, PERCHANCE, HER HUSBAND HAD GONE SOMEWHERE DISTANT, SHE SAID: 'NOW HE COMETH, FOR HE HATH KICKED OVER MY TORTILLA.'"

SAHAGÚN. *FLORENTINE CODEX*, BOOK 5: THE OMENS, APPENDIX, FOURTEENTH CHAPTER.

In any market, you'll find vendors, baskets in hand, selling *tortillas caseras*, homemade tortillas, by the dozen. In the same markets, you can also find the famous blue tortillas that retain the original color of the maize. Some regions in the North, especially San Luis Potosí, boast red tortillas, which take their color from the ground chile mixed into the meal, usually from *ancho* or *guajillo* chiles. A variety of ingredients may be added to corn masa: dried *nopal*, amaranth flour, or soy flour as a nutritional supplement that reduces carbohydrates. Other specialty tortillas contain condiments or ingredients that add flavor to the tortilla dough, such as *huitlacoche* (corn fungus), chile, cilantro, parsley, oregano, sesame—or whatever takes the cook's fancy, for corn masa welcomes all.

"HOT, WHITE, DOUBLED TORTILLAS ARRANGED IN A LARGE BASKET; LARGE TORTILLAS; LARGE, THICK, COARSE TORTILLAS; FOLDED TORTILLAS OF MAIZE TREATED WITH LIME, PLEASING [TO THE TASTE]; TORTILLAS FORMED IN ROLLS; LEAF-SHAPED TORTILLAS [...]."

SAHAGÚN. *FLORENTINE CODEX*, BOOK 8: KINGS AND LORDS, THIRTEENTH CHAPTER.

It's surprising to see how both the comal and metate were used and, in fact, changed little until the end of the nineteenth century, when they began to be replaced by machines: mechanical *nixtamal* mills and tortilla makers. As strange as it may seem, today's tortilla press and the automated tortilla machines are recent inventions.

THE VIRTUES OF NIXTAMAL DOUGH

Without the process of *nixtamalization*, maize would not be as nourishing as it is. "In its natural state, as a grain, maize is nutritionally inefficient as a cereal staple. It is deficient in niacin, which is essential for vitamin absorption. This deficiency can lead to malnutrition and pellagra, a potentially fatal condition. [...] A complete utilization of [the nutritional advantages of] maize would not have been possible without the invention of the process of *nixtamalization*, likely another contribution made by women and one of the great technological achievements of Mesoamerica. Its invention made maize a more easily digestible food [...] and permitted the development of Mesoamerican civilizations. Soaking it in alkaline water increases its protein value and the presence of calcium and niacin. [...] We can deduce that [this] was a technique invented at the beginnings of Mesoamerican civilization. The oldest evidence of this technique comes from the Mid Pre-Classical Period [...] in the south of Guatemala, between 1000 and 800 B.C."

Long. *Tecnología Alimentaria Prehispánica*, pages 131–132.

A NOURISHING FOOD

Nutritional Facts

Approximate amount per serving
(Serving size 3 tortillas at 1¼ oz/35 g) each

Water	45.89 g
Calories	218 kcal
Protein	5.70 g
Total fats	2.85 g
Ash	0.93 g
Carbohydrates	44.64 g
Fiber	6.3 g
Total sugars	0.88 g

Minerals

Calcium	81 mg
Iron	1.23 mg
Magnesium	72 mg
Phosphorous	314 mg
Potassium	186 mg
Sodium	45 mg
Zinc	1.31 mg
Copper	0.154 mg
Manganese	0.326 mg
Selenium	6.1 µg

Vitamins

Thiamin	0.094 mg
Riboflavin	0.065 mg
Niacin	1.498 mg
Pantothenic acid	0.109 mg
Vitamin B6	0.219 mg
Folic acid	5 µg
Vitamin E	0.28 mg

Fats

Saturated fats	0.453 g
Monosaturated fats	0.692 g
Polyunsaturated fats	1.419 g
Cholesterol	0 mg

Amino Acids

Tryptophan	0.042 g
Phenylalanine	0.285 g

The first tortilla maker machine made in Mexico was built by Everardo Rodríguez Arce and Luis Romero. The first automated machine was developed in 1947 by Fausto Celorio, whose company kept tweaking the design through the next fifty years. Even so, tradition holds some sway: the grindstones in modern *nixtamal* mills are still hand-carved out of volcanic rock before being laid into the machines.

All this brings us to the modern tortilla factory, where tortillas are classified by their diameters: the 6-inch (16 cm), considered the norm; the 4-inch (10 or 11 cm) are referred to as *taqueras* because they're made especially for tacos. Among the variety of shapes and sizes we should mention *memelas*, long and tapered tortillas; and the enormous Oaxacan *tlayudas*, or *clayudas*, that can have a diameter of up to nearly 16 inches (see page 259).

The tortilla clearly has a long tradition behind it, but with the spread of mills, tortilla machines, and industrial production of *nixtamal* flour, the way tortillas are made and eaten is somewhat different in the present day. Today there are vast Mexican food consortia that distribute tortillas by the packet, available for purchase in supermarkets, stores, and practically anywhere else. There is also talk of square tortillas served up in a *taquería* in Mexico City South, along with tortillas made of flour rather than maize, the last recourse of the hungry and a nostalgic consolation for those from the other side of the Maize Curtain. Flour tortillas are prepared with wheat flour instead of corn masa. Though they serve the same function, flour tortillas have a very different texture and flavor.

Each person has an intimate relationship with tortillas: some go to their neighborhood's tortilla mill with their own cloth napkin to bundle them up, while others wrap their tortillas in paper. The warmth of this precious bundle is, in a way, a pleasant preview for the pleasure to come. Often, the customer finds the half-hour wait in the line rewarded with a courtesy salted taco. There is also the custom of displaying the tortillas in a great variety of woven baskets and tortilla containers—*chiquihuites* (see page

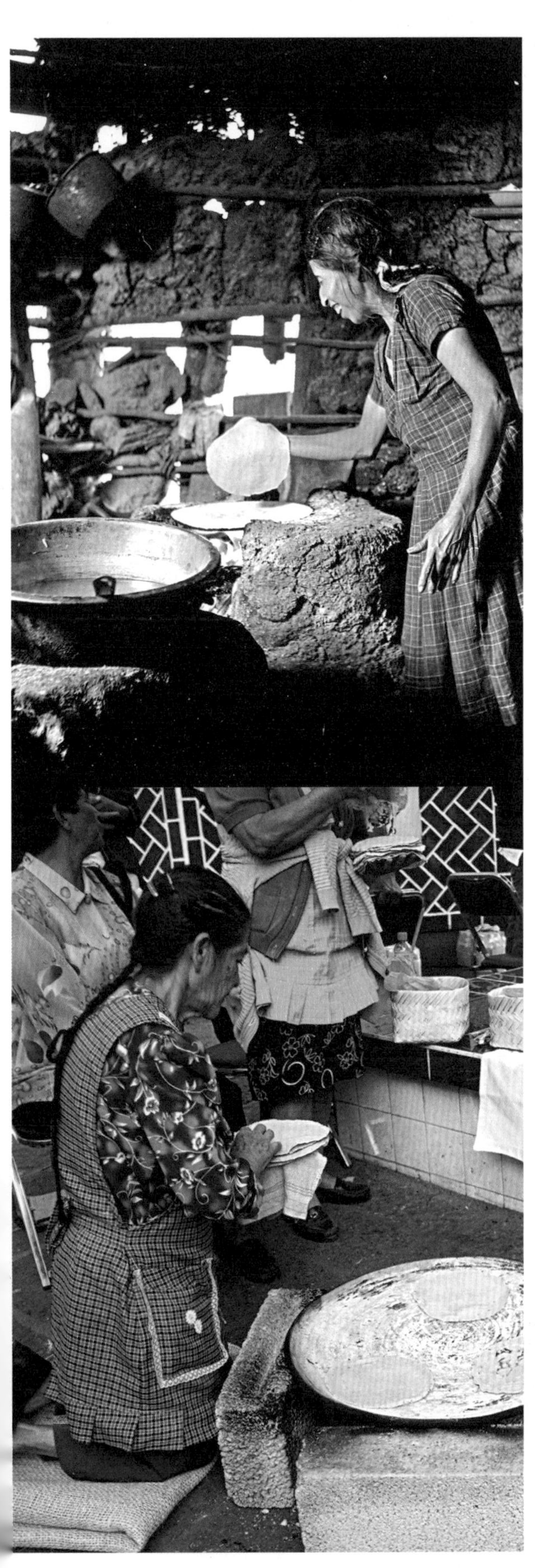

THE

POOR

SPEND ALMOST

10%

OF THEIR FOOD & DRINK BUDGET ON

TORTILLAS;

THE

RICH

ONLY

3.1%.

THE AVERAGE MEXICAN CONSUMES

135 POUNDS

OF TORTILLAS PER YEAR.

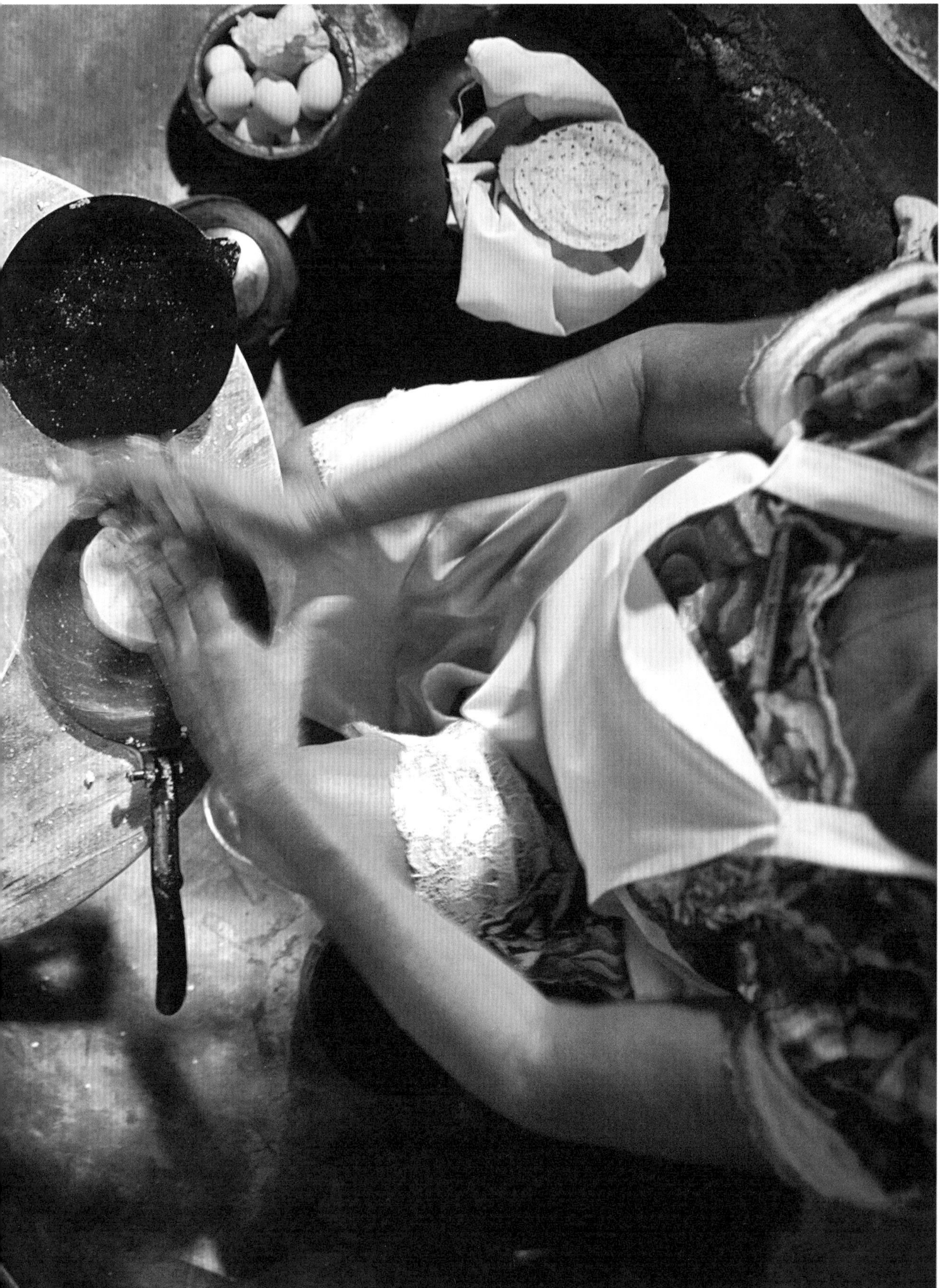

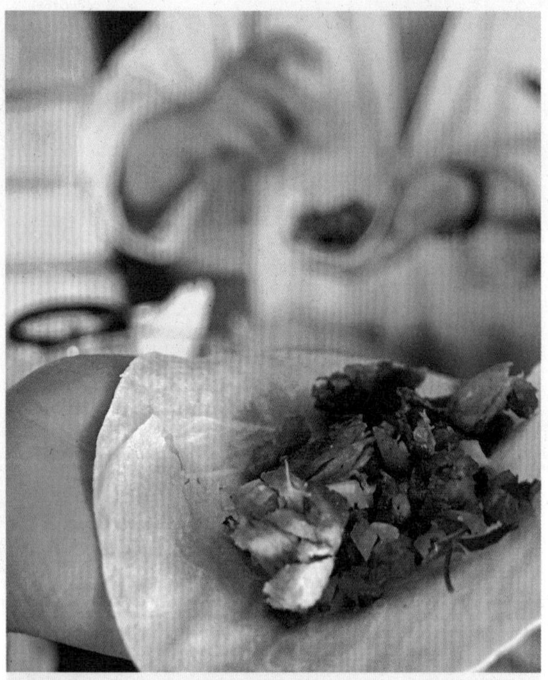

FLOUR TORTILLAS

Flour tortillas came into being when the conquistadors brought their provisions of wheat flour into the arid zones of what is now the north of Mexico. Their cooks naturally took this new product and made tortillas out it. Flour tortillas are easy to make, mixing wheat flour with water until it has a doughy consistency, then shaping and heating up the tortillas on the comal. The mixture, however, needs a little lard to give the tortillas their soft texture and add some flavor. Flour tortillas vary markedly both in size and quality: in Sonora, they are huge and thin, like the singular tortilla *sobaquera*, which can be up to three feet in diameter; in Nuevo León, on the other hand, tortillas are small and thick. You can find sweet tortillas, fried crisp tortillas, and packaged tortillas sold in supermarkets.

50), *tenates* (page 49), or *tompeates* (page 51)—lending an air of tradition and tasteful decoration while keeping the tortillas warm in a hygienic environment.

Freshness is of the utmost importance. Once tortillas have cooled off, they lose much of their charm, though old tortillas can have a second life as *totopos*, *tostadas*, or *chilaquiles* (see page 278). Fresh tortillas are used not only for tacos, quesadillas, and enchiladas, but also to accompany soups or stews in place of bread. In Mexican homes, it's common to dunk a salted taco in soup for a few seconds before eating it. And if the tortilla is cut or torn into triangles, it can be used as a kind of spoon to scoop up food and salsa. That a tortilla can pass for an edible utensil is especially obvious when it's used to pinch up meat. From tortillas you get big tacos and little tacos, half- and quarter-tacos; you can pick up meat or other food with it, slop up some salsa, spoon it up, move it around, and mop the plate clean. If there is no napkin lying around, a tortilla can wipe the hands and mouth till no traces are left. Plate, utensil, napkin, meal…is that enough tortilla for you?

The long process that corn undergoes to become a tortilla is a curious one; it has defined Mexican daily life for centuries, and it entails year-round work. While men looked after crops, women prepared the tortillas, a daily chore that involved cooking and grinding the *nixtamal* on the metate to make the dough, and heating the tortillas on the comal three times a day. Today, these exhausting tasks have largely been delegated to specific branches of the agricultural and commercial sectors. Still, the importance of this food lives on, not only in its enormous economic contribution to Mexico, but also in its cultural legacy: maize, tortillas, and tacos are an integral part of Mexican identity.

FAUSTO CELORIO
INVENTED
THE FIRST
AUTOMATED
TORTILLA MACHINE
IN 1947.

TODAY
THERE ARE
NEARLY
79,000
MILLS
AND
TORTILLA
OUTLETS
IN MEXICO.

1

TACO

TACOOO... LOTERIA!

Lotería is a Mexican game of chance, similar to bingo, but using images on a deck of cards. The world of tacos is as diverse as the images that represent it. Familiar objects like the plastic tomato-shaped salt shaker and the thick log used as a chopping-block are but two of the many iconic items that make up this colorful compilation.

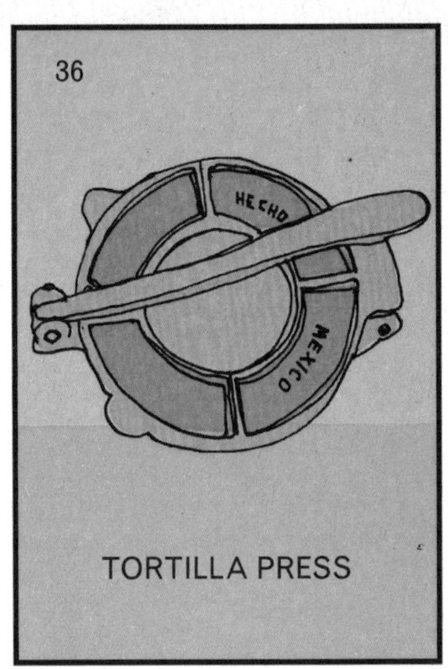

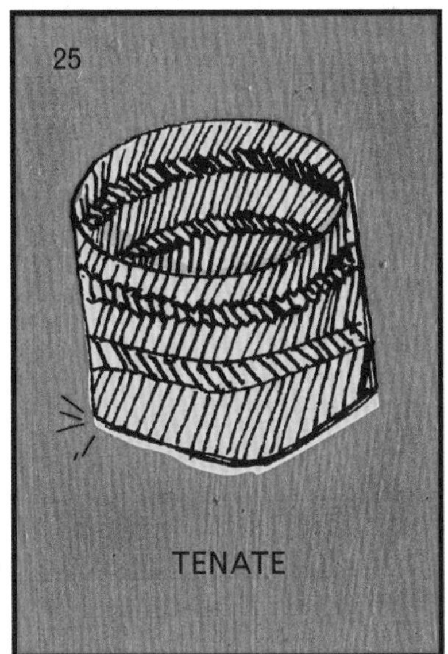

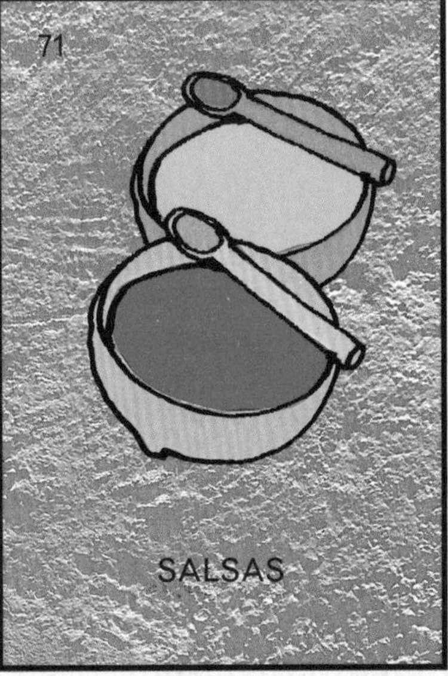

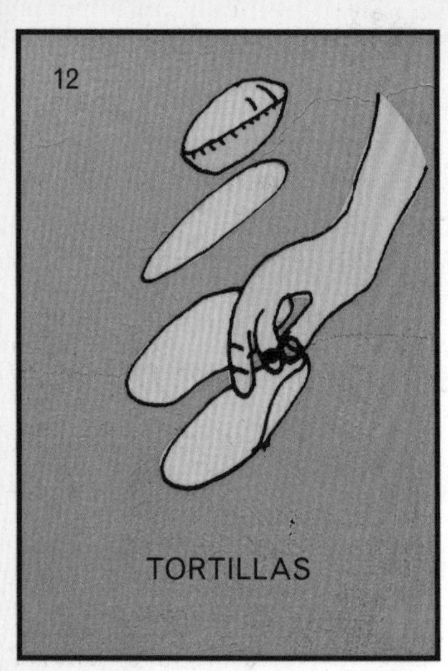
12
TORTILLAS

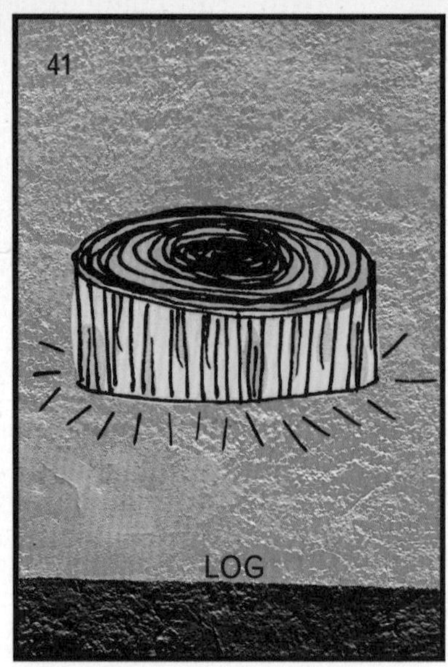
41
LOG

64
SALT SHAKER

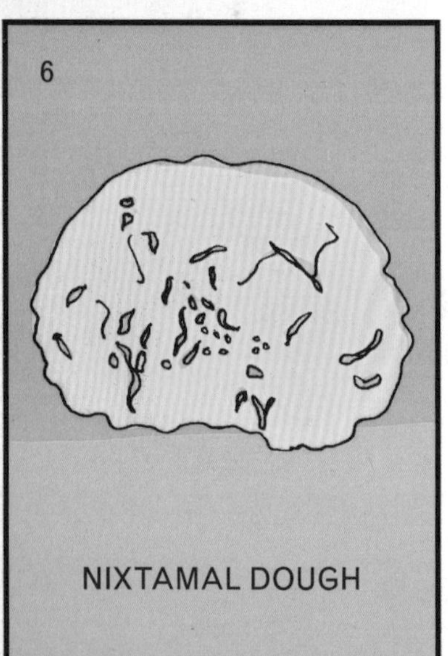
6
NIXTAMAL DOUGH

35
EMBROIDERED
NAPKINS

52
BIG
CARNITAS PAN

73
STEAM TRAY

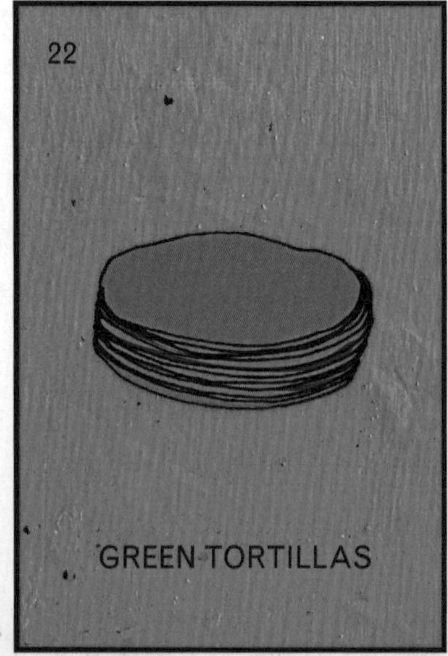
22
GREEN TORTILLAS

16
CHIQUIHUITE

70
TOMPEATE

46
MACHETE

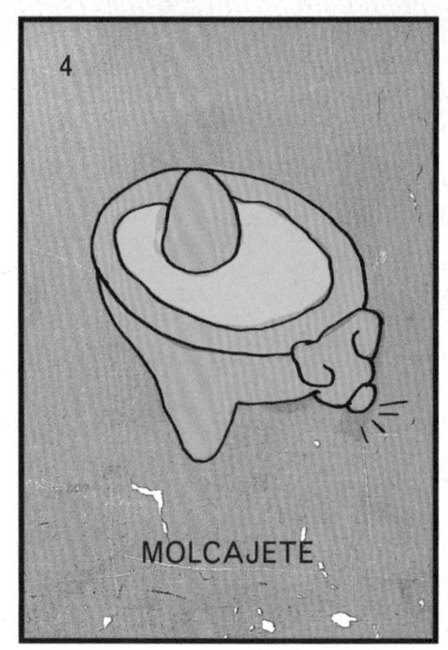
4
MOLCAJETE

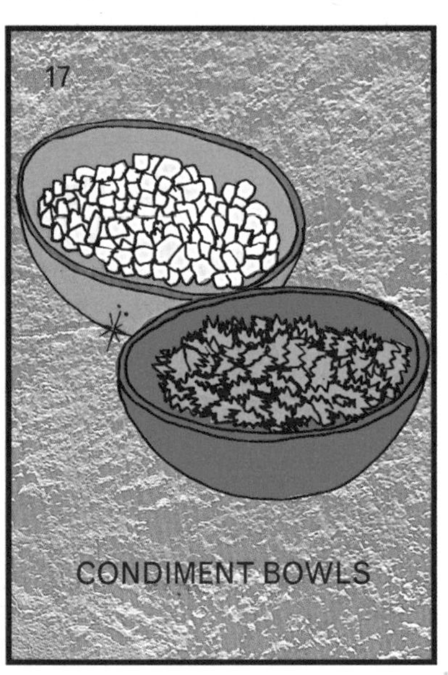
17
CONDIMENT BOWLS

28
COW

31
METATE

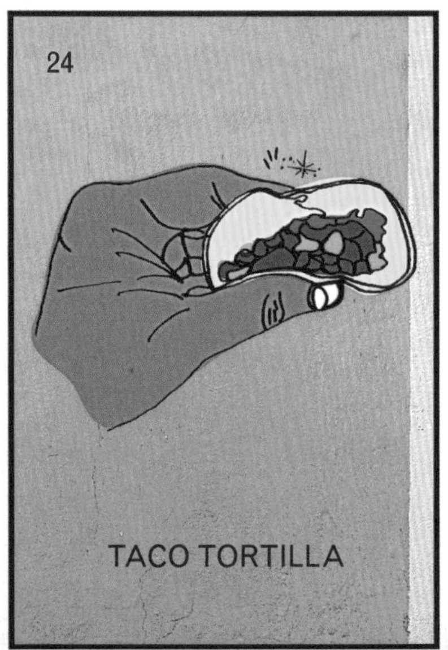
24
TACO TORTILLA

51
FRYING PAN

68
GREEN ONIONS

38
BASKET

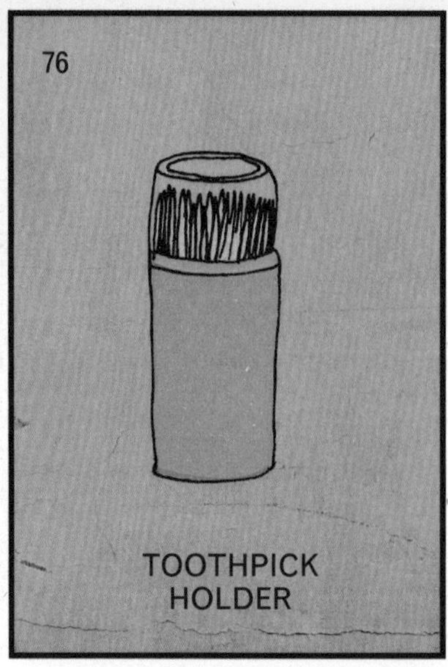
76
TOOTHPICK
HOLDER

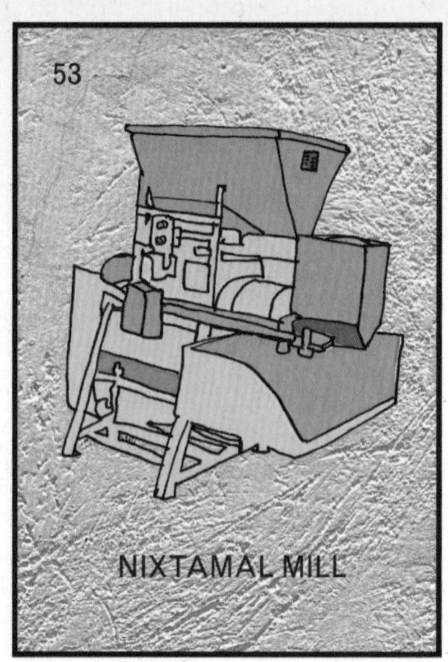
53
NIXTAMAL MILL

2
PIG

42
CONVEX-CONCAVE
TACO COMAL

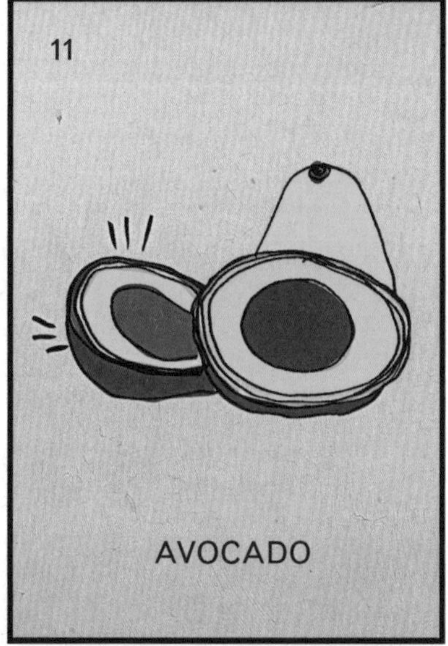
11
AVOCADO

21
PLASTIC PLATES

67
CLAY POT

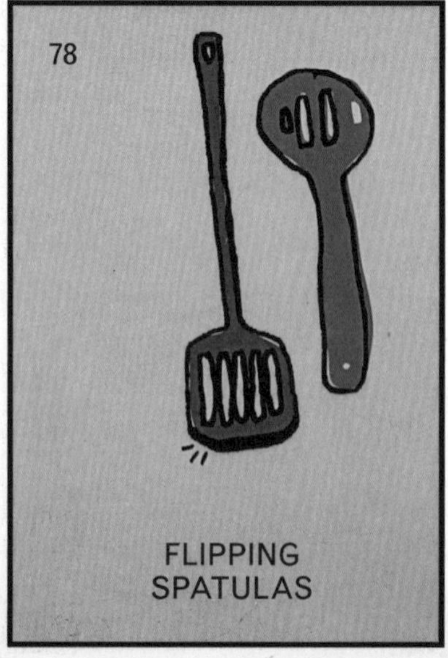
78
FLIPPING
SPATULAS

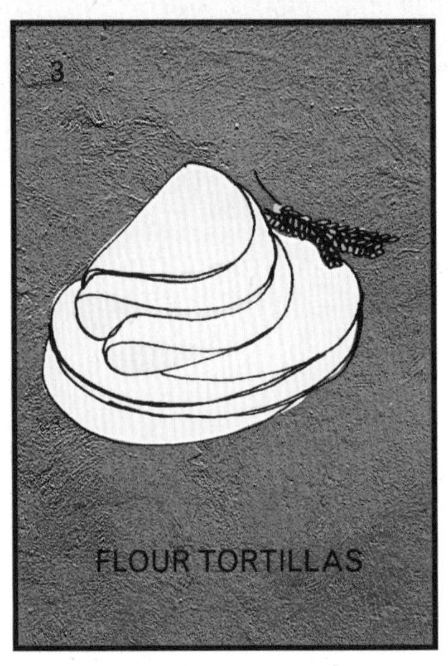
3
FLOUR TORTILLAS

14
LIMES

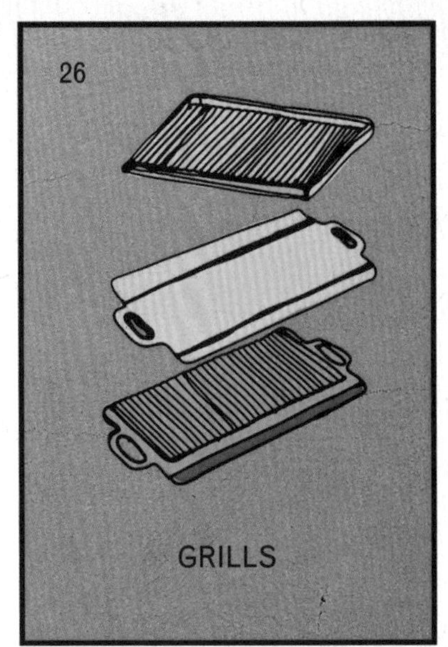
26
GRILLS

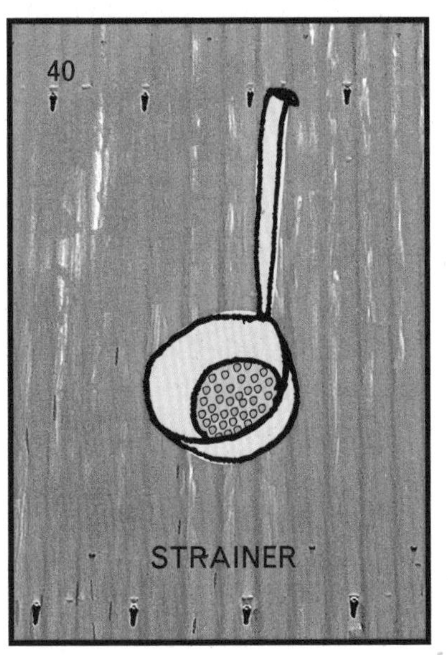
40
STRAINER

79
BARBACOA PIT

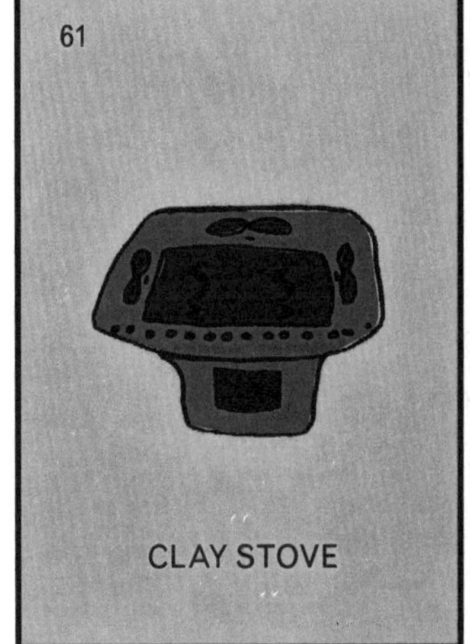
61
CLAY STOVE

59
MOOCHER DOG

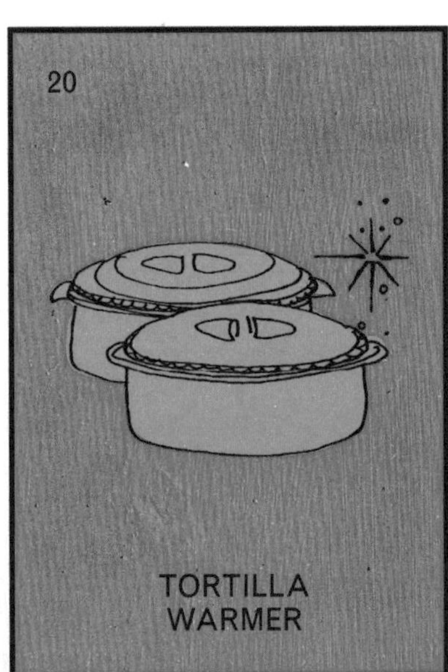
20
TORTILLA
WARMER

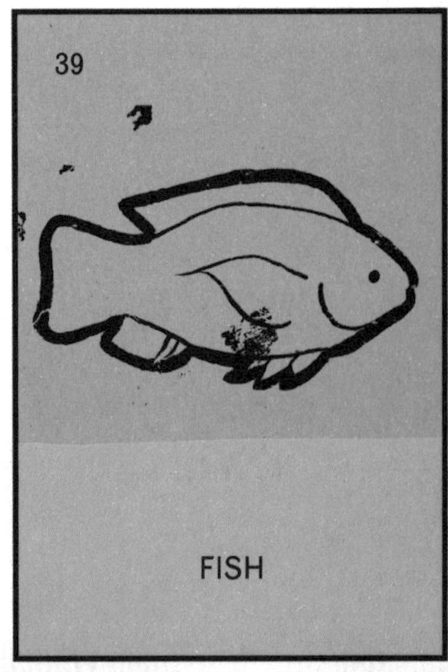
39
FISH

77

KNIVES

15

APRON

33

FOLD-OUT TABLE

8

TORTILLA SOBAQUERA

27

COUNTER

49

UPRIGHT GRILL

55

METAL COMAL

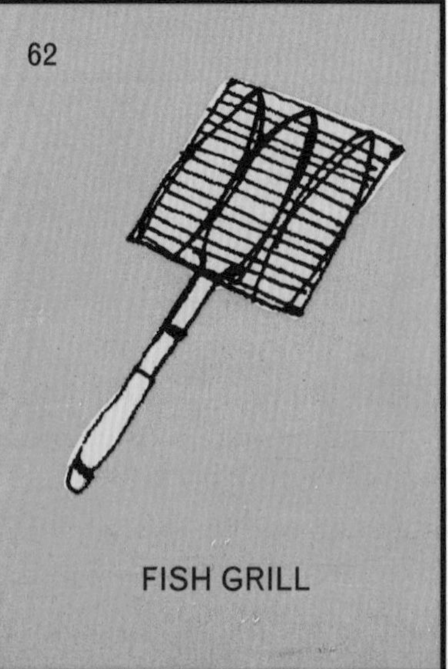

62

FISH GRILL

37

TACO BASKET

9
SODA

34
STEAMER

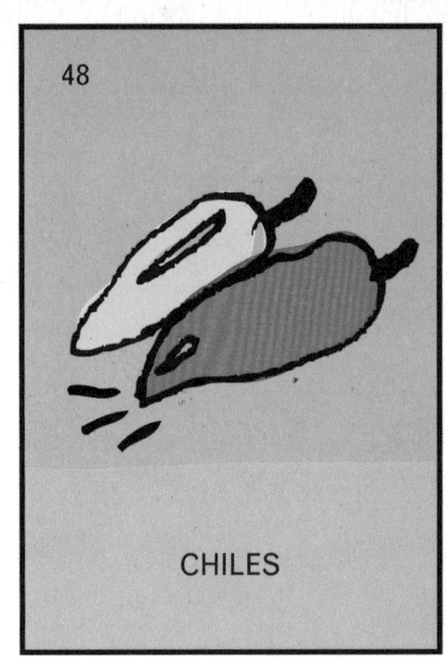
48
CHILES

23
RABBIT

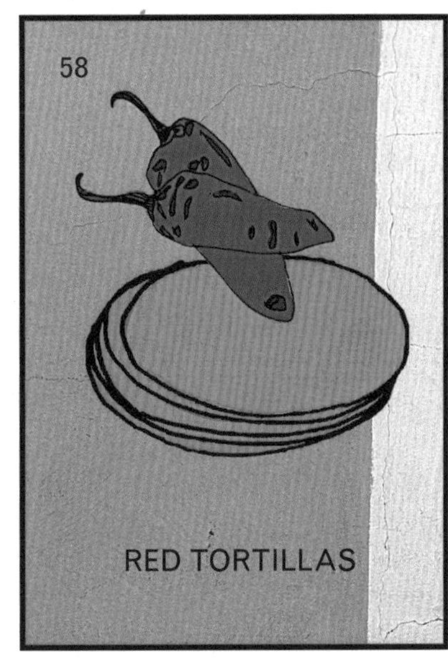
58
RED TORTILLAS

72
WOODEN SPOON

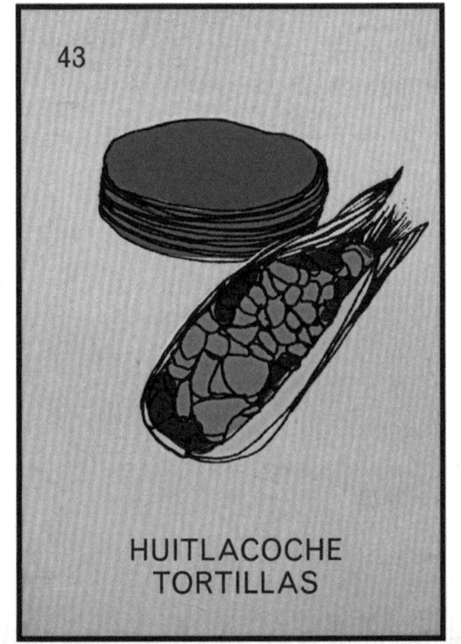
43
HUITLACOCHE
TORTILLAS

65
RAM

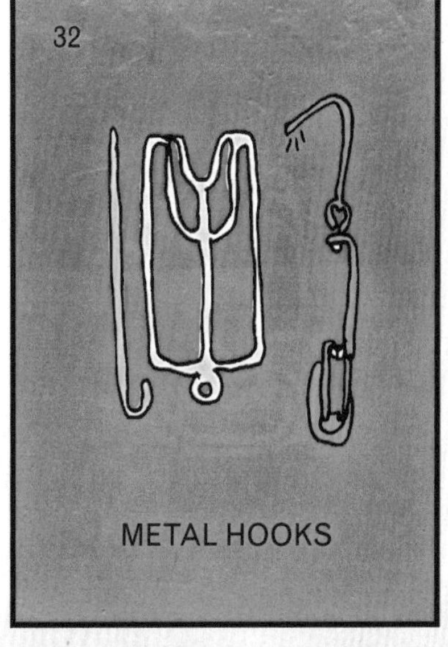
32
METAL HOOKS

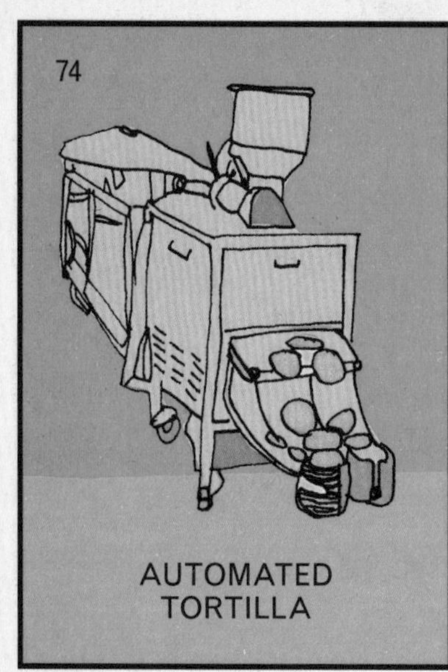
74
AUTOMATED
TORTILLA

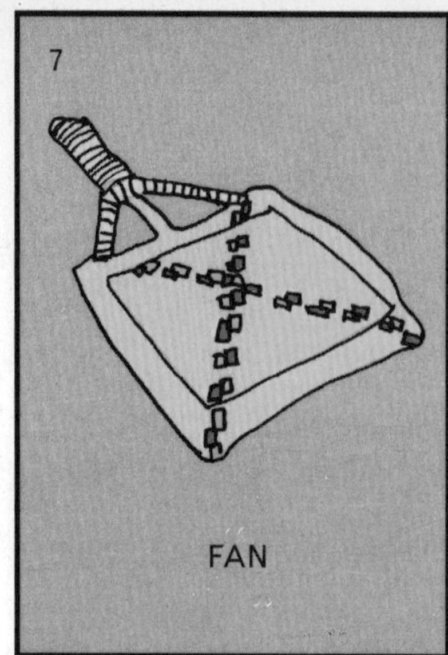
7
FAN

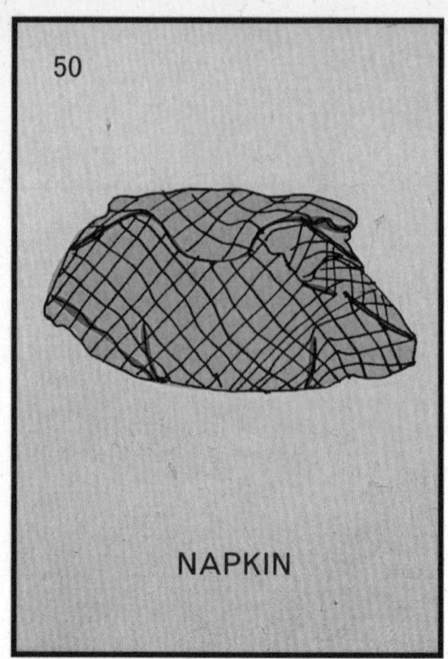
50
NAPKIN

54
GOAT KID

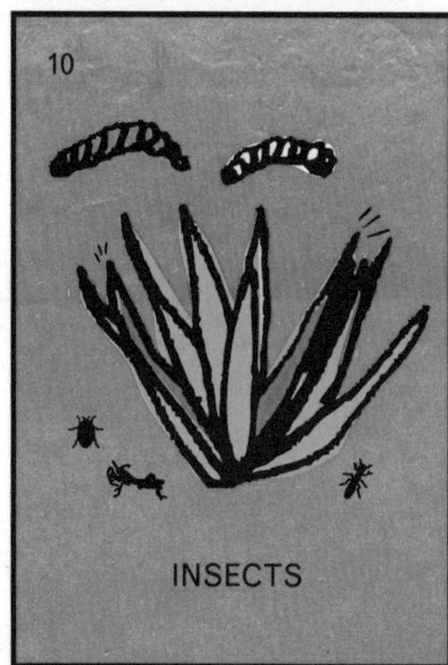
10
INSECTS

29
STEEL GRIDDLE

66
NAPKIN HOLDER

13
CYCLING
TACO MAKER

56
TACO STAND

60
TLAYUDA

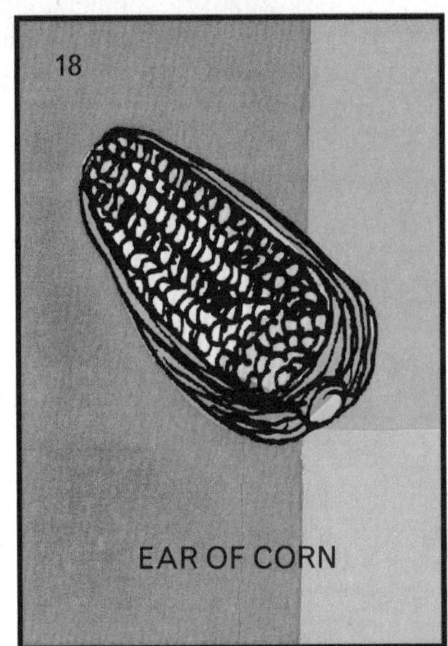
18
EAR OF CORN

45
CLAY COMAL

47
MEMELAS

75
CHICKEN

30
PRESSURE
COOKER

69
FRYING COMAL

57
TACO EATER

80
CARVING FORK

THE TACO MENAGERIE

ROUND TIP: THE CENTRAL LEG MUSCLE, THE TASTIEST AND LEANEST CUT OF THIS PART OF THE COW.

TOP AND BOTTOM ROUND: WHERE THE MOST MEAT IS ON A COW, THE LEG MUSCLES. THE TOP ROUND IS THE FRONT PART OF THE LEG, THE OUTER SIDE, WHILE THE BOTTOM ROUND IS ON THE INSIDE.

SHANK: THE CUT CLOSEST TO THE JOINT HAS BONE AND NERVES THAT NEED TO BE COOKED FOR A LONG TIME.

LOIN: THIS IS THE CLEANEST, TENDEREST MEAT ON THE COW. THE NAMES OF SPECIFIC CUTS DEPEND ON WHERE THEY ARE.

TENDERLOIN: A LONG MUSCLE OF TENDER TASTY MEAT. THIS PART GIVES US BEEF TIPS, FAJITAS, *GAONERAS*, ALAMBRES, SKEWERS, AND FILLET TACOS.

SIRLOIN: THIS IS FOUND IN THE PART FARTHEST BACK OF THE TENDERLOIN AND HAS SOME BACKBONE. THESE TACOS ARE VERY REFINED, EXPENSIVE, AND HARD TO FIND.

T-BONE: A CUT THAT HAS SOME TISSUE AND VERTEBRA. IT COMES FROM THE MIDDLE PART OF THE COW TO THE TAILBONE. IT HAS A 'T-SHAPED BONE AND MAKES FINE, EXPENSIVE TACOS.

LEG: THIS IS THE BACK QUARTER, FROM WHICH WE GET MANY CUTS. THE NAME OF EACH GROUP OF MUSCLES CHANGES DEPENDING ON THE REGION, THE BUTCHER, OR EVEN THE TACO STAND. IT'S EATEN IN GRILL TACOS, GRIDDLE TACOS, STEAK TACOS, BARBACOA, ETC.

RUMP: JUST BELOW WHERE THE TENDERLOIN MEETS THE UPPER PART OF THE LEG IS THE RUMP, THE HIPS OF THE COW.

HINDSHANK: THIS IS THE BACK OF THE LEG

ENTRAILS

RIBS: THE VARIOUS PARTS ARE DISTINGUISHED BY THICKNESS, THE PRESENCE OR ABSENCE OF BONE, AND THE QUALITY OF THE MUSCLE TISSUE.

RIB STEAK: A LARGE AND THICK CUT OF BEEF ON THE BONE. A FINE CUT.

RIB EYE: A PORTION OF MEAT NEXT TO THE BONE. THIS INCLUDES SIX MAIN PARTS OF THE ANIMAL, INCLUDING THE OFFAL.

BEEF RIBS: THE PORTION OF RIBS, GENERALLY A THIN CUT FOR GRILLED, GRIDDLE, STEAK AND BARBACOA TACOS.

ENTRAILS: THESE ARE THE RESPIRATORY AND DIGESTIVE ORGANS OF THE ANIMAL. THEY TASTE STRONGER THAN THE MEAT, AND ARE EASIER TO CHEW.

LIVER: LIVER IS USUALLY PREPARED WITH ONION IN STEWED-MEAT TACOS.

INTESTINES: THE LARGE AND SMALL INTESTINES, STUFFED WITH OTHER OFFAL (E.G., LIVER, STOMACH, AND LUNG), HIGHLY SEASONED, AND DEEP FRIED, GRILLED OVER COALS, ON THE GRIDDLE, IN *SUADERO* TACOS, OR STEAMED ALONGSIDE HEAD TACOS.

TRIPE AND MARROW GUT: TRIPE IS THE SMALL INTESTINE OF THE COW, MARROW GUT COMING FROM MILK-FED CALVES. ONCE CLEANED, THEY ARE FRIED AND PREPARED IN CHARCOAL-GRILLED AND SUADERO TACOS.

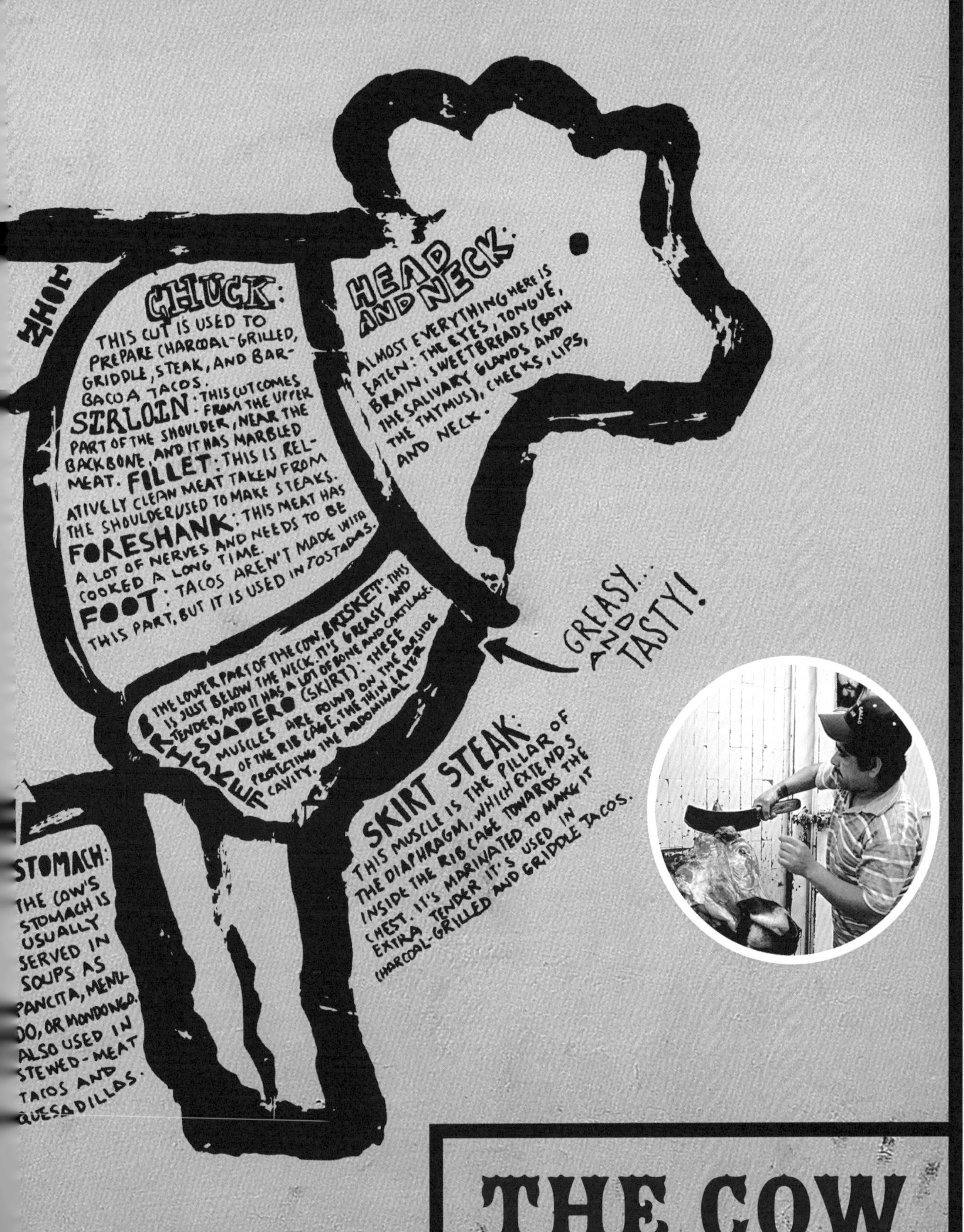

CHUCK:
THIS CUT IS USED TO PREPARE CHARCOAL-GRILLED, GRIDDLE, STEAK, AND BARBACOA TACOS.
SIRLOIN: THIS CUT COMES FROM THE UPPER PART OF THE SHOULDER, NEAR THE BACKBONE, AND IT HAS MARBLED MEAT.
FILLET: THIS IS RELATIVELY CLEAN MEAT TAKEN FROM THE SHOULDER USED TO MAKE STEAKS.
FORESHANK: THIS MEAT HAS A LOT OF NERVES AND NEEDS TO BE COOKED A LONG TIME.
FOOT: TACOS AREN'T MADE WITH THIS PART, BUT IT IS USED IN TOSTADAS.
HEAD AND NECK:
ALMOST EVERYTHING HERE IS EATEN: THE EYES, TONGUE, BRAIN, SWEETBREADS (BOTH THE SALIVARY GLANDS AND THE THYMUS), CHEEKS, LIPS, AND NECK.
GREASY... AND TASTY!
BRISKET
BRISKET: THIS IS THE LOWER PART OF THE COW. IT IS JUST BELOW THE NECK. IT'S GREASY AND TENDER, AND IT HAS A LOT OF BONE AND CARTILAGE.
SUADERO (SKIRT): THESE MUSCLES ARE FOUND ON THE OUTSIDE OF THE RIB CAGE. THE THIN LAYER PROTECTING THE ABDOMINAL CAVITY.
SKIRT STEAK:
THIS MUSCLE IS THE PILLAR OF THE DIAPHRAGM, WHICH EXTENDS INSIDE THE RIB CAGE TOWARDS THE CHEST. IT'S MARINATED TO MAKE IT EXTRA TENDER. IT'S USED IN CHARCOAL-GRILLED AND GRIDDLE TACOS.
STOMACH:
THE COW'S STOMACH IS USUALLY SERVED IN SOUPS AS PANCITA, MENUDO, OR MONDONGO. ALSO USED IN STEWED-MEAT TACOS AND QUESADILLAS.

THE COW

THE
TORTILLA
WENT INTO
OUTER SPACE
WHEN
THE ASTRONAUT
JOHN GLENN
ADDED IT
TO THE MENU
FOR
THE SPACE SHUTTLE
DISCOVERY,
IN 1998.

LOC N. 4

SIDE: THIS PART GIVES US PORK CHOPS AND RIBS.

CHOPS: THIS IS A THIN SLICE OF THE RIB CAGE, CUT FROM RIB TO RIB, USING THE MEAT CLOSEST TO THE BACKBONE, THOUGH IN TACO STANDS ANY THIN CUT IS CALLED A COSTILLA, OR PORK CHOP. IT'S USED IN CHARCOAL-GRILLED AND GRIDDLE TACOS. CURED AND SMOKED, THESE CHOPS ARE ALSO EATEN IN GRIDDLE TACOS.

LEG: THIS IS THE MAIN SOURCE OF LEAN MEAT ON A PIG. IT IS USED FOR STEAK, BONELESS FILLETS, COCHINITA PIBIL*, TINGA** AND OTHER RECIPES. THIS MEAT IS SERVED IN CHARCOAL-GRILLED AND GRIDDLE TACOS, AS WELL AS TACOS AL PASTOR AND COCHINITA TACOS, AMONG OTHERS.

RIBS: THIS CUT IS FROM THE TIPS OF THE RIBS, THE PART FARTHEST FROM THE BACKBONE. CUT LENGTHWISE, PARALLEL TO THE BACKBONE, IT'S EATEN IN CARNITAS TACOS.

ENTRAILS: ALMOST EVERYTHING IS EATEN FROM THIS PART, ESPECIALLY IN →

LIVER: THIS ORGAN IS EATEN IN CARNITAS TACOS OR COOKED WITH ONIONS IN STEWED-MEAT TACOS.

HEART: THIS IS USED IN CARNITAS TACOS.

STOMACH: REFERRED TO AS BUCHE, THIS IS USED IN CARNITAS TACOS

UTERUS: REFERRED TO AS NANA, THIS IS ALSO PUT IN CARNITAS TACOS.

SKIN OR FATBACK: THE PIGSKIN GIVES US PORK RINDS—A CHARCOAL-GRILLED TACO'S BEST FRIEND AND AN ESSENTIAL INGREDIENT IN STEAMED AND STEWED-MEAT TACOS.

*(P. 163)
**(P. 182)

ORK TENDERLOIN:
HIS IS A PORK FILLET. IT
OMES FROM THE RIBS, BUT
AS NO BONE OR FAT THIS
S ONE OF THE FINEST CUTS
ROM THIS ANIMAL,
SED IN GRIDDLE
CHARCOAL-GRILLED
ACOS.

HEAD:
THE HEAD PROVIDES MANY INGREDIENTS FOR **CARNITAS TACOS**: SNOUT, CHEEKS, EAR, TONGUE, AND BRAIN.

NECK:
A CUT WITH THE IDEAL PROPORTION OF MEAT AND FAT FOR TACOS AL PASTOR.

ARNITAS
TACOS

THE PIG

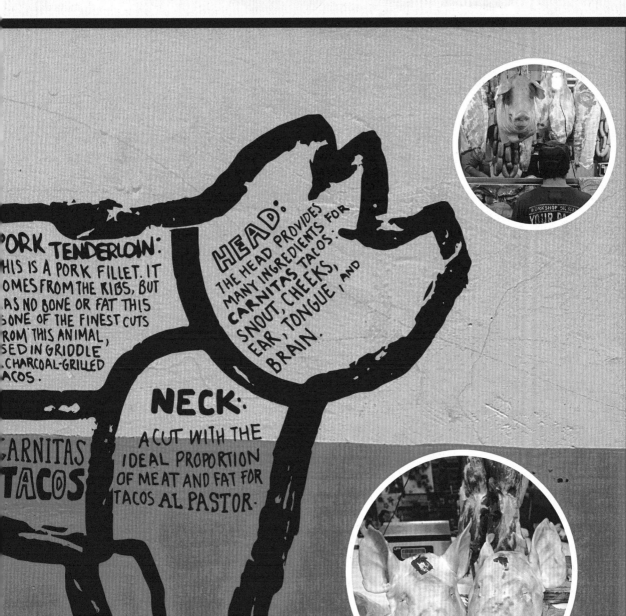

RAM, EWE, AND LAMB

THESE ARE ALL DIFFERENT NAMES FOR SHEEP, OF WHICH THERE ARE OVER 600 VARIETIES AROUND THE WORLD. THIS ANIMAL'S MEAT PLAYS AN IMPORTANT ROLE IN LOCAL GASTRONOMY, ESPECIALLY IN THE HIGHLANDS OF MEXICO, WHERE THE MEAT IS MOSTLY COOKED BARBACOA STYLE, IN UNDERGROUND OVEN PITS. IT CAN BE COOKED IN CONVENTIONAL OVENS OR CHARCOAL-GRILLED ON UPRIGHT AL PASTOR SPITS OR, OF COURSE, STEWED, AS IS THE CASE WITH LAMB BIRRIA STEW.

STILL, THERE'S SOME CONFUSION OVER HOW TO NAME THIS ANIMAL; THE DIFFERENCES REFER TO ITS AGE OR STAGE OF DEVELOPMENT.

NURSING LAMB: IS THE ANIMAL LESS THAN 45 DAYS OLD, FED SOLELY ON MILK. IT WEIGHS FROM 9 TO 15 LB, AND HAS VERY TENDER MEAT.

LAMB: IS THE ANIMAL BETWEEN A MONTH AND A YEAR OLD, ALREADY FED ON GRASS OR OTHER FOOD BESIDES MILK. IT WEIGHS BETWEEN 11 AND 66 LB. THIS IS THE ANIMAL MOST OFTEN USED IN THE KITCHEN BECAUSE IT HAS ABUNDANT, TENDER MEAT THAT IS NUTRITIOUS AND FLAVORFUL.

YEARLING: IS THE ANIMAL OVER A YEAR OLD AND WITH A WEIGHT ABOVE 55 LB. ITS STRONGER FLAVOR MAKES IT BETTER SUITED TO WOOL PRODUCTION.

EWE: IS THE ADULT FEMALE, WITH A WEIGHT BETWEEN 44 AND 88 LB. IT HAS THE SAME CULINARY CHARACTERISTICS AS THE YEARLING, SO IT IS USED FOR MILK AND WOOL PRODUCTION.

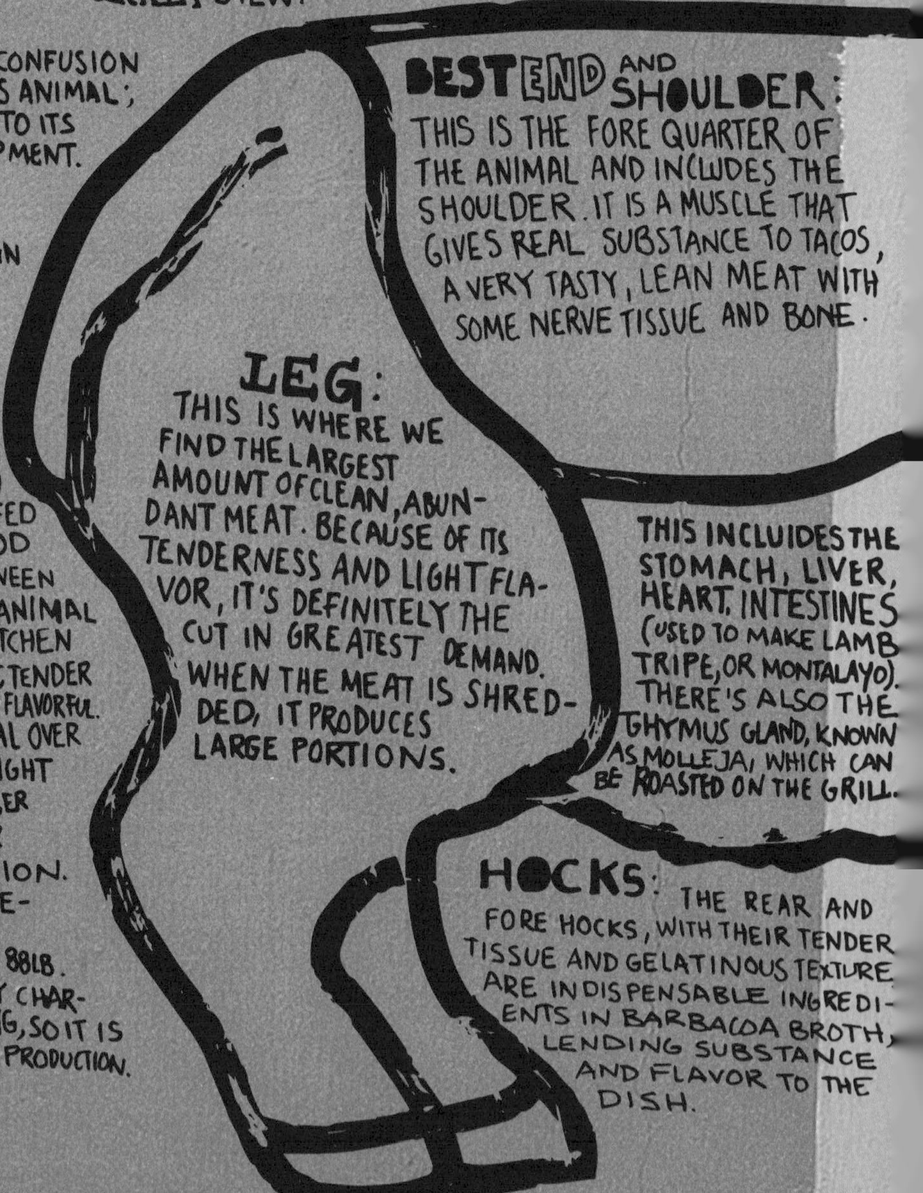

BEST END AND SHOULDER: THIS IS THE FORE QUARTER OF THE ANIMAL AND INCLUDES THE SHOULDER. IT IS A MUSCLE THAT GIVES REAL SUBSTANCE TO TACOS, A VERY TASTY, LEAN MEAT WITH SOME NERVE TISSUE AND BONE.

LEG: THIS IS WHERE WE FIND THE LARGEST AMOUNT OF CLEAN, ABUNDANT MEAT. BECAUSE OF ITS TENDERNESS AND LIGHT FLAVOR, IT'S DEFINITELY THE CUT IN GREATEST DEMAND. WHEN THE MEAT IS SHREDDED, IT PRODUCES LARGE PORTIONS.

THIS INCLUDES THE STOMACH, LIVER, HEART, INTESTINES (USED TO MAKE LAMB TRIPE, OR MONTALAYO). THERE'S ALSO THE THYMUS GLAND, KNOWN AS MOLLEJA, WHICH CAN BE ROASTED ON THE GRILL.

HOCKS: THE REAR AND FORE HOCKS, WITH THEIR TENDER TISSUE AND GELATINOUS TEXTURE ARE INDISPENSABLE INGREDIENTS IN BARBACOA BROTH, LENDING SUBSTANCE AND FLAVOR TO THE DISH.

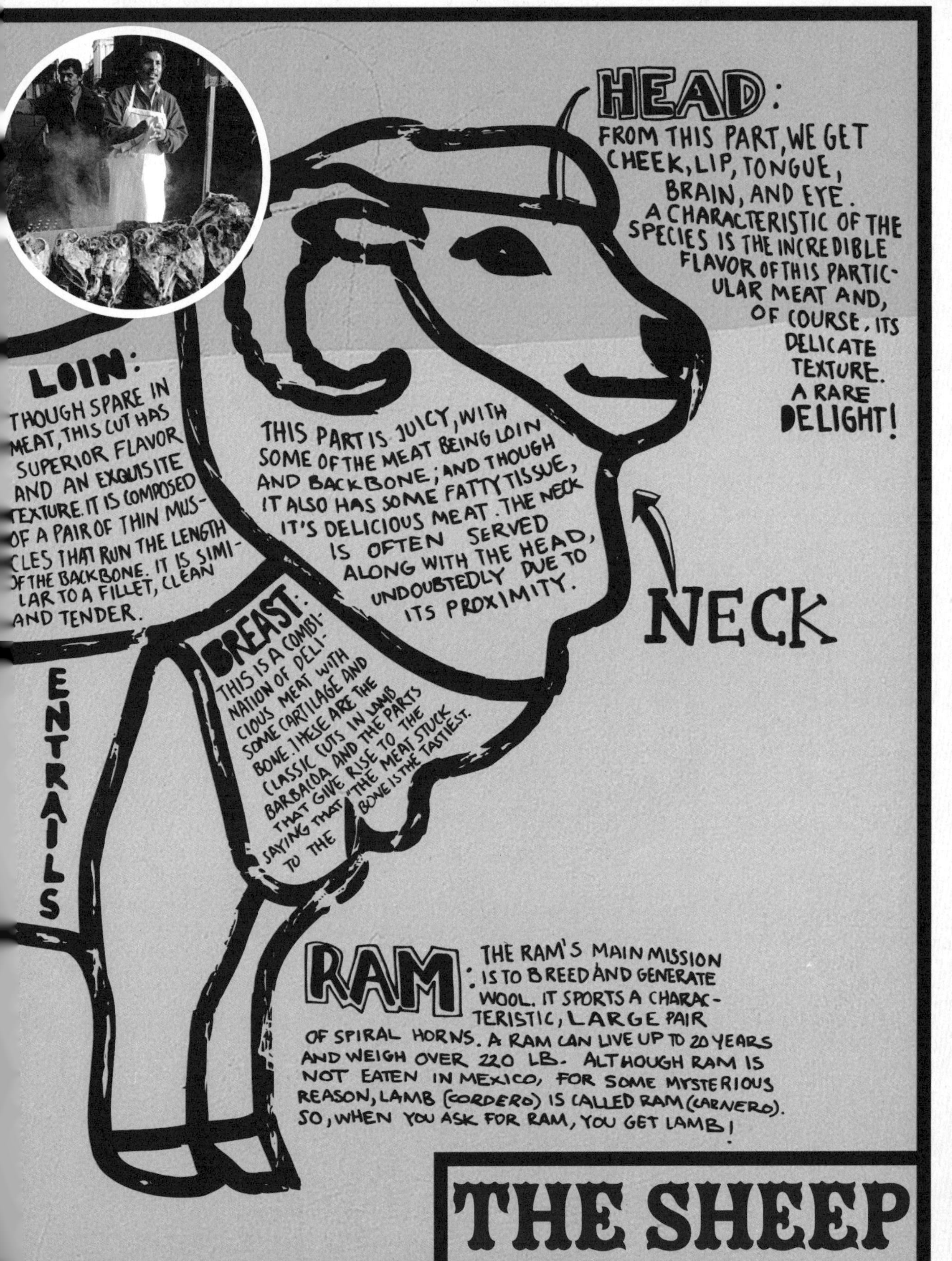
HEAD:
FROM THIS PART, WE GET CHEEK, LIP, TONGUE, BRAIN, AND EYE. A CHARACTERISTIC OF THE SPECIES IS THE INCREDIBLE FLAVOR OF THIS PARTICULAR MEAT AND, OF COURSE, ITS DELICATE TEXTURE. A RARE DELIGHT!
LOIN:
THOUGH SPARE IN MEAT, THIS CUT HAS SUPERIOR FLAVOR AND AN EXQUISITE TEXTURE. IT IS COMPOSED OF A PAIR OF THIN MUSCLES THAT RUN THE LENGTH OF THE BACKBONE. IT IS SIMILAR TO A FILLET, CLEAN AND TENDER.
THIS PART IS JUICY, WITH SOME OF THE MEAT BEING LOIN AND BACKBONE; AND THOUGH IT ALSO HAS SOME FATTY TISSUE, IT'S DELICIOUS MEAT. THE NECK IS OFTEN SERVED ALONG WITH THE HEAD, UNDOUBTEDLY DUE TO ITS PROXIMITY.
NECK
BREAST:
THIS IS A COMBINATION OF DELICIOUS MEAT WITH SOME CARTILAGE AND BONE. THESE ARE THE CLASSIC CUTS IN LAMB BARBACOA AND THE PARTS THAT GIVE RISE TO THE SAYING THAT "THE MEAT STUCK TO THE BONE IS THE TASTIEST."
ENTRAILS
RAM:
THE RAM'S MAIN MISSION IS TO BREED AND GENERATE WOOL. IT SPORTS A CHARACTERISTIC, LARGE PAIR OF SPIRAL HORNS. A RAM CAN LIVE UP TO 20 YEARS AND WEIGH OVER 220 LB. ALTHOUGH RAM IS NOT EATEN IN MEXICO, FOR SOME MYSTERIOUS REASON, LAMB (CORDERO) IS CALLED RAM (CARNERO). SO, WHEN YOU ASK FOR RAM, YOU GET LAMB!
THE SHEEP

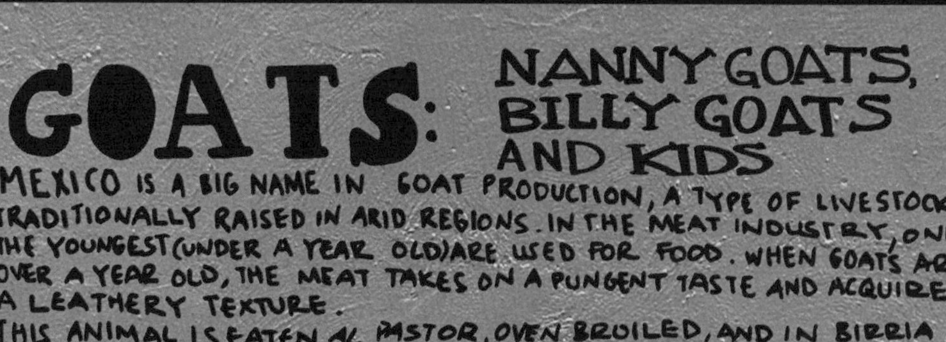

GOATS: NANNY GOATS, BILLY GOATS AND KIDS

MEXICO IS A BIG NAME IN GOAT PRODUCTION, A TYPE OF LIVESTOCK TRADITIONALLY RAISED IN ARID REGIONS. IN THE MEAT INDUSTRY, ONLY THE YOUNGEST (UNDER A YEAR OLD) ARE USED FOR FOOD. WHEN GOATS ARE OVER A YEAR OLD, THE MEAT TAKES ON A PUNGENT TASTE AND ACQUIRES A LEATHERY TEXTURE.

THIS ANIMAL IS EATEN AL PASTOR, OVEN BROILED, AND IN BIRRIA STEW. HERE ARE THE DIFFERENT NAMES GOATS GO BY:

KID: IF NURSING AND UNDER 25 DAYS OLD, A KID IS REFERRED TO AS A CABRITO AND USUALLY WEIGHS 11-22LB. IF OVER 25 DAYS BUT UNDER A YEAR OLD AND NO LONGER NURSING, THEN IT IS CALLED A *CHIVO*. THEY ARE USUALLY FATTENED BEFORE SLAUGHTERED, TO REACH A WEIGHT OF 15-45 LB.

NANNY-GOAT: THIS IS THE FEMALE ADULT GOAT, USUALLY RESERVED FOR BREEDING AND MILK PRODUCTION.

BILLY-GOAT: THIS IS THE MALE ADULT GOAT, USED ONLY FOR BREEDING AND NOT FOOD PRODUCTION.

LEG: IN THIS PART, WE FIND THE LARGEST SUPPLY OF MEAT IN A GOAT KID. WHEN PREPARED CORRECTLY, IT IS JUICY, VERY TENDER AND HAS AN EXCELLENT TASTE.

LOIN: THIS CUT IS THE BACK, OR UPPER PART OF THE ANIMAL, FROM SHOULDER TO HIPS. THERE IS QUITE A LOT OF BONE HERE, BUT THE MEAT ALONG EACH SIDE OF THE BACKBONE IS CONSIDERED A FINE CUT.

SHOULDER: THIS FRONT PART OF THE LOIN, THE SHOULDER, WITH A VARIETY OF CUTS, COVERS A QUARTER OF THE ANIMAL. IT HAS EXQUISITE MEAT WITH SOME BONE.

ENTRAILS: GOAT KIDNEYS ARE A RENOWNED DELIGHT, AND GOAT'S BLOOD IS USED TO PREPARE THE *FRITADA*, A BROTH MADE FAMOUS IN NUEVO LEON. WITH THE OMENTUM (A DELICATE FATTY TISSUE INSIDE THE RIB CAGE THAT WRAPS AROUND THE INTESTINAL ORGANS) AND THE INTERNAL ORGANS IT PROTECTS, AS WELL AS HEART, LIVER, AND LUNG, IT'S POSSIBLE TO MAKE MACHITO, A DISH SIMILAR TO HAGGIS.

HOCKS: THE LEGS OF THIS ANIMAL ARE THIN AND, AS SUCH, HAVE NO CULINARY USE ASIDE FROM ADDING FLAVOR AND NUTRITIONAL VALUE TO A BROTH, AS IS THE CASE WITH BIRRIA STEW.

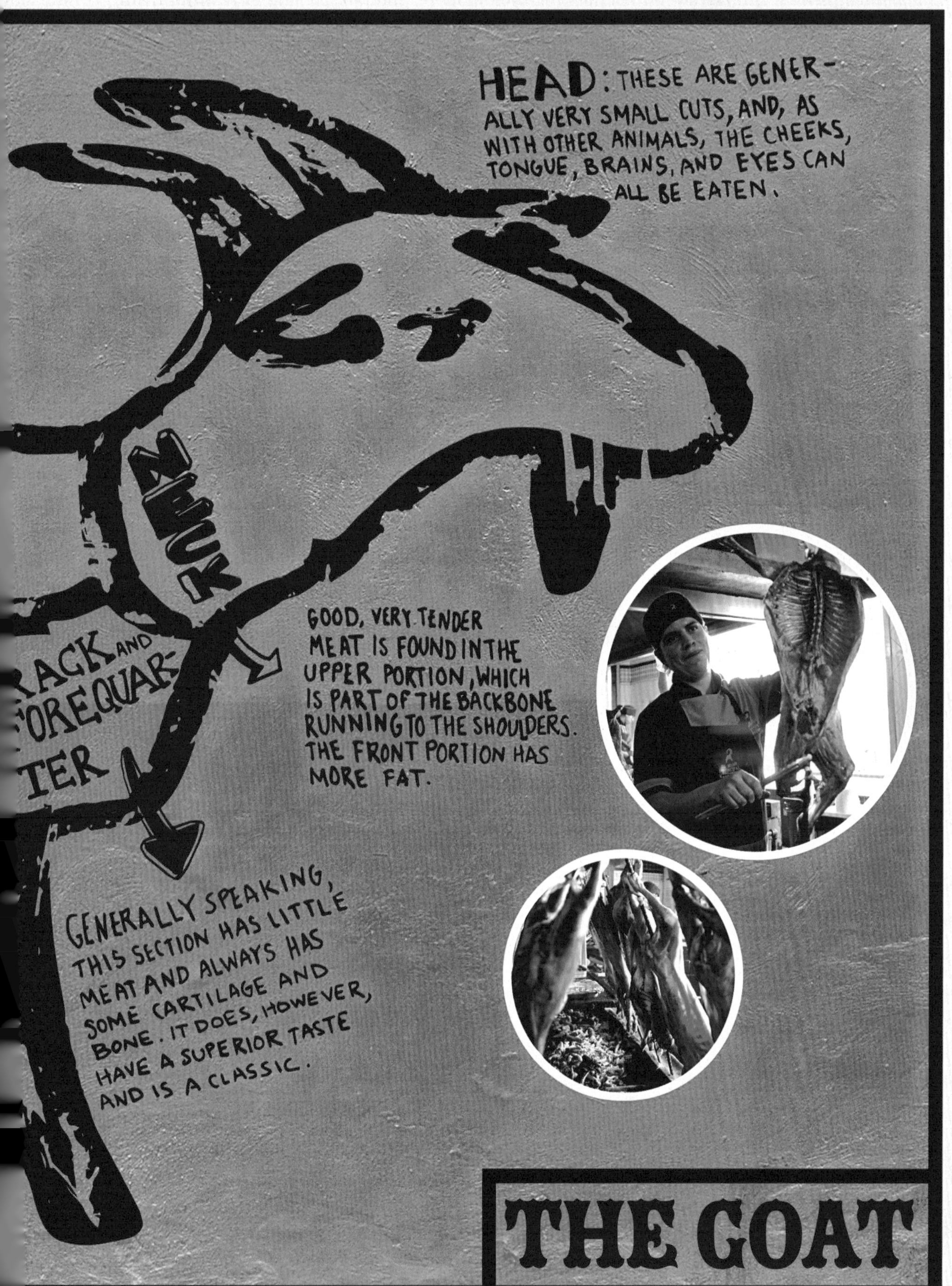
HEAD: THESE ARE GENERALLY VERY SMALL CUTS, AND, AS WITH OTHER ANIMALS, THE CHEEKS, TONGUE, BRAINS, AND EYES CAN ALL BE EATEN.
NECK
RACK AND
OREQUAR-
TER
GOOD, VERY TENDER MEAT IS FOUND IN THE UPPER PORTION, WHICH IS PART OF THE BACKBONE RUNNING TO THE SHOULDERS. THE FRONT PORTION HAS MORE FAT.
GENERALLY SPEAKING, THIS SECTION HAS LITTLE MEAT AND ALWAYS HAS SOME CARTILAGE AND BONE. IT DOES, HOWEVER, HAVE A SUPERIOR TASTE AND IS A CLASSIC.
THE GOAT

PART 2

IT'S

TACO

TIME

TACOS ON THE GRILL

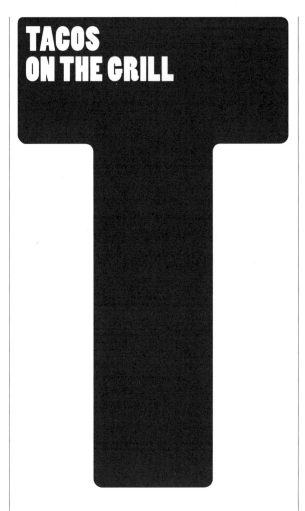

There are two giveaways that prove these tacos aren't of pre-Hispanic origin: beef and grilling, since both came over with the Spanish. In antiquity, all cultures did have one thing in common—ritual sacrifice of animals to the gods. The pungent aroma that wafts up from meat in contact with burning coals is so alluring that it's easy to understand why people treated it as sacred for thousands of years. Indeed, the most ancient way to prepare an animal for eating is to roast it over hot coals; and if this was pleasing to the gods, surely there could be no better dish.

NORTHERN ORIGINS

It's well known that pre-Hispanic Mexicans roasted many kinds of animals over the coals—birds, fish, frogs, and dogs—and the meat was very likely served in tacos. The fundamental difference between then and now lies in the use of a metal grill, a cooking tool unknown in the Americas before the arrival of the Spanish. Before that time, people probably used wooden skewers and griddles made of wood or palm leaves, known as *tapescos*, or else use the old trick of putting the meat next to the coals. Grilling beef is a popular method of cooking throughout the north of Mexico, a region that, for many years, was in fact defined as "a grilled-beef culture."

TYPICAL IN SONORA, CHIHUAHUA, COAHUILA, TAMAULIPAS

MADE WITH BEEF

COOKED ON A GRILL

The famous charcoal-grilled tacos arrived in Mexico City as late as the 1950s, though today they are found throughout the country. Perhaps the biggest difference between the two lies in the northern tradition of referring to meat cuts using "American-style" terms; in the capital of the country, meanwhile, the choice is basically reduced to either steak tacos or rib tacos.

Compared to the great variety of tacos on offer, at first glance this simplistic distinction may seem less imaginative, but in reality, for many meat lovers, beef tacos cooked on the grill need no further explanation.

ON THE RACK

A grill is a tool that consists, quite simply, of a rack of metal bars, which allows the heat from below to toast or roast whatever is placed over them. The metal bars separate the meat from direct contact with the coals but allow the heat to move upwards while immediately dispersing any moisture. Meat cooked using this method ends up golden brown on the outside, juicy on the inside, and smoked with the characteristic aroma of the coals. All kinds of meat can be roasted on the grill without the need for oil, though there is a tradition of marinating or seasoning it beforehand to tenderize the meat and bring out its flavor. Once cooked, the meat is chopped up on a cutting board and placed on tortillas. The entire process is simple, so the flavor mostly depends on the meat itself more than anything else.

STEAK, RIBS, AND CURED MEAT

Many people are surprised to discover that the word *bistec* (a term derived from the English "beefsteak") refers to the cut, rather than which part of the animal it comes from. So, *bistec* in tacos can be any piece of meat cut into thin slices. The meat is often pounded to make it even thinner, and some real pros go so far as to use a food slicer on a frozen cut to get uniform, wafer-thin slices.

The cuts themselves can easily be broken down into two categories: select and regular. Certain select cuts are much in demand—sirloin, blade steak, eye round, and tip steak—while some cuts come from other leg muscles or different parts of the cow altogether—tip round, bottom round, blade roast, shank cross-cut, and neck. Besides steak and rib cuts, other varieties of meat have their place in these tacos: *arrachera*, *cecina* (both beef and pork), chops, pork chorizo sausages (see page 76), as well as a taco mainstay, *alambre*. Ribs or pork chops are thin cuts that come from the ribcage and have some bone; thick pork chops are nearly impossible to find at a taco stand. Many taco makers can be found using other pork cuts (from the leg, neck, backbone, blade, or loin) under the label *chuleta*, or pork chop.

In charcoal-grilled or griddle tacos, it's rare to hear people talking about pork ribs, since they belong to the world of *carnitas* (see page 143) and refer to a cut near the chest of the animal at the tip of the rib cage, American-style short ribs. *Cecina* is a term that refers to a method of seasoning rather than a particular cut. It is generally lean beef from tip roast, bottom round, or top round steaks, thinly sliced, salted, and then cured in a dry and well-ventilated place. In this preparation, it is also known as *tasajo*, which comes from the state of Oaxaca and resembles beef jerky.

There is also a version of *cecina* made from pork, known as *cecina enchilada*. Usually from the leg of the animal and, though salt-cured as well, it undergoes a different process, since it's also marinated in achiote (annatto paste) together with ground chiles, such as guajillo or ancho. Whether used on beef or pork, the seasonings dehydrate the meat and protect it from bacteria, so that after a week in a dry, cool, ventilated place, it is perfectly preserved and has a texture and flavor different from that of fresh meat. It can then be safely stored for many weeks.

Whatever the meat filling, charcoal-grilled tacos are often accompanied by fried green onions, grilled *nopales*, slow-roasted green serrano chiles, as well as an assortment of fresh, cooked, or mixed chile salsas (see recipes 1–4, 7, 8, 10, 14, 17–19, 21, 22, 28–30, pages 296–307).

These tacos are traditionally accompanied by *charro* beans (see page 77), which are served in miniature ceramic casserole dishes to keep them warm. Be sure to find some lime wedges and salt on the side, as well as slices of avocado, cucumber, or radish.

THE CHARCOAL'S THE THING

These tacos are defined by how they're cooked, so the charcoal is essential. However, red meat is not the only filling: anything put onto the grill is a worthy addition, from chicken to fish to rabbit, and even grilled vegetables, such as *nopales* or peppers, which, despite their novelty, undoubtedly make for a delicious alternative.

ALAMBRES OR SKEWERS

The classic combination for *alambres* or skewers is beef cubes, strips of smoked bacon, poblano chile, and onion. The ingredients are alternately threaded onto a skewer that is slowly moved

"DECÍA EL BUEN CARNICERO: 'DE LA CABEZA A LA COLA, TODO ES BISTEC DE BOLA.'"

"Said the butcher, 'I'm no fake: Top to tip, it's tip-top steak.'"
Meaning that the butcher is so handy with his knife that he can make any cut of meat look good.

toward the heat of the coals. Patience is the key here: too much heat, and the outside will be scorched, while the inside is left raw; too little, and the whole brochette dries out, tough and lifeless. This ancient cooking method has endless possibilities: surf-and-turf, chicken, shrimp, mushroom, and so on. Obviously, the ingredients can be slid off the skewer and into a taco. Indeed, many taco places have broken the rules altogether and their *alambres* have lost their skewers completely; instead, the ingredients are prepared right on the griddle. Some replace the poblano with red or green chiles, while others like to top it all off with cheese. Any of these tacos could be done on a griddle, but that's for the next chapter.

BURRITO PERCHERÓN

Perhaps the best example of the use of flour tortillas is the so-called *burrito percherón*. These tacos consist of an oversized, 12- to -16–inch diameter *tortilla sobaquera*—perhaps so-called because it can be carried under the arm in the armpit, or *sobaco*—with mayonnaise spread on top, avocado slices, a pound of finely chopped grilled meat, and a little grated Chihuahua cheese. It's finished off like any burrito: fold one side over, close the ends, and roll it up from the other side to seal in all the flavor.

PIRATE TACOS

If you can't find those huge tacos that are so typical in Baja California, Sonora, and Chihuahua, then there's a consoling possibility: you can use flour tortillas of any size. Be forewarned, though that these will be considered "pirate tacos," the name they are given in the states of Coahuila, Nuevo León, and Tamaulipas with no documented reason. They are usually made with grilled meat and cheese, and accompanied by a fresh avocado garnish.

THE
FIRST THING
IN THE MEXICAN
BASIC
FAMILY BASKET
IS THE

BEEF;

THEN THE

TORTILLAS;

AND THEN THE

BEER.

"THIS IS A TOUGH NEIGHBORHOOD, BUT WE'LL GET AHEAD."

We've got charcoal-grilled beef, pork chop, and *longaniza* tacos here, as well as quesadillas, and beef-with-cheese, pork chop-with-cheese, and *longaniza*-with-cheese tacos.

The tacos are good because they're charcoal-grilled and the tortillas are freshly made by hand. The secret ingredient is the seasoning of the salsas, which are made right here every day. The tortillas, salsas, and charcoal give the tacos a different flavor from other charcoal-grilled tacos. They're prepared in a special way to give the meat its unique taste. All kinds come here... we've had some names here too—the singer Paquita la del Barrio and the attorney general of Chiapas, and others. The business started in 1970. My husband founded it. When we got married, he had already started here and knew the business. They are the same tacos we serve today. The truth is that I have never kept count of how many we sell, but it's a lot. The beef tacos are the most popular, but the beef-with-cheese and pork-chop tacos and quesadillas also sell well. The tacos are good because of their beefy flavor.

The pork chop is also very good, but some people don't eat pork. The *longaniza* sausage is good too because it's not the type you regret afterwards. It's a special type of sausage, not the usual kind. A person can eat these and they're just fine. My husband is the one that knew all the stories about the business, not me. We've had robberies just like everyone else—no, you can't avoid it, but lately they've left us in peace. We thank God for the business. We love it. One of our workers has been with us for over twenty years. Two others have been here eight and nine years. They are happy working with us, and we're happy with them. We have an understanding, and I feel comfortable here. This is a tough neighborhood, but we'll get ahead.

Lidia Segura Rosas
TAQUERÍA LAS BRASITAS
210 EJE 1 PONIENTE, GUERRERO,
MEXICO CITY

CHORIZO SAUSAGE

Chorizo is a spicy pork sausage that's associated with Toluca, though it's made all over Mexico. Its preparation consists of five steps: it's chopped, seasoned, left to sit, stuffed in casings, and then cured. Naturally, the first thing to do is to wash the pork intestines, then fill them with a mix of pork meat liberally seasoned with chiles, paprika, garlic, cumin, and vinegar, though every establishment has its secret recipe. It's important that the meat cures in the right conditions for at least 20 days before going on sale because the flavors need time to blend perfectly. Chorizo sausage usually has a deep red color, but there are also green chorizo sausages, their color due to the different seasonings—green pepper, cilantro, marjoram, etc.—though the taste is similar.

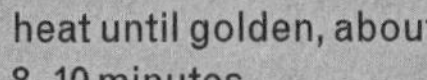

MELTED CHEESE WITH CHORIZO AND POBLANO CHILE SLICES

Serves 2

—1 medium poblano chile
—2 tablespoons (30 g) unsalted butter, plus extra for greasing
—2 tablespoons corn oil
—3½ oz (100 g) chorizo, crumbled or diced small
—9 oz (250 g) Oaxaca or string cheese, grated or finely chopped
—Freshly ground black pepper
—4–6 flour tortillas, to serve

1. Roast the poblano chile on a griddle or over an open fire until blackened, then place it in a plastic bag to sweat for 15 minutes.
2. Carefully peel off the burnt skin. Remove the seeds and veins, and then cut the chile into thin slices.
3. Melt the butter in a skillet over low heat. Add the chile and cook for around 3 minutes. Transfer chiles to a plate and set aside.
4. Add a little oil in a skillet, then fry the chorizo on a low heat until golden, about 8–10 minutes.
5. Grease two small ovenproof ramekins with butter.
6. Put the chile and half the cheese in the ramekins, and the sausage and the rest of the cheese in the other. Season with a little pepper.
7. Heat for 5 minutes on the stovetop, grill, or griddle, or else warm in the oven at 350°F/180°C/Gas Mark 4 until the cheese just begins to bubble. (Be careful not to overheat the cheese mix.)
8. Serve immediately with flour tortillas.

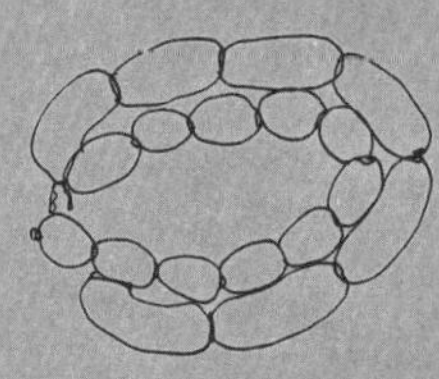

CHARRO BEANS

Serves 4

—2 tablespoons corn oil
—3½ oz (100 g) chopped chorizo
—3½ oz (100 g) bacon, finely diced
—2 cloves garlic
—1 medium onion, finely chopped
—1 large tomato, peeled and diced
—A pinch of ground cumin
—4 bay leaves
—2 medium jalapeño chiles, sliced
—4 cups (about 1 liter) broth from the cooked beans (if preparing with canned beans, use water or vegetable broth)
—4 cups (2¼ lb/1 kg) cooked bayo, pinto, or chili beans
—3½ oz (100 g) crispy fried pork rinds, cut into medium-sized chunks
—3 sprigs cilantro
—½ teaspoon dried oregano
—Apple cider vinegar
—Sea salt

1. Put a little oil in a large pot, then fry the sausage and bacon together on low heat until both are golden brown.
2. Add the garlic to the pot and cook for 2–3 minutes.
3. Add the onion and sauté until translucent for 2–3 minutes.
4. Add the tomato and sauté on high heat for 2–3 minutes.
5. Add the cumin, bay leaves, and chiles. After 1 minute, add the bean broth and the cooked beans.
6. Add the pork rinds to the mixture as soon as it starts to boil, along with the cilantro, oregano, and a few drops of vinegar and bring to a simmer.
7. Let simmer for 10 minutes at low heat and add salt to taste. The mixture should be loose.
8. Serve in bowls or individual casserole dishes.

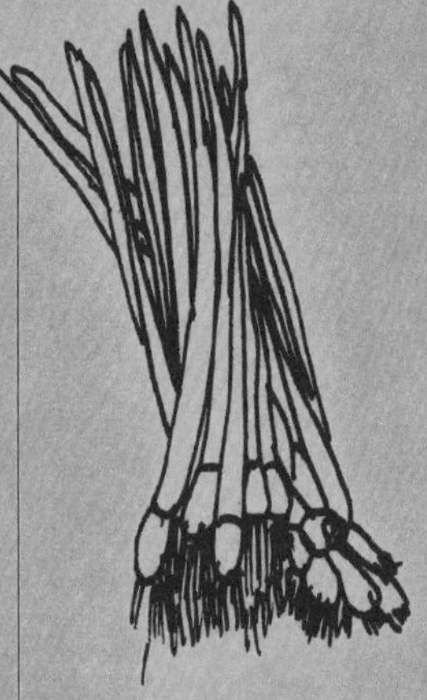

FRIED GREEN ONIONS

Serves 4

—½ cup (120ml) corn oil
—1 clove garlic, finely chopped
—1 tablespoon sea salt, plus more as needed
—Apple cider vinegar
—20 green onions
—Lime wedges, for serving

1. Stir the oil, garlic, salt, and a few drops of vinegar together in a small bowl. Let sit for 1 hour at room temperature.
2. Thoroughly clean the onions, then cut off the root ends from the heads, discarding the green stalks.
3. Put the onion heads in the garlic oil and fry on a grill or griddle, turning until golden brown.
4. Serve with a sprinkling of lime and salt.

THE BEST

Bellinghausen
95 LONDRES, ZONA ROSA, MEXICO CITY
The oven-roasted goat alone is worth making the trip to the Zona Rosa, a neighborhood that's certainly seen better days.

Casa Ávila
8 MIGUEL ÁNGEL DE QUEVEDO, COL. CHIMALISTAC, MEXICO CITY
Though you can have traditional Spanish fare as well, you can't miss the charcoal-grilled goat at Casa Ávila, served with roasted chiles, guacamole, and all the tortillas you could possibly eat.

Casa Regia
39 ARQUÍMEDES, COL. POLANCO, MEXICO CITY
Promoting Monterrey cuisine among the business class in Polanco, Casa Regia offers goat meat tacos *al pastor*, as well as charcoal-grilled lamb.

El Chilo
268 HIDALGO PONIENTE, COL. MITRAS SUR, MONTERREY, NUEVO LEÓN
Famous in Monterrey for its "pirate beef tacos": roast beef, avocado, and grilled cheese in corn or flour tortillas, served with onion, roast sausage, guacamole, and refried or charro beans.

El Farolito
19 ALTATA , COL. CONDESA, MEXICO CITY
This restaurant recently celebrated half a century in business, placing it among the first in Mexico City to offer steak, rib, and pork chop tacos.

El Rey del Cabrito
817 CONSTITUCIÓN ORIENTE, CENTRO, MONTERREY, NUEVO LEÓN
You can order kidney, leg, brisket, chuck, half the animal, or the whole thing in this typical Monterrey eatery, with all the salsa and tortillas you could ask for.

Los Bomberos
CALLEJÓN AGUSTÍN LARA (CORNER OF AQUILES SERDÁN), CENTRO CULIACÁN, SINALOA
The main attraction of this Sinaloan taco stand is its *tacos Pirulí*, made of roast beef with anaheim chile (a regional pepper made for grilling) and filled with Chihuahua cheese.

Los Picudos
230 MORAS, COL. DEL VALLE, MEXICO CITY
The tortillas are small, the prices expensive, and the place cramped—still, people keep coming in order to enjoy some of the best charcoal-grilled steak tacos in Mexico City.

Sonora Grill
1955 COYOACÁN (CORNER OF UNIVERSIDAD), COL. XOCO, MEXICO CITY
The success of Sonora Grill lies in combining a night club atmosphere with an extensive menu of meat cuts, including New York tacos, chopped flank steak seasoned with garlic, cilantro, and chiltepin chiles.

Tacos Fonda Argentina
431 PARROQUIA, COL. DEL VALLE, MEXICO CITY
The success that this business had with steak restaurants led it to open up a taco restaurant. They also serve *chinchulines*, Argentine-style tripe.

TACOS ON THE GRIDDLE

Every taco place in Mexico has a griddle to make tortillas or heat them up. Many specialized businesses prepare the entire menu on the griddle: from established restaurants to taco shacks to the taco stands wheeled into neighborhood markets, where you can find *campechano* tacos and other less well-known variations. Any grilled-meat tacos can be made on the griddle; other snacks, such as *huaraches* and *sopes* (see page 277), are usually cooked on the griddle, along with the famous *gaoneras* (see page 82) and *cecina* tacos. On this hot metal plate, tortillas and meat can be cooked side-by-side in a way that has surely benefited the world of tacos.

THE COMAL RELOADED

The griddle—a hot, flat surface to cook food on—is little more than a modern version of the pre-Hispanic clay comal. In fact, the tortilla itself got its start with the comal, placing the origin of the tortilla in the Classic period in Mesoamerica (see page 29). The comal is still an essential utensil in Mexican cuisine, and is so familiar to anyone claiming to be a cook in Mexico. They adapt to its particularities and skillfully learn to get the most out of it in any culinary situation.

With the comal so firmly established in Mexico, the steel griddle felt right at home when it came over from Spain. In fact, it might be said that here any sheet of metal can lend itself to this purpose, heating up the food that would be cooked on a comal, plus anything else that takes your fancy.

Since the heat is more evenly distributed over a metal sheet, a griddle is an improvement on a clay comal; what's more, a griddle becomes non-stick after repeated use, so it's easier to clean thoroughly every time. At places serving tacos in Mexico, you'll find griddles that range from a modest strip of metal to colossal sheets, with its size as a fair indicator of how business is going.

And though it's easy to find a metal comal in any market in Mexico with different colored tacos sizzling away on it—tacos for every taste, quesadillas, and the like—the origin of modern griddle tacos as a specialty remains a mystery.

HOT OFF THE GRIDDLE

When food hits the griddle, the scorching-hot surface uniformly sears it on contact, leaving it juicy inside. The griddle is heated from below by either a gas stove or charcoal. As mentioned, the griddle is essential equipment for a taco stand, since it's used for heating or making the tortillas. High-quality griddles are stainless steel, but other materials will do. Beef, pork, cheese, and vegetables are the mainstay fillings of the griddle taco, though it has its own variants, such as *alambres*, *gaoneras*, and *campechanos*.

> "How were those *arrachera* tacos? Would you like some more, or should I get the *cecina* ones going? So, it was a Friday and there were a lot of drunks. And one of them didn't wanna pay, he was like 'You're overcharging me,' and stuff like that. What's that? Hold the onion, you say? No problem, boss! And a horchata drink? Comin' right up! And so he was all 'I'm calling Immigration,' and so on... and there was some pushing and shoving, and next thing I know that guy and his friends were lying on the floor! They had to carry the drunk guy away because I knocked him out cold!"
>
> **GERARDO CÁRDENAS.**
> "Gallito Bravo," in ***A Veces Llovía en Chicago***. Mexico: Libros Magenta, 2011.

STEAK TACOS

Although steak tacos come in different styles, they're all based on the same principle: thin strips of beef on a griddle. Once the meat has been cooked, it's finely chopped up and made into a taco. The steak-and-bacon taco, *bistec con tocino*, is a classic, with both meats cooked side-by-side. Another way to make steak tacos, one that first appeared in the 1970s and is popular at both restaurants and street stands, consists of cooking up a heap of finely chopped, seasoned steak meat, then leaving it warming on the griddle, ready for the next customer. The order is placed, the meat is portioned onto tortillas, and you're ready to roll. This method may have originated at the Taquería Brasil Copacabana, where tacos are served like this, with a slice of tomato and avocado. At El Charco de las Ranas, meanwhile, they add onion, also preprepared on the griddle in another hot pile. Of course, cheese versions of these specialties are out there too. To continue listing more places would fill an entire book. Each establishment and every taco chef brings out the best subtleties that this piece of equipment allows.

GAONERA STEAK TACOS

You also find beef in the famous *gaonera* tacos, but only quality cuts are used. In principle, it should be a fillet, though any fine cut will do: sirloin, chuck, or rib eye, for example. And while the thinness of the meat is essential, the heat of the griddle is important too: the metal needs to be so hot that the meat is cooked in a quick one-two-and-once-over flip, then tossed whole onto the tortilla, without being chopped up. Recipes vary, but fresh tortillas and tasty hot salsas are of the highest importance. At El Califa de León, they've developed a great variation: every slice of meat is left to soak in pork lard and coarse salt, then kept chilled till the moment it goes on the griddle. Simply delicious.

PORK TACOS

You can make typical pork tacos with rib, pork chop, or chorizo sausage—meats that the griddle treats with the utmost respect. As is often the case with taco recipes, anything goes well with cheese, but cheese with chorizo is the best of all possible combinations. Among other pork products served on the griddle, smoked bacon deserves special mention, since it goes

THE COMAL AND THE POT

The Comal said to the Pot:
"Oh, Pot! Oh, Pot! Oh, Pot!
If you think that I'm just here for you
to lean on, well, I'm not!
Find someone else to prop you up."

And the Pot turned to the Comal:
"Stupid brute, stupid boor!
Can't you see my beans are boiling o'er?
And don't think I'm putting up
With you hogging the coals."

The Comal said to the Pot:
"O' all this push-an'-shove, I'm tired.
An' with your filthy soot from the fire
Look how you've ruined—and for good!—
My elegant attire."

And the Pot just about fainted:
"Oh, really, Hotshot! Is that so?
They brought you—I happen to know—
From the market just as dingy as you are,
And my eyes are all I need
To see you're no movie star."

The Comal said to the Pot:
"Don't come any closer,
There's nothing that's grosser!
I say it morning, noon, and night;
But you just can't get it right!"

So the other shot back, taunting him:
"Hey, stupid, we're not done!
This'll end with you in little pieces—
And don't even think of the police."

The Comal stared at his partner:
"What'd ya say, ya shriveled shrew?
If you can't even make potato soup,
How you gonna make stew?"

And the Pot lit into him livid:
"Look here, 'young man,' that's all just beans!
The potter made you a hundred years back,
Don't think that you can hide
What everyone here has seen."

FRANCISCO GABILONDO SOLER, CRI-CRÍ
Francisco Gabilondo Soler was a Mexican singer-songwriter, born in Veracruz in 1907. He died in 1990. He wrote more than 200 children's songs and created over 300 characters.

well with beef steak tacos and is also used in *alambres* (see page 70). You can make smoked pork rib tacos too: the ribs are griddled to a golden brown, chopped up, then slipped onto a tortilla.

CURED CECINA

Cured beef or pork *cecina* is traditionally cooked on the griddle. When it's ready, you chop it up on a cutting board, then distribute over tortillas. The custom of accompanying *cecina* with sour cream or avocado comes from the state of Morelos, but a new way of serving *cecina* is along with a side of fries or *nopales*.

ALAMBRES

This dish is based on the classic charcoal-grilled skewer, with a variation: the chopped ingredients are cooked separately. First, the bacon and vegetables (poblano chile or else red, yellow, or green peppers) are cooked, then the meat (steak or fillet, for example) goes on the griddle. Another version comes with cheese (see page 70).

FAJITAS

This internationally renowned dish probably owes its fame to its presence in Tex-Mex cuisine, but it is widespread in the north of Mexico. The word *fajita* comes from *faja*, meaning belt or ribbon, and refers to the resemblance between the pieces of grilled meat and strips of leather. This meat can be roasted on a griddle or a grill, but traditionally the steel griddle is preferred, hence the dish's inclusion in this chapter. The meat can be cut up prior to cooking or just before serving. Lastly, the meat is usually served on a sizzling cast-iron platter together with julienned onions or jalapeño or serrano chiles, all done on the griddle.

Griddle tacos are served with green onions, *nopales*, peppers, chiles, mushrooms, and other griddled vegetables. These vegetables can also be a taco filling in their own right, alone or with melted cheese. Raw vegetables, like avocado, tomato, or onion, often make an appearance in these cases, as well as fresh cheese and herbs, like *papaloquelite* or cilantro. Griddle tacos are open to variation: they go perfectly with any salsa or chile.

VARIATIONS ON THE VARIATIONS

There are more versions of griddle tacos out there—in Mexico, the culinary imagination knows no limits!

DISCADAS

This dish is named after the plow or harrow disc it was originally cooked on, and is traditional fare in the north of Mexico. The recipe allows for many variations, but it essentially consists of adding many different diced ingredients to a griddle: bacon, chorizo sausage, onions, chiles, pork, beef, tomatoes, salt, pepper, cumin, beer, cola, or other sodas. These tacos go hand in hand with competitions, bonfires, and parties—and the *charro* beans shouldn't be too far off.

CHEESE AND TACOS

Volcanes are toasted tortillas with grilled beef served with melted cheese. You can also find *queso fundido*, cheese melted on the griddle or in a little clay ramekin served along with tortillas for the diner to prepare tacos. Also common is the *chicharrón de queso* or cheese crackling, a thin slice of cheese cooked on the griddle till it's crunchy and golden. And we can't forget griddle quesadillas: folded tortillas with cheese inside that melts once on the griddle. The tortillas can be made from maize or all-purpose flour, as the quality of a quesadilla mostly depends on the cheese used.

TACOS CAMPECHANOS

The term *campechano* means an unusual or improvised mixture, and this taco is based on beef *cecina*, but is served with *longaniza* pork sausage and deep-fried pork rinds. Versions revolve mostly around the pork rinds, which are commonly crispy but may be pressed (see page 139). Traditionally, these tacos are served with morita chile salsa (see recipe 20, page 302). A new variety of *campechano* tacos, popular in street markets, is special because it's the customer who decides on the meat—beef steak, pork ribs, beef or pork *cecina*, pork cutlets, smoked pork chops, chicken breast, or sausage (either *longaniza* or chorizo)—and the accompanying vegetables—french fries, grilled *nopales*, fried onions, roasted chiles, or refried beans. The option of adding cheese widens the range even further.

SMOTHERED TACOS

The smothered taco, or *chorreada*, has a fresh corn tortilla with a smear of lard, a sprinkling of fried pork rinds, and griddled meat on top. This famous dish originally hails from Mazatlán, Sinaloa, and though it's become better known as a taco, purists insist that it be eaten as a *sope* (see page 277). Some add cheese, which may seem redundant and certainly makes it even greasier. It's usually served with a side of cucumber slices, topped with finely chopped cabbage and *salsa cruda* which, in Sinaloa, is made with chiltepin peppers.

Why are the tacos from Chupacabras so famous?

Because of our history. Guide books say that to come to Coyoacán and not stop by Los Chupas is like not going to Coyoacán. A young guy that worked here came up with the name. His grandfather started working here, and he was always making these dirty jokes, and he'd say, "Without chorizo there is no *Chupas*!"—no sausage, no sucking! The tacos here are made from pork *cecina*, steak, and chorizo. And then there's the *Chupacabras*, our "goatsucker" taco, which has pork, steak, and chorizo, as well as our secret recipe— more than 127 spices! But, if I told you the recipe... well, it wouldn't be a secret anymore! We make the tacos on a griddle so they're ready in a flash, cooked to perfection, which makes them different from other tacos, like *suadero*, where the beef is slow-cooked in broth; or tacos *al pastor*, seasoned pork on a spit. We are open 24 hours a day, 365 days a year. The tacos come with potatoes, *escamoles* (see page 192), beans, green-bean broth, and

"COMING TO COYOACÁN AND NOT VISITING US IS LIKE GOING TO CHAPULTEPEC PARK AND NOT SEEING THE MONKEYS."

chicadriles, a mix all our own, with some onion to give it flavor. And whatever else you want to put on them! We have green and red salsas—every taco gets some. We also have a salsa made with habanero chile and onion. And you can have whatever you want on the side: lime, potato, onion, beans, *nopales*. All this with a good soft drink: *Jarritos*—tasty! Our tacos are like sandwiches—because if you can't close the tortilla, it's a sandwich! This is a family restaurant, and guess what—just for today, kids don't pay—their parents do! This is our third site. Our first spot was on Mayorazgo Street, and then we moved under the bridge. If you don't know these tacos, then you don't know Mexico. I always say, coming to Coyoacán and not visiting us is like going to Chapultepec Park and not seeing the monkeys. You can't miss it!

Carlos Carreño
TACO MAKER AT SUPERTACOS EL CHUPACABRAS, JUNCTION OF CHURUBUSCO AND AV. COYOACÁN (UNDER THE BRIDGE), MEXICO CITY

IN

1979

THE
MEXICAN
VISUAL ARTIST

MARIS BUSTAMANTE

REGISTERED THE

TACO

AS LEGALLY HERS
AND CLAIMED
THE PATENT
RIGHTS.

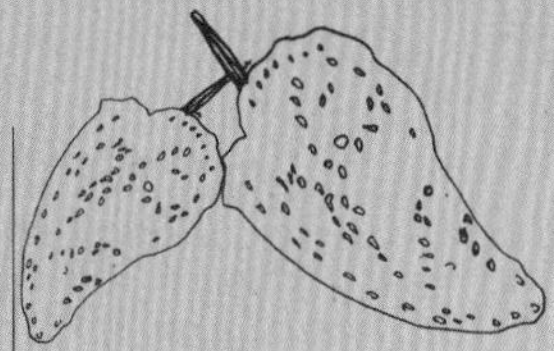

VILLAMELÓN-STYLE CAMPECHANO TACOS

Serves 4

—2 tablespoons corn oil
—1 lb (450 g) *longaniza*, cut into pieces
—1 lb (450 g) cured beef *cecina*, thinly sliced
—6–12 2¾–4⅓-inch (7–11 cm) corn tortillas
—9 oz (250 g) crispy, fried pork rinds, chopped
—3 cups (750 ml) Morita Chile Salsa (see recipe 20, page 302)

1. Heat the oil in a large pot over low heat. Add the sausage and fry for 3–5 minutes, until golden brown.
2. Transfer the meat to a cutting board and chop or shred.
3. Sauté the beef on high heat in the same pot the sausage was fried in, stirring constantly, for 2–3 minutes, until cooked through.
4. As soon as the beef is done, prepare the tacos. Place some strips of beef on a tortilla, a heaping spoonful of sausage, some crushed pork rinds, and some Morita Chile Salsa.

Another way to make this dish would be to fry the beef first, add the sausage, pork rinds, and salsa, with all the ingredients in the same pot. Cook for 1 minute, then serve heaping portions over fresh corn tortillas.

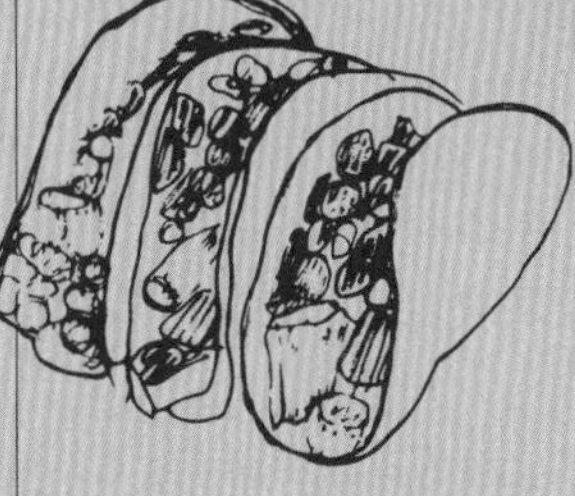

CALIFA DEL LEÓN STYLE GAONERA TACOS

Serves 4

—2¼ lb (1 kg) beef fillet (ask your butcher to slice it into 10 thin, even steaks)
—5 oz (150 g) pork lard
—Coarse salt
—6–12 2¾–4⅓-inch (7–11 cm) corn tortillas
—Halved limes, for serving

1. Melt the lard in a frying pan.
2. Place the steaks one by one on a tray until the surface of the tray is covered.
3. Using a pastry brush, brush the melted lard on the steaks and generously season with salt.
4. Place second layer of steaks on the tray, and repeat with the lard and salt. Continue until all the steaks are on the tray. Cover the tray with plastic wrap or a damp cloth, then chill, at least 2 hours.
5. Cook the steaks, one at a time, on a griddle or in a skillet, over very high heat, 1 minute per side.
6. Serve the steaks, without cutting the meat, on corn tortillas with limes on the side.

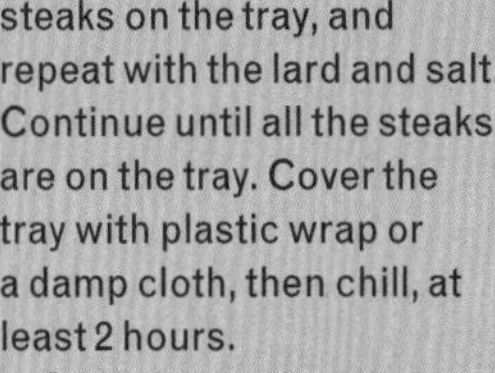

ALAMBRE ON THE SKILLET

Serves 4

—2 tablespoons corn oil
—7 oz (200 g) smoked bacon, cut lengthwise into strips
—9 oz (250 g) raw poblano chile, deseeded and diced small
—4 oz (120 g) diced onions
—14 oz (400 g) thin beef steaks, cut into strips or diced
—Sea salt
—6–12 2¾–4⅓-inch (7–11 cm) corn tortillas, for serving

1. Put a little oil in a skillet, and cook the bacon over low heat until it just starts to sizzle.

2. Add the poblano chile and onion and cook until the onion is translucent.
3. Raise the heat and when the skillet is very hot, add the steak, stirring until the meat is cooked to your preferred taste. Season to taste with salt.
4. Serve on tortillas and accompany with salsa (see recipes 8, 9, 11–13, pages 297–301).

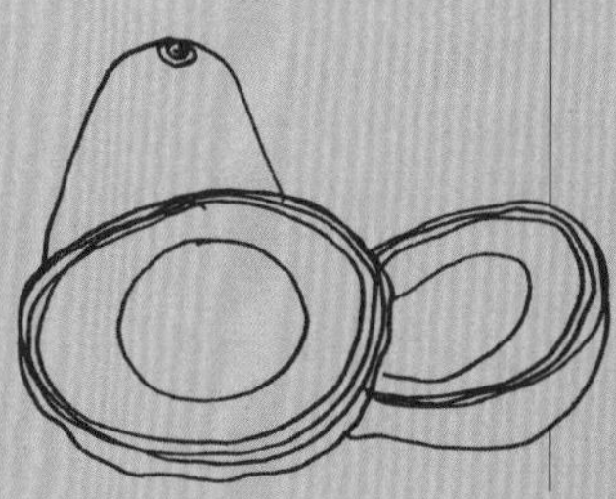

THE BEST

El Califa de León
56 RIBERA DE SAN COSME, COL. SAN RAFAEL, MEXICO CITY
More people associate the word *gaonera* with their beef taco than with the bullfighting move this word comes from. The special flavor of the tacos here comes from the lard and salt marinade.

El Villamelón
123 TINTORETTO (CORNER OF AUGUSTO RODIN), COL. CIUDAD DE LOS DEPORTES, MEXICO CITY
For over half a century this place has been selling *campechano* tacos (cured meat, *longaniza* sausage, and pork rind) in front of Mexico City's bullfighting arena, and they are loved by fans and critics of the sport alike.

Don Beto
1023 DOCTOR VÉRTIZ, COL. NAVARTE, MEXICO CITY
They serve up *los de cochinada*, "the grubby tacos," so named for the extra lard from the grill added to your taco—something that has made this eatery something of an urban legend. Shock treatment after a night's clubbing.

Fonda Km 107
KM 107 ON, MEXICO CITY-ACAPULCO HIGHWAY, ALPUYECA, MORELOS
Previously known as Fonda de Cuatro Vientos, this roadside diner has achieved mythical status for its cured meat and locally made sour cream, all served on long communal tables.

Los de Bucareli
BUCARELI (NEAR CORNER OF DONATO GUERRA), CENTRO HISTORICO, MEXICO CITY
Alberto González, a former butcher, applied his art to a taco stand just outside the offices of the newspaper *Excélsior*, where customers testify to the quality of the beef served in their tortillas.

Los Parados
333 MONTERREY (CORNER OF BAJA CALIFORNIA), COL. ROMA SUR, MEXICO CITY
Essential eating for any self-respecting night owl thanks to generous opening hours, efficient service, and quality food—especially the flank steak tacos and the delicious salsas.

Los Sifones
2804 DIVISIÓN DEL NORTE, COL. PARQUE DE SAN ANDRÉS, MEXICO CITY
This place stands out for two reasons: the enthusiastic use of avocado (two dishes are even called *bistecate*, a "beef-cado," and *arréchate*, a "steak-cado"), and the eatery's unique square-shaped tortillas.

Mochitacos Merino's
1883 CHIHUAHUA SUR, COL. CAMPESTRE, CIUDAD OBREGÓN, SONORA
Excellent taco choices: marinated meat, beef ribs, or stewed beef, all served with cheese, grilled onion, and cabbage, a mix known there as *repollo y frijoles*.

Suntory
14 TORRES ADALID, COL. DEL VALLE, MEXICO CITY
A traditional Japanese restaurant with a gastronomic rarity, the "tacos checa," made from griddled teppanyaki beef, which a customer once requested with tortillas, an item that initially was served only on the sly but is now a main attraction.

Xanto
44 JUAN SALVADOR AGRAZ, SANTA FE, MEXICO CITY
The gourmet version of *tacos campechanos*, made by the famous chef Daniel Ovadia: flank steak, pork rind, and green chorizo sausage from Toluca, artfully garnished with a dab of guacamole.

exa
104.9
exa
COTESCO
PONTE
exa
104.9
SOBRE TODAS LAS COSAS
¡La más perrona!

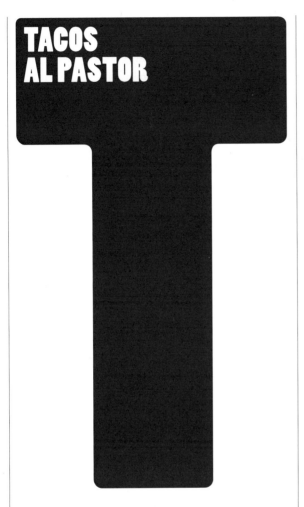

Tacos *al pastor* have a curious name, since, as everyone knows, pigs aren't put out to pasture. Be that as it may, the key to the origins of this taco reside in the upright grill. Originally from Asia, the upright grill spread in popularity and has been used from India to Greece for roasting lamb. This roasted meat goes by different names—doner kebab, shawarma, *doneraky*, or gyros—but they all come from the same grill, with the meat placed on some kind of "bread" and accompanied by various salsas and garnishes.

FROM ASIA WITH LOVE

This grill arrived in Mexico via the city of Puebla, undoubtedly stowed away in the baggage of a Middle-Eastern immigrant. By the 1930s, the evocatively named "Oriental tacos" were part of the local vernacular, and were served either on pita bread or a corn tortilla, with a chipotle chile salsa. The widespread and instant success of these tacos was such that imitators were soon producing variations on the "original" recipe. Several businesses claim paternity: in Puebla, the Antigua Taquería La Oriental and Tacos Árabes Bagdad (both founded in 1933), as well as Tacos Tony (founded in 1942); in Mexico City, El Huequito (founded in 1950) has served it for the longest. These establishments all have an Asian decor, and none use chile marinades for the meat or add pineapple to their tacos. When the upright grill moved on from Puebla, the imitators were left by the wayside, and the taco *al pastor* as we know it today gradually came into being. The fundamental changes were that marinated pork replaced lamb on the spit, and cilantro and onion were added to the tacos. The upright grill got its Mexican papers, and tacos *al pastor* became famous. So where did the pineapple come from? That remains a mystery, though the tradition of adding some fruit is a classic way for many cultures to give pork dishes a sweet-and-sour tang. And in the case of tacos, it was a stroke of genius. The first restaurant to add pineapple to these tacos was probably El Tizoncito, founded in 1966—or at least so say the taco chefs who work there, and no one has ever come forward to say otherwise. One thing's for sure: this particular variation first appeared in Mexico City, where it now can be found on any street corner between noon and the early morning hours.

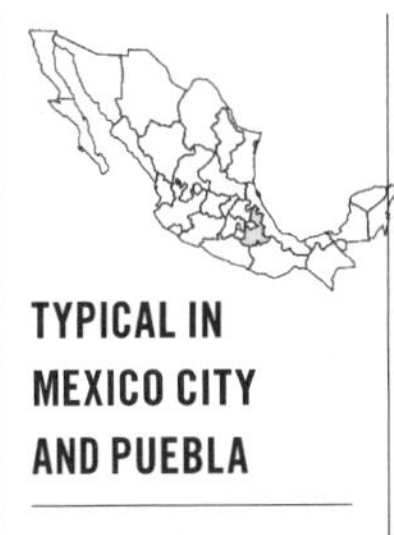

TYPICAL IN MEXICO CITY AND PUEBLA

MADE WITH PORK

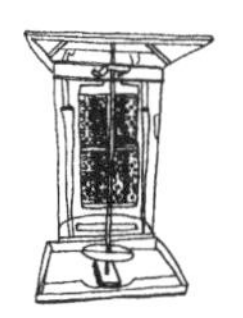

COOKED ON A VERTICAL GRILL

TOP THAT!

Nowadays, the ingredients required for a good taco *al pastor* are the marinated pork grilled upright and served on small corn tortillas, with a pinch of cilantro and chopped onion, along with chipotle chile salsa and some pineapple on top. It's only two or three mouthfuls, but the flavors blend so well they leave you wanting more—a pleasure so tempting that, though you may start off by ordering just one, you'll soon find you've wolfed down half a dozen. To prepare tacos *al pastor*, the pork must be cut into thin slices and then marinated for hours on end. The meat can be from the leg or back, but lean cuts are alternated with fatter ones, like those from the neck, shoulder, or brisket. Once all the meat has been sliced and marinated in *adobo* (see page 203), it is placed piece by piece on a thick metal spit that becomes the axis of a ball of meat, called a *trompo* for its resemblance to a spinning top. A large onion is pierced by the bottom of the spit, and a whole peeled pineapple is speared by the top end. The meat roasts as it revolves in the vertical grill under the watchful eye of an experienced taco maker, who cuts thin slices from the outer layer when they are done. The trick is to cook the pork thoroughly without losing its distinctive tenderness. The tortillas should invariably be small (around 4 inches/5 cm). Some taco restaurants are famous for the dexterity of their taco maker, among them El Tizoncito. They deftly slice off portions of meat, then nimbly sliver a chunk off the pineapple that flies through the air to land squarely on the taco in his waiting hand. And if the traditional red chipotle chile salsa isn't your thing, there's a different salsa for everyone (see pages 296–309).

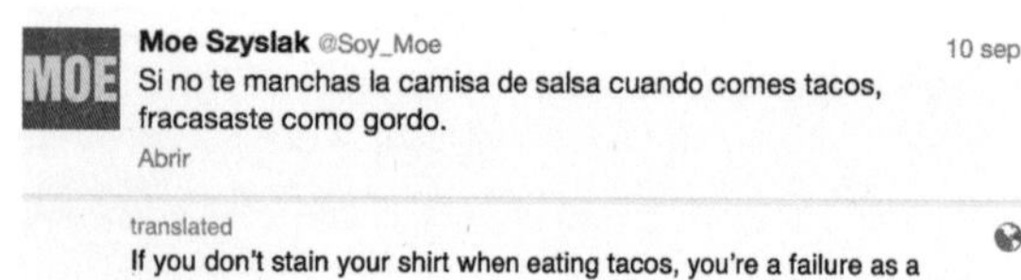

MOE
Moe Szyslak @Soy_Moe
10 sep
Si no te manchas la camisa de salsa cuando comes tacos, fracasaste como gordo.
Abrir
translated
If you don't stain your shirt when eating tacos, you're a failure as a glutton.

FOREIGN, BUT SO MEXICAN

The Mexican culinary imagination brazenly feeds on whatever it discovers, borrowing freely from other cuisines, adding or altering ingredients at will, trying another meat in a dish, while respecting other "traditional" aspects of once-foreign dishes that are now not only proudly Mexican but even considered defining elements of Mexican cuisine. In the case of tacos *al pastor*, we find three main variations.

ARAB AND ASIAN TACOS

Arab and Asian tacos still live on in Puebla, where they are prepared as they always have been. However, these tacos would have little success in Arab countries, since pork has definitively ousted mutton in Mexico. The meat is seasoned with garlic, pepper, onion, and salt, without dried chiles, and is served in pita bread made of all-purpose flour instead of maize. So-called "Arab tacos" are sold throughout Mexico, following neither the original recipe nor that of tacos *al pastor*. It seems that pita bread is enough to make them Arab tacos—even if this is in fact a wheat-flour tortilla—and any kind of meat can be used, even when done on a charcoal grill or griddle.

GRINGAS

A variation on the above is the *gringa*: *asadero* cheese melted over meat *al pastor* in flour tortillas. The origin of this curious name, which basically means "foreign," is unknown, but the most probable explanation stems from mixing something "Swiss" (like the fondue-style cheese used in these tacos) with pork and flour tortillas. There's definitely a logic in there somewhere.

CHICKEN AND FISH TACOS AL PASTOR

There are also chicken and fish varieties of tacos *al pastor*. The meat goes through the same marinating process and can be roasted on a *trompo*, just like regular tacos *al pastor*, though some establishments cook the marinated meat on a regular grill or griddle and serve them with the added touch of pineapple. The overall flavor and seasoning are very much like the original, evenif the consistency is different.

El Tizoncito

ARAB TACOS ARRIVED IN PUEBLA IN THE FORTIES, TOGETHER WITH THE LEBANESE COMMUNITY.

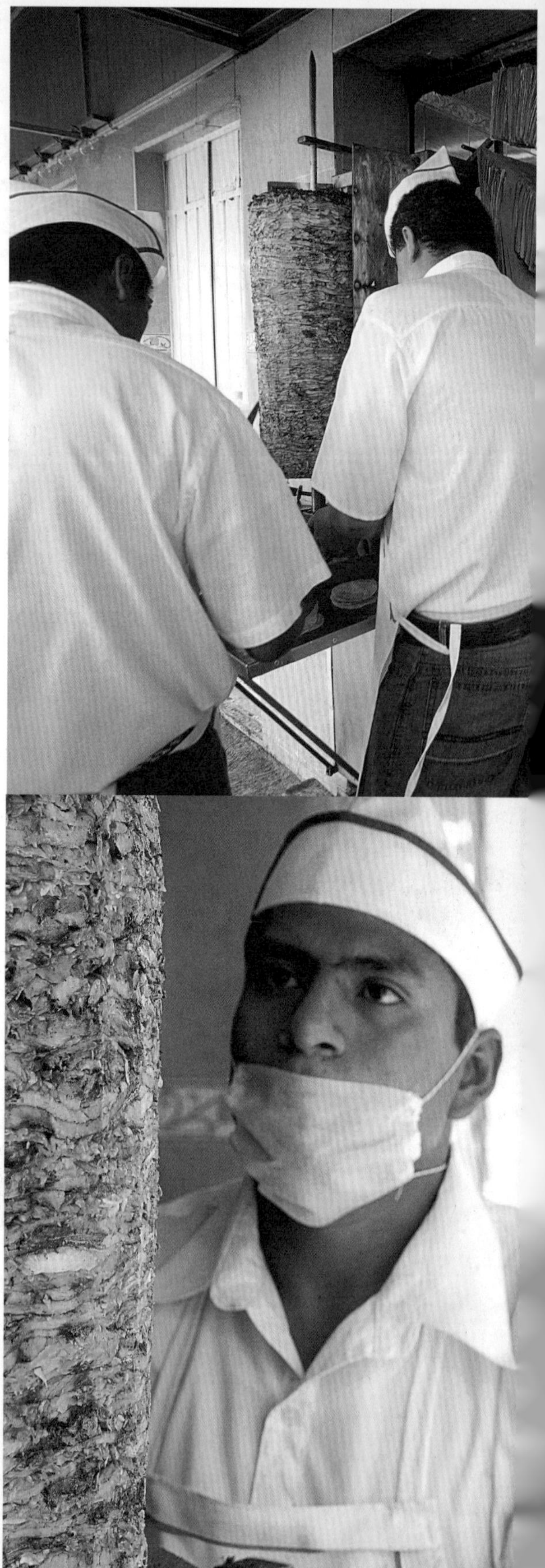

Most of those who sell tacos *al pastor* nowdays garnish them with cilantro, onion, and pineapple: a huge mistake!

The authentic *al pastor* doesn't have pineapple, cilantro, or anything of the sort because the taco's Arabic and, if my memory from my school days serves me, there's no pineapple in the desert because it's a tropical fruit. The authentic taco *al pastor*, the Arabic one, is made with lamb meat and pita bread, called *pan árabe* here in Mexico. Anyway, the flavor of El Huequito's tacos is a mix of Arabic and Mexican because we use pork marinated with natural spices. And we use corn tortillas, not wheat ones. Over there, they use lamb because their religion forbids eating pork, because the animal eats garbage. But, look, truth be told, I do have customers from the Middle East, and they sneak in here to eat their tacos. And no, I'm not going to give up their names! A lot of people who know their food agree that the tacos *al pastor* here taste completely different than those from other places, and that these are the best. Tacos *al pastor* don't have any secret per se. It's all about working the meat well, and marinating it for the right time. I think that every taco place marinates the meat its own way, and I don't say this because I work here, but I do think we serve tacos *al pastor* pretty much how it was in the beginning. It's the owners' secret recipe, and it was passed down from their parents. This is my thirty-fourth year working here and the business has been here for fifty-five, so I've been working here more than half that time! This is a chain restaurant, so it belongs to the owners. They don't really need to open franchises because they have control of their product, their taco. If they want to open another taco restaurant, then they'll do it themselves, and create new jobs.

"I DO HAVE CUSTOMERS FROM THE MIDDLE EAST WHO SNEAK IN HERE TO EAT THEIR TACOS."

Guillermo "El Mayor" Gonzàlez
EL HUEQUITO TACOS
21 AYUNTAMIENTO, CENTRO HISTÓRICO, MEXICO CITY

HAVING TACOS AL PASTOR WITH A "GARDEN" OF ONION, CILANTRO, PINEAPPLE, AND SALSA IS A MEXICO CITY ORIGINAL.

HOME-STYLE MARINATED TACOS AL PASTOR

Serves 4

—2¼ lb (1 kg) pork steak, sliced very thin
—2 cups (500 ml) annatto or ancho chile marinade (see recipes 33, 34, page 309)
—Corn oil, if frying
—Sea salt
—6–12 2¾–4⅓-inch (7–11 cm) corn tortillas
—Roasted pineapple chunks, chopped onion, lime wedges, fried green onions, guacamole, and chipotle or Mexican salsa (see recipes 1, 7, 16, pages 296–302), to garnish

1. Place the meat in the marinade. Cover and refrigerate for at least 3 hours.
2. Roast the meat on the grill or a griddle, for a little more than 1 minute, or until golden brown. (If not working with a grill, sauté the meat in a skillet with a little oil. The steaks should be cooked individually for the best results.)
3. On a cutting board, slice the meat into strips, season, and keep warm.
4. Serve on the warm tortillas with a selection of garnishes.

ROASTED PINEAPPLE

Serves 4–6

—1 small pineapple, peeled, cored, and thinly sliced
—Sugar
—Sea salt
—Corn oil, if frying

1. Dust both sides of the pineapple slices with a little sugar and salt.
2. Roast the slices on a hot grill or griddle, or else fry in a skillet with a little oil, on each side for about half a minute, or until golden.
3. Cut the slices into small chunks and serve on a plate next to the salsas.

TACOS AL PASTOR (VARIATION)

Serves 4

With the marinade from the first recipe, it's possible to make home-made tacos *al pastor* using 2¼ lb (1 kg) of other meat fillings (chicken, rabbit, or dogfish) or vegetarian fillings (such as eggplant, mushrooms, or zucchini).

1. Cut depending on the filling: chicken breast into fillets or tenders; fish into thin fillets; rabbit into thin boneless cuts; vegetables into very thin slices.
2. Place in the marinade, cover, and refrigerate for at least 3 hours.
3. Roast on the grill or griddle, or else fry in a skillet. Once the food has been cooked to taste, finely chop and serve with the usual *al pastor* garnishes.

GRINGAS

Serves 4

—9 oz (250 g) Oaxaca, Chihuahua, or *asadero* cheese (or another melting cheese)
—6–12 4⅓-inch (11-cm) flour tortillas
—11 oz (300 g) meat prepared *al pastor*–style
—Salsa, roasted pineapple, chopped onion, and fresh cilantro, to garnish

1. Make a quesadilla: put some cheese in a flour tortilla, fold the tortilla in half, then warm both sides on a hot griddle until the cheese has melted.
2. Open the quesadilla and add the prepared meat to the melted cheese.
3. Serve immediately with garnishes of your choice.

THE BEST

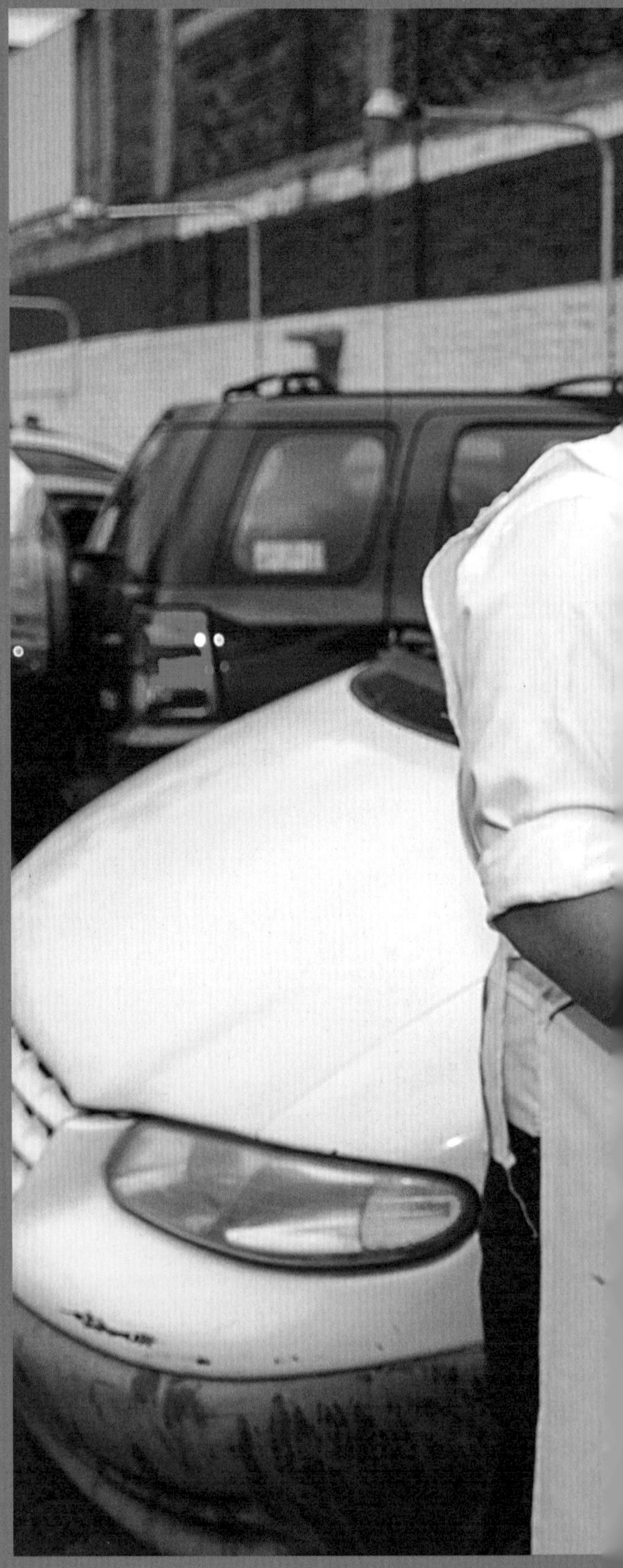

Al Andalus
171 MESONES, CENTRO HISTORICO, MEXICO CITY
A restaurant set up near the famous La Merced market, popular with the local Jewish and Arabic communities, which should give you an idea of the quality of their *tacos árabes*.

Antigua Taquería la Oriental
101 HUMBOLDT, CENTRO, PUEBLA
Al pastor archeologists declare this site to be among the first. It's been in business in Puebla since 1933. The pork is served in pita bread.

Chih'ua Tacos y Cortes
UNIVERSIDAD AT JUNCTION WITH PASCUAL OROZCO, COL. MAGISTERIAL, CHIHUAHUA
Located in front of the Autonomous University of Chihuahua, it boasts the Guinness World Record's biggest spit of meat *al pastor*, weighing in at a certified 3,745.8 kg (almost 8,260 lb).

El Borrego Viudo
REVOLUCIÓN (JUNCTION WITH VIADUCTO HIGHWAY), COL. TACUBAYA, MEXICO CITY
This culinary heritage site in Mexico City leaves no one indifferent: either you love it or you hate it. They even have their own version of a drive-thru service. Many attribute the Borrego's success to its chipotle salsa.

El Faraón
5TH AVENUE BETWEEN 20 ST. AND 22 ST., PLAYA DEL CARMEN, QUINTANA ROO
Thanks to this establishment's opening hours, it is perfect for snacking after a night's clubbing, with a few surprises, like its chicken *al pastor* instead of pork. They also have branches in Cancún and Mexico City.

El Tizoncito
122 TAMAULIPAS, COL. CONDESA, MEXICO CITY
Serving the Condesa neighborhood since the mid-seventies, they are considered the inventors of the tacos al pastor with the now-classic image of a spit crowned with a whole peeled pineapple.

El Zorrito
212 COSTERA MIGUEL ALEMÁN, ZONA DORADA, ACAPULCO
Its strategic location and opening hours (open all week and almost all day) makes it essential eating after a day at the beach or a night on the town.

La Cervecería
40 JUAN SALVADOR AGRAZ, SANTA FE, MEXICO CITY
Don't be fooled by the name, this brewery has a large selection of fish tacos, including fish tacos *al pastor* with a unique flavor thanks to the lean meat seasoned in the traditional style.

La Suprema Salsa
56 ALJOCUCA, COL. LA PAZ, PUEBLA
This restaurant offers meat cooked *al pastor* on pita bread, on tortillas (corn, flour, and whole-wheat flour, as well as toasted), and in *tortas* and *cemitas*, a traditional bread roll from Puebla.

Tacos Serafín
85 CIRCUITO CIENTÍFICOS, CIUDAD SATÉLITE, STATE OF MEXICO
These tacos *al pastor* have a unique taste because of a special marinade—a mixture of garlic, pepper, and cinnamon— that gives the filling its white color.

BARBACOA TACOS

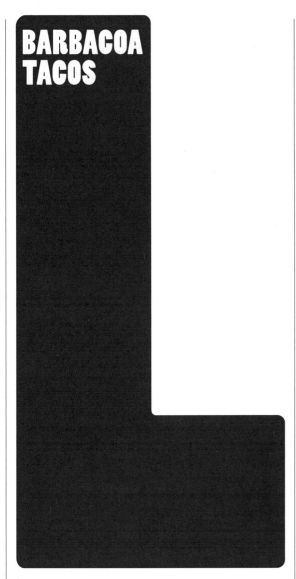

Like a religious ritual, on Saturday and Sunday mornings, the hungover masses sit down to warm broth, a few tacos, and *barbacoa* for breakfast, though this is a tasty delight that can also be savored at weddings and other get-togethers. The ritual begins the night before, while the party's barely underway, in a distant ranch where lamb is about to be put in an oven pit. The meat, having sweltered in the depths of the earth, is taken out the following day to revive the bleary-eyed partygoers with a sumptuous banquet. It should be clarified that *barbacoa* is, beyond one dish, a method of preparation: the oven pit is used to cook not only mutton but all kinds of livestock and fish—including rabbit, opossum, frog, and squirrel, too.

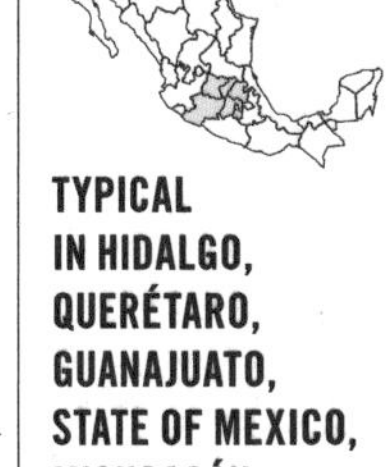

TYPICAL IN HIDALGO, QUERÉTARO, GUANAJUATO, STATE OF MEXICO, MICHOACÁN, MORELOS, MEXICO CITY

MADE WITH LAMB OR MUTTON

COOKED IN AN OVEN OR IN A PIT

FIRE UNDER THE GROUND

Barbacoa is an ancient method of cooking used by peoples around the world. The ancient inhabitants of Mexico were no exception, handling these underground ovens with great mastery.

The word *barbacoa* is said to have come from a Taino dialect, a language spoken in Cuba before the Spanish colonization. It referred to a grill made of sticks and logs to roast meat and other foods by the heat of a fire burning in a hole. This is not to be confused with the kind of grills found in gardens and on terraces, also called *barbacoa*, barbecue, or BBQ in other countries. When the Spaniards sailed from the Caribbean islands to the mainland, they found that the natives there likewise cooked with a fire in a hole in the ground.

In their galleons, the Spanish brought pigs, sheep, goats, cows, and chickens—and sooner or later these animals all found their way to the oven pits, radically changing ancient cooking traditions. Nevertheless, traces of the ancient, pre-Hispanic cooking methods are still present in the chile and spice seasoning, and in the fine art of eating these delicacies in tortillas and tacos. In the central region of Mexico, *barbacoa* means the meat from a lamb, yearling, ewe, or ram (see page 102), which when cooked using this method reaches new gastronomic heights with its pure flavor. This traditional *barbacoa* exists in many states of Mexico—Puebla, Hidalgo, Querétaro, Guanajuato, State of Mexico, Michoacán, Morelos—all of them places where pulque production developed over centuries, because, not surprisingly, there is an intimate relation between *barbacoa* and the white or *pulquero* maguey plant. In other regions of Mexico, there are other dishes of great repute that are cooked in a barbacoa oven. Some of the best known of these is perhaps *cochinita pibil* from Yucatán state (see page 163); and another would be goat *birria* from the state of Jalisco (see page 113).

MEAT FROM MAGUEY BLOSSOMS

In this fine, complex gastronomical art known as *barbacoa*, the whole animal is cooked, so the diner has a delicious choice to make: leg, rib, brisket, shoulder, neck, or parts of the head—lips, cheek, tongue, brains, or eye—though the *taco surtido*, or mixed taco, is an option that always delights. The traditional preparation of this dish involves first digging a hole in the ground, 3 to 5 feet deep and 6½ feet wide. A layer of rocks, preferably volcanic, are then placed in the bottom as a hearth. Wood for a fire is laid over these rocks and lit. Once the wood is burned off and the rocks are very hot, the thick leaves of a maguey plant are laid over them so the meat isn't in direct contact with the heat source. Next up is a large pot to catch all the juices, and the lamb meat is placed inside, seasoned and wrapped in pre-grilled maguey leaves, scraped out to make them more flexible. In some regions, the meat is dipped in a chile marinade; in others, just lard and salt are used. Everything is covered well with more maguey leaves to let the plant's distinctive aroma seep into the meat and also to separate it from the soil that is then used to fill the hole. Lastly, a fire is lit above the covered hole to keep everything underground warm.

After ten hours or so, the hole is carefully re-opened so that no dirt gets in the meat. The package of maguey leaves is lifted out with all the cooked meat inside, where it will stay warm for a few more hours. The pot with the precious lamb broth is then retrieved from the bottom of the pit. In many places, *barbacoa* is ordered by the kilogram (about two pounds), with half a pound being the typical amount for one person. It's a tradition that the portion of meat be presented on the table in a maguey leaf to keep it warm. Another option, especially in markets, is to eat the *barbacoa* tacos individually, either as *suaves* (in a fresh tortilla) or *duros*, which is a variety of *flauta* served with lettuce, cheese, and sour cream inside (see page 228). As far as the accompaniment goes, the broth can prove a feast in itself. As strange as it may seem, it traditionally consists of a delicious mutton broth, a soup that always delights with its strong flavor. The base of the broth is the juice from the *barbacoa* meat, collected in the pot

THE NAME GAME

Barbacoa all comes from the same animal, but what's the animal called? For animals under a year, it's lamb; over a year, it's yearling. For the full-grown animal, a distinction is drawn between the female ewe and the male ram. The meat is another matter: if the animal was over a year old, then its meat is mutton; under a year, then it's lamb, just like the young animal.

“BARBACOA.

Of the many ways invented to cook meat, none is like that employed for *barbacoa*. Indeed, without the mingling of any liquid, which may diminish the meat’s substance or flavor; without any contact with fire, which dries out the meat’s juices; with no more than the steam from the heated earth, whilst preserving all its nourishing qualities, the meat is so well-cooked and delicious that not only does it excite the appetite but is easily digested by even the weakest stomachs.”

Nuevo Cocinero Mejicano en Forma de Diccionario.
Mexico: Liberia de la Viuda de Ch. Bouret, 1894, page 62, S.V. Barbacoa.

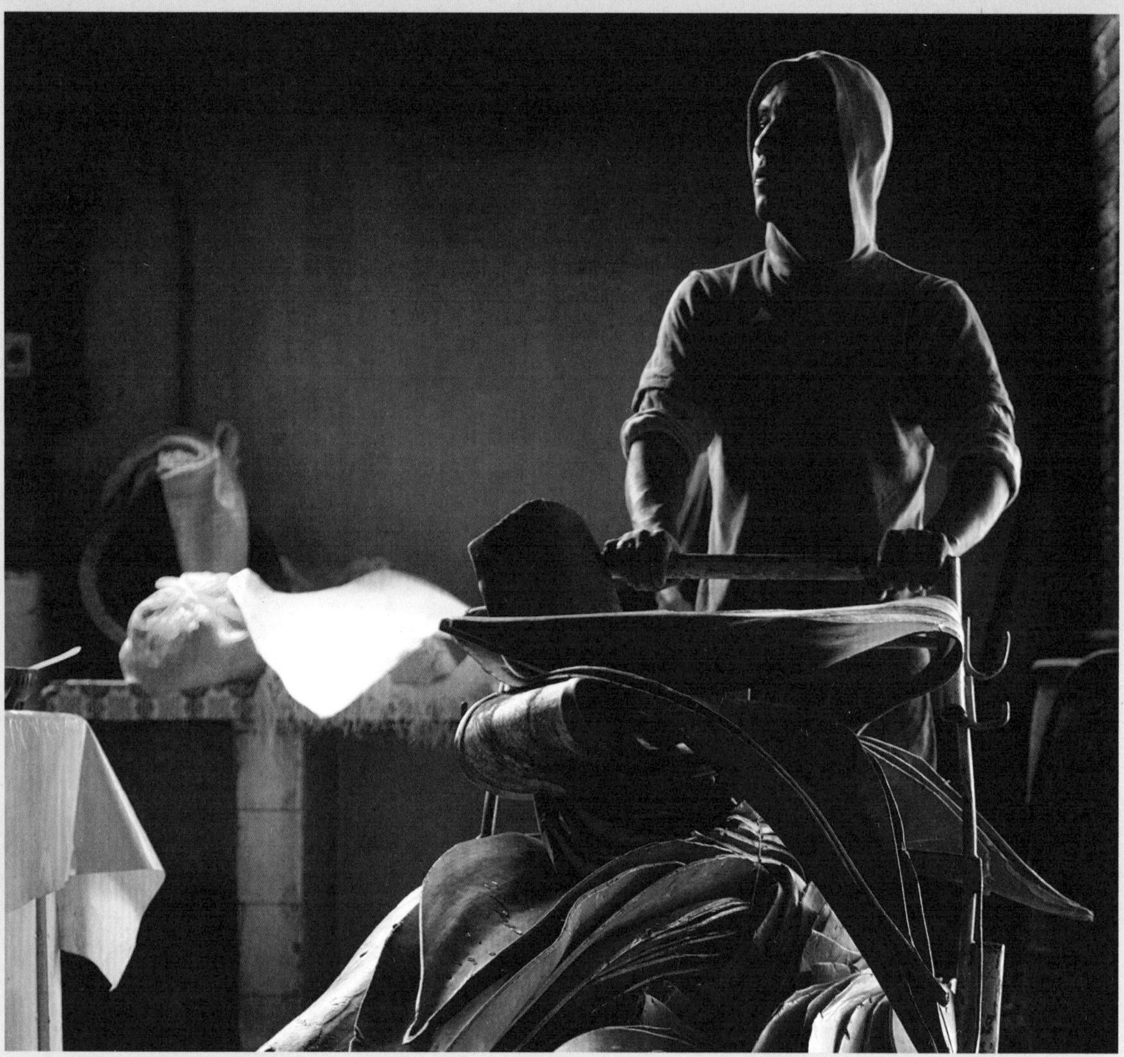

THE MAGUEY PLANT

A special plant is needed to make *barbacoa*— the agave, or maguey, plant. The *manso* or *pulquero* maguey (Agave salmiana) is of vital importance to the process and is used throughout the preparation of *barbacoa*, with its distinctive aroma permeating the cooked meat. Maguey is cultivated mostly for pulque, a pre-Hispanic alcoholic beverage, but the plant has so many and so varied uses that nothing is left of it by the end of the day: the leaves are used in the oven pit and also to transport and serve the meat; the cuticle is used in *mixiotes* (see page 199); and red and white Maguey worms are extracted from the roots, depending on the season. This is why, wherever *barbacoa* is sold, you'll often find pulque, *mixiotes*, and maguey worms. The pulque business hasn't died out— not yet anyway—though little is left of a once bustling industry that supplied *barbacoa* producers on the side. With the enormous growth of *barbacoa* in the last few years, however, the maguey itself may be endangered—the price of fame?

THE HOLE

THE OVEN

Dig that hole!

Light that fire!

TWO WAYS TO COOK BARBACOA

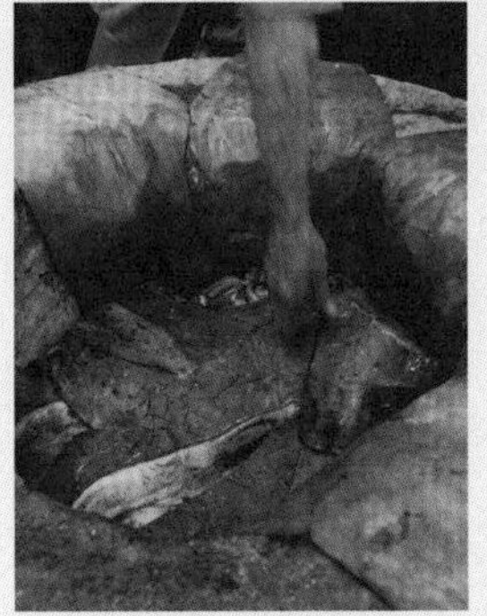

The hole is covered with maguey leaves...

...and the meat too.

Ten hours later...

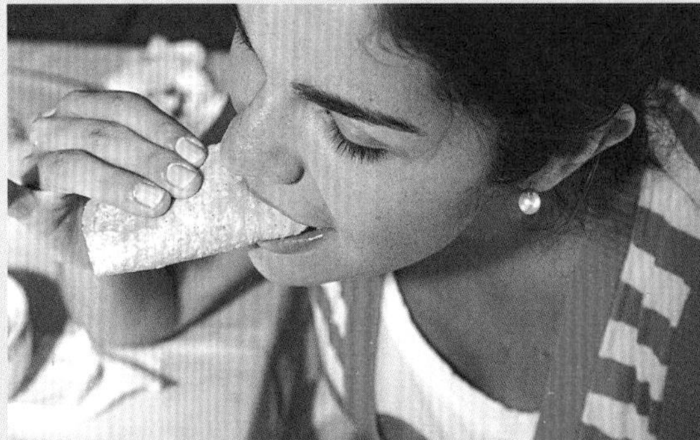
...yuuummm!!! That's some great lamb!

that was placed in the oven pit. Traditionally, when the pot goes in the pit, it already has chickpeas, onions, garlic, bay leaves, chiles, and scrubbed sheep hooves to give extra flavor to the broth. Both the broth and the *barbacoa* tacos come with onion, cilantro, and limes. The tacos may also come with *papaloquelite*, salt, and a variety of salsas. Purists opt for pasilla chiles, though no salsa can be ruled out with such a choice morsel (see recipes 18, 26, 27, 29, pages 302–307). Avocado also makes for a fine accompaniment, as does a good ranchero cheese. As for deep-fried tortillas, they usually come with sour cream, salsa, and white or Cotija cheese.

LIGHTENING THE LOAD

The art of cooking in an oven pit is so complex that alternatives have been developed to make life easier for the intrepid *barbacoa* chef, while still preserving the exquisite flavor and tenderness of the meat. In some cases, the use of the oven pit is complemented with a pressure cooker, allowing for interesting variations.

PRESSURE-COOKER BARBACOA

One variation consists in putting the meat in a pressure cooker instead of an oven pit, making preparation much easier, since it can be done at home and in smaller quantities. The seasoning depends on the recipe, with preferences differing from region to region, and practically from household to household. Even so, these home recipes can also make for memorable tacos. To make this *barbacoa*, the desired cut is steamed for hours, but with a strainer between the meat and the bottom of the cooker so as to produce the broth. And of course *barbacoa* can be made with beef, goat, chicken, rabbit, venison, or armadillo—in fact, any meat on hand.

STEAMED LAMB TACOS

In some establishments, lamb meat already cooked in a *barbacoa* oven is shredded and kept warm on a steam tray like the one used for head-meat tacos. The meat is then served on fresh tortillas so that the lamb keeps all of its taste. Though the meat comes already in a mix, this method has its merits. Normally, these tacos come without broth.

BEEF BARBACOA TACOS

In the north of Mexico, beef *barbacoa* is cooked almost the same way as head-meat tacos (see page 123). The method consists of taking the head and various beef cuts (loin, leg, and ribs, for example) and steaming them for a long time. The meat is then shredded and, before serving, it's reheated again with steam. These extremely tender tacos can be served in either corn or flour tortillas; they come with onion, cilantro, lime, and piquin or chiltepin chile salsas (see recipe 10, page 300). In the state of Morelos, beef *barbacoa* consists in boiling the beef in a pot with tomato and guajillo chiles. Different beef cuts (head, loin, and leg) are cooked in this broth for over six hours. After that, the meat is chopped up on cutting board and heated on a steam tray, like the one used for head-meat tacos. A mild guajillo chile marinade is added, and the tacos are prepared with a little diced onion. A broth is served on the side, similar to the one served with the lamb tacos, with chickpeas and rice. The condiments are usually onion, cilantro, lime, sliced radish, chiles in vinegar, and a salsa (see recipes 2, 4, 8–9, 13–14, 16, and 20, pages 296–303). Other dishes cooked in a *barbacoa* oven get the treatment they deserve in the chapters on *Cochinita Pibil Tacos*, *Birria Tacos*, and *Mixiote Tacos*.

SHEEP TRIPE

In Mexico, the well-known *montalayo*, or sheep's stomach, is prepared by stuffing a mince of the sheep's seasoned entrails into the previously washed stomach of the animal. The red variety uses cinnamon, cumin, pepper, clove, onion, and guajillo or arbol chiles, while the green variety uses onion, oregano, epazote, and jalapeños. This magnificent specialty is cooked alongside the other cuts from the animal in the same oven. Wherever you find sheep *barbacoa*, you'll likely find *montalayo* tacos, with the tripe either served alone or mixed in with the meat.

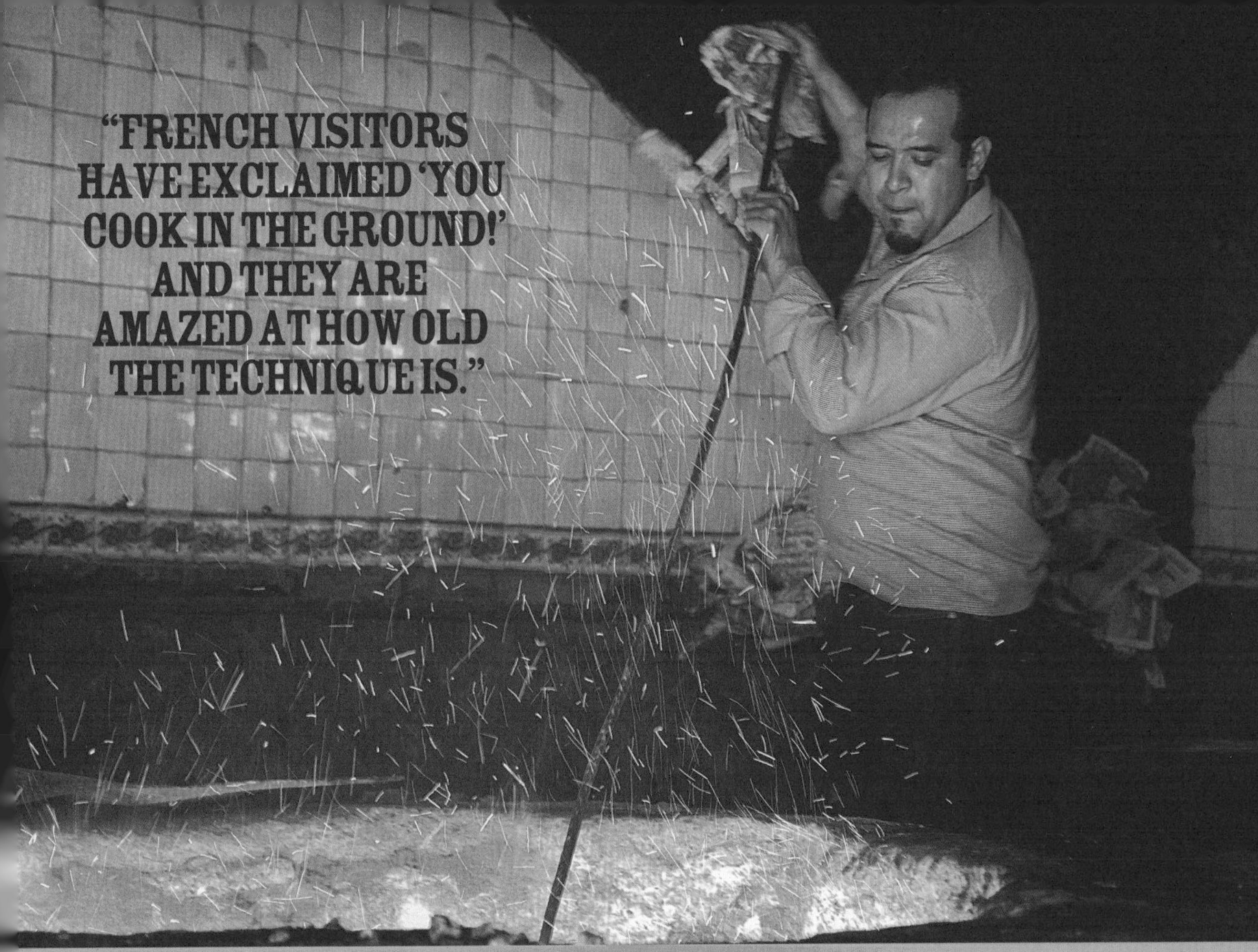

"FRENCH VISITORS HAVE EXCLAIMED 'YOU COOK IN THE GROUND!' AND THEY ARE AMAZED AT HOW OLD THE TECHNIQUE IS."

The house secret is the way we do it. The type of wood is important.

The red eucalyptus and pine give the food its woody taste while the bricks we use add a special aroma. The salsas are good too. Everything is made right here. The meat is brought from the slaughterhouse and is prepared here. There are soft tacos and fried tacos; *barbacoa*, tripe and *campechanos*. The soft, slow-cooked *barbacoa* tacos are most popular, but there are customers that come from far away for our tripe and *barbacoa* broth too. This type of restaurant is rare in the city. You usually have to get out of Mexico City to find the home-cooked stuff. Sometimes it takes up to four days to prepare the *barbacoa*: from choosing the meat to cleaning and seasoning it... The next day it's put in the oven, then taken out the following day. You get locals, celebrities, foreigners—all kinds come here. On Saturdays, when the oven's lit, it's an attraction in itself, people love to see it. Some people come just to grab a quick taco while others buy three kilos. Families also come to celebrate birthdays and other events. The business is fifty-five years old. My grandparents started it. I'm the third generation. My grandfather went all over the place. Some of his *barbacoa* recipe comes from Hidalgo state. This kind of cooking doesn't have much in the way of variations, but you can use it for turkey, pork leg—whatever you want to put in the oven. Sometimes customers order their Christmas dinner from us. We've had professional soccer players and even politicians, like López Obrador. When Fox was president, we sent him his *barbacoa*. Some French visitors that came by here said, "You guys cook in the ground!" And they were amazed at how old the technique is. One of my grandmother's favorite clients was the actor Emilio Fernández. He'd come by once a week and always asked for the corner table and handmade tortillas. He even asked my grandmother to come to his house and cook, but she'd just say, "Crazy old nut," and never went.

Victor Hugo Álvarez
CHEF AT EL CALANDRIO
22 EL ROSARIO, COL. SAN MARTÍN XOCHINÁHUAC, MEXICO CITY

ZAPATA
TIED UP HIS
HORSE
AT THE DOOR
OF TACOS BEATRIZ
AND
ORDERED
"TACOS
FOR
THE ANIMAL"
SINCE
IT DIDN'T EAT
"JUST
ANYWHERE."

HOME-STYLE BARBACOA

Serves 8

—4½ lb (2 kg) lamb (pork, beef, or chicken), cut into large chunks
—2 cups (500 ml) ancho chile *adobo* (see recipe 34, page 309)
—12 dried avocado leaves or Mexican pepperleaf (*hoja santa*, Piper auritum [root beer plant])
—Sea salt
—12–20 4⅓-inch (11 cm) corn tortillas, for serving
—Chopped cilantro, diced onion, papaloquelite, lime wedges, sea salt, diced avocado, white cheese, or salsas (see recipes 2, 3, 18, 24, 26, and 27, pages 296–307), for garnish

1. Place the meat with *adobo* in a deep casserole dish, cover, and chill overnight.
2. Put a grill at the bottom of a 6-quart pressure cooker to separate the meat from the water.
3. Spread half the dried leaves on a piece of aluminum foil large enough for the meat.
4. Place the meat on the remaining foil, and cover with the remaining leaves.
5. Wrap the meat and place in the pressure cooker. Cover tightly with a lid and let the pressure come up to 15 psi; then cook for 45 minutes to 1 hour.
6. Remove from heat and let sit for 15 minutes to let the pressure cooker return to normal pressure. Unlock the lid and carefully place the meat in a large dish, along with some of the broth. (The rest of the broth can be served in a sauce dish for your guests to pour.)Season to taste and serve with corn tortillas and garnishes on the side.

LAMB BROTH

Serves 8

—2¼ lb (1 kg) mutton with bone (neck, leg, ribs, or shoulder meat)
—8 well-scrubbed lamb trotters, ready to cook
—14 oz (400 g) beef stew bones (with marrow or with porous bones)
—2 medium carrots, peeled
—2 medium tomatoes
—2 medium onions, plus extra chopped for garnish
—1 small leek
—1 celery rib
—5 cloves garlic
—1 dried ancho chile

—1 dried sweet guajillo chile
—1 dried pasilla chile
—3 bay leaves
—1 sprig epazote
—1 sprig cilantro, plus extra for garnish
—1 sprig parsley
—Sea salt
—Pinch freshly ground black pepper
—1 lb 2 oz/500 g cooked chickpeas
—12 oz/350 g uncooked rice, rinsed
—12–20 4⅓-inch (11 cm) corn tortillas
—Green serrano chiles and quartered limes, for garnish

1. Put the meat in a large pot, along with the lamb trotters, stew bones, carrot, tomato, onion, leek, celery, garlic, and chiles.
2. Add enough cold water to cover and bring to boiling. Skim off any grey scum on the surface.
3. Add the bay leaves, epazote, cilantro, parsley, salt, and pepper, and reduce heat to low.
4. Let the broth simmer, uncovered, for at least 1½ hours. Ideally, the meat should almost come apart on its own.
5. Using a ladle, remove the meat and the trotters and set them aside in a covered container.
6. Pour all the broth through a coarse-mesh strainer into a large bowl to separate it from the large ingredients (bones, onion, carrots, etc.), then pour the broth through a fine-mesh strainer into a new pot to separate it from the small ingredients (chiles, seeds, condiments, etc.). Discard the strained ingredients.
7. If the broth is thick after straining, dilute with water. Return the broth to pot and bring to a boil. Lower the heat to a medium heat and add the chickpeas and rice, and cook until the grains of rice swell, about 10–15 minutes. Add salt to taste. You'll need around 12 cups of broth to serve 8.
8. Shred the meat from the bones and dispose of the bones and hooves.
9. On each plate, serve some shredded meat, a spoon of rice and chickpeas, and a ladle of broth. Serve hot with tortillas and garnishes.

THE BEST

Aquí está Texcoco

97 CALIFORNIA,
COL. PARQUE DE SAN ANDRÉS,
MEXICO CITY

The star dish here is prepared, as the name says, Texcoco-style: oven-roasted slowly over mesquite coals, giving it a slightly smoky taste.

Arroyo

4003 INSURGENTES SUR, TLALPAN,
MEXICO CITY

It's hard to imagine that this eatery, where the multitudes come for the oven-cooked *barbacoa*, started out as a roadside stand on the highway out of Cuernavaca.

Barbacoa de Santiago

KM 152.1, MEXICO CITY–QUERÉTARO HIGHWAY,
PALMILLAS, QUERÉTARO

Thousands of travelers heading north from Mexico City take a break at this sprawling rest stop located at the toll booth just outside Querétaro.

Caballo Bayo

360 DEL CONSCRIPTO, COL. LOMAS HIPÓDROMO, MEXICO CITY

Certain customers used to ride over by horse from the nearby racetrack to enjoy the oven-cooked, Hidalgo-style *barbacoa*.

El Hidalguense

155 CAMPECHE,
COL. ROMA, MEXICO CITY

This is one of the most renowned establishments in the city, partly because the owner, who lives near Tulancingo, raises the very animals served in the restaurant.

Humberto's

1440 PATRICIO SANZ,
COL. DEL VALLE,
MEXICO CITY

Between the *cochinita* and the *salbutes* offered on its traditional Yucatecan menu, we find the *barbacoa*-style beef tongue.

La Adelita de Tlalpan

1111 VIADUCTO TLALPAN, COL. LA JOYA, MEXICO CITY

On the road parallel to the highway for Cuernavaca, this colorful restaurant specializes in serving up *barbacoa* and other typical Mexican food.

Mercado de San Antonio

FRAY PEDRO DE GANTE (OPPOSITE PLAZA BICENTENARIO), TEXCOCO, STATE OF MEXICO

Texcoco's fame is in good part earned from its *barbacoa*, making the town's market one of its main culinary attractions.

Restaurante Don Horacio

24 HIDALGO, CENTRO,
PACHUQUILLA, HIDALGO

This place is found in a town that's now a suburb of the state capital, Pachuca. Both local politicians and tourists on the lookout for regional specialties frequent the restaurant.

Restaurante La Blanca

201 MATAMOROS, CENTRO,
PACHUCA, HIDALGO

Its location in front of the monumental clock in downtown Pachuca makes it a must-visit spot for *barbacoa*, served up with all the proper taco garnishes.

SONY

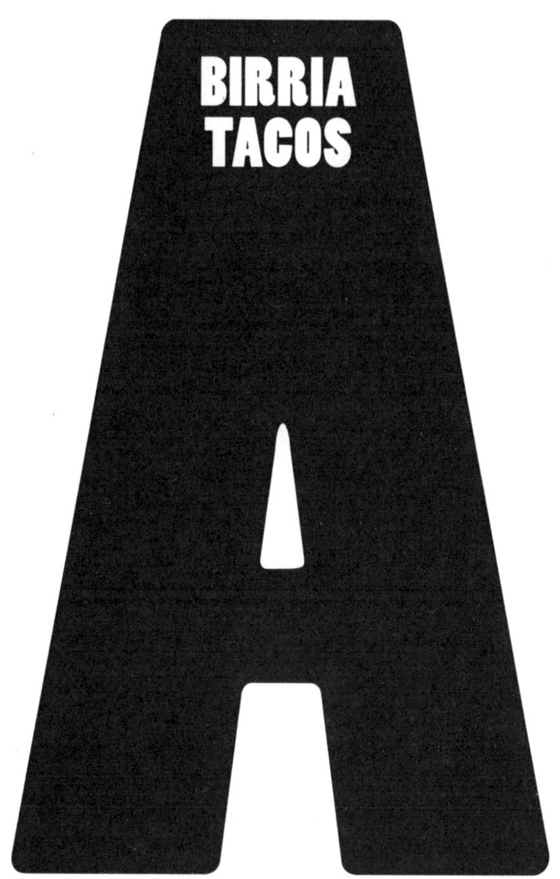

According to the dictionary of the Royal Spanish Academy, *birria* is not only "goat *barbacoa*" but also "a person of little value or importance." Be that as it may, this dish, alongside *tortas ahogadas* and *carne en su jugo*, is the pride of people from Jalisco state. *Birria* is a dish from the west of Mexico and is particularly associated with Jalisco. It's a dish that, to be done properly, requires *barbacoa*-style oven pit cooking. Depending on the town, *birria* can be goat, or chicken, beef, pork, fish (fresh or saltwater), and, of course, lamb. Versions abound even within the state of Jalisco, with one *birria* from Arenal, another from Ameca, yet another from Cocula, each using different chiles, or chocolate, or sesame seeds. There are a thousand ways to prepare *birria*.

DISPUTED ORIGINS

To uncover the origins of a dish so deeply rooted in popular culture, we can only rely on speculation, but it's likely that it started out as meat cooked by shepherds—a rustic beginning that, little by little, entered households and eventually made its way into posh restaurants and pretty much everywhere else. A bitter and long-standing feud has raged among the residents of several towns in Jalisco over the paternity of this dish, and it has gone on at such a pitch that holding the claim to *birria* is clearly a prize of some importance to people: anecdotes, recipes, and even personal letters have been brought forward as proof. As for those of us outside the debate, we can just relax and savor this versatile culinary creation.

TYPICAL IN JALISCO, DURANGO, ZACATECAS, AGUASCALIENTES, MICHOACÁN

MADE WITH GOAT MEAT

COOKED IN A BARBACOA OVEN

HONEY, I ATE THE KIDS

Traditionally, *birria* is made of either goat or goat kid meat, though in the end, it's one and the same animal, just in different stages of development. Meat may be used from goats that have stopped suckling but haven't mated. (If using adult goats, their meat—due to the testicles and certain glands behind the ears—is said to cause the *birria* to stink.) Goat kid meat is supposed to be wholly raised on milk, though in practice, as long as the animal's no more than 45 days old, it's included in this category, even if it's been put out to pasture. When eating *birria*, the taco diner chooses the cut: head (brain, tongue, and cheek meat), neck, shoulder blade, leg, kidneys, shoulder, or sirloin, which has delicious cuts of round between the bone and the fatty tissue, a part of the backbone. To make *birria*, the meat must be seasoned and marinated for a long time in a mix of chiles and condiments. Afterward, everything is cooked in a pot with a sealed lid inside a *barbacoa* oven pit. The key to the preparation is that the meat cooks in its own juices. The result is a dish that is succulent and, though certainly rich in broth, it's meaty and ready to be eaten in a taco. Beyond that, the "authentic" recipe for this dish remains shrouded in mystery—that is, if such a thing even exists. Some say that the main ingredient is black pepper; for others it is ginger or cumin; still others insist that pulque, vinegar, and grilled maguey leaves are essential; some go so far as to reject cooking it in a pit because the authentic method, they maintain, involves cooking the meat and the salsa in a brick oven. Still, be it in an oven or a pot, once served, the *birria* is seasoned with oregano, chopped onion (which lends a sweet taste to each mouthful), and a salsa, invariably a very spicy one. This kind of taco is tender, with a fine texture and an intense flavor. Put a generous portion of well-chopped meat on a tortilla—and dig in! Of course, don't forget to add a red salsa (see recipes 2, 9, 11, or 15, pages 296–301), oregano, salt, chopped onion, cilantro, and lime. The refried beans are optional but, again, some will say that the dish just isn't the same without them.

IT'S ALL IN THE TECHNIQUE

A characteristic of *birria* is that it's served with its juice, be it broth or soup, which has led to endless confusion because in some regions it's served almost as a soup. In some cases the main ingredient changes: for example, it's not unusual to find it made with beef, lamb, or rabbit. The first way to tell these different styles of *birria* apart is, necessarily, to start with the different cooking methods.

IN AN OVEN PIT

The animal, once it has been carved up and seasoned, is cooked for a long time in a *barbacoa* pit (just like lamb) and, similarly, the flavorful broth is saved (see page 101). There are two ways of serving this dish: the first is in tortillas, as tacos; the second is in a bowlful of meat and broth, as a stew.

IN A BRICK OVEN: SEARED BIRRIA

All the cuts of the animal can be cooked in a brick oven too, but in this case they make two journeys through the oven. The first time round, the animal is put in a pot with a little salt and cooked until tender. The meat is then separated from the broth, which is left to cool in the covered pot. Selected pieces are placed on a ceramic dish and "painted," or daubed, with a red *adobo* (always a household secret, but often with ancho and pasilla chiles, garlic, onion, black pepper, allspice, cloves, cinnamon, and salt). Once done, the meat is placed back in the oven until perfectly browned on the outside, retaining its characteristic tenderness inside. Lastly, the meat is served up sizzling hot, and everyone prepares their tacos, accompanying the taco with the indispensable broth served on the side. The broth is made from the juices gathered from the first roasting and a mix of bay leaves, allspice, garlic, and tomato.

POT OR CASSEROLE BIRRIA

Casserole *birria* can be prepared with goat meat or, as mentioned earlier, with the meat of any animal. In fact, some daring chefs mix the meat of several different animals. With lots of different recipes, the big differences lie in whether the meat is braised in a broth or steamed; if pulque is added or not; and if one kind of chile is used instead of another, as well as the choice of other seasonings. Listing all the possible recipes here, apart from offering no more than a rambling enumeration, would be an endless endeavor. Finally, when the meat is cooked to a point, it is taken out of the broth and left to cool, covered, before it is used in tacos. This meat is also served along with the broth, in a big mishmash of a stew—a *birria*. The combination, obviously, is stupendous.

GUADALAJARA, GUADALAJARA

Guadalajara, Guadalajara...
Guadalajara, Guadalajara...

With the heart of a provincial maiden,
Pure, fragrant rose in the early sun.
Fresh blossoms by the river green.
Flocks of doves, your hamlets seem...
Guadalajara, Guadalajara...
Fragrant like the moist, damp earth.

Ay, ay, ay, ay! My forest of Colomos...
Ay! Where the springs do flow.
Ay! Unforgettable Colomos,
Like the afternoon shower that rolled
Down from the slope that day,
Not letting us go down Zapopan way.

Ay, ay, ay, ay! Gentle, little Tlaquepaque...
Your many redolent jars of clay
Keep cool the sweet *tepache*
By the *birria*, and the mariachi,
Who, among the stalls and pottery,
Serenade their songs so very sadly.

Ay, ay, ay, ay! Chapala, your lake...
Like a fairy tale at the day's break.
At dusk's fall the same magic, soon
Followed nightly by the loving moon.
So still, Chapala, is your romantic water,
Like a bride the equal of no other.

Ay, ay, ay, ay! Zapopitan I love so well,
Nowhere else have I heard such bells
Like those at the convent that deeply toll
And lull the burdens of my soul.
Sad Zapopan, an open missal
My feelings like friars, restful.

Ay, ay, ay, ay! Lovely Guadalajara
I still have one last thought:
Yours, the waters of your wells,
The shawls of your devoted belles,
Guadalajara, Guadalajara
You have the most Mexican heart.
Guadalajara... Guadalajara...

PEPE GUÍZAR
In 1954, Guízar penned the song *Guadalajara*,
considered a veritable ode to the city.
The song gained international renown and has been performed
by the likes of Elvis Presley and Edward Kennedy.

FROM THE FIFTIES ON, THE TACO STARTED TO GET

FANCY,

EVEN **SNEAKING** INTO

ELEGANT

RESTAURANTS.

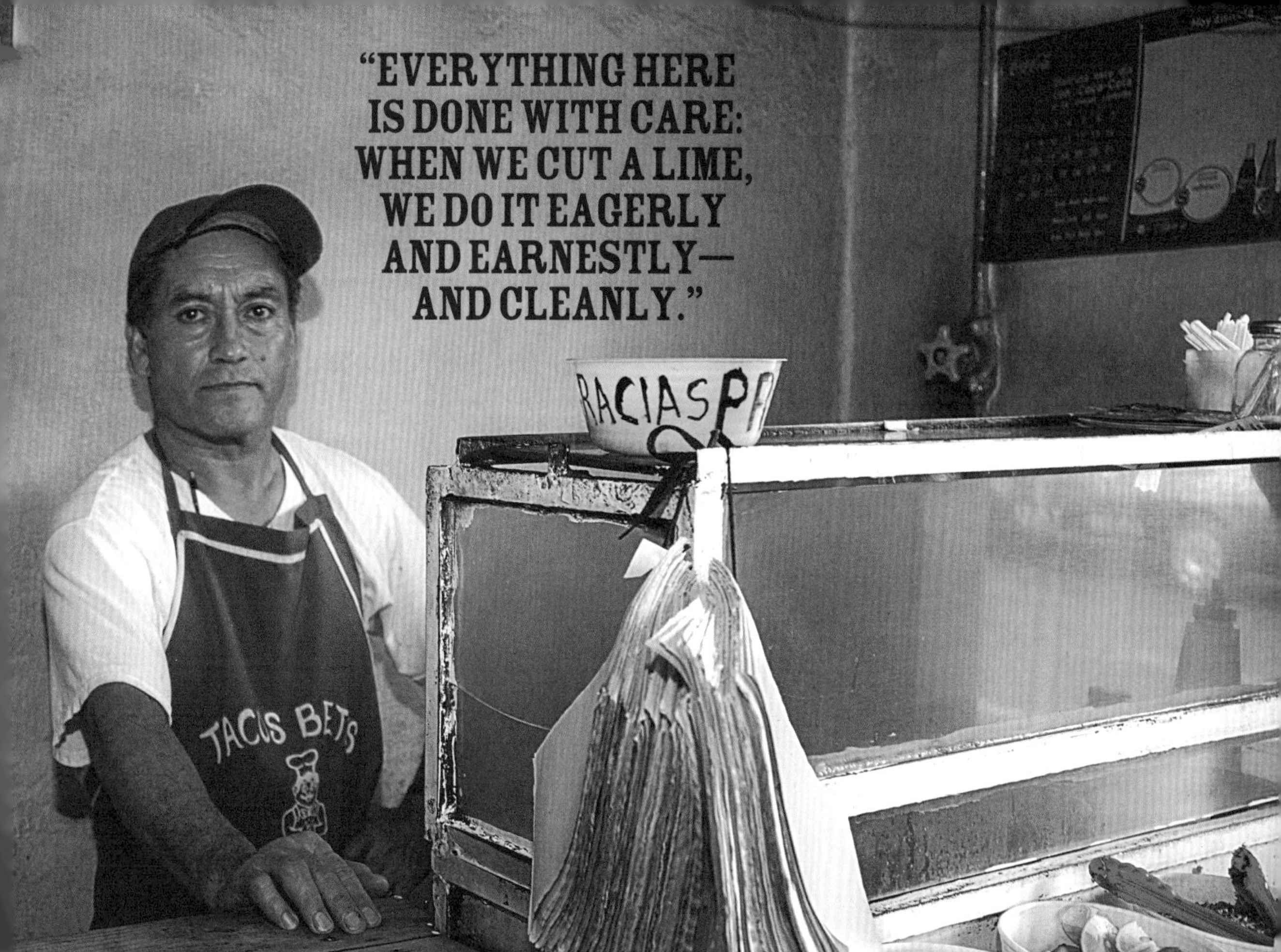

"EVERYTHING HERE IS DONE WITH CARE: WHEN WE CUT A LIME, WE DO IT EAGERLY AND EARNESTLY— AND CLEANLY."
RACIAS PA
TACOS BETS

The origin of the *birria* that we sell was a bit of improvisation.

We came up with a *birria* that only uses cow's head-meat, and we've made it like that for thirty years. These tacos are different from other head-meat tacos for a few reasons: the recipe, the taste, the seasoning... that's all! Tacos made from head meat are traditionally steamed, but ours aren't. Ours are made in broth, which makes them *birria*—that's the big difference. As you know, the word *birria* means a "mishmash." And here we use meat from the cow's cheek, the lean meat, and all the rest of the meat in the head. This *birria*, this mishmash, is made to be finished up quick. The recipe comes from all over—but it turned out best here! It's like someone inventing something—like a soccer player with a special move, that's what it's like. *Birria* is from the state of Jalisco and it's usually made from goat, although what makes it *birria* is the red meat. If you ever ask me, "What style of *birria* do you do?" I always answer, "D.F. style." Here the secret is that everything is done with care. It's a family business. When we cut a lime, we do it eagerly and earnestly, and cleanly. The *birria* is served with a hefty amount of meat and broth—it's really a decent portion—and our customers always leave satisfied. We've had TV personalities, soap-opera stars, athletes (swimmers, track stars, soccer players—I'm a huge sports fan!). They've all eaten here. There is a famous TV presenter who orders his tongue tacos here—if he didn't, how would he be able to talk so well? Seriously though, we've had many famous people in here. The house specialty is this taco that I invented called Betu's Special. It comes with everything, and with more filling, of course, to make it a "Special." The customers think, "It must be good if it's a Special," and after eating one, that's all they'll order afterwards.

Floriberto Ramos Serimiento
OWNER OF TACOS BETU'S
97 RAFAEL MARTÍNEZ "RIP-RIP," COL. SAN SIMÓN TICUMAC, MEXICO CITY

IN

1997

THE 31ST OF MARCH
WAS DECLARED
INTERNATIONAL

TACO DAY.

JALISCO STYLE BIRRIA

Serves 6

—3 ancho chiles
—3 cloves garlic
—2 whole cloves
—½ tablespoon sesame seeds
—½ cinnamon stick
—A pinch of freshly ground black pepper
—1 cup (250 ml) beer
—3 bay leaves
—½ tablespoon dried oregano
—½ tablespoon dried thyme
—Sea salt
—Apple cider vinegar
—3¼ lb (1.5 kg) meat, cut into chunks (goat, mutton, beef, chicken, etc.)
—1 cup (250 ml) beer or water, if needed

1. Roast the chiles to release the aroma, then remove the stems, seeds, and veins.
2. In a skillet set over low heat, toast the garlic, cloves, sesame seeds, cinnamon, and pepper until fragrant.
3. Add the roasted chiles, beer, bay leaves, oregano, thyme, salt, and a few drops of vinegar. Bring to a boil and let simmer vigorously for 10 minutes.
4. Remove from heat and process all the ingredients in a blender to make a smooth marinade.
5. Pour the marinade over the meat in a large dish, cover, and refrigerate overnight.
6. Preheat the oven to 325°F/160°C/Gas Mark 3. Put the meat in a large pot and cover with aluminum foil. Put the lid on the pot, sealing the edges with more aluminum foil.
7. Roast the meat for 1½–2 hours, until soft.
8. Remove from the oven and uncover once it has cooled slightly. If the meat is very dry, add a cup of beer or water, then let boil for 15 minutes.
9. To make tacos, serve the meat with some of its broth, along with salsa, tortillas, and garnish on the side.

SEARED BIRRIA

Serves 6

—Sea salt
—1 (9–13 lb/4–6 kg) goat kid, chopped
—3 cups (750 ml) *adobo* (see previous recipe)
—3 medium tomatoes
—2 heads garlic
—2 medium onions
—3 dried arbol chiles
—2 dried mulato chiles
—Corn oil
—4 cups (1 litre) goat, chicken, or beef broth
—12–20 4⅓-inch (11 cm) corn tortillas, for serving
—Chopped onion and salsa (see recipe 8, page 297), for granish

1. Generously rub the meat with salt in a large baking dish and brush with a little marinade.
2. Preheat the oven to 350°F/180°C/Gas Mark 4.
3. Put the tomatoes, garlic, onion, chiles, a splash of oil, and the meat in a very large pot. Close tightly and seal the pot with aluminum foil.
4. Cook the meat in the oven, allowing 45 minutes per 2 pounds of meat. (A 10 pound animal, for example, should be cooked for 4½ hours.)
5. Once the meat is cooked, remove it from the pot, but keep the oven on. Cover with clean tea towels and let cool inside another covered pot so that the meat doesn't cool too quickly and dry out.
6. Pour the meat juices into a smaller pot. Add 4 cups (1 litre) of broth and a heaping tablespoon of *adobo* to the juices. Add salt to taste and bring to a simmer. Strain before serving. Increase the oven heat to 400°F/200°C/Gas Mark 6.

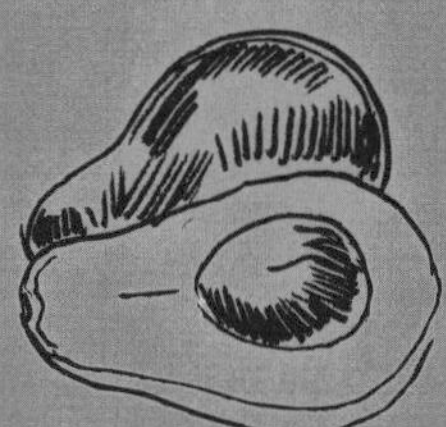

7. Once the meat has cooled (after about 35–40 minutes), baste the meat generously with the remaining *adobo* in a large ovenproof dish. Place the meat in the oven, uncovered, until the meat is well browned and hot.

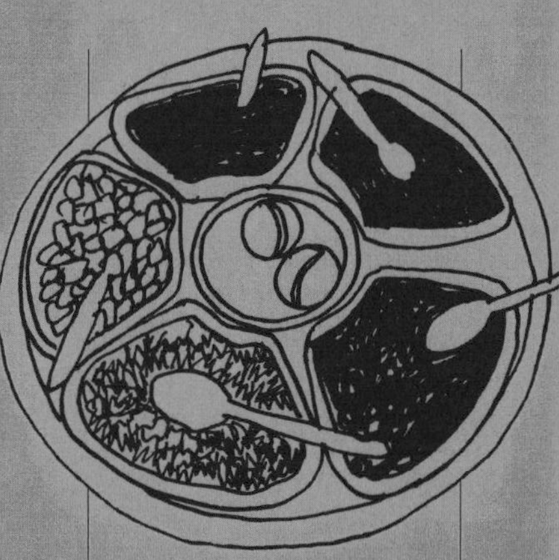

8. Serve along with the broth and the garnishes and assemble tacos tableside.

THE BEST

Arrebirria

22647 PANAMERICANO, TIJUANA, BAJA CALIFORNIA

The influence of immigrants from Jalisco state can be felt in this establishment that serves tacos and an unmissable soup.

Birrería Chololo

MOJONERA 20-A, COL. LAS JUNTAS, TLAQUEPAQUE, JALISCO

Politicians, artists, and other *birria* lovers come down the old road to Chapala to enjoy the seared goat *birria* prepared here.

Birrería David

PINO SUARÉZ (BETWEEN ANGULO AND HERRERÍA AND CAIRO), CENTRO, GUADALAJARA

In the centrally located Alcalde market in Guadalajara, three generations of restaurateurs have served customers in this popular family business.

Birrería las 9 Esquinas

COLÓN (CORNER GALENA), CENTRO, GUADALAJARA

Found in one of the most picturesque corners of Guadalajara, this business specializes in seared goat *birria* simmered over low heat in the purest Jalisco style.

El Borrego Tatemado

GUILLERMO PRIETO (CORNER M. ORDÓÑEZ), CENTRO, LOS MOCHIS, SINALOA

This place is considered one of the attractions in Los Mochis for its lamb *birria*, seared mutton, and lots of handmade tortillas.

El Pialadero de Guadalajara

332 HAMBURGO, COL. JUÁREZ, MEXICO CITY

This restaurant is known as the best place in Mexico City for Guadalajara-style cuisine. Its three claims to fame are its *tortas ahogadas*, *birria*, and meat served in its own juice.

La Polar

129 GUILLERMO PRIETO, COL. SAN RAFAEL, MEXICO CITY

Few places offer only a single item on their menu, as is the case in here, the most famous *birria* restaurant in Mexico City. There's a reason why it's open 365 days a year and always full.

La U. de G.

258 GUERRERO, COL. GUERRERO, MEXICO CITY

This long-standing cantina is tucked away in a busy neighborhood on the edges of downtown Mexico City. Its Friday specialty is Jalisco-style *birria*.

Mercado San Camilito

5 REPÚBLICA DE ECUADOR, CENTRO HISTÓRICO, MEXICO CITY

Though all kinds of food are on sale here, the mariachi ambience of nearby Plaza Garibaldi means the Jalisco-style *birria* stalls stand out. Open 24 hours.

Tacos Betu's

97 RAFAEL MARTÍNEZ "RIP-RIP" (CORNER LUIS SPOTA), COL. SAN SIMÓN TICUMAC, MEXICO CITY

The owners started out with a taco stand outside this building that backs onto Eje Central; now they're inside the building, serving a wide range of clientele.

HEAD MEAT TACOS

Head-meat tacos are part of a deeply rooted popular tradition. And it's all about cattle now, be it a heifer, a calf, a cow, an ox, or a bull. In establishments serving head-meat tacos, eyeball tacos can also be found, a morsel that's not to be looked down upon. Other palates may prefer one of the following: tongue, brain, cheek, neck, sweetbreads, lips—or a mix of all of the above (here you can't go wrong). Despite their intense—or extreme-sounding—origins, these are, in fact, select cuts of meat whose qualities any real gourmet knows full well: tenderness, texture, and, above all, an exclusive flavor that, in this Mexican specialty, can be found at its purest.

THE HEADLESS COW

The origin of head-meat tacos is unclear. In *Las cocinas de México*,[1] historian José N. Iturriaga assures us that these tacos come from the central Bajío region but unfortunately says no more. What we do know is that this kind of taco, though traditionally cooked in the central states in Mexico, can be found all over the country with the same name and similar preparation. A nineteenth-century cookbook[2] includes a recipe with cow's head cooked in a *barbacoa* oven—one way that head-meat is still cooked today. At any rate, despite variations, the preparation of head-meat tacos always involves a long cooking time; and, though they can be found at any time during the day in the city, they are usually enjoyed as a late-afternoon or early-evening snack.

TYPICAL IN GUANAJUATO, JALISCO, MICHOACÁN, QUERÉTARO

MADE WITH COW'S HEAD

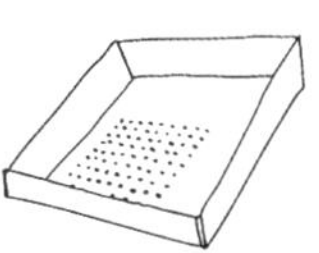

COOKED ON A STEAM TRAY

STEAM HEAT

This is a world of steam. The meat is cooked in a water bath for hours on end, then, when ready, it's served from a steaming tray, which is simply a stainless steel box with holes for the steam. It keeps the meat at the perfect temperature once covered with a piece of cloth or a sheet of plastic. The tacos that can be eaten from this part are divided into two groups: offal and actual meat, referred to as *maciza* or "solid" meat. Tacos made from the offal include eye (sliced in half, then chopped up with some meat), tongue (a generous couple of slices on two tortillas), brain, sweetbreads (which could be the thymus or the salivary glands of the cow, cut up with a bit of other meat), or the *machitos* (finely chopped beef intestines, which, though not part of the

[1] JOSÉ N. ITURRIAGA. *LAS COCINAS DE MÉXICO II.* MEXICO: FONDO DE CULTURA ECONÓMICA, 1998, PAGE 12.
[2] *NUEVO COCINERO MEJICANO EN FORMA DE DICCIONARIO.* MEXICO: LIBRERÍA DE LA VIUDA DE CH. BOURET, 1894, PAGE 63.

CONTRARY TO WHAT MOST PEOPLE THINK, IT'S ONLY BEEN OVER THE LAST

200 YEARS

THAT EATING TACOS HAS BECOME A

POPULAR

TRADITION.

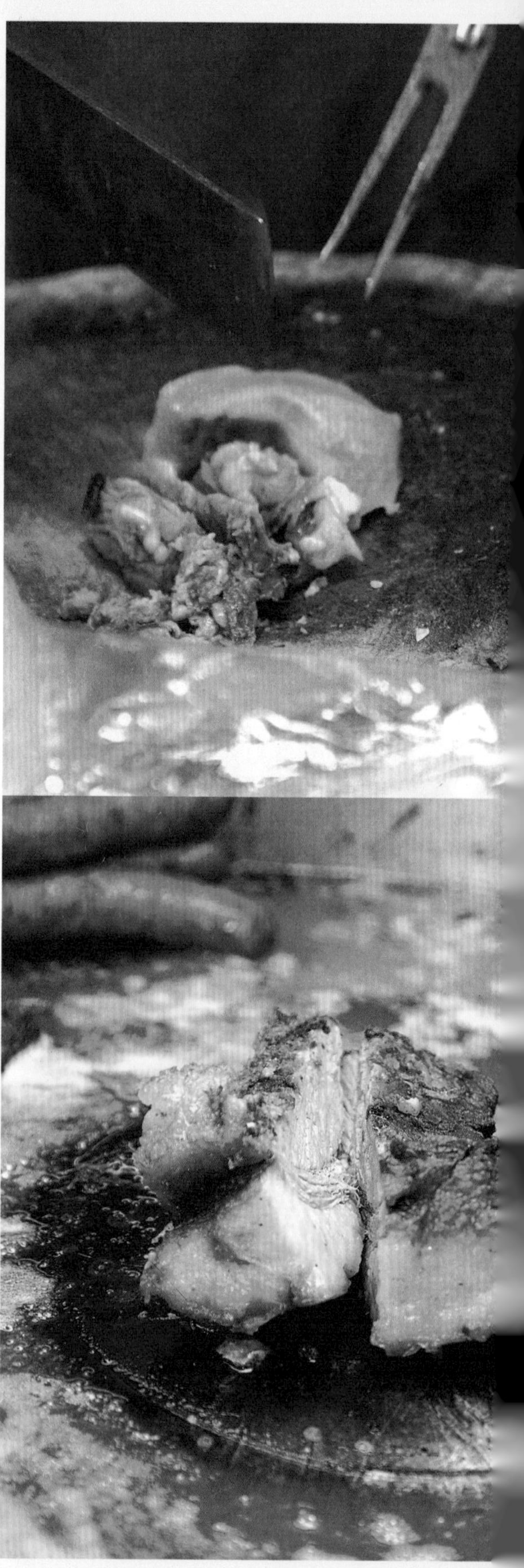

LA TAQUIZA

That lovely girl who ate and ate

A table of tacos outdid me
An' put out my amorous fire;
For when I got on bended knee,
To eat was her sole desire. [...]

As we strolled by the *taquería*,
I thought, "It's time to tell her!"
But you just looked at the plates
An' sat at a bench in the corner.
So, to offer you my love's praise,
I marched in to declare my ardor
Meanwhile you asked, eyes a-glazed,
For tongue tacos—three for a starter—
An' beef sirloin—all well braised.

I struggled at the verge of tears
To describe my endless passion,
As the eye tacos disappeared—
Stomach an' heart, in like fashion.
And while I set the date for that year
When God an' State might make us one,
You gulped down cheek and ear,
Lord, like I'd never seen it done. (...)
Then tripe they did haul out—
And did I ever start to worry—
Then brain an' lung an' even snout,
Porky rinds an' womb-o-piggy.
She'd keep it up, I had no doubt:
"Two liver here," she said "for me!"

Then the sausages did come around
An' the cured an' the lean an' the kidneys too.
And as she gulps, well, there's this sound:
She belches out this, "Nope. Not you."

Seeing I would surely have a fit,
She swilled three pints of ice-cold beer
An' gobbled up all the little bits.
Then came the bill, just as I'd fear'd,
For you know I paid the whole of it.
Then in her sweetest voice so dear,
Heavenly, silver and moonlit:
"As snacks go, well, that was fine...
Now ask me out to wine and dine."
Supper! Why, you'd bankrupt the state!
Oh, that lovely girl who ate and ate.

CHAVA FLORES (1920–1987)
Chava Flores was born in La Merced, Mexico City.
His songs are an unsurpassed account of daily life in Mexico.

head, are cooked in similar fashion). The actual meat, properly speaking, has different cuts: cheek (an extremely tender, clean, and flavorful cut), lips or mouth (with a taste all its own), and neck

Donaí Valencia @KitziaSV 26 de sep
Me voy a comer unos tacos de cabeza... ¡A ver si no me tuerzo el cuello!
Abrir

translated
These tacos are really going to my head... I'm getting dizzy!

(somewhat marbled meat with a strong taste). For the hesitant and undecided out there, the solution lies in the *taco surtido*, which comes with a bit of everything. Once the cut has been chosen, the taco maker chops it up on a cutting board, places a portion on a pair of tortillas that have been steam-heated alongside the meat, and lastly sprinkles a handful of onion and cilantro on top, together with a dash of salsa. This brings out a play of intense contrasts: the flavor of the meat, the bitterness of the lime, the crunch of the onion, and the scent of the cilantro—a perfect combination.

OUT OF THE FRYING PAN AND ONTO THE GRIDDLE

Steamed meat comes out so clean, tender, and tasty that you'll find this same method of preparation used in a variety of tacos. An alternative is to heat the tacos on a comal with some oil or lard. The end result is different, since the characteristics that the steam bestows on the tacos are lost, but the now browned tacos have their own unique merits. You can also fry the meat up a second time in a skillet or on a griddle, giving it a golden texture on the outside that's delicious and crunchy. Sliced up, it is then served in taco tortillas together with the usual condiments. It goes with saying that *flautas* and deep-fried tacos (see page 228) can also be made with this meat, extending still further the range of mouthwatering choices. The beef *barbacoa* served in the north of Mexico and Texas (see page 101) is prepared in the same way, but with flour tortillas and chiles—typically piquin or chiltepin chiles, which in Mexico are also known as *chile de monte* or wild chiles (see recipe 10, page 300).

EVERYTHING IS EATEN FROM A COW'S HEAD—

EYES, TONGUE,

LIPS, SWEETBREADS,

BRAINS,

CHEEKS. NOTHING GOES TO WASTE.

> "THEY LOVE THE EYE, BRAIN, AND TONGUE TACOS. THEY JUST FLY OUT THE KITCHEN."

The head-meat tacos we've got are cheek, lips, tongue, eye, sweetbreads, ear, neck, brain, and a mix of all the head meat from the animal.

Everything is used and it all tastes great. Would you like an eyeball taco? Sure, just tell me which you'd like—the left one or the right one. Customers order the eye, brain, and tongue tacos more than anything else. They just fly out the kitchen. Really, those eyeball tacos fly! Honestly, I have no idea how many cow heads we go through in a day. I've no time to count them, because it never stops. The difference between our tacos and the rest is that ours don't have any fat, so they're not bad for you. It's because of the steam—just steam, not an ounce of fat. They're cooked in a pot like the one used for tamales, just a bain-marie, that's it. Everything is boiled. Since the place is small, the meat comes already cooked, ready to be heated up and served... but it's a long process, about seven or eight hours of cooking with nothing but water, no oil. That's how it gets that special flavor. Condiments include saltpeter—it's a type of salt. It's not like the table salt that people eat at home. It gives the meat this pinkish color. If you use table salt the meat goes purple. Generally, head-meat tacos sell better in the afternoon, from about four or five o'clock until the late evening. That's how it usually is, but it depends on where the taco place is located, what neighborhood it's in. Here in downtown, you can sell tacos all day because there are a lot of people in the area. The secret of the tacos is the quality, hygiene, and good salsas—can't be beat! We sold tacos round the corner from a stand for twelve years, but here we have more space. Clients don't get wet when its raining. They can take their time eating. It's safer, too. And we sell quality products—only the best.

Daniel González
TACO MAKER AT LOS GÜEROS
93-B LÓPEZ, CENTRO HISTÓRICO, MEXICO CITY

IN

2010

THE TOTAL
PRODUCTION OF

BEEF

IN MEXICO
WAS IN
EXCESS OF

3.3 MILLION

TONS.

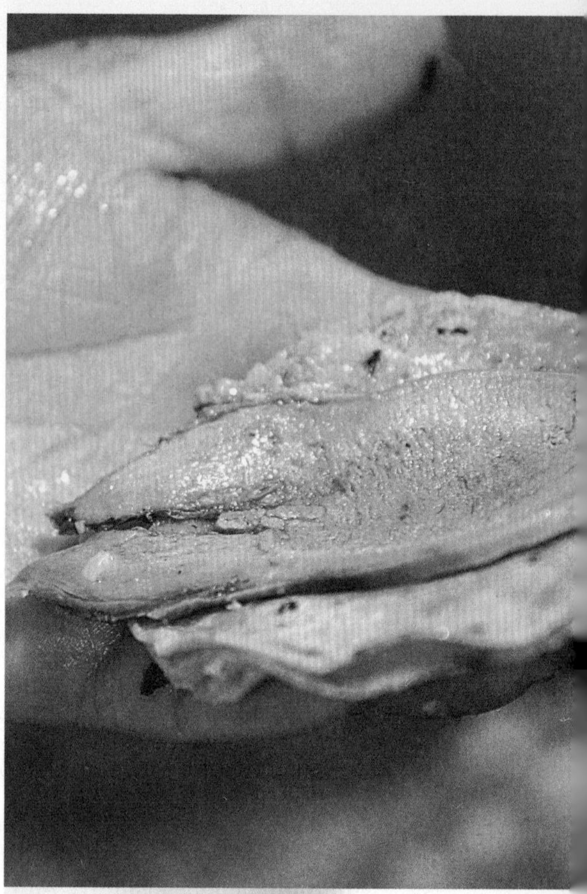

HOME-STYLE HEAD-MEAT TACOS

Serves 8

—1 lb (450 g) beef cheek
—1 lb (450 g) beef neck
—9 oz (250 g) beef lip
—1 beef tongue
—1 beef brain
—2 cow eyes
—½ medium onion
—2 cloves garlic
—5 whole black peppercorns
—3 bay leaves
—Sea salt
—12–20 4⅓-inch (11 cm) corn tortillas, for serving
—Chopped onion, chopped cilantro, lime wedges, salsas (see recipes 11–13, pages 300–301), and sea salt, for garnish

1. Rinse all the meat thoroughly, dry it, then salt lightly. Wrap each piece of meat in a clean tea towel. (Aluminum foil can be used instead of a dishcloth.)
2. Put the meat in a large pressure cooker, like those used for tamales. The water (around 2–3 cups/475–750 ml) should be strongly seasoned with at least a onion, a little garlic, peppercorns, bay leaves, and salt.
3. Cook over low heat for 5 or 6 hours, adding a little warm water when needed. Remove from heat and let the meat cool in the same pot, covered, for at least 30 minutes.
4. Once the meat is cool enough to handle, separate the different cuts and remove any excess fat from the broth in the pot.
5. Place a strainer above the pot containing the broth, line the strainer with a tea towel, place the meat inside, and cover with the tea towel. After 1 hour, remove the meat and finely chop it on a cutting board.
6. Steam the tortillas in small batches so they don't absorb too much humidity and fall apart. Serve the meat and tortillas together, accompanied by chopped onion and cilantro, limes, salt, and salsas (see recipes 11–13, pages 300–301).

HEAD-MEAT TACOS WITH OTHER ANIMALS

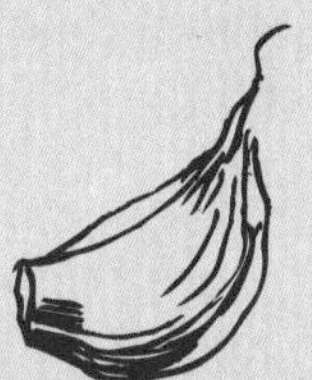

You can prepare head-meat tacos from nearly any other animal, such as goat, lamb, calf, or suckling pig. The most substantial cuts are neck, cheek, tongue, and brain.

1. Since the pieces are small, plan on one, two, or even three heads per person.

2. At the butcher's, ask for heads that have already been cleaned and are nearly ready to be prepared. At home, rinse them again and, once they're dry, sprinkle with salt. Wrap in aluminum foil and steam by placing a strainer above the pot containing the broth the meat was cooked in on the bottom. Cover with a tea towel and put the meat inside. Cook for 1 hour per 2 pounds (1 kg) then remove the meat and finely chop on a cutting board until the meat comes off the bone easily.
3. Once the meat is cooked, separate it into in small piles (one for chopped tongue, the other for diced cheek, etc.). Wrap the piles in aluminum foil and steam them until warm.
4. Warm some corn tortillas for serving, and garnish each taco with cilantro and chopped onion, a few drops of lime, and a generous serving of salsa (see recipes 11–13, pages 300–301).

THE BEST

Cantina la Ribera

140 CUAUHTÉMOC (CORNER DR. ERAZO), COL. DOCTORES, MEXICO CITY

This traditional cantina, located between the neighborhoods of Roma and Doctores, serves fried tripe and tongue tacos that come five per order off the menu.

El Afán

339 MONTERREY, COL. ROMA, MEXICO CITY

This cantina has a successful concept that mixes a modern look with good service and traditional dishes, including tongue tacos that come three per order.

El Tigrín

20 DE NOVIEMBRE (NEAR CORNER OF PÍPILA), CENTRO, JALAPA, VERACRUZ

Here the cow's head-meat is steamed *barbacoa* style. They also have four salsas available: green tomato, avocado, ranch-style, and dried chile.

Fonda Mexicana

775 SAN JERÓNIMO, COL. SAN JERÓNIMO LÍDICE, MEXICO CITY

Among the varied options from its snack food menu of regional dishes, connoisseurs will find tongue tacos, two per order.

La Imperial

245 LAGO ZURICH, COL. AMPLIFICACIÓN GRANADA, MEXICO CITY

This cantina in the Plaza Carso—conferring it a certain sophistication—offers beef tongue tacos on its menu.

Los Cocuyos

56 BOLÍVAR (CORNER OF URUGUAY), CENTRO HISTÓRICO, MEXICO CITY

What better place to set up a stand serving head, tongue, and eye tacos than in a cantina like Los Portales deTlaquepaque in Mexico City's historic downtown?

Tacos de Abogado

COLIMA (CORNER OF MORELIA), COL. ROMA, MEXICO CITY

A mischievous little stand found on the corner opposite Pushkin park. If you ask for a couple of "*abogado*," or "lawyer," tacos, you get tongue tacos with a bit of brains.

Tacos Don Luis

CHAPULTEPEC (CORNER OF MEXICALTZINGO), COL. AMERICANA, GUADALAJARA

These tongue tacos are offered sliced or chopped; with cilantro or onion; and with spicy salsas—red chile salsa or green tomato with green chiles.

Taquería Arandas

15-B MESONES (NEAR CORNER OF BOLÍVAR), CENTRO HISTÓRICO, MEXICO CITY

Here you find little head-meat tacos prepared in the style of the Jalisco municipality that this eatery is named after: smothered in hot arbol chile sauce, tempered with green tomato.

Taquería El Paisa

5435 NICOLÁS COPÉRNICO (CORNER OF MARIANO OTERO), COL. PASEOS DEL SOL, GUADALAJARA

They serve head, tongue, tripe, brain, and over half a dozen high-octane salsas to satisfy the "Pearl of Jalisco's" night clubbers.

JADERO
DE
CABEZA
BIRRIA
TAQUERIA LOS GÜEROS
2978-4016
BIRRIA
NO

Wilson

BASKET TACOS

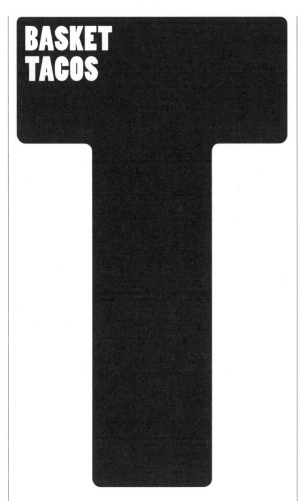

These tacos take up so little space that they usually fit in a basket on the back of a bicycle. And wherever you find basket tacos served, there's always a corner store nearby to provide the perfect beverage to accompany them. In fact, since the tacos are there every morning, it's almost like they are a permanent fixture and it is the store that sets up beside them every day. Between basket tacos and corner stores, a symbiotic or even parasitic relationship develops—the basket tacos waiting in the smallest nook or cranny, on the sidewalk or across the street from the store so that the ever-important cold drinks are nearby. The end result: an exquisite buffet of flavors and a hungry patron satisfied in seconds.

A MOVABLE FEAST

Seeking the inventor of *tacos de canasta* or basket tacos means going back to pre-Hispanic times. The modern basket was, back then, known as a *chiquihuite* or *itacate*. Though it's only guesswork, it wouldn't be hard to imagine the ancient Mexicans taking similar food to work from their homes. No one really knows the origin of these tacos, but some say they come from the mining towns of Hidalgo and Guanajuato, which would explain why they were known for years as *tacos mineros*, or miners' tacos. What distinguishes these tacos is their preparation, which allows them to be kept warm for hours. Their charm is rooted in their special flavor and portability, which means there's never a vendor too far away—and they go down the hatch just as easily. Not long ago, they were also known as *tacos de albañil* or "construction workers' tacos," which emphasizes their blue-collar origins and explains the nomadic wandering since basket taco vendors cycle around looking for entrances to construction sites, parks, and street corners to sell their fare. Because the food fits in a basket, these tacos lend themselves to all kinds of roving set-ups, from cars to bicycles, any corner offering a bit of shade. There are also those who have established more formal premises exclusively dealing in this kind of taco, but these are relatively rare. These days, basket tacos are gladly gulped down by the dozen without giving much thought to the origin of the tacos, or to who is eating them, because, rich or poor, everyone loves them. Usually, these tacos are savored in the morning hours; and, since the freshness and taste of basket tacos makes them an ideal option for lunchtime, they're very hard to find later in the afternoon, with the exception of their appearances at weddings and neighborhood events. These

TYPICAL IN MEXICO CITY

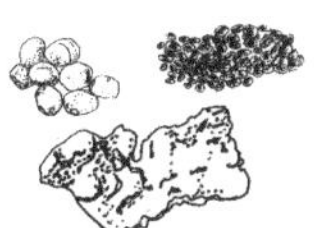

MADE WITH BEANS, POTATOES, PORK RINDS, CHORIZO

FINISHES COOKING IN A BASKET

tacos are typical of Mexico City, but they're found in nearly every state, where many advertise them as "Mexico-style"—referring to the capital—to lend them greater credibility.

BASKET STYLE

Even though these tacos aren't fried, they certainly look greasy enough, and that is exactly the quality that endows them with their incomparable taste. Another characteristic of these tacos is that the cooking process is completed in the basket. Keeping the food warm for hours as it is hawked from corner to corner is no small feat, and it is precisely the close contact of tightly packed tacos, sweating in the steam and imbibing their own aroma, that brings out their best qualities: softness, flavor, and lightness. In fact, despite being so greasy, they do have a light taste—the customer's "I'll just have one" almost always ends up being "Go on then, just one more." The classic fillings are mashed potatoes, refried beans, *adobo*, and of course pressed pork rinds, accompanied with chiles in a vinegar marinade called *escabeche* and a variety of salsas. The best and most elegant mode of presentation is in a traditional reed basket, though there are places that have them displayed on steam trays. The chiles in the *escabeche* are essential to fully appreciate this specialty, but it has to be freshly made, with plenty of carrots (see recipe 31, page 308). These tacos are also often eaten with raw green salsa (see recipe 3, page 296), which includes an avocado variation.

IT'S THE LITTLE THINGS THAT COUNT

In practically every state of Mexico, there are minimal differences in how basket tacos are prepared: it might be a question of a different filling, a local flavor, or a different selection of chiles for the salsa. The basket tacos from the north of Mexico show the biggest variation: these tacos are heated in a steaming tray, as if they were head-meat tacos (see page 123). With this piece of equipment the tacos are infused with steam, staying warm until the moment they are ready to be served.

7:55
They line the basket with plastic, dishcloths, and butcher's paper. The fillings are all ready.

8:00
They put the pressed pork rinds on low heat so that the fat melts off.

8:10
They make the tacos with warm tortillas, layering them in the basket and coating them with the fat from the pork rinds.

8:30
They cover 250 tacos with raw onion rounds.

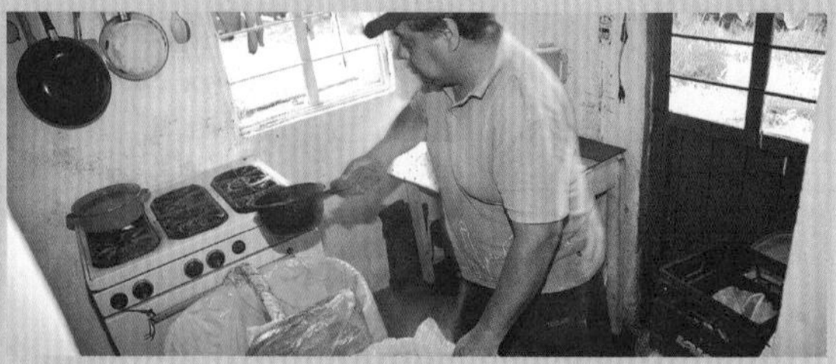

8:35
They put a cup of oil on the stove-top.

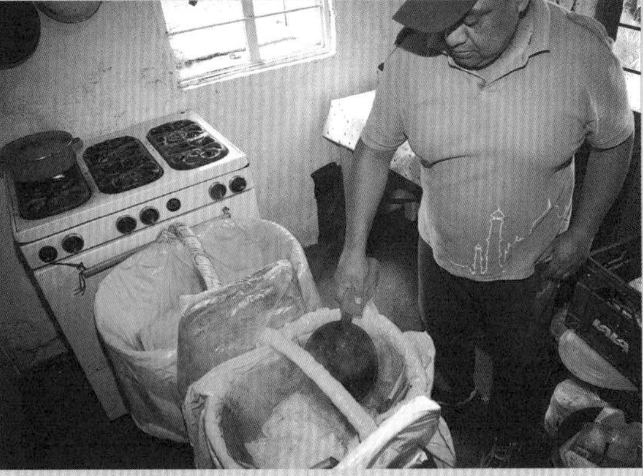

8:40
They coat the tacos with the oil.

8:45
Jaime says a prayer to the Virgin of Guadalupe before leaving.

BREAKFAST ON WHEELS

**IT IS AN ORDINARY MORNING.
THIS HARD-WORKING COUPLE WAKES UP VERY EARLY TO PREPARE THE BREAKFAST
THE RESIDENTS OF COYOACÁN ARE HUNGRILY WAITING FOR.**

8:41
They tightly close the basket so that the tacos start to sweat.

8:46
He pedals off to Coyoacán. It's going to be a long day.

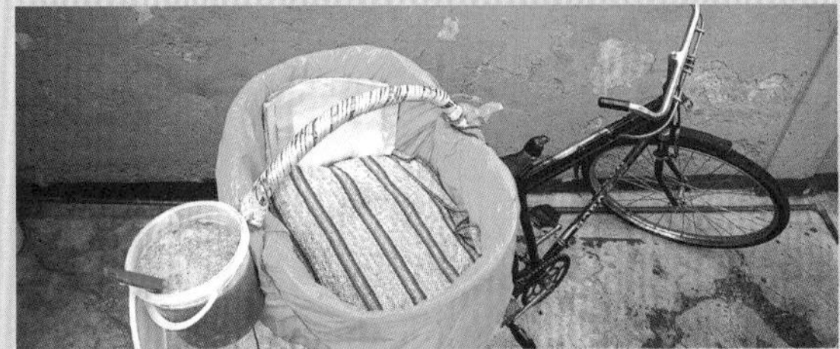

8:42
They put the basket on the bike.

9:00
Five with potato and four with pork rinds. Coming up!

BASKET TACOS WERE INVENTED IN THE MINING AREAS OF HIDALGO AND GUANAJUATO, WHICH IS WHY THEY WERE KNOWN AS MINERS' TACOS.

I started making these basket tacos about twelve years ago.

My buddies—they're from Oaxaca—showed me how. A bit before eight in the morning, we get the baskets ready by putting in the plastic, the cloth, the paper, and then we get on with the tacos. My wife cooks the fillings. On Sundays we just do the basics: the potatoes, the beans, and the pork rinds; the rest of the week we do the other fillings: sliced poblano chiles with eggs, *cochinita pibil*, *adobo*, picadillo, or green *mole* sauce—every day's a different filling. They say that these tacos were invented by a guy who was so poor that all he had was a basket, some potatoes, and some beans. So, he says to himself, "Let's see if I can sell all this stuff." And he did. Later, he started filling the tacos with pork rinds. I think the man was from a town called San Vicente Xiloxochiltla, in Tlaxcala, because most guys selling these tacos are from there, but me, I'm from Mexico City, a *chilango*. I cycle all round Coyoacán, Los Reyes, San Lucas, La Candelaria, Atlántida, Ciudad Jardín, and San Pablo Tepetlapa. Lots of my customers work in restaurants, and since they always get given the same for lunch, they wait for me to come around. A lot of my work comes in on my cell phone: "Hey, I'm waiting for you!" I've got different customers for the different fillings each day of the week too. We've got three bicycles: I take out 250 tacos, but my kids only take a hundred a piece because they're going to school too. We make some 450 tacos a day—and I'm glad to say they all sell. We're usually finishing up between one and two in the afternoon but, to tell you the truth, there are days when it's five o'clock and we're still at it. There are basket-taco vendors all over the place here, but there's enough business for all of us.
Us Mexicans, we love these tacos. Customers say to me, "You must be lacing these with something: I wolf them down, I'm full, and then it's 'Hey, give me two more!'" Then they joke around, saying, "Stop comin' round here!" But they're always the first ones to be calling me up again on the phone.

Jaime Jasso
BASKET TACO MAKER, COVERING COYOACÁN BY BICYCLE

TACOS STANDS STARTED TO POP UP AROUND MEXICO CITY DURING THE REVOLUTION, TO FEED THE TROOPS.

BASKET TACOS

Serves 10

REFRIED BEANS

—3 tablespoons lard
—½ a medium onion, finely chopped
—1 lb (450 g) cooked black beans
—1 cup (250 ml) chicken broth (as needed)
—1 sprig epazote
—Sea salt

1. Melt the lard in a medium pot over medium heat, then fry the onion until translucent.
2. Add the beans and fry them for 1 minute while adding just enough broth to get to the consistency of a thick paste when mashed.
3. Taste and season with the epazote and bring to a boil, stirring constantly, until the paste thickens, about 1–5 minutes.
4. Season to taste with salt. Discard the epazote and serve.

BEEF IN ADOBO

—1 lb (450 g) flank or loin steak
—¼ medium onion, plus extra sliced onions to serve
—3 bay leaves
—3 whole black peppercorns
—3 tablespoons apple cider vinegar
—Sea salt
—1 cup (250 ml) ancho chile *adobo* (see recipe 34, page 309)

1. Place the beef in a large pot and add enough water to cover. Add the onion, bay leaves, peppercorns, vinegar, and salt.
2. Heat over high heat until the water boils. Reduce heat to low, cover, and simmer for 1 hour or until the meat is tender.
3. Remove from heat and allow to cool for about 1 hour, covered. Transfer the beef to a cutting board and carefully shred by hand.
4. In a second pot, bring the *adobo* to a boil, then add a little water to loosen.
5. Add the shredded beef to the *adobo*, and allow to simmer until it thickens. Discard the bay leaves before serving.

PRESSED PORK RINDS WITH SAUCE

Serves 10

—1 lb (450 g) pressed pork rinds, finely chopped
—½ cup (120 ml) cooked guajillo chile salsa (see recipe 21, page 303)
—Sea salt

1. Put the chopped pork rinds in a pot set over low heat. Cook the rinds in their grease until browned.
2. Transfer the rinds to a cutting board and chop into smaller pieces. Return to the pot set over low heat.
3. Add the salsa and stir well. Let simmer for a couple of minutes until thickened. Season to taste with salt.

MAKING A TACO BASKET

1. Once the fillings are ready, line the inside of a basket with plastic wrap, a large tea towel, and parchment paper, so that the tacos stay warm.
2. Prepare the tacos by adding a portion of the fillings to the tortillas, fold in half, then place along the bottom of the basket, to form a single layer.
3. Once the bottom of the basket is covered by the first layer of tacos, lightly baste the tacos with hot oil with a brush.
4. Arrange another layer of tacos on top of the first and repeat the process as many times as required.
5. Cover the tacos tightly to seal in the heat so that they stay at the right temperature, allowing them to sweating for 1 hour before serving.

THE BEST

El Gallo

167 PRISCILIANO SÁNCHEZ, CENTRO, GUADALAJARA

Basket tacos are called "steamed tacos" here (*al vapor*). Aside from the traditional choices of beans and potatoes, "meat chunks" can be ordered too.

El Negro

REGIDORES (CORNER OF AMERICAS), COL. CHAPULTEPEC COUNTRY, GUADALAJARA

Their secret resides in reheating refried beans, mashed potato, and pork rinds after they've soaked in a red tomato salsa for two days.

Flavio's

342-A 13TH AV. PONIENTE NORTE, CENTRO, TUXTLA GUTIÉRREZ, CHIAPAS

The capital of Chiapas boasts this establishment that offers traditional taco choices accompanied with pickled carrot, guacamole, and cabbage with green tomato salsa.

Los Especiales

NEAR TO 52 AYUNTAMIENTO, CENTRO HISTÓRICO, MEXICO CITY

The landmark for finding this taco stand is nearby radio station XEW, which explains why so many of the stand's patrons come from the cultural scene.

On Palmas avenue (itinerant)

PALMAS (CORNER OF SIERRA MOJADA), COL. LOMAS DE CHAPULTEPEC, MEXICO CITY

Setting up shop from a bike or a little table is the essence of basket tacos. An umbrella marks our spot of choice in the Lomas neighborhood.

Capuleto basket tacos

441 ENRIQUE OLIVARES SANTANA, COL. BOULEVARES, AGUASCALIENTES

A variety of choices: pork in green salsa (or is it *mole*?), *tinga*, and beans with chorizo—to name just a few—served with oregano, pickled onion, and grated carrot.

La Pantera basket tacos

17 FERNANDO BELTRÁN Y PUGA, COL. AMPLIACIÓN, MIGUEL HIDALGO, MEXICO CITY

The plus in this operation roving around Tlalpan is the *nopales* salad that comes with tacos served with *adobo*, beans, potatoes, pork rinds, and green *mole*.

Tacos Joven

199 UNIVERSIDAD, COL. NAVARTE, MEXICO CITY

You'll have no trouble finding them if you head for the junction with Doctor Vértiz—the snack food area par excellence. Bigger than average tacos, too.

Tacos Lara

120 SUDAMÉRICA, COL. VISTA HERMOSA, MONTERREY

"Sweated" tacos with beans, potato, pork rind, or shredded meat, served on a corn or flour tortilla with cabbage, tomato, and a roasted green tomato salsa.

Taquería La Mexicana

244 VICENTE GUERRERO, CENTRO, MONTERREY

Set up in the market in Monterrey, they serve *carnitas*, picadillo, pork rinds, potato, and shredded meat in handmade, oil-free tortillas.

CARNITAS TACOS

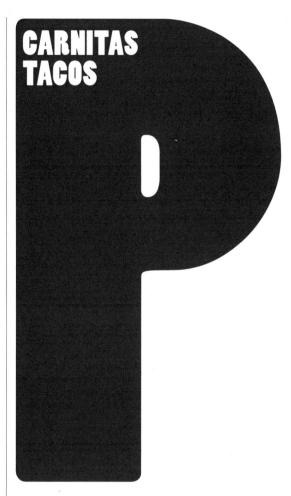

Pork *carnitas* is one of the most famous dishes in Mexican cuisine. It's something that arouses passions—from love and lust to regret and repentance—because of the boundless pleasure of our enjoyment and the shame of our gluttony, the pleasing taste of its grease and the knowledge of its consequences. Without a doubt, the flexible tortilla and the tender pork come together to provide an unparalleled culinary performance: that corn dough with which the gods created the first man in the Americas meets the pig, an animal that in New Spain in the sixteenth century was eaten as proof of adherence to the Catholic faith.

PORK COMES TO THE NEW WORLD

Carnitas tacos represent one of the best examples of culinary cultural intermixing. In these tacos, we find ingredients that Mediterranean peoples have used for centuries (onions, cilantro, and limes, for example) combined with local American produce (such as green tomato, avocado, and chiles) that have a privileged place in salsas. The combination is perfect: little wonder that *carnitas* have reached monumental importance in the national identity. It's customary to prepare this dish in great copper pots, a metallurgical marvel in themselves, wrought with great mastery in the state of Michoacán. This is why thc most famous *carnitas* are the ones done "Michoacán style," easy to recognize by the sweet flavor and dark color that appeals to everyone (with variations in Zamora, La Piedad, Uruapan, Puruándiro, and other towns elsewhere in Michoacán). The copper pots and distinctive style strongly suggest that these tacos themselves come from Michoacán, a claim reinforced by the excellent quality and numerous makers of these tacos in this part of Mexico, as well as a lengthy oral tradition. There is, however, another version gleaned from the lines of the book written by conquistador Bernal Díaz del Castillo. In the chronicle, he sets down the events of a celebration held in Coyoacán that some consider the stamped and signed birth certificate of our famous pork *carnitas*. This banquet, ordered by their leader Hernán Cortés, took place on August 13, 1521, the day the city of Tlatelolco fell to the Spanish, bringing the Aztec Empire to an end. With war shortages and the urgency of the moment, it's thought that the only way to prepare the pork was to fry it in its own lard; and since wheat had yet to be planted in the New World and only corn tortillas were available, the menu at that

TYPICAL IN MICHOACÁN

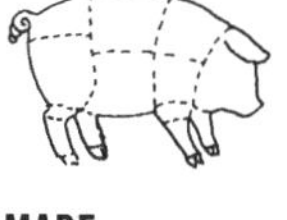

MADE WITH PORK

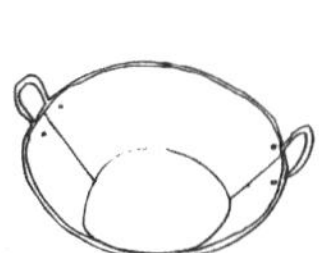

COOKED IN A COPPER POT

banquet must have consisted of *carnitas* tacos. The excesses indulged in during the festivities in question called for several masses and even solemn processions to invoke divine pardon for the gluttony committed. Still, the event itself is of less import than the unquestionable success of the dish that was served there. Pigs arrived in Mexico along with the first conquistadors, and it seems altogether probable that the first piggy to set its trotters on the beaches of Veracruz was quickly led to a pot to make *carnitas*. Indeed, there's nothing strange in the idea of frying pork in its own lard either, given the large amount of fat the animal has. Although considered a typically Mexican technique, it is found around the world, wherever pork is eaten. The ingenious local touch was to put the pork on a tortilla and add chiles. This specialty is sold all day and can be found even into the late hours of the night—and this is where light bulbs come in handy, hot light bulbs having been used to keep meat warm a good fifty years before microwaves came on the scene. That's why these carnitas tacos are also called *tacos de foco*, or "light bulb tacos."

THIS LITTLE PIGGY WENT TO THE POT

The traditional method to cook *carnitas* is to fry the meat in a large casserole or copper pot, and to do so with the pig's own fat, its lard. The proportions should be such that the lard covers the meat completely. After, the meat is cooked on slow burn until it browns to perfection, usually for an hour or two, depending on how much meat there is. You can make variations by adding different ingredients and seasonings to the pot (but not by dumping them all in together!): sugar, caramel, brown sugar, water, *tequesquite* (natural mineral salt), fragrant herbs, whole oranges (or just the peel or the juice), milk, sodas... every household has a secret recipe. In another variation, the meat is boiled first, then fried afterwards—a recipe that strays from the straight and narrow, but is more convenient and easier to make. As an animal, the pig is so noble, gastronomically speaking, that nearly all of it goes into the copper pot and, since some parts have a nomenclature all their own, the naive diner may not know what's being eaten when gulping down a *taco de pera*. So, beside the leg, the shoulder, and the loin (together referred to as *maciza*), we have the whole head, including snout (*trompa*), cheeks, ears, and tongue (or *nenepil*, a word also used to describe a mix of stomach and uterus); all the offal and other parts, including the ribs, intestines (*moño*, *trenza*, or *tripa*), throat (*perilla*), neck, shank (*chamorro*), liver, pancreas (*pajarilla*), heart, tail, stomach (*buche*), lungs (*bofe*), uterus (*nana*), anus (*pera*), and penis (*viril*). And if that wasn't enough, from

> "The Zouaves [...] accused us of trying to poison them [...] when the truth of it is that they don't know how to eat, they stuff themselves with *chirimoyas* and pork rinds and guava at the same time, and later, of course, they rush around dirtying themselves all over the place, but it's very hard, I told him, my child, to get used to this food, I almost gave my soul up to the Lord twenty years ago when I was assigned the parish at [...] Tzitzipandacuri, I almost died, as I was telling you, from the *carnitas* binge that I went on, and the truth of it is that it took a lot of effort to get used to all those chiles and spices, I was so homesick, my child, but so homesick for my Donostiarra-style eel and the *pil-pil* cod."
>
> **FERNANDO DEL PASO.**
> *Noticias del Imperio*. Mexico: Diana, 1987.

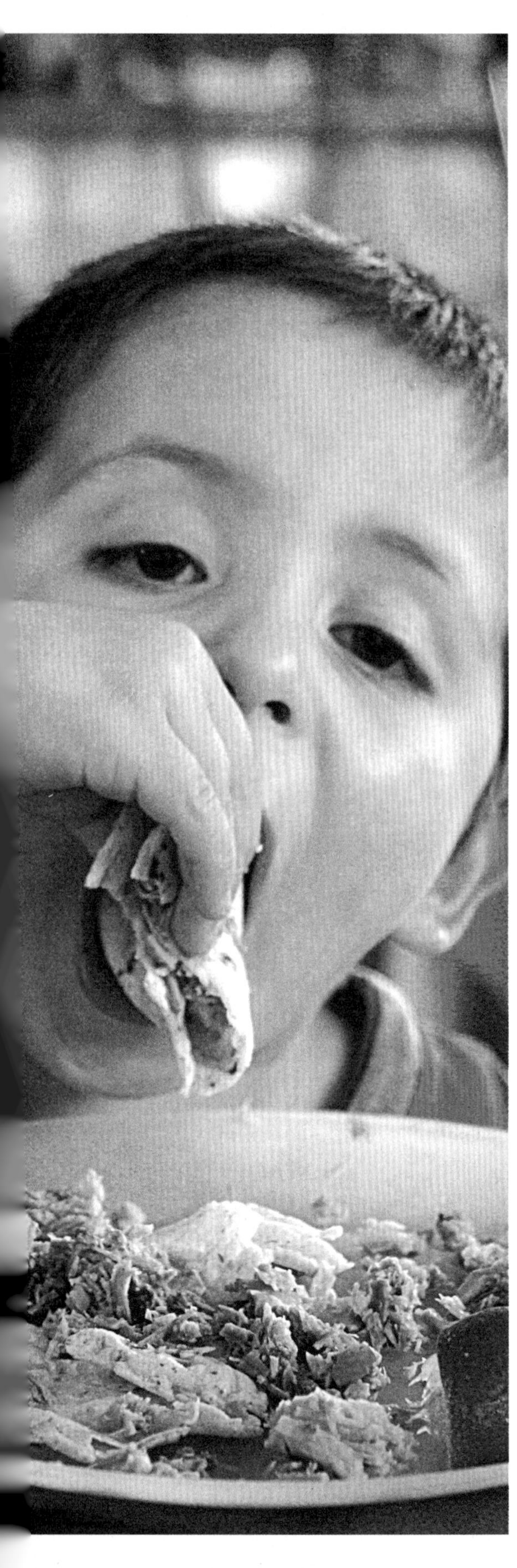

THE
BIGGEST
TACO
EVER MADE
WAS CREATED ON
NOVEMBER
20, 2011,
IN QUERÉTARO.
IT MEASURED
246
FEET LONG
AND WAS
FILLED WITH
CARNITAS.

out of the bottom of the pot comes the *chiquita*, *achicalada*, or *cochinada*, which could be described as the fried-to-a-crisp leftover bits, regardless of where they came from. Lastly, the pigskin provides *cueritos*, of paramount importance in *carnitas* tacos; and pork rinds or cracklings, the preparation of which is so special it gets an explanation all its own (see page 150). Once the meat's been cooked, two or three pieces are selected, then finely chopped with a machete on a chopping block. The meat is then generously spread on a pair of small, warm tortillas, ready to be topped off with onion, cilantro, salsa, a few squirts of lime, and a dash of salt: the authentic *carnitas* taco. Period. The classic combinations—ask anyone in the know—are lean meat with pork rinds, ribs with *chiquita*, stomach with uterus, and, lastly, *surtido*: with a little bit of everything. *Carnitas* tacos are accompanied with diced onion, chopped cilantro, and *papaloquelite*; fried *nopales* with onion, garlic, and arbol chiles; sliced avocado, cucumber, and radish; and, finally, a long list of salsas (see recipes 1–3, 6, 8–9, 17, 20–22, 24–29, among others, pages 296–307).

FEATHERS AND SCALES

From out of the copper pot, we also get brain quesadillas, nicknamed *sesadillas* (*sesos* = brains). These are folded tortillas that have been fried golden brown in the grease of the copper pot. They have a soft filling with a very special flavor. They are eaten with chiles in vinegar or with the same salsas already mentioned. Another close relative of *carnitas* tacos are known as *pepena* tacos. These are native to the state of Michoacán and made from pork offal, which is slowly fried in the pig's own lard until it is golden. Still, the most interesting variations have feathers and scales, and we can now turn to these.

DUCK TACOS

There are a few clues as to where the inspiration for duck tacos comes from: its beginnings can be traced back to Peking duck, a classic in Chinese cuisine in which the meat is placed on wheat pancakes, then seasoned with a special plum sauce, green onion, and cucumber cut lengthwise. Although the similarity between Peking duck and *carnitas* is superficial, since the meat is roasted in an oven and the concept of the dish is quite unlike Mexican tacos, the method of slowly cooking the meat in its own fat—as they also do in France with duck confit—is very close to the method used for *carnitas*. Something of both styles seems to have permeated the spirit of contemporary Mexican

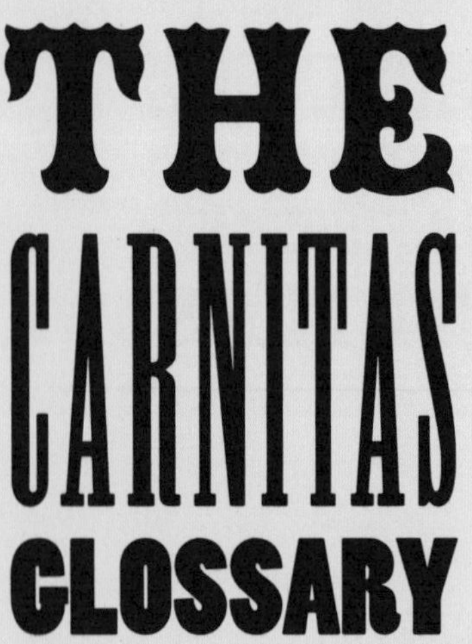

MACIZA lean meat from the leg, loin, and shoulder blade
COSTILLA rib
CUELLO OR PAPADA neck
CHAMORRO cross-cut veal shank
HÍCADO liver
CORAZÓN heart
RABO tail
CACHETE cheek
OREJA ear
BUCHE stomach
NANA uterus
PERA anus
VIRIL penis
BOFE lung
MOÑO, TRENZA, OR TRIPA tripe (intestines)
PERILLA throat
PAJARILLA pancreas
SESOS brain
NENEPIL tongue (also a mix of stomach and uterus)
CUERITOS skin
CHIQUITA, ACHICALADA, OR COCHINADA the crunchy leftovers at the bottom of the pot
CHICHARRÓN crispy pork rinds

chefs, together with a certain capricious ingenuity, too, and with excellent results: the duck meat is gently cooked in its own fat until golden on the outside and tender and juicy on the inside. It's cut up onto corn or flour tortillas, to the discerning patron's taste. It's garnished with chopped cilantro and parsley, then finished off with a chile salsa, a few drops of lime, and some salt. There are different recipes with slight variations that play on the basics, but they all have one thing in common with *carnitas* tacos: the succulent combination of greasy meat, corn masa, taco garnishes, and the "spirit" of the moment—satisfying a craving.

Seleno Gómez Leyva. @Perro_Macizo 13
Yo también dije "no gracias, no tengo hambre"", y me chingue doc tacos.
Abrir

translated
Me too, I said "thank you, I'm not hungry", and then gulped down twelve tacos.

TUNA CARNITAS

A method that has proven an unmitigated success: frying up food so that the outside is crisp to the tooth, with a slightly dry texture, while the inside reveals the exquisite contrast of fresh, flavorful meat. Not many types of animal lend themselves to this method of cooking, and the prerequisite is, above all, that the meat be high in fat content. And that's how tuna made its way into the world of *carnitas*. Tuna *carnitas* are prepared just like pork ones, though obviously the cooking times are shorter. They are also presented and eaten the same, in corn tortillas, with guacamole and different salsas, onion, cilantro, and a squirt of lime. Tuna's not the only fish that could be prepared like this, but the others have yet to make their way into the nation's kitchens. For the time being, we'll just have to wait.

"Cortés ordered a banquet to be held at Coyoacán in celebration of the capture of the city [the battle of Tlatelolco] and had already procured plenty of wine for the purpose out of a ship which had come from Spain to the port of Villa Rica, and he had pigs which they had brought him from Cuba."

Bernal Díaz del Castillo, *The History of the Conquest of New Spain,* Albuquerque: University of New Mexico Press, 2008, page 306.

4 OUNCES
(120G)
OF
PORK LOIN
CONTAINS

ONLY 2.4G

OF SATURATED

FAT

(LESS THAN 10%
OF THE RECOMMENDED
MAXIMUM
DAILY INTAKE).

Carnitas carmelo is named after José Carmen Rivera Márquez, our dad.

This business has been in the family for a century. My great-grandfather started it, and now we all sell *carnitas*. I started out in this little stand in the plaza, and it's my favorite; but we also have four proper restaurants in Morelia, another four in Quiroga, one in Zamora, one in Jalisco state, and another in Arlington, Texas. They're all called Carnitas Carmelo, and we ten brothers and our children run them. Our restaurants are trademarked and patented, so we can sell vacuum-sealed bags of our food at Oxxo, Superama, and Walmart. The only thing we need now is a permit to send our products to the U.S. for export, but we'll get that soon enough. The secret to good flavor is in processing the meat quickly—it's the only real difference that I've found. The animal isn't dead more than twelve hours before it's in the pot: we slaughter the animal at 5 p.m. and by 4 a.m. the next day, it's cooked. Also, everything is natural. We don't use anything else, like they do elsewhere, to give the meat its color—no sodas or sugar or stuff like that. We just let the meat fry. You need to give it enough time to fry so that it seasons itself and turns the right color. Tourism has dropped off some, but we still sell the same. We've got how much we sell daily figured out, so we just prepare what we can sell, and there you go. On a Sunday, we sell two or three pigs. My clients include many politicians and celebrities. Governors come here, and presidents too… Cuauhtémoc Cárdenas and his son, Lázaro Cárdenas Batel. I have photos of them eating here, and photos of other people off the TV. Marco Antonio Solís, the singer, and the sports anchor Enrique Bermúdez de la Serna—he even sends us his greetings when he's on air.

"EVERYTHING IS NATURAL HERE. WE DON'T ADD SODAS OR SUGAR TO THE MEAT."

Rodolfo Rivera Aguirre
OWNER OF CARNITAS CARMELO TACO STAND IN THE TOWN SQUARE IN QUIROGA, MICHOACÁN

I'M THE TOP HOG HERE

The preparation of this delicious specialty has given rise to a profession all its own: the *chicharronero*, the person in charge of the production and sale of lard, of which *chicharrón* —pork rinds or cracklings— are a much-prized derivative.

There are three main types of pork rinds:

1. Crunchy, crackled, or puffed
These pork rinds can go in tacos, eaten just with salsa, avocado, guacamole, cheese, *papaloquelite*, or tomato. This culinary creation begins by salting pigskin and leaving it to dry for a day. Next, it's cut and cooked very slowly in lard in a process known as parboiling the rinds. The result gives hardened sheets that are pressed and left to sit for a while. When about to be eaten, the sheets are fried in sizzling lard, which inflates and expands the skin, a step called "crackling" or "puffing" the rinds. This product is commonly found in outlets selling *carnitas*. It's eaten as a snack accompanied with guacamole or cooked in salsa. Likewise, it can be used as a side or garnish in regional dishes such as charro beans, tortilla soup, pozole, and so on.

2. Loaded
This product is found nearly everywhere pork is eaten. It's prepared by putting the pigskin, dewlap, and fatty cuts of the animal in water, then boiling it all till the water has evaporated and the pork fat or lard can be extracted. The leftover chunks are fried until they are golden brown all over, and are known as *chicharrones*, *migajitas*, *grasitas*, or *tlalitos*, though they go by other names in different parts of Mexico (for example, *chicharrones de* Montemorelos, in Nuevo León). These are finely chopped and fried in a skillet in their own grease along with onion, chile, tomato, and a little lime juice to make for a nice snack.

3. Pressed
This specialty is made by heavily seasoning the prepared crunchy or loaded fatty rinds with dried chiles and different spices. Next, the rinds are pressed in special molds and left to cure to remove the excess grease. Over time, the process produces a delicious cured morsel that is an essential component of many different *antojitos*.

CRACKLINGS THAT DON'T COME FROM PORK

In Mexico, other types of cracklings are eaten that don't come from pork but are fried golden brown and crunchy like pork rinds are. We can find "beef cracklings" (a specialty in Hidalgo and Querétaro states), which consist of frying beef offal in pork lard; "prawn cracklings" (a specialty from Sinaloa state); and "cheese cracklings" (see page 70).

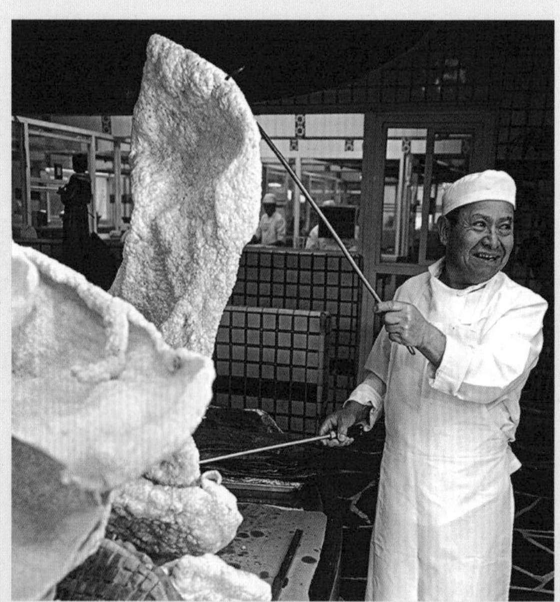

MICHOACÁN -STYLE CARNITAS

Serves 4

—1 lb (450 g) pork leg, cut into 2-inch dice
—1 lb (450 g) pork ribs, cut into 2–3 bone segments
—¼ medium onion
—2 cloves garlic
—Sea salt
—4 tablespoons lard
—½ cup (120 ml) whole milk
—½ cup (120 ml) fresh orange juice
—12–20 4⅓-inch (11 cm) tortillas
—Chopped radishes, cilantro, and lime wedges, for serving

1. Place the meat in a large pot and add enough water to cover it completely.
2. Add the onion, garlic, and a pinch of salt. Bring to boil, reduce heat to low, and simmer for an hour or until the meat is tender.
3. Transfer the meat to a cutting board.
4. Melt the lard in a large skillet set over medium heat and, once the lard is hot, add the meat. When the lard begins to sizzle again, add the milk and orange juice.
5. Cook for around 20 or 30 minutes, until the pan is dry and the meat is golden brown.
6. Place the meat in a strainer set over a bowl, letting the liquid drain off.
7. Chop the meat on a cutting board, and serve with plenty of fresh tortillas and garnishes.

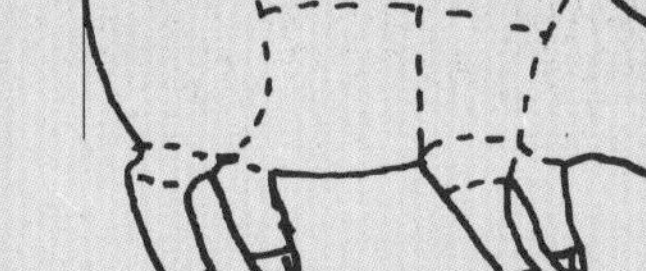

SESADILLAS (PORK BRAIN QUESADILLAS)

Serves 10

—2 tablespoons corn oil
—5 oz (150 g) lean ground pork
—4 oz (120g) chopped onion
—1 clove garlic, finely chopped
—1 small potato, diced
—1 small carrot, diced
—Sea salt and freshly ground black pepper
—9 oz (250 g) ground pork brain
—1 sprig epazote, chopped
—20 mint leaves, chopped
—2 or 3 green chiles, seeded and finely chopped
—12–20 4⅓-inch (11 cm) corn tortillas
—9 oz (250 g) lard
—Chiles in vinegar and salsa (see recipe 31, page 308), for serving

1. Heat the oil in a large skillet. Add the lean ground pork and fry over a medium

heat for 5 minutes. Add half the chopped onion and the garlic. Add the potato, carrot, and around 1 cup (250 ml) water. Season with salt and pepper, and leave on the heat until the mixture is cooked through. Remove from heat and allow to cool.
2. Mix the cooled picadillo with the pork brain in a medium bowl. Add the mint, the remaining onion, chiles, and epazote.
3. Place the mixture in fresh tortillas, then fold tortillas in half and secure with a toothpick.
4. Melt the lard in a large skillet set over medium heat. Fry the quesadillas in the skillet until crisp on both sides, about 2–3 minutes. Serve with chiles in vinegar and salsa.

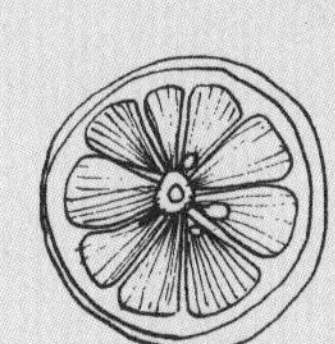

CARNITAS IN BEER SALSA

Serves 4

—2 tablespoons corn oil
—1 medium onion, sliced
—3 jalapeño chiles, seeded and sliced
—1 small clove garlic, finely chopped
—2 large tomatoes, peeled and diced
—1 12-oz (350 ml) bottle of beer
—Sea salt and freshly ground black pepper
—Ground cumin
—1 lb (450 g) pork *carnitas*, chopped
—1 sprig cilantro, chopped

1. Heat the oil in a large skillet over low heat. Add the onion and cook until translucent. Add the chiles and garlic, and cook for 2–3 minutes, until cooked through.
2. Increase the heat to medium and add the tomatoes. Cook until

softened, then add half of the beer. When it starts to boil, stir and press the mixture until it becomes a thick sauce. Season to taste with salt, pepper, and cumin. Let simmer at medium heat, until the sauce begins to thicken. Add the meat, stir, and let simmer until thick (stirring occasionally), for 3–5 minutes.
4. Sprinkle the cilantro on top and serve. (Tacos can be made with this mixture, without other condiments, unless you prefer to spice it up with salsa [see recipes 15 and 30, pages 301 and 307].)

THE BEST

Bajío
2709 CUITLÁHUAC, CLAVERÍA, MEXICO CITY
When foreign chefs come to Mexico City, this is where their local colleagues bring them to try out its renowned Michoacán-style *carnitas*.

Carnitas Don Valente
360 LAGUNA DE TÉRMINOS, COL. VENTURA PUENTE, MORELIA, MICHOACÁN
This is a family business where they prepare their tacos exclusively with young pigs—you'll notice the difference in the consistency and the flavor.

Carnitas El Azul
CHAPULTEPEC (CORNER OF INSURGENTES METRO), ZONA ROSA, MEXICO CITY
A humble establishment frequented by the extravagant residents of the Zona Rosa district and some of Mexico City's best chefs, like Mikel Alonso and Pedro Martín.

El Cerdo Mareado
KM 7.7 ON THE PANORAMIC HIGHWAY TO AJUSCO, TLALPAN, MEXICO CITY
The cuts of meat roasting over the coals are already a reference point for those on afternoon drives to Ajusco, stopping by for the "Cuban-style pork tacos."

El Kioskito
6 SONORA (CORNER OF CHAPULTEPEC), COL. ROMA, MEXICO CITY
Since 1948, this has been one of the best places for *carnitas*. Especially tasty is their *Especial Kioskito*: pork rinds, rice, enchiladas with *mole* sauce, and *charro* beans.

El Rincón Tarasco
142 JOSE MARTÍ, COL. ESCANDÓN, MEXICO CITY
A family from Zacapu, Michoacán, came to run this restaurant, where the spicy condiments can't be missed. Try the pickled chopped onion and manzano chile.

El Venadito
1701 UNIVERSIDAD, COL. CHIMALISTIAC, MEXICO CITY
You can still recognize the vestiges of the country club where this famous *carnitas* establishment has been operating for decades.

La Hacienda de los Morales
525 JUAN CARLOS DE MELLA, COL. DEL BOSQUE, MEXICO CITY
Duck *carnitas* stands out as one of the special creations of this restaurant, where you step back in time when you walk inside.

Los Cochinitos
1519 REVOLUCIÓN, SAN ÁNGEL, MEXICO CITY
These are staunch defenders of the nutritional merits of pork and carefully prepare it with an eye to hygiene, inviting patrons to see the kitchen for themselves.

Quiroga
20 MINS. BY CAR FROM MORELIA, MICHOACÁN, HEADING TO PÁTZCUARO
Many towns in Michoacán are dedicated to making *carnitas*: the stands around this town square are not to be missed.

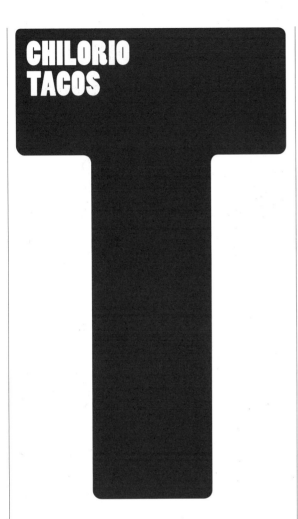

CHILORIO TACOS

The most famous food in Sinaloan cuisine is, without a doubt, *chilorio*. It could be considered simply chorizo sausage prepared in a pot, which is to say that it's heavily seasoned pork, but with the difference that *chilorio* meat isn't stuffed into tripe casings. As a regional, typically homemade specialty, this dish has come to represent Sinaloa, mostly due to the commercial success of canned *chilorio*, which can be found in any Mexican supermarket and has catapulted its fame far beyond national borders.

A SOPHISTICATED SINALOAN PRESERVE

For centuries, the defining characteristic of Sinaloa was that it was very far away from anything else, so it was vitally important to the inhabitants to acquire what was necessary to survive. *Chilorio* was, in fact, a method of preservation, like cold cuts and sausages, but with the marked difference that the fat and spices are the curing agents that preserve the food from harmful bacteria. A carefully prepared jar of *chilorio* is good for a month or longer, depending on storage conditions. The many different methods of preparing pork meat have always traveled with it wherever it has been taken, and two ancient preservatives in Mexican cuisine are chiles and salt. It seems that in this case the culture of Spanish explorers and colonists shook hands with the culinary wisdom of the native peoples of these fertile regions. Sinaloa is a state that from the start was renowned for its agricultural and livestock production, but not all of the pork production could be sent to other parts of the country for sale, so the Spanish methods of preservation—cold cuts, sausages, and cured meat—found a ready home there and settled in. This is a dish that evokes grandma, the childhood home, and family life: the intimate surroundings where these tacos have always had their place as snacks.

TYPICAL IN SINALOA

MADE WITH PORK

COOKED IN CERAMIC POTS

A SIMPLE YET TASTY DISH

This food is shredded meat infused with the intense flavor of red *adobo*. Given the nature of the ingredients, it may be a bit greasy, but, even so, once served in tortillas, it makes for a very special combination indeed. It makes no difference if *chilorio* tacos are eaten with corn or flour tortillas, or even in the form of a burrito. In fact, it's all about heating the meat to serve it up on fresh tortillas and gulping it down straightaway. *Chilorio* tacos can be accompanied with Mexican-style salsa (see recipe 1, page 296) or with nothing more than some finely chopped tomato, onion, and green chile. They can also be eaten with sliced onion and tomato, typical condiments that give contrast and freshness to each mouthful, or else some avocado, if preferred. These tacos are good with a red salsa with green chiles or else a salsa with *arbol* chile (see recipe 15, page 301), to provide them with a bit of fiery oomph. In questions of taste there are no hard-and-fast rules, and there is no doubt that *chilorio* goes well with any kind of cheese, it's entirely your choice: panela, asadero, Chihuahua, Oaxaca, or any other string cheese. Each cheese gives the taco a different flavor and style: fresh, melted, in strips, grated—some people even spread on sour cream! Refried or casserole beans—be they black beans, bayo beans, or red beans—are all excellent garnishes to go with these mouthwatering tacos.

BREAK SOME EGGS

The most common variation is likely *chilorio* with scrambled eggs, which is a simple but unique delight. To prepare it, you need only break the eggs into the same pot that the chilorio is heated in, then stir the mixture until the eggs have reached the desired cooking point. Some people add potatoes to *chilorio*, and these can be diced and boiled, or just plain fried. The potatoes are mixed in with the *chilorio* and fried together, creating a great-tasting variation with an exquisite combination of flavors and textures. Frying tortillas filled with *chilorio* is not unusual, either: the tortillas can be rolled or folded up, then deep-fried for as long as desired. If deep-frying isn't your thing, the tortillas can be folded and heated up on the griddle. Done this way, it is the greasy filling that helps to turn the tacos golden brown. Serve each taco with its respective slices of tomato, avocado, onion, sour cream, and salsa to taste. Nowadays, it's possible to find turkey, chicken, and even soy *chilorio*, among other innovations. In the end, these tacos, like the traditional *banda*-style music from Sinaloa known as *chirrines*, are a style that people all over the country (and outside it too) have taken to—and one that sells.

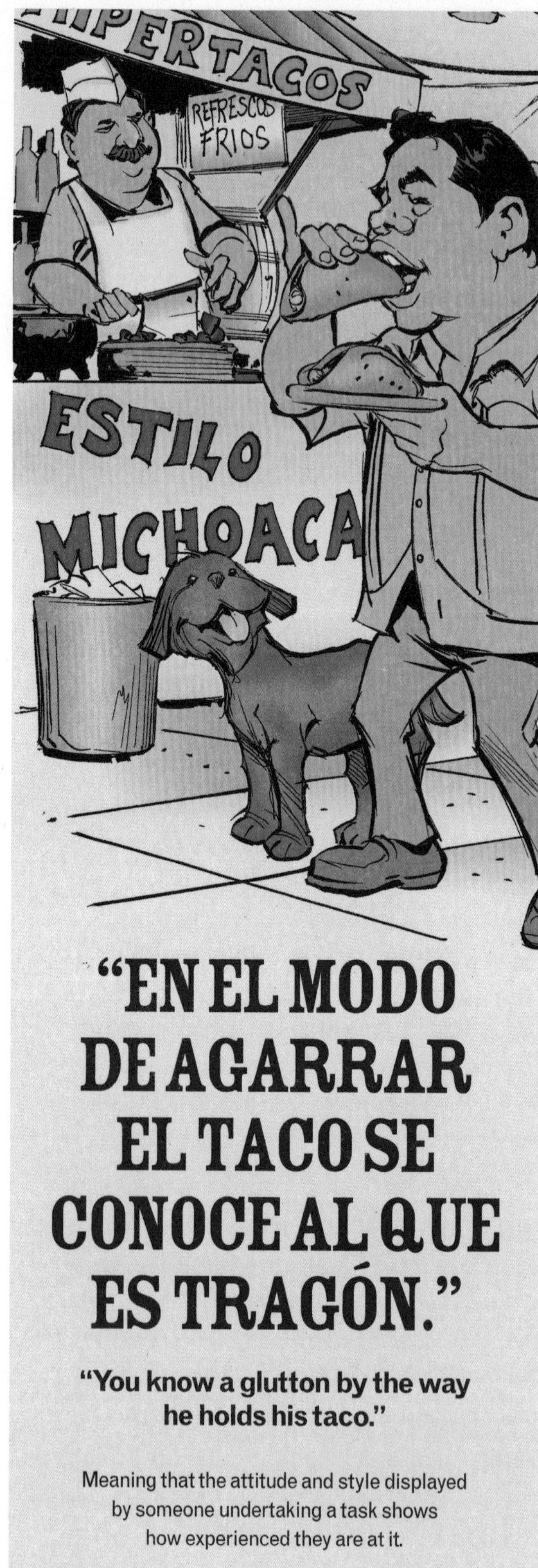

"EN EL MODO DE AGARRAR EL TACO SE CONOCE AL QUE ES TRAGÓN."

"You know a glutton by the way he holds his taco."

Meaning that the attitude and style displayed by someone undertaking a task shows how experienced they are at it.

This place was my father's ranch and we had guests over every weekend.

He served delicious food using my grandma's recipes: creams, soups with eggs, ground *molcajete* salsa, chorizo, *chilorio*, chile cheese, and so on. One day he told his friends that this would be their last free meal. The next Sunday, we had all these tables, and every friend asked for the bill. Everything was improvised, so we set up under the trees and had to move the tables around to keep people in the shade. The business grew through friends of friends of the people we'd invited. What's characteristic about this place is that it brings back the Sinaloa ranch culture of the last century. There's nostalgia everywhere. It's an open-air restaurant and it used to be outside the city, but now it's surrounded by new homes because Culiacán has grown fast. It's become a refuge for iguanas, raccoons, possums, armadillos, squirrels, snakes, and birds. People come here on their own or with big families, mostly on the weekends; during the week, it's mostly business people. People on the arts and cultural scene also really like the place.
The cooking process is slow. We don't use canned food or preprepared seasonings: everything is made by hand and with the simplicity that our regional cuisine is known for. We make *chilorio* like our grandparents taught us, with pork leg and back cuts, making sure to strip off all the fat. The *chilorio* is especially tasty when we've just slaughtered a little piggy in the backyard. As far as gastronomy goes, this is an important moment for Culiacán: the first gastronomy students from the four or five universities offering that degree are going to be graduating soon. I also run the Café Marimba, which is a cultural center. The menu there includes some contemporary takes on the dish like spaghetti in a *chilorio* sauce and *chilorio* burritos with caramelized onion.

"THE CHILORIO IS ESPECIALLY TASTY WHEN WE'VE JUST SLAUGHTERED A LITTLE PIGGY IN THE BACKYARD."

Jorge Pereza Sato
OWNER OF LA CHUPARROSA ENAMORADA KM 3, CULIACANCITO HIGHWAY, PUEBLO BACURIMÍ, NEAR CULIACÁN, SINALOA

MEXICANS EAT
AN AVERAGE OF
22 POUNDS OF
FISH
33 POUNDS OF
BEEF
33 POUNDS OF
PORK
AND
68 POUNDS
OF
CHICKEN
EACH YEAR.

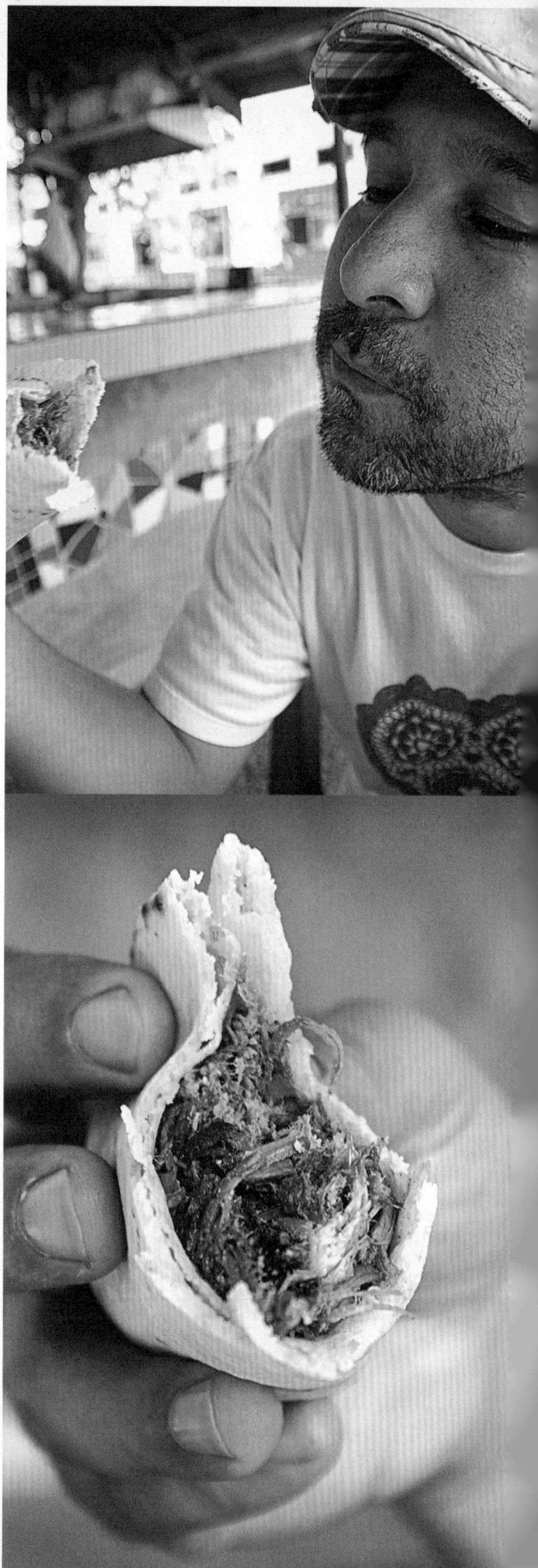

CHILORIO TACOS

Serves 6

—3¼ lb (1.5 kg) pork (leg or loin), coarsely diced
—Sea salt
—2 tablespoons lard or shortening
—3 dried ancho chiles, seeded
—2 dried guajillo chiles, seeded
—5 cloves garlic
—4 sprigs parsley
—1 tablespoon dried oregano
—1 tablespoon apple cider vinegar
—½ tablespoon ground cumin
—Freshly ground black pepper
—12–20 4⅓-Inch (11 cm) corn or flour tortillas

1. Place the meat in a large pot with enough water to cover, add a pinch of salt and bring to a boil. Reduce heat to medium-low and simmer until very soft, about 30–45 minutes.
2. Let the meat cool in the pot, then thinly shred on a cutting board into a bowl. Reserve the broth.
3. Melt the lard in a large skillet over low heat. Fry the shredded meat until it begins to brown.
4. Bring 1 cup of the broth to a boil in a small pot. Add the chiles and boil for 10 minutes. Stir in the garlic, parsley, oregano, vinegar, and cumin.
5. Add the chile mixture to the meat, cover, and cook for 1 hour on low heat, making sure that the meat doesn't stick or burn.
6. If necessary, add more of the reserved brot. The meat should be cooked to the point where it easily comes apart with a fork, and the sauce should be thick. Stir it into the meat to fully incorporate.
7. Serve with tortillas and accompany with the usual garnishes.

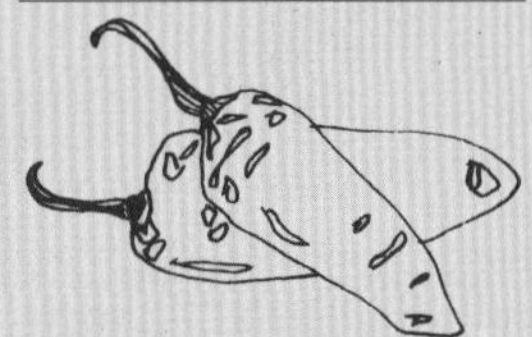

CHILORIO BURRITOS

Serves 6

—2 fresh anaheim or poblano chiles, deveined and cubed
—4 oz (120 g) onion, finely chopped
—3 medium tomatoes, peeled and chopped
—1 lb (450 g) *chilorio* (canned or home-made)
—9 oz (250 g) refried beans (see page 139)
—12 flour tortillas
—Chiles in vinegar and salsa, for serving

1. Fry the ingredients individually in a large skillet: first, the chiles until tender, about 1 minute; then, the onion until translucent, 1 minute; and lastly, the tomato until it changes color, 1 minute.
2. Add the *chilorio* and cook on low heat, covered, until simmering, about 3–5 minutes.
3. Heat the refried beans in a pot or skillet over low heat until warm. Warm the flour tortillas.
4. Make the burritos: thinly spread some beans on the tortilla, scoop on generous amounts of hot *chilorio*, then roll the tortillas into burritos.
5. Place the burritos together under a clean tea towel for 5 minutes to let them continue to sweat.
6. Serve with chiles in vinegar and salsa.

CAFÉ MARIMBA-STYLE CHILORIO TACOS WITH CARAMELIZED ONION

Serves 6

—6 tablespoons (90 g) unsalted butter

—2 medium white or red onions, thinly sliced
—Sugar, optional
—Marjoram, thyme, bay leaf
—1 lb (450 g) Sinaloan pork *chilorio*
—2 tablespoons balsamic vinegar
—12–20 4⅓-inch (11 cm) corn or flour tortillas
—black *molcajete* salsa (see recipe 28, page 307), for serving

1. Melt the butter on low heat in a medium skillet, then add the onions. If the onion tastes too sharp, then add sugar and a sprinkling of water.
2. Wait for the onion to caramelize, stirring occasionally over a very low heat, for 15–20 minutes. Stir in the herbs to taste, as well as the *chilorio* and vinegar.
3. Serve on a large plate and make tacos with the tortillas and black *molcajete* salsa.

THE BEST

Café Marimba

1203 EL DORADO, COL. LAS QUINTAS, CULIACÁN, SINALOA
How about *chilorio* tacos with a beer and a movie showing? This is the place for local art lovers and culture enthusiasts.

Casa Regia

39 ARQUÍMEDES, COL. POLANCO, MEXICO CITY
In this Polanco restaurant, the Northern-style items on the menu include *chilorio* among its appetizers.

Churros El Dorado

1793 CALZADA DE TLALPAN, COL. CHURUBUSCO, MEXICO CITY
Despite the incongruent name referring to the classic dessert, this restaurant offers Sinaloan specialties including *chilorio* tacos prepared *al pastor* with cheese and pineapple.

El Mirador

1 LAS PALMAS, COL. GUADALUPE, CULIACÁN, SINALOA
This is the restaurant in the San Luis Lindavista Hotel, where they offer *chilorio* tacos with onion, green tomato, and chiles, as well as salad or refried beans with cheese to garnish.

El Rincón de Analco

257 ORIENTE 20 DE NOVIEMBRE, CENTRO, DURANGO
This restaurant in the state capital's Gobernador Hotel has *chilorio* tacos on the menu. The building has the curious charm of having been a penitentiary.

La Chuparrosa Enamorada

KM 3 ON THE CULIACÁN-CULIACANCITO HIGHWAY, CULIACÁN, SINALOA
Not only do they prepare the tortillas for their tacos—husking the corn themselves to make the dough—but they also make the *chilorio* filling.

Las Lupitas

PLAZA SANTA CATARINA (CORNER OF FRANCISCO SOSA), COYOACÁN, MEXICO CITY
Established in the heart of Coyoacán, this is one of the few places in the capital where they make *chilorio* tacos, which can also be filled with *machaca*, a dried, spiced meat.

Restaurante Regio

CORNER OF GONZALITOS AND VANCOUVER, COL. VISTA HERMOSA, MONTERREY
Its starters menu is a repertoire of Northern cuisine, where *chilorio* appears with cured meat, tripe, and goat-kid head-meat, as well as grilled marrow.

Santa Bárbara Grill

3070 PONIENTE ANTONIO L. RODRÍGUEZ BLVD, COL. SANTA MARÍA, MONTERREY
Another showcase of regional cuisine (with tripe, *atropellado*, etc.), where the shredded meat prepared with red chile is served in tacos or quesadillas.

Sonora Taco Grill

911 DIVISIÓN DEL NORTE, COL. DEL VALLE, MEXICO CITY
They offer three tacos per order, with flour tortillas and garnishes to choose from the menu (French fries and grilled asparagus, among others).

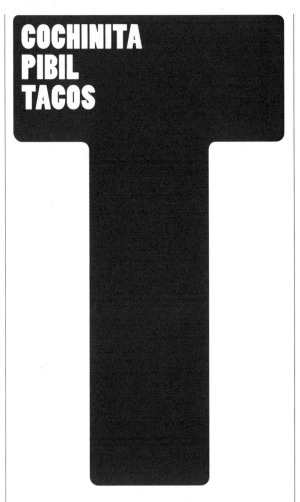

COCHINITA PIBIL TACOS

The nature of this specialty is revealed in the first part of its name, *cochinita*—the little pig demanded by the recipe. The second part, *pibil*, comes from the Mayan language, and means "buried" or "cooked underground." So, it follows that this dish is a young pig cooked in an oven pit, much like *barbacoa*, but with its own traditional seasonings. Eating *cochinita pibil* tacos, besides keeping alive ancestral Mayan customs, is a delight, and the preparation is nearly a ritual in itself, since, as we'll see, it has its own peculiarities, its special touches, a few rules, and a particular order to it.

A DISH FOR THE LIVING... AND THE DEAD

Cochinita pibil is a traditional dish from the Yucatán Peninsula, and brings together a whole series of methods and ingredients that, while illustrating the drama of the Spanish Conquest, also express a new identity and culture. In Yucatán, there is an annual celebration that runs from October 31 to November 3: the *Hanal Pixan*, or Feast of the Souls. These festivities are considered a remnant of an unaltered Mayan tradition for remembering the dead: altars are erected and offerings are left, *the pibes,* local food, along with portraits of the dead. All things *pib*, or *pibil*, are cooked underground in a Yucatecan *barbacoa* oven. Using this method, any meat can be cooked, from the humble corn-on-the-cob, or *pibinales*, to anything that flies, swims, or walks: deer, paca, iguanas, pheasants, and fish—all animals known to have been eaten in pre-Hispanic times. After the Conquest, room was made for chickens (prepared as *pibipollo*, or *mucbipollo*, a casserole-cooked tamale), goats, sheep, and of course, little piggies.

TYPICAL IN YUCATÁN STATE

MADE WITH PORK

COOKED IN A BARBACOA OVEN

SEASONINGS FROM HERE AND ABROAD

Now it's clear that the technique's the *pib* and the food's the *cochinita*, let's take a look at the achiote marinade, the sauce that seasons the dish. To give this recipe its flavor, not only pigs but also many other necessary ingredients came sailing across the ocean: onions, garlic, bitter orange, black pepper, cumin, cinnamon, cloves, anise, oregano, vinegar, and sugar. These are all ground together with the achiote (annatto), a seed that has a very delicate flavor but that also acts as a potent coloring agent to give this dish its distinctive orange color.

AFTER THE **CONQUEST** THE FIRST **INDIGENOUS MEXICANS** TO **TASTE PORK** WERE THOSE LIVING IN WHAT IS NOW **YUCATAN.**

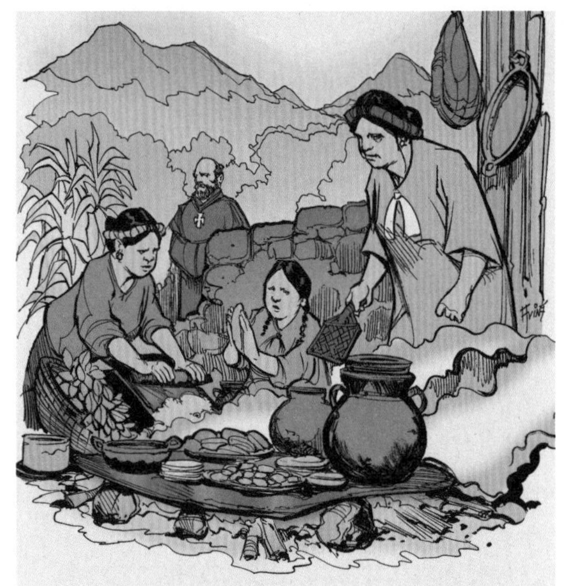

"They make meals of vegetables and venison and fowl, wild and domestic, of which there are many, and fish, of which there are many, and thus have good supplies, especially since they have been raising swine and fowl from Castile [...]; and if there is no flesh, they make their sauces with peppers and vegetables."

De Landa
Yucatán before and after the conquest.

The local ingredients that go in the marinade are the chiles—piquin (for extra hot dishes), guajillo, ancho, and pasilla—and allspice, too. Be it a whole young pig or just a few cuts (the leg being the most common cut, along with some ribs), the preparation is the same: the meat is marinated overnight in the traditional Yucatecan achiote mixture. After that, the meat is wrapped up tightly in a banana-tree leaf, placed in a pot, and cooked with all the care required for the oven-pit method. The combination that results from the cozy contact of banana-tree leaf, meat, and marinade was, of course, one of the most important discoveries in Mexican cuisine, and its fame is well-founded. Though this dish turns out best when cooked in the authentic *barbacoa* oven pit, it's also common to find it cooked in wood-fired stoves in big-city and small-town bakeries around the Yucatán peninsula. These days it can also be done in a conventional oven or even in a pot on the stovetop, though on a more modest scale and sometimes even without the banana-tree leaves. Once the meat comes out of the oven, the ritual of eating may begin. This involves a whole new set of ingredients: red onion marinated in vinegar, as well as an extensive range of habanero chile salsas (a real specialty in Yucatán, which multiplies the options); onion-based salsas (see recipes 4 and 6, pages 296–297); mortar-ground or roasted salsa; an oil emulsion; store-bought or bottled sauces; or simply nibbles from a green habanero chile, the rare pleasure of connoisseurs. All in all, it's quite simple: all that is required is to take a good-sized serving of the prepared meat, place it on a warm tortilla, add some red onion and the preferred choice of salsa, then dig in. These tacos can also be served with a layer of refried black beans, another option to take into consideration.

PIBIL WITHOUT PIG JUST AIN'T COCHINITA

What's the main variation on *cochinita pibil* tacos? As far as tacos go, there is none, since the *cochinita pibil* sandwich doesn't fall within the scope of our study. So, really, these tacos have no variations, and instead it may be more appropriate to speak of chicken *pibil*, rabbit *pibil*, iguana *pibil*, tuna *pibil*, and the rest, since all of these dishes are prepared the same way, but, in the end, none of them is *cochinita pibil*. As for the famous *panuchos* and *salbutes* (see pages 275–6), they aren't really variations on these tacos either. Even though *cochinita pibil* figures as a star ingredient in their recipes, these are *antojitos* in their own right and get their own section further on (see page 275).

ACHIOTE
—OR ANNATTO—
A FRUIT
USED AS A
COLORANT,
IS ALSO
SAID TO HAVE
MEDICINAL
PROPERTIES.

La Tradición began in 1991 as a deli. In 2003, we sold only *panuchos*, *salbutes*, tamales, and *tortas*.

After that we opened a small restaurant, specializing in Yucatecan cuisine. We grew, and we have been at this location since 2006. Our benefactor was Don Armando Manzanero, and he set the standard so that people would know the quality products that we offer. The name La Tradición comes from my being the third generation in my family involved in gastronomy. That's also why—in an effort to preserve Valladolid's haute cuisine— we cook everything over wood and coals, just like it was done eighty years ago, using my grandmother's recipes and my mother's too. We have even made commercials aimed at Europe, and we have been on TV programs. I still get nervous when I have to cook in front of a camera. The camera doesn't like me! Here, the *cochinita* is traditionally made, to keep the regional dishes alive. The key ingredients of our *cochinita* are achiote, bitter orange, and condiments and spices—which are secret, so I'm not going to tell you! *Cochinita pibil* is cooked in the ground. That's where it gets its name. (*Pib* means underground.) It can also be cooked in an oven, but here we cook it in the ground like it should be. We serve it with refried beans, tortilla chips, handmade tortillas, and *xnipec*, which is similar to *pico de gallo* salsa (see recipe 36, page 309). Our secret is in professionalism and dedication in preparing the dishes. It shows the great love we have for food. I wake up at 5 a.m. and head for the central market. Every ingredient we use I select myself. The same goes for the meat. We like to use organic products. At about 9 a.m., we arrive at the restaurant and get ready to open. At 6 p.m., we close the kitchen but I'm usually there until 9 p.m. You could say that it's an eighteen-hour day, but I'm happy and glad to be the one doing it.

"COCHINITA PIBIL IS COOKED IN THE GROUND. THAT'S WHERE IT GETS ITS NAME: 'PIB' MEANS UNDERGROUND."

David Cetina Medina

CHEF AT LA TRADICIÓN RESTAURANT
60TH STREET NORTH, CORNER
OF 25TH, COL. ALCALÁ MARTÍN,
MÉRIDA, YUCATÁN

IN THE

SECOND

WORLD WAR,

THE PILOTS

OF THE MEXICAN

201ST SQUADRON

WROTE ON THE SIDE

OF A MISSILE

"TAKE THIS

TAQUITO

HIROHITO."

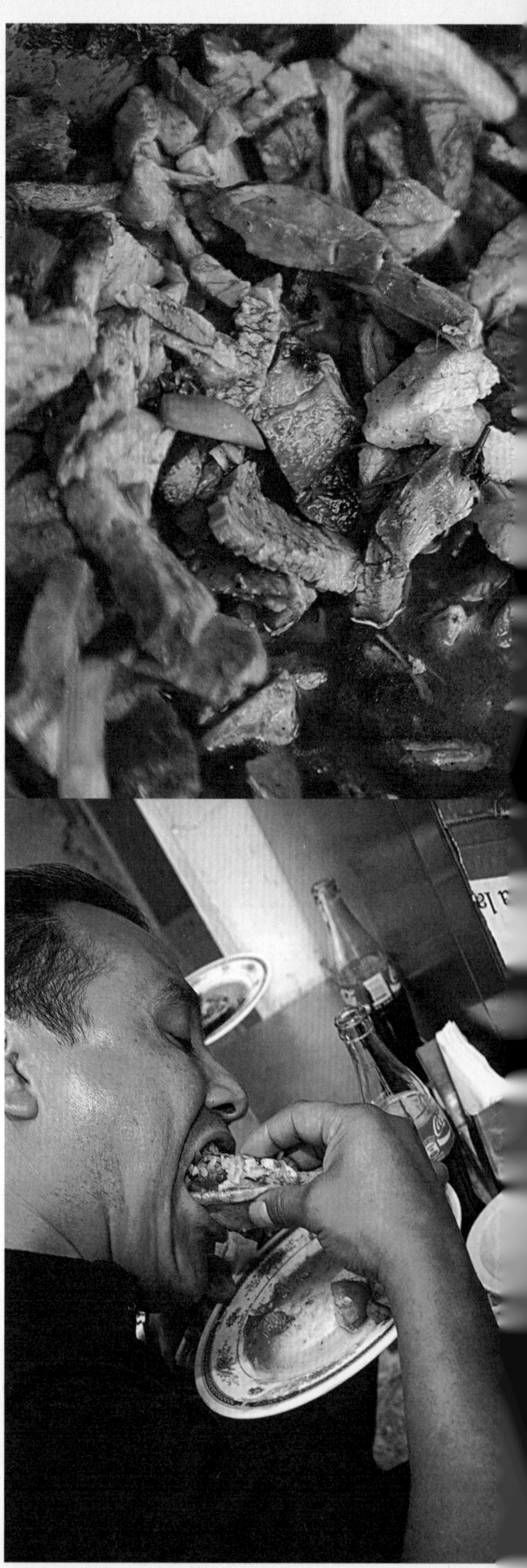

COCHINITA PIBIL TACOS

Serves 6

—2¼ lb (1 kg) pork leg
—1 lb (450 g) pork ribs
—1 cup (250 ml) achiote or red *adobo* (see recipe 33, page 309; commercially sold achiote or *adobo* will do if diluted in 1 cup of orange juice and a good amount of apple cider vinegar)
—2 large banana-tree leaves
—4 oz (120g) lard
—Sea salt
—Pickled onions, refried beans (page 139), and Yucatecan habanero chile salsa (see recipe 5, page 297), for garnish

1. Place the meat in a large pot. Pour the sauce over the meat, cover, and chill overnight or for at least 8 hours, turning the meat occasionally so the *adobo* penetrates the meat.
2. Warm the banana-tree leaves over direct heat to soften them. Set aside.
3. Grease a large pot with 1½ oz (40 g) lard. Preheat your oven to 300°F/150°C/Gas Mark 2.
4. Grease the leaves with 1½ oz (40 g) lard, then line the insides of the pot with them. Leave enough of the leaves sticking out over the edges to cover the meat afterwards.
5. Place the meat on the leaves in the bottom of the pot, then baste with the remaining lard and marinade. Season with salt and wrap the meat with the leaves. Cover the pot and seal the edges with aluminum foil.
6. Cook in the oven for 2½ hours. Add ½ hour for every extra pound (half kilo) of meat, and then cook an additional ½ hour.

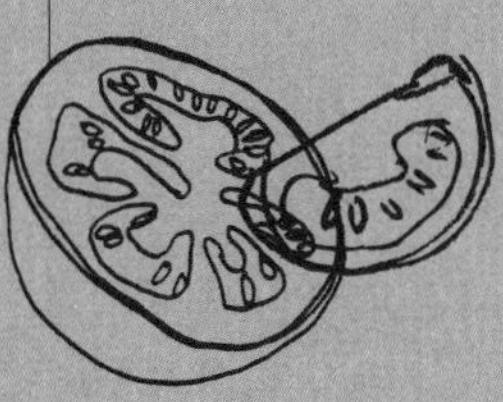

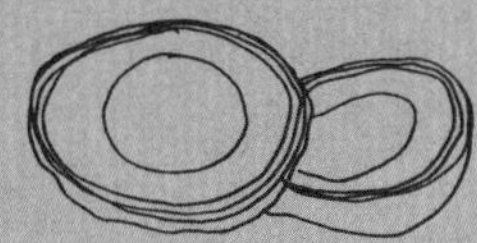

7. Remove from the oven and let cool, covered, for a few minutes. Take out the pieces of meat. Shred the meat and serve garnished with pickled onion, refried beans, and habanero chile salsa, or in individual portions wrapped in the cooked banana leaves.

PICKLED ONIONS

Serves 6

—3 medium white or red onions, sliced into rings or small dice
—1 cup (250 ml) cider vinegar
—1 teaspoon muscovado sugar
—1 teaspoon whole black peppercorns
—2 allspice berries
—1 teaspoon dried oregano
—3 sprigs thyme
—Juice of 1 lime
—Sea salt

1. Bring a large pot of water to a boil. Blanch the onions in the boiling water for just under 1 minute. Strain the onions and transfer to a glass bowl.
2. Immediately add the vinegar, sugar, spices, herbs, lime juice, and a little salt, stirring slowly.
3. Let sit, mixing occasionally. If possible, let marinate overnight.

COCHINITA SALBUTES

Serves 6

For the Salbutes
—1 lb (450 g) corn masa
—3 tablespoons all-purpose flour
—1½ tablespoons lard
—A pinch of sea salt
—Corn oil

For the fillings and condiments
—18 oz (500 g) cochinita pibil (see recipe at left), shredded
—9 oz (250 g) pickled onion
—1 small head of iceberg lettuce, finely chopped
—2 medium tomatoes, thinly sliced
—1 medium ripe avocado, sliced
—Habanero chile salsa (see recipe 4, page 296)

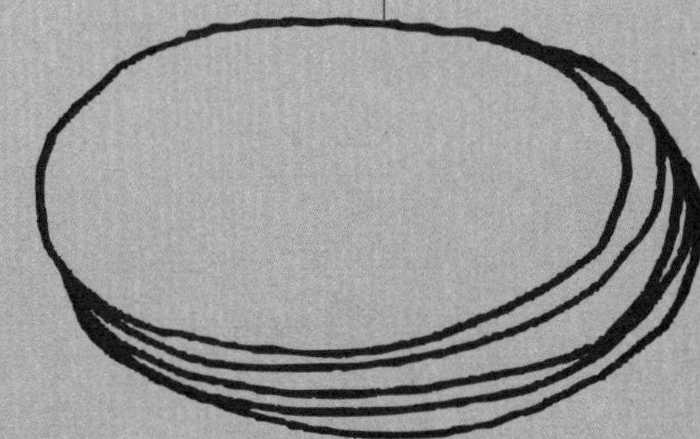

1. Mix the masa, flour, lard, and salt in a large bowl, and knead until you have a smooth dough.
2. Make the dough into small, thick tortillas (about 2–3 inches (5–8 cm) in diameter).
3. Heat plenty of oil in a deep skillet. When hot, fry the tortillas until they just begin to brown, about 1 minute. Remove the tortillas from the oil and allow to drain on a paper towel-lined plate.
4. Place three hot tortillas on a plate and place a generous serving of *cochinita* over them, adding pickled onions, lettuce, tomato, avocado, and salsa to taste.

THE BEST

COCHINITA PIBIL TACOS

Bar Montejo
261 BENJAMÍN FRANKLIN, COL. CONDESA, MEXICO CITY
This is an odd combination of Yucatecan restaurant and cantina, where they offer *cochinita pibil* tacos and *panuchos*, as well as a proper main course.

Cochinita Country
1503 ÁNGEL URRAZA, COL. LETRÁN VALLE, MEXICO CITY
An unlikely name for this Yucatecan restaurant that set up in the capital and is still running three decades later, which says something about the quality of the food.

Coox Hanal
83 ISABEL LA CATÓLICA, CENTRO HISTÓRICO, MEXICO CITY
Some consider this the best place for Yucatecan eats— a place so traditional that its Mayan name is impossible for Mexico City natives to pronounce.

El Turix
212 EMILIO CASTELAR, COL. POLANCO, MEXICO CITY
It started out as a tin-shack street stand and went on to become *the* reference point for people in the city who have a hankering for proper *cochinita* tacos.

Fonda 99.99
347 MORAS, COL. DEL VALLE, MEXICO CITY
You'll have to take all necessary precautions to get yourself a spot in this restaurant in Colonia Del Valle if you want to sink your teeth into their *panuchos*, *papadzules*, and *cochinita*.

Hacienda Teya
KM 12.5 MÉRIDA–CANCÚN HIGHWAY, MÉRIDA, YUCATÁN
Part of the prestige of this hotel on the outskirts of Mérida resides in the regional delights that can be eaten there, including, naturally, its *cochinita*.

Hostería del Marqués
203 39TH STREET, VALLADOLID, YUCATÁN
A restaurant at El Mesón del Marqués Hotel, where the food is always exquisite and served in an attractive colonial courtyard.

Los Almendros
451 PASEO MONTEJO (CORNER OF COLÓN), MÉRIDA, YUCATÁN
Yucatecans themselves vouch for the quality of the local dishes in this restaurant located in the Fiesta Americana Hotel Mérida, in the heart of the city.

Mi Taco Yucateco
CORNER OF AYUNTAMIENTO AND DOLORES, CENTRO HISTÓRICO, MEXICO CITY
Modest in appearance, this is a marvelous stand next to San Juan Market, attracting multitudes in search of its *cochinita*, served both in tacos and *tortas*.

Tacos Casablanca
CORNER OF 16 PONIENTE AND 3 NORTE (FACING THE MUNICIPAL DIF OFFICE), TUXTLA GUTIÉRREZ, CHIAPAS
They prepare a local take on *cochinita* (though the people from Chiapas take issue with the comparison), using ancho chile marinade instead of achiote paste.

BIEN
FRIA

STEWED TACOS

The outstanding characteristic of this kind of taco is perhaps its variety, for here we find the whole range of culinary classics in the Mexican repertoire. These dishes are usually served up in ceramic casserole pots, creating an impression of abundance—a landscape that is a feast for the diner's eyes and surely a case of love at first sight. Another reason it's so attractive is its swift preparation: you simply make your choice, and in seconds you're enjoying a deluxe taco. In this regard, stewed tacos are the closest we come to fast food in Mexican cooking.

VARIETY IS THE SPICE OF LIFE

This ancient style of taco is as old as the tortilla itself, since nothing could be more natural than scooping out the contents of a pot to make a taco. It's easy to imagine an Aztec prince taking on a taco the same way that a conquistador might have done. And today you find people from all social classes peering into the casserole pots with the same hungry look. These tacos are a universal favorite and yet, in their infinite variety, leave a wide margin for personal expression. A prestigious establishment may offer up to thirty different preparations to choose from, though more modest operations will offer only three or four.

ALL THAT FLIES, WALKS, AND SWIMS... AND WHATEVER GROWS TOO!

All the *moles*, *pipianes*, and *entomatados* (see page 242) that are found here liven up a diverse array of food: beef, pork, chicken, sausages, eggs, cheeses, seafood, vegetables, seasonal ingredients, and exotic ingredients from around the world, too. Traditionally, the meat should first be "purged," removing any bones or spines before serving, so that the taco can become a carefree morsel. To eat these tacos, you don't need to watch out for anything. Behind this apparent ease though, their preparation demands a profound understanding of Mexico's culinary heritage; for, if these tacos are to have any success at all, they'll first need the approval of a knowing public that has grown up with these flavors. Preparation couldn't be any easier: ladle up a generous spoonful from the casserole pot of your choice, drop the filling on the tortilla, and... *bon appétit!* It should be mentioned that these tacos are usually served on a pair of tortillas or, in slang, *con copia*, so that the food goes further, or maybe so that the soupy contents don't soak through a single tortilla

TYPICAL THROUGHOUT MEXICO

MADE WITH BEEF, PORK, CHICKEN, EGGS, CHEESE, POTATOES, PEPPERS

FINISHES COOKING IN A BASKET

and cause it to disintegrate. There's invariably some rice and beans near the casserole pots as well, since many people see these as essential complements. Traditionally the rice is red, Mexican-style rice, with tomato, carrot, peas, onion, garlic, cilantro, and green chiles. The beans can be of any kind or color, refried or from the pot; in many places the broth is served as a soup, in little ceramic jars or mugs. Lastly, there are the indispensable salsas: the red and green standards should be there, as well as an onion salsa with manzano chile, or a habanero salsa with lots of lime juice, though every establishment has its own specialty (see recipes 2, 4, and 12, among others, pages 296–300).

AS MANY VARIETIES AS STATES

There are as many variations on this kind of taco as there are regional dishes in Mexico. Here are a few that stand out, each with its particular name.

ARMORED TACOS

Originally from the state of Morelos, *tacos acorazados* are known for their gross excess. They start off with rice and beans, then half a hard-boiled egg, then the main filling. The filling is typically a *milanesa* (breaded fillet) or a stuffed chile, though pork rinds in salsa, shredded chicken with *mole poblano*, and *tortitas de colorín* are other alternatives. They are usually accompanied with squash seeds and marinated chiles. A double tortilla is a must.

HOME-MADE TACOS

In Mexico, "sneaking" a tortilla from the kitchen to make a taco is a traditional custom that requires no particular ingredients nor certain time of day. It can be slapped together for breakfast or for supper or even between meals, but it's always on the go. It consists of throwing a couple tortillas on the griddle and scavenging around for some filling. Obviously, there are the classics, like the thousand varieties of scrambled-egg tacos: alone or with cheese, beans (refried or from the pot), fresh pork rinds, chorizo, bone marrow. Each house has its customs, and that's probably the big plus with homemade tacos: they have leeway for improvisation for they can be thrown together with the leftovers of any meal and, in just a few minutes, they're ready to eat. Also, we should take a serious look at "real" homemade tacos, that is, when tacos are the meal of the day. The most common are surely *flautas* or deep-fried tacos, which are important enough to get a chapter of their own (see page 227); but there are also enchiladas, usually made at home with a range of possibilities (see the chapter *Enchiladas*). And then there's always grandma's traditional recipe, the birthday specialty, and that rare dish only dad knows how to make. These might be dishes that harken back to the family's roots, perhaps from another state or city, though sometimes they're ingenious inventions or the free interpretation of novel dishes from some cantina, taco stand, or restaurant.

Laura Ochoa @lausaysmeow
6 sep
Situación sentimental: Instagrameando unos tacos de chile relleno.
Abrir Responder Retwittear Favorito
translated
Relationship status: posting a pic of my stuffed chili tacos on Instagram.

CONSTRUCTION WORKERS' TACOS

At construction sites all over the country, workers can be seen gathering in small groups at lunchtime to eat tacos. This is a very particular way of eating, characterized by a profusion of chiles, since the key to this way of eating tacos lies in almost everything being seriously hot. The idea is that everyone contributes something: each brings a different filling in a container, and they all chip in for the tortillas. As a result, what would be a dull lunch, with each person eating a single filling, spreads out into a buffet of options with as many choices as there are people eating together. The preparation involves, without the need to ask permission, making tacos from each of the fillings, as well as a mix of them all—always a tasty option. So, what is the

"BUENA PARA EL PETATE, PERO MALA PARA EL METATE."

"Good for the mat, but she'll never get you fat."

Meaning that a woman is good in bed but doesn't know how to cook. (In rural communities, instead of sleeping on a mattress, some people use a *petate,* a woven palm mat).

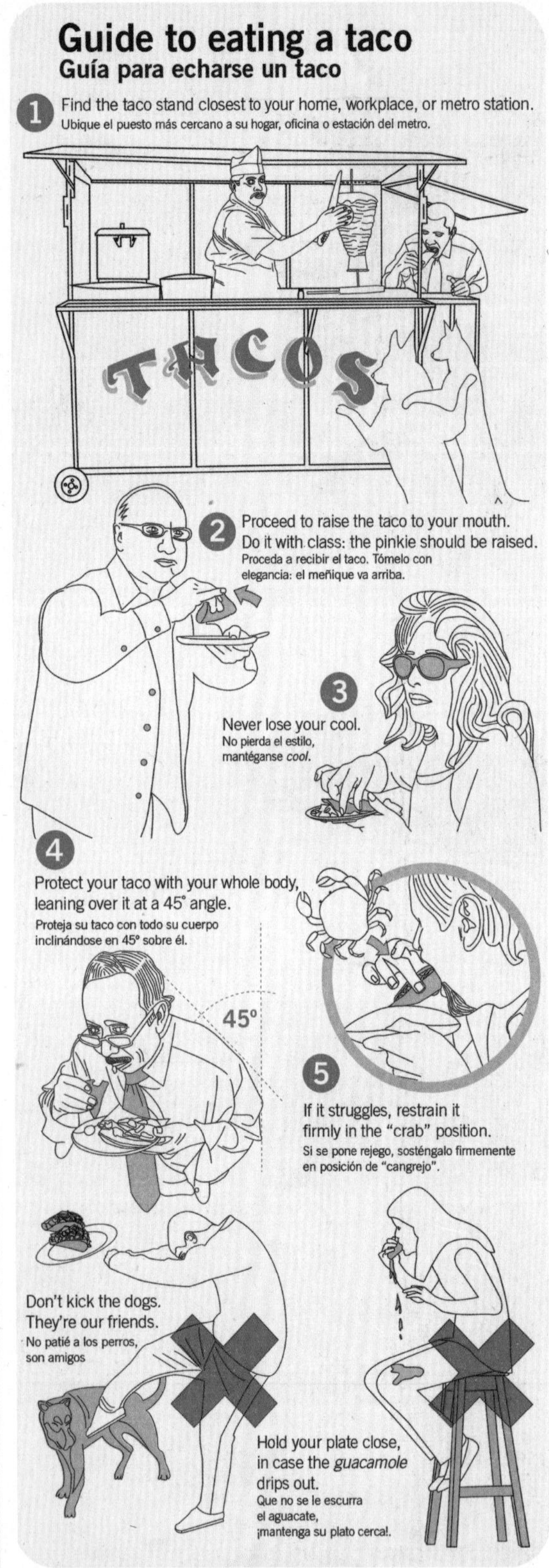

Guide to eating a taco
Guía para echarse un taco
1
Find the taco stand closest to your home, workplace, or metro station.
Ubique el puesto más cercano a su hogar, oficina o estación del metro.
TACOS
2
Proceed to raise the taco to your mouth.
Do it with class: the pinkie should be raised.
Proceda a recibir el taco. Tómelo con elegancia: el meñique va arriba.
3
Never lose your cool.
No pierda el estilo, mantéganse cool.
4
Protect your taco with your whole body, leaning over it at a 45° angle.
Proteja su taco con todo su cuerpo inclinándose en 45° sobre él.
45°
5
If it struggles, restrain it firmly in the "crab" position.
Si se pone rejego, sosténgalo firmemente en posición de "cangrejo".
Don't kick the dogs.
They're our friends.
No patié a los perros, son amigos
Hold your plate close, in case the guacamole drips out.
Que no se le escurra el aguacate, ¡mantenga su plato cercal.

difference between these tacos and others in this chapter? The difference lies in the location, the flavor, the company—the shared feast. As mentioned earlier, the term "construction workers' tacos" used to refer to basket tacos (see page 133), because of the vendors' routine of selling their fare at the gates of worksites. Nowadays, though, these tacos are known for their spicy, shared repast that makes room for any ingredient a workmate happens to bring along: steak, pork rinds, *longaniza*, sausage, chicken, *nopales*, potatoes, eggs; ingredients that may be spiced up with sliced poblanos, pasilla or morita chiles, and some red or green salsa. There should also be rice, beans, and a few things from the corner store or supermarket: a can of chiles, pork rinds, avocado, ham, headcheese, a can of sardines… all ingredients that make for an emergency menu when unexpected occasions come up.

LAGUNERO TACOS

These modest tacos from Coahuila suggest that there is such a thing as culinary evolution, with each region using the ingredients with full creative license. These tacos are, quite simply, tortillas with slices of poblano chiles previously stewed with tomato. Just before being served, they are put in the oven to melt the generous cheese topping. Their quality depends entirely on the freshness of the ingredients used.

EGG AND DRIED-BEEF TACOS

For rich and poor alike, the classic breakfast dish in Nuevo León is *machacado con huevo. Machacado* (so called in Nuevo León, Tamaulipas, and Coahuila) or *machaca* (as it is known in Chihuahua, Sonora, Baja California, and Sinaloa) is simply shredded dried beef, but it's a product that is exceptionally well-made, and can be used in soups and snacks. An important point to remember when making these tacos is to rehydrate the meat, letting the flavor seep into the dish until everything's perfectly integrated. The dried beef is cooked with tomato, chiles, onion, and scrambled eggs;

the tortillas can be made of flour or maize.

BURRITOS

Legend has it that the curious name "burrito" comes from a man who would go on a little donkey—*burro*—to a certain street corner every day to sell his big flour tortilla tacos. That flour tortilla is what defines this well-known version of the taco, which is a favorite in the north of Mexico and the south of the United States, and it is named after that little donkey. Since burritos are completely closed, they can be kept awhile, then reheated, so a big batch can be whipped up to be eaten later on. Flour tortillas can be filled with a long list of ingredients, but three tidbits top the list: grilled meat, beans, and cheese. Once the ingredients for the filling are placed on the tortilla, it's folded once lengthwise, the ends are closed up, and finally the whole thing is rolled up to make a sealed package. From these simple beginnings, we plunge into a world of possibilities: whole beans in their broth or refried, added in or as a side dish for the principal ingredient, which can run the full gamut from grilled beef and picadillo, to shredded beef (in different *adobos*, *moles*, and salsas), to pork, chicken, cold cuts (ham or sausages), bacon, seafood, or eggs prepared in a whole range of different ways. As for the cheese, it can be Chihuahua cheese or any other melting cheese, such as manchego, Monterrey Jack, cheddar, or gouda. Sour cream and mayonnaise can also be added, along with rice, or different chile salsas, particularly green or chipotle salsa. Finally, we cannot forget the fresh guacamole or avocado, as well as tomato, onion, and even lettuce. Sizes vary too: though homemade burritos are usually small, modest affairs, at the other extreme there are burritos that have been known to measure over three feet and weigh more than six-and-a-half pounds. And lastly, from what starts out as a handmade, artisanal snack prepared with choice ingredients, at the opposite end of the scale we come to the prepackaged burritos found in convenience-store coolers all over the world, ready to be heated up in the microwave.

> "Under an inclement sun, his eyes inflamed and his heart spent from the coke comedown, the journey was an unending ordeal that almost caused him to abandon the plan. Arriving at the junction of Río Churubusco and Eje 3, near the Palacio de los Deportes, he stopped at a stand to eat some tacos with *longaniza* accompanied with a large Lulú soda. Revived by the blast of calories, he continued his expedition without paying attention to the traffic, trying to figure out Lima's motivations."
>
> **ENRIQUE SERNA.**
> *El Miedo a los Animales.*
> Mexico: Joaquín Mortiz, 1995.

FROM THE OVEN

There are a number of preparations of meat fillings that come out of the oven and go into "stewed tacos" too and should consequently be considered variations: roast ham, chicken, and turkey, among others. One of the few places traditional turkey tacos are found is on Motolinia street in downtown Mexico City. The preparation is simple: strips of this tender meat are placed in a hot tortilla spread with guacamole. What's more, many recipes for chicken can be adapted to this exceptionally flavorsome meat: turkey *tinga*, turkey *mole*, shredded turkey, and, of course, roast turkey. Likewise, roast ham slices, a classic ingredient in sandwiches, have naturally migrated to tacos, laid on a simple guacamole spread. Some establishments also sell roast chicken, a delicious morsel in a fresh tortilla, with some rice inside and a touch of fresh salsa.

COOKED

CHICKEN

CONTAINS

UP TO

35%

PROTEIN;

BEEF

UP TO

27%

AND

PORK

24%.

We have more than twenty types of stewed tacos.

There are stuffed chiles, poblano chiles, ancho chile, manzano chile, cauliflower, shrimp, chard. In fact, fifty percent of what we offer is vegetarian, and the other fifty is for the meat-lovers. These tacos are a hundred percent homemade. You go to your kitchen in the morning, see what you have, and prepare what you come up with. The secret is in the seasoning and making healthy tacos. We also offer organic and low-fat products.
All sorts come to our restaurant: from the people that make this city beautiful—those sweeping and cleaning the streets in the early morning—to business owners, people who change laws, and others, even artists and designers. The business was launched in '68. It's a tradition we inherited from our parents. In the beginning, they forced it on us, but, after a while, I saw its good side. During the warm season, we sell *salpicón*, and salad is in high demand. During the cold months, people tend to order pressed pork rinds, beef steak, or

"CUSTOMERS FORMING A LINE A HUNDRED FEET LONG JUST TO HAVE ONE OF OUR TACOS—THAT'S QUITE SOMETHING!"

something grilled. What makes us special is the quality of the service and products, and our effort with the flavors. Another ingredient that this restaurant adds to the mix is the use of local products, buying things directly from farms—organic products—and this gives a little something extra to the flavor of our food. Also, there has been a change to improve the recipes. For example, years ago pressed pork rinds didn't sell; now they sell like hot cakes. These days we put olive oil and avocado on *nopales*. Something that I'll never forget is the hundreds of people that came when we reopened. Police had to block off the street in front, with squad cars and tow trucks to get the traffic moving again. Customers forming a line a hundred feet long just to have one of our tacos, that's quite something!

Gustavo Millán
OWNER OF TACOS EL GRAND GUS
56 OMETUSCO, COL. CONDESA,
MEXICO CITY

AMERICAN
JOEY CHESTNUT
WON
$5,000
FOR EATING
53 TACOS
IN
10 MINUTES
AT AN
EATING CONTEST
IN PUERTO RICO.

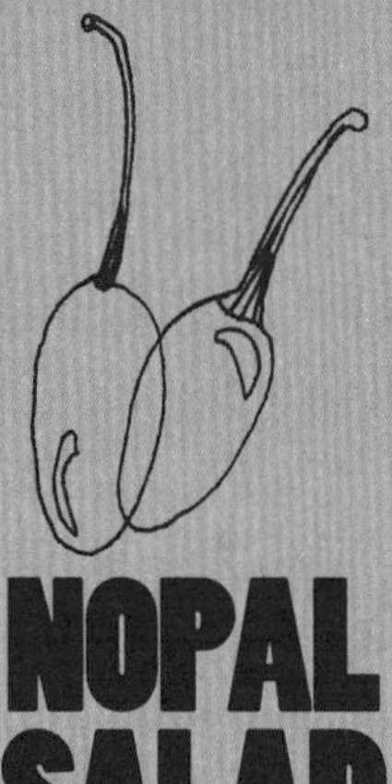

NOPAL SALAD

Serves 12

—10 tender *nopales,* spines removed, cut into diamonds
—1 medium onion, thinly sliced
—2 cloves garlic
—Sea salt
—Apple cider vinegar
—Pinch of baking soda
—5 oz (150 g) broad beans, shelled
—2 green serrano chiles, thinly sliced
—1 medium tomato, thinly sliced
—4 sprigs cilantro, chopped
—Pinch of dried oregano
—Olive oil
—3½ oz (100 g) white cheese, like Cotija or Sierra, optional
—12–20 4⅓-inch (11 cm) corn tortillas
—Sliced avocado, arbol chile red salsa, and chiles in vinegar, (recipes 9 and 31, pages 300 and 308), for serving

1. Bring a large pot of water to boil. Add the *nopales,* along with a half of the onion, 1 garlic clove, salt, a splash of vinegar, and a pinch of baking soda, for 10 minutes. Strain and rinse the *nopales* well under cold water. (To remove the *nopal* "slime," some suggest using a strainer made from a natural fiber like palm, cane, or bamboo.) Set aside the onion and garlic to cool.
2. Bring a separate pot of salted water to a boil. Add the broad beans and boil for 10–15 minutes until tender. Strain and rinse the beans well under cold water. Let cool, then peel. If the beans are large, split them in half. Set aside.
3. Toss the *nopales* with the broad beans, chiles, half of the tomato, half of the remaining onion, and cilantro. Dress with the oregano, salt, olive oil, and a few drops of vinegar.
4. Garnish with the remaining tomato, cilantro, remaining onion, and, if desired, the cheese on top, diced.
5. Serve a heaping spoonful of salad on a fresh corn tortilla accompanied by sliced avocado, chiles in vinegar, and arbol chile red salsa.

MEXICAN-STYLE BEEF TIPS

Serves 6

—2¼ lb (1 kg) tenderloin or rib eye, sliced into small strips
—3 cloves garlic, crushed
—½ tablespoon freshly ground black pepper
—½ tablespoon ground cumin
—Sea salt
—1 tablespoon corn oil
—9 oz (250 g) diced onion
—2¼ lb (1 kg) medium tomatoes, peeled and diced
—6 serrano chiles, sliced into rings
—12–20 4⅓-inch (11 cm) corn tortillas
—Sliced avocado, rice and beans, for serving

1. Mix the meat with the garlic, ground pepper, cumin, and a pinch of salt. Cover and chill marinate for 3 hours.
2. Heat the oil in a large pot over low heat. Add the onion and fry for a few minutes, until translucent.
3. Raise the heat, add the meat and marinade, and sauté for 7 minutes.
4. Add the tomato and chiles, and season to taste. Simmer until the liquid thickens.
5. Serve in heaping spoonfuls on doubled fresh tortillas, with rice, beans, or avocado.

PORK RINDS IN SALSA

Serves 4

—3 cups (750 ml) red, green, mixed, or ancho chile salsa (see recipes 11–13, 17, pages 300–302)
—11 oz (300 g) crunchy pork rinds, cut into medium-size chunks
—Sea salt
—12–20 4⅓-inch (11 cm) corn tortillas, rice, or beans, for serving

1. Simmer the salsa in a large pot set over low heat, adding a little water to thin out the sauce.
2. When the salsa begins to boil, stir in the rinds and continue stirring gently.
3. Let simmer for 3 minutes to thicken the salsa and season to taste with salt.
4. Serve generously on doubled tortillas so that the taco doesn't fall apart. Accompany with rice or beans, as desired.

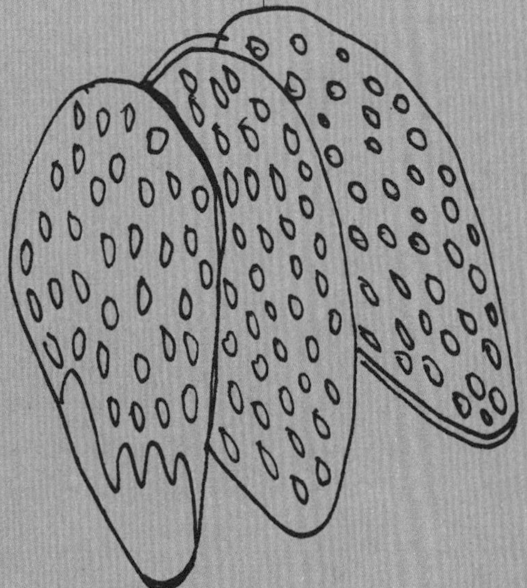

PUEBLA-STYLE TINGA

Serves 8

—9 oz (250 g) pork leg cut into chunks*
—9 oz (250 g) pork brisket cut into chunks
—2 cloves garlic, one left whole and one minced
—3 bay leaves
—Sea salt
—2 tablespoons corn oil
—1 lb (450 g) pork chorizo sausage, casing removed and cut into coarse cubes
—1 medium onion, thinly sliced
—1 lb 9 oz (750 g) tomatoes, peeled and finely chopped
—½ tablespoon dried thyme
—½ tablespoon dried marjoram
—½ tablespoon dried oregano
—3 chipotle chiles in vinegar, seeded and sliced, plus ½ cup (120 ml) of the surrounding liquid
—½ tablespoon freshly ground black pepper
—12–20 4⅓-inch (11 cm) corn tortillas, rice, or beans, for serving

*Chicken *tinga* can also be made using 2¼ lb (1 kg) of chicken breast in place of the pork leg, brisket, and chorizo.

1. Put the pork leg and brisket in a large pot and cover it with cold water.

2. Add the whole garlic clove, 1 bay leaf, and salt. Bring to a boil, reduce the heat to medium, and simmer 1 hour, or until the meat is tender.
3. Let the meat cool in the pot, then shred in thin strips on a cutting board. Set the broth aside.
4. Heat the oil in a separate pot. Fry the sausage about 4-6 minutes until browned and cooked through. Transfer to a cutting board, peel the sausage, and dice.
5. Add the onion and minced garlic, and fry until golden brown.
6. Add the tomatoes, remaining bay leaves, thyme, marjoram, oregano, chipotle liquid, and some of the remaining broth to cover and boil 5 minutes.
7. Carefully stir the shredded meat into the mixture. If the sauce thickens too much, thin it with more broth.
8. Serve the meat and vegetables on a large plate; discard the bay leaves. Garnish with the sliced chipotles and season with salt and pepper.
9. Spoon a generous serving on a fresh tortilla and accompany with rice or beans, as desired.

BONE MARROW TACOS

Serves 4

—Sea salt
—1 lb (450 g) beef bones with marrow
—½ medium onion
—1 clove garlic
—3 bay leaves
—3 whole black peppercorns

—Sliced onion, fresh cilantro leaves, and green salsa (see recipe 3, page 296), for serving

1. Bring a large pot of salted water to a boil. Add the bones, onion, garlic, bay leaves, and peppercorns, and boil for 45 minutes.
2. Remove the bones and spoon out the marrow.
3. Serve a spoonful of marrow on a tortilla, spread, and add sliced onion, cilantro, and green salsa, as desired.

MORELOS-STYLE ARMORED TACOS

Serves 6
—12 4⅓-inch (11 cm) fresh corn tortillas
—9 oz (250 g) refried beans (see page 139)
—9 oz (250 g) Mexican-style rice
—6 hard-boiled eggs, peeled and halved lenthwise

—1 cup each of cooked *nopales*, pork rinds, *tinga*, or other stewed dish
—1 cup (250 ml) sliced chiles in vinegar (see recipe 31, page 308)
—9 oz (250 g) squash seeds, shelled and salted
—Sea salt

Using double tortillas, make the tacos by spreading a layer of refried beans, 2 tablespoons of rice, half of a hard-boiled egg, 1 tablespoon of your filling of choice, chile slices, squash seeds, and salt to taste. (Place the remaining squash seeds and chile slices on the table for your guests to help themselves.)

CONSTRUCTION WORKER-STYLE EGG TACOS

Serves 2

—4 large eggs
—Sea salt
—2 tablespoons corn oil
—1 cup (250 ml) ranchera salsa (see recipe 14, page 301)
—8 4⅓-inch (11 cm) corn tortillas

1. Beat the eggs with a pinch of salt in a small bowl.
2. Heat the oil in a skillet. Add the eggs and fry, stirring vigorously over a medium heat until cooked, about 3–5 minutes.
3. Add the salsa to the skillet and cook for a couple minutes until it thickens.
4. Serve the eggs and salsa in the corn tortillas.

LAGUNERO TACOS

Serves 6

—4 poblano chiles
—1 cup (250 ml) plus 2 tablespoons corn oil
—½ medium onion, thinly sliced
—1 clove garlic, finely chopped
—2 medium tomatoes, peeled
—Sea salt and freshly ground black pepper
—6-12 4⅓-inch (11 cm) corn tortillas
—7 oz (200 g) Chihuahua cheese, grated
—Sliced tomato, avocado, refried beans, and salsa (see recipes 1, 2, 11, or 15, pages 296–301), for serving

1. Grill the poblanos or roast them over an open flame until they are charred on all sides. Seal the chiles inside a plastic bag 10 minutes to make them easier to peel. Peel, seed, and devein the chiles, then slice.

2. Heat 2 tablespoons oil over low heat in a large pot. Add the onion and fry until translucent. Add the garlic and cook with onion for 12 minutes.
3. Puree the tomatoes in a blender until smooth. Add to the pot, and cook with the garlic and onion for 5 minutes.
4. Season the sauce with salt and pepper. Let simmer for 5 minutes or until the sauce is thick.
5. Add the sliced chiles, and cook on low heat for 3–5 minutes.
6. Heat the remaining oil in a large skillet or comal. Heat the tortillas, one by one, in the hot oil, very quickly, without browning them.
7. Preheat your oven to 350°F/180°C/Gas Mark 4.
8. Make the tacos, by rolling the chile sauce tightly inside the tortillas. Place the tacos on a heat-resistant glass dish, and cover with the cheese.
9. Bake tacos for 15 minutes. Accompany with tomato, avocado, beans, and salsa.

BEAN-FILLED PORK BURRITOS

Serves 4

—2 tablespoons corn oil
—9 oz (250 g) ground pork
—1 cup (250 ml) ancho *adobo* (see recipe 34, page 309)
—9 oz (250 g) cooked black beans
—Sea salt
—6–12 4⅓-inch (11 cm) flour tortillas
—7 oz (200 g) Chihuahua cheese, grated
—½ medium onion, sliced
—Chopped lettuce, sliced tomato, sliced onion, shredded cabbage, and Mexican salsa (see recipe 1, page 296), for serving

1. Heat the oil in a large pot over medium-high heat. Add the meat and brown, stirring constantly to break apart, 3–5 minutes.
2. Add the *adobo* and let simmer for 1 minute, stirring constantly. Add the black beans and ½ cup of water. Season to taste with salt and let simmer until thick, about 3–5 minutes.
3. To make tacos, place the filling inside tortillas; top with the grated cheese and onion.
4. Serve with the lettuce, tomato, onion, cabbage, and salsa, if desired.

THE BEST

STEWED TACOS

Carnicería Atlixco
CORNER OF ATLIXCO AND JUAN ESCUTIA, COL. CONDESA, MEXICO CITY
You can get sirloin by the kilo here or hearty tacos from a variety of dishes displayed in ceramic casserole dishes.

El Acorazado
7 JARDÍN JUÁREZ, CENTRO, CUERNAVACA, MORELOS
The best armored tacos are here, where they serve a local variety with potatoes and marinated pepper slices instead of salsas so your tortilla doesn't get soaked.

La Burrería
171 ORIZABA, COL. ROMA, MEXICO CITY
A self-proclaimed "northern-style cantina," its menu boasts burritos both from "land" (meat) and "sea" (shrimp), as well as vegetarian burritos, all wrapped in large flour tortillas.

Le Lah Tho
456 PATRIOTISMO, COL. SAN PEDRO DE LOS PINOS, MEXICO CITY
Among the Yucatecan delights served here, special kudos goes to the *papadzules* on corn tortilla filled with hard-boiled eggs in cucumber and tomato sauce.

Los Güeros
303 RODRÍGUEZ SARO, COL. DEL VALLE, MEXICO CITY
Locals from the neighborhood and people from outside come here for the *moronga*, beef tips, pork and purslane, among many other kinds of tacos.

Tacos Beatriz
34 TUXPAN, COL. ROMA, MEXICO CITY
This place opened the year the Mexican Revolution started. Though they now specialize in catering, they still have a place to come in and savor their tacos.

Tacos Chava
1640 A FRAY SERVANDO PADRE MIER, COL. OBISPADO, MONTERREY
The biggest demand here is for tacos with marinated slices of peppers, which come with cheese, picadillo, shredded meat, and beans, all served on flour tortillas an impressive 10 inches across.

Tacos El Güero
146 RÍO ORINOCO, COL. CENTRITO VALLE, SAN PEDRO GARZA GARCÍA, NUEVO LEÓN
Their *papadillo* tacos (potato mixed with picadillo) are strongly recommended, served on either wheat or corn tortillas.

Tacos Hola
135 AMSTERDAM (CORNER OF MICHOACÁN), COL. CONDESA, MEXICO CITY
Feeding those visiting and working in the Condesa for four decades now, they offer some twenty-odd succulent choices, including an outstanding liver and onion option.

Tacos La Bici
147 CIRCUITO CIRCUNVALACIÓN ORIENTE, CIUDAD SATÉLITE, TATE OF MEXICO
The story goes that this started out on a humble bicycle, hence the name. This place, with over twenty dishes to choose from, is the pride of people from the suburb of Satélite.

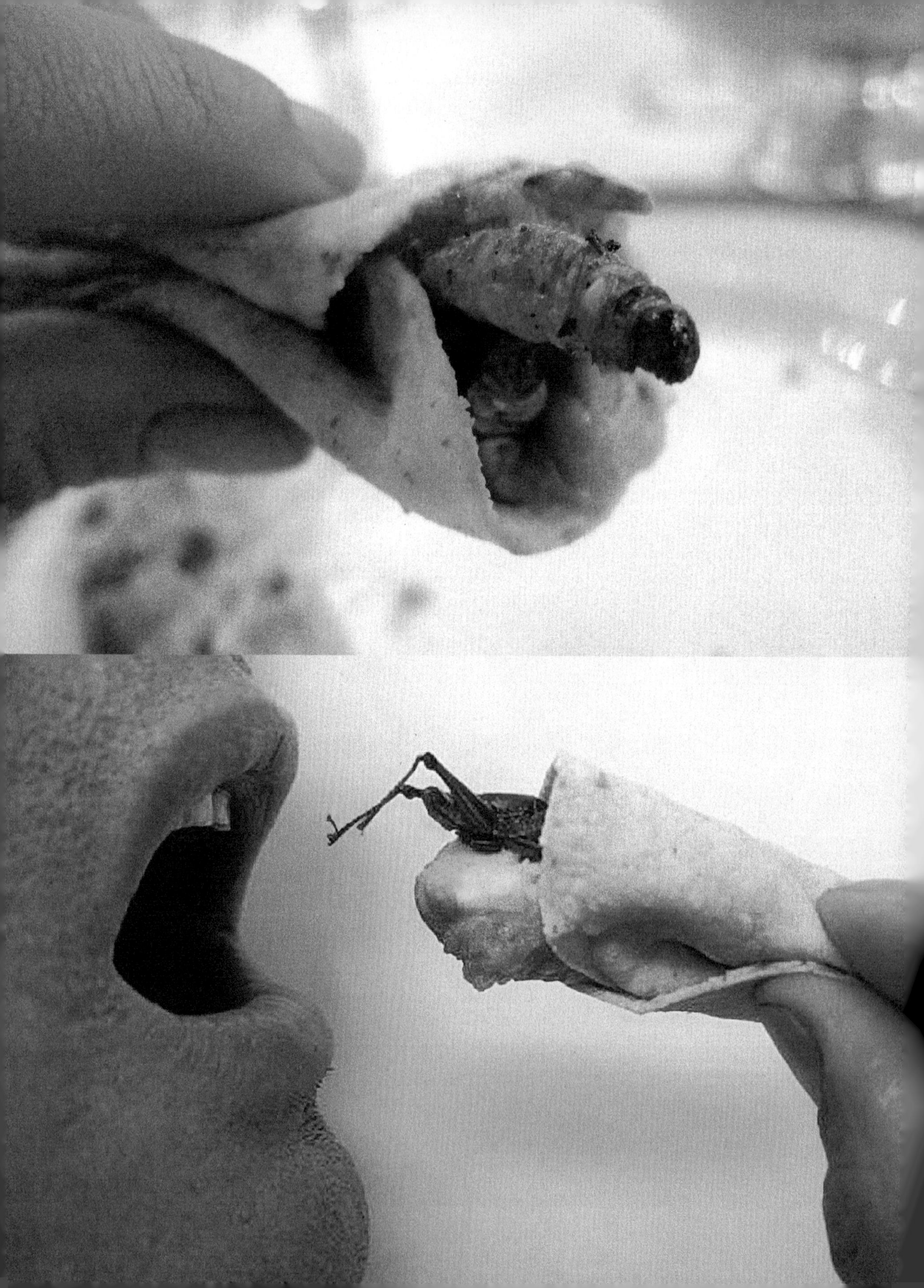

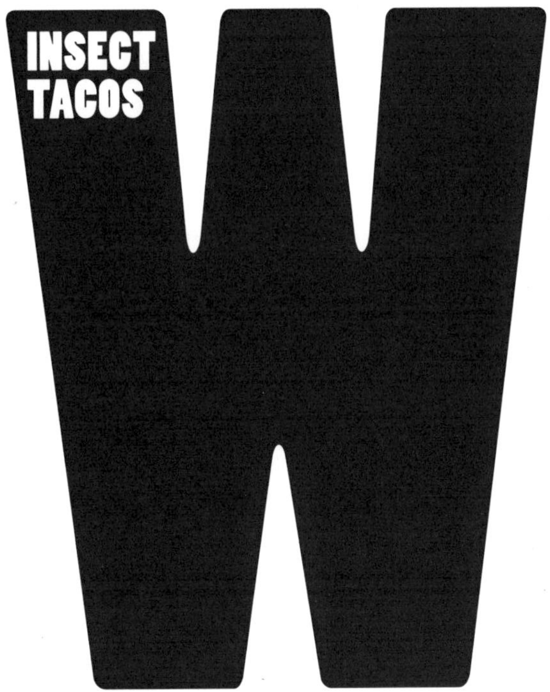

INSECT TACOS

When you bite down, the food escapes, fleeing towards your face—but you guide it back towards your mouth with a calm finger. This is a taco with *jumil*, a scented insect that should be eaten alive to be fully appreciated. There are 549 edible insects recorded in Mexico, among them ants, grasshoppers, and crickets, as well as eggs, larvae, ticks, and a variety of caterpillars. It's a truly exotic culinary repertoire that goes into main courses, *antojitos*, and tacos; and they always leave the diner with a strong impression. This food is an excellent source of vitamins and protein (about half the insect's weight is protein), making them a nutritious choice as well. The main ways to prepare this authentically pre-Hispanic food consist of either boiling the insects in salted water for a few minutes or else tossing them on the griddle. Once cooked, they can be gulped down in a taco with a little salsa or prepared in ways reminiscent of the remote past, in *mixiotes*, *moles*, or salsas. Nevertheless, some connoisseurs claim that the less cooked, the better.

OTHERWORLDLY PLEASURES

The first chroniclers of the Conquest took the time to write about the food and customs of these lands, so it's well documented that in those days our society cultivated a refined taste and enjoyed forms of pleasure that seem otherworldy. On the pre-Hispanic menu we find amphibians, fish, and birds, along with farm and game animals, all unknown to the Europeans when they arrived. It wasn't only the fauna but also the flora that was new to the Europeans, who found a garden full of unfamiliar vegetables, fruit, flowers, and seasonings. Today, some of those native flavors have attained worldwide renown, such as turkey, tomatoes, chiles, chocolate, and vanilla. Other edibles from the New World include armadillos, *biznaga* cactus, the volcano rabbit, manatees, and various kinds of turtle, all now listed as endangered species and, as such, illegal to eat. All the same, this restriction doesn't extend to the *axolotl* or Mexican salamander, iguana, spotted *paca*, or a wide array of flowers, all of which are prepared in their native regions and were surely part of the pre-Hispanic diet. Nor do any restrictions apply to insects, so eating them is fairly easy. Perhaps that's why they have the honor of being the authentic pre-Hispanic taco filling.

TYPICAL FROM CENTRAL TO SOUTHERN MEXICO

MADE WITH CATERPILLARS, GRASSHOPPERS, ANTS, AND JUMILES

COOKED ON A COMAL

THE LESS COOKED, THE BETTER (AND STILL KICKING IS BEST)

It's recommended that this food be eaten in its natural, uncooked state to enjoy its true flavor. Insects can be eaten raw, even if they're traditionally served dried, grilled, fried, in tamales or with salsa. Of course, eating insects drops us straight into the universe of

"[And] a species of bread made of a kind of mud or slime collected from the surface of this lake, and eaten in that form, and has a similar taste to our cheese."

Bernal Díaz del Castillo. *The History of the Conquest of New Spain.* Albuquerque: University of New Mexico Press, 2008, page 237.

"*Yectli Chapolín*: It is of average size. Its lower legs are chile-red, its breast chile-red. It appears when it is harvest time. It is edible. It becomes chile-red, ruddy."

Sahagún. *Florentine Codex,* Book 11: Earthly Things, fifth chapter, 12th paragraph.

"Black ant: It is also called *tzicatl.* These live in cold lands. They are very small; they breed underground, in maguey pith. And also they are rather inclined to bite one. And when it is summer, its young are dug out; they are gathered. They are white, like white worms. They are eaten; they are savory. Many are cooked in an olla. Their name is really *tzicame,* or else they are called *azcamolli.*"

Ibid., 9th paragraph.

Mexican *antojitos* and, more particularly, into the world of tacos. Unfortunately, some of the original methods of preparation have been lost over time, as is the case with *ahuautle* and *axayacatl.* These fly eggs, according to the conquistadors and chroniclers of the day, were bred in lagoons, gathered to make a preserve, and eaten at different stages of maturity, much like cheeses that are aged to acquire a more pungent flavor. Today, insects are sold fresh or frozen, and they command a high market price: supply depends on the amount that can be gathered once predators have had their share. The techniques behind breeding and gathering insects have been completely lost, and recent scientific research has garnered little support from either the authorities or those living in the villages where these succulent delights thrive. Let's take a look at those insects that are easiest

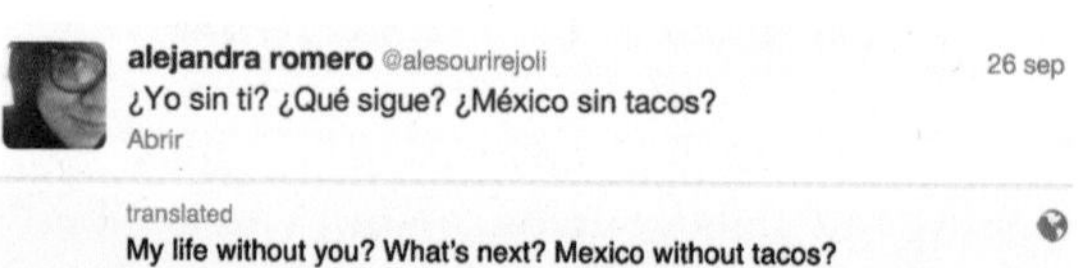

alejandra romero @alesourirejoli
26 sep
¿Yo sin ti? ¿Qué sigue? ¿México sin tacos?
Abrir
translated
My life without you? What's next? Mexico without tacos?

to come by. Remember—to really appreciate them, you should eat them in season.

CHAPULINES (GRASSHOPPERS)

The scientific names for this insect are *Sphenarium purpurascens* and *Sphenarium histrio.* They come out from May to December, especially at the start of the rainy season in the center and south of Mexico, but, given the many edible varieties, they can be found throughout the country. This is perhaps the insect the Mexican palate appreciates the most, and it is certainly the most in demand. In the state of Oaxaca, grasshoppers are a veritable tradition, but they can be easily found in markets in Mexico City, Puebla, Morelos, and in the State of Mexico too. The term is used to include a wide variety of crickets and locusts. These critters are considered a pest to farmers, so their place in tacos is widely supported. The most common varieties are known as the *chapulín de milpa* and the *chapulín de los arbustos*—the field and bush grasshopper,

MORE THAN
A THIRD
OF ALL KNOWN

INSECTS

IN

THE WORLD

ARE

EDIBLE

AND THEY ARE

VERY RICH

IN

PROTEIN.

respectively. You'll often come across different sizes sold in bulk in Oaxacan markets. They are eaten on a tortilla with guacamole, with some lime and salt to taste.

WHITE MAGUEY WORMS

The *Aegiale hesperiaris*, also known as *meocuil* or *meoculin*, and above all as the white maguey worm, is a delight for the refined palate. The worms appear in May and August, but can be preserved in fermented maguey sap and frozen, making them available year-round. They are traditionally eaten in all pulque-producing regions and, as such, have a special relation with lamb *barbacoa*, *mixiote*, and, naturally, pulque itself (see page 104). Maguey worms are actually the larvae of a nocturnal butterfly that deposits its eggs in the maguey plants. Once the insects are born, they slowly burrow through the thick maguey leaves, feeding on the pulpy insides to complete a phase in their development leading to metamorphosis. As the pulque industry fell deeper into its slump, these worms got harder and harder to come by. Some street vendors and those selling alongside highways took advantage of this by passing other caterpillars off as maguey worms. You can, however, find these worms on the menus of posh restaurants, where authenticity hopefully shouldn't be an issue, meaning it's still possible to savor this delight. And now that pulque is starting to show the first signs of recovery, and has found new favor among the younger generation, this situation may change.

RED MAGUEY WORMS

The red maguey worms are also known as *chinicuiles* and are unlike the white worms in that, besides their different color, they are moth larvae; also, they grow in the maguey stem rather than in the leaves. Their scientific name is *Comadia redtenbacheri*. They are found from July to September in the pulque-producing regions (Hidalgo, State of Mexico, Morelos, Oaxaca, Querétaro, Guanajuato, Michoacán, Puebla, Veracruz, and Tlaxcala). The plants hosting these worms take on a withered appearance, and this is the sign those hunting for the worms are hoping to spot. If the worms are gathered at too early a stage of their development, they are kept alive and fed on tortillas by the locals until they reach maturity. Today, the greatest demand for red worms comes from the mezcal industry: that's right, they are the classic little worm at the bottom of the mezcal bottle. They also comprise the main ingredient in the famous "worm salt" that accompanies mezcal, frosting the rim of the glass or accompanying the drink with lime. To prepare the worms in this way, griddle them with salt, and then string them together in the sun to dry. Once dried, they should be milled with salt and ground guajillo chiles. They can also be cooked and eaten in a similar manner to the white worms.

JUMIL

The *jumil* (*Euschistus sulcacitus* in the state of Morelos, *Edessa cordifera* elsewhere in Mexico) is considered sacred for its intercession with divine powers. On the first Monday after the Day of the Dead, thousands of pilgrims climb Mount Huixteco near the city of Taxco, Guerrero, to venerate this insect and eat any they come across along the way. What's more, the insect has also been attributed certain medicinal properties. So, the *jumil* is sacred, curative, and delicious too—it really has everything going for it! There are also other *jumiles*, particularly the "Morelos *jumil*," or *chumil*, which is a species of mountain tick that's similar in shape, behavior, and diet. It's also eaten as a taco filling or condiment. In fact, the *jumil* itself is not only eaten as a taco filling: *jumil* is used in various salsa recipes with the bugs ground up live in a *molcajete* (see page 290) in a blend of green tomato and chiles; the dried, ground *jumil* can also be used in a powder as a condiment for tacos; and lastly, the insect can be cooked and smothered in a sauce, the best known being *mole de jumil*. Insect tacos are often accompanied with guacamole (see recipe 7, page 297) and different chile salsas.

White maguey worm

YUMMY!

Grasshoppers

Red maguey worm

Chicatana ants

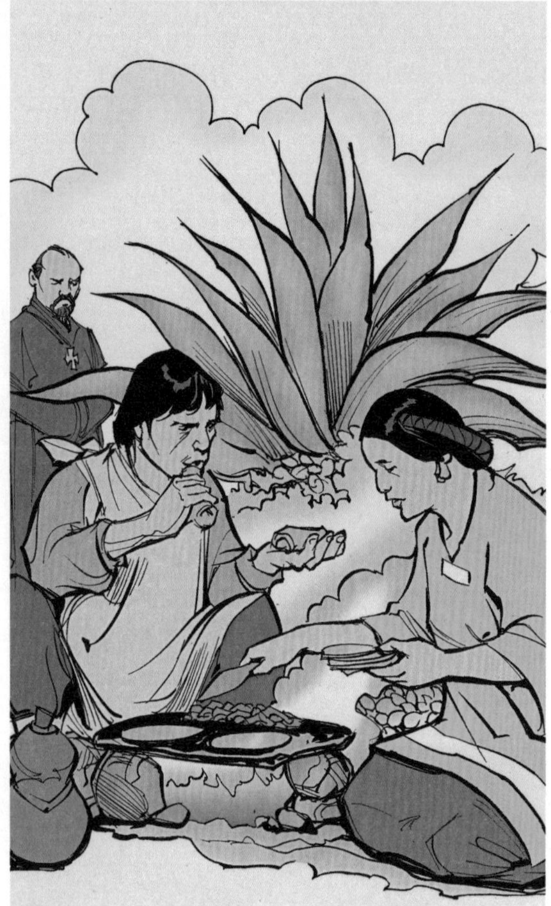

"*Meocuilin*:
**It is like the *cinocuilin*
—white, very white, exceeding white.
It occurs within the maguey plant.
It presents itself in the manner:
wherever it rests, it bores a hole
into the maguey leaf;
it makes an exit opening in it.
There it lies excreting,
and it lies eating the maguey.
[It is edible, savory, good-tasting]."**

Sahagún.
Florentine Codex, Book 11: Earthly Things,
fifth chapter, 13th paragraph.

ANT LARVAE

Escamoles—the larvae of an ant species whose scientific name is—*Liometopum apiculatum*—are one of the world's most extraordinary culinary marvels. They are often mistakenly referred to as "Mexican caviar," an honor that in fact was originally granted to the eggs of certain water bugs by the conquistadors, who observed them being eaten as a delicacy in Tenochtitlán (see page 188). Most people think that *escamoles* are the eggs of the ant, which is not completely off, but the reality is a little more complex: this insect is, in fact, at an immature stage of development (the larval or pupal stage). Only those that belong to the reproductive caste are collected and used for food, since drones at an identical stage can be found in the same nest but are not considered *escamoles*. This type of ant can be found all over Mexico during the months of March and April, but the larvae only tend to be offered as a dish in the finest restaurants and are considered both luxurious and exotic. The most widespread preparation is to fry them in butter with a pinch of salt and to enjoy them *au naturel*. However, recipes abound: some chefs add onion, chile, cilantro, or epazote (sometimes frying the larvae, sometimes leaving them raw) before using them as a filling in tacos with a garnish of guacamole; others prepare them with garlic or salsa. In the end, they are an ingredient that always receives the respectful treatment any fine delicacy deserves.

WAITER, THERE'S A FLY IN MY SOUP

Besides being eaten "raw" in tacos, all these insects can be found as ingredients in a broad range of culinary preparations, depending on the dish, be it quesadillas, tamales, or *mixiote*. They can also be served as the main ingredient in thick sauces, such as *mole* or *adobo*, as well as in soups. Finally, the *chicatana* ant is renowned for its use in a unique salsa from Oaxaca. They are collected when they take flight with the first rains, grilled and ground up with garlic, chile, and salt in a *molcajete*.

Althought the most famous edible insects in Mexico are grasshoppers, maguey worms, ant larvae, and *jumil* beetles, in our country people eat whatever insects they come across.

Wasps, for example, which are even sold at markets. When wasps begin their own colony, the hives are small and the wasps don't bite. People can take the hive to their homes and hang them there. One time, I came across a house in Tizapán, Hidalgo, that had eighty hives and one of them was huge, over six-and-a half feet. The wasps are eaten roasted. Here on campus, when it's grasshopper season, I've seen the workers eat the grasshoppers roasted off the comal. The insects are gathered up in large numbers in a huge net dragged across the alfalfa fields by several men in the early hours. The grasshoppers just fly into it. But all this is directed by a woman. She's the one who gets permission from the farmers, explains how many they are going to catch, how many they are going to sell, where the grasshoppers will be distributed, everything. It's a matriarchy, just like with the *jumiles*. In the countryside, the white maguey worm is usually roasted, as it has a lot of fat, up to thirty-eight percent depending on its stage of development. When they're cooked on a griddle the flavor is concentrated, it's exquisite and unique, but they have to be fed on the maguey plant; otherwise they lose their flavor. There are also many types of edible beetle larvae that live in fallen tree trunks and are delicious —but they're not quite like the maguey worms, which have a very refined taste. The demand for this insect is enormous because there has to be at least one in each bottle of mezcal. If it's not there, the bottle won't sell! It really does change the flavor. The worm is actually red but turns white in the alcohol because its pigment dissolves in the ethanol. When you eat them straight out the dried trunk of the maguey, they're spicy! If you give them a bite, you'll find them as hot as a chile. Cooking salt is put on them to dry them out a bit, and that mixture is then ground up. Sometimes chile is added. The maguey worm is also used for salsas, but the *jumil* beetles make the best salsas—a real delight, those salsas! There are sacred *jumil* beetles and also the Morelos type. They are both pretty potent and are known as "stink bugs." They are eaten alive in tacos with guacamole. I personally prefer the *jumil* beetles from Taxco and, even though they're eaten without condiments, they have a flavor that gives a real kick—it's super strong... your gums, tongue, and cheek all go numb for about three hours. Some people call *escamoles* the Mexican caviar, but that's not quite right: Mexican caviar would be the water-bug eggs that they used to have in Tenochtitlán, still found today in some bodies of water. People used to make fritters with them, which the conquistadors described as "cheeses." The dish has a religious aspect to it as it's popular over Easter (even if more eggs are produced during the summer rainy season), and they're served like shrimp fritters. It was the Spanish who actually gave them the name "Mexican caviar." But anyway, even if the ant larvae aren't the real Mexican caviar, they're still one of the world's most unusual ingredients. The problem with insect tacos is that people always put loads of spicy salsa and guacamole on them and it swamps the flavor, because the tortilla has a neutral flavor, but the salsas are really powerful.

"THEY ALWAYS PUT SALSA OR GUACAMOLE ON INSECT TACOS, AND IT SWAMPS THE FLAVOR."

Julieta Ramos-Elorduy B.
STUDIED BIOLOGY AT THE UNAM, EARNED HER DOCTORATE AT THE SORBONNE, NOW A RESEARCHER AT THE ETHNOBIOLOGY DEPARTMENT OF THE UNAM'S INSTITUTE OF BIOLOGY

IF
YOU WANT
TO SHOW OFF,
THERE IS
NOTHING
CLASSIER
THAN

ANT LARVAE,

THE
MISTAKENLY
NAMED
"MEXICAN
CAVIAR."

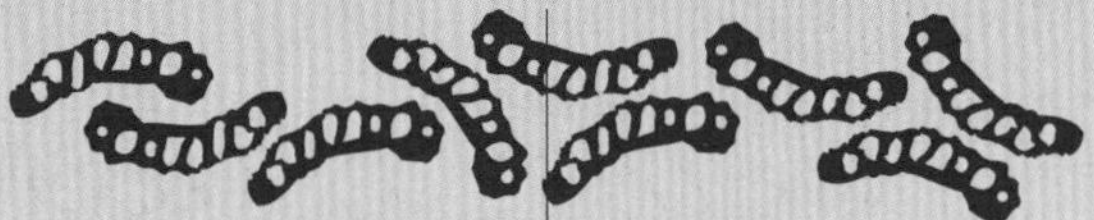
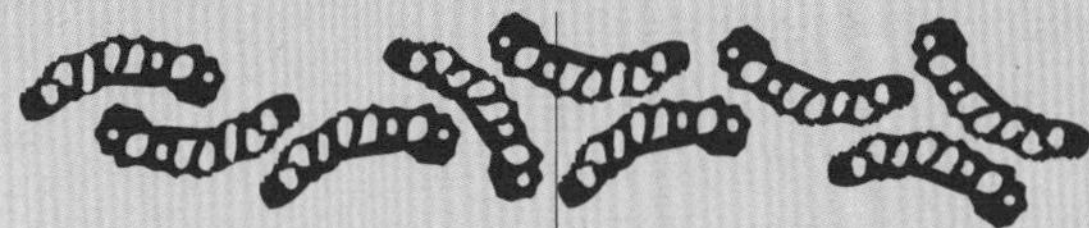

ANT-LARVAE TACOS

Serves 4 as an appetizer

—7 oz (200 g) ant larvae (*escamoles*)
—1 tablespoon (15 g) unsalted butter
—¼ medium onion, finely chopped
—1 clove garlic, minced
—2 green serrano chiles, seeded and deveined
—3 epazote leaves, finely chopped
—Sea salt
—1 cup (250 ml) guacamole

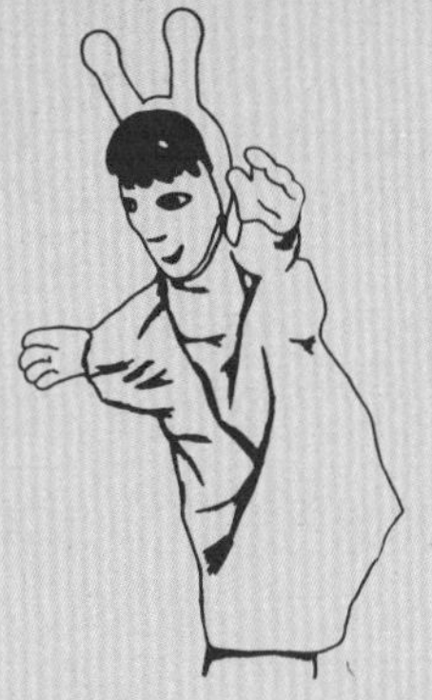

(see recipe 7, page 297)
—Green-tomato salsa and "drunken" salsa (see recipes 12, 26, and 27, pages 300 and 306–307), for serving

1. Rinse the ant larvae and drain completely in a strainer.
2. Melt the butter in a medium pot set over medium. Add the onion and fry for 1 minute. Add the garlic and let cook for 1 minute. Add the chiles to the mixture. Cook, stirring 1 minute without letting the vegetables brown.
3. Add the ant larvae and sauté for a minute.
4. Add the epazote and salt to taste.
5. Immediately prepare the tacos with a spoonful of guacamole, then another of ant larvae on top.
6. If desired, serve with green-tomato salsa or "drunken" salsa when serving.

MAGUEY WORM TACOS

Serves 4

—7 oz (200 g) white maguey worms
—1 teaspoon lard or oil
—Sea salt
—8 4⅓-inch (11 cm) corn tortillas
—1 cup (250 ml) guacamole (see recipe 7, page 297)
—Green-tomato salsa (see recipe 12, page 300) or "drunken" salsa (recipes 26 and 27, pages 306–307), for serving

1. Rinse the worms and drain in the strainer.
2. Put the worms in a heat-resistant ceramic casserole dish with lard or oil. Set the heat to low so that the worms fry turning regularly until browned and crispy. Season to taste with salt.
3. Compose the tacos, putting a spoonful of guacamole in a tortilla, then adding a generous serving of worms.
4. If desired, accompany with prepared green-tomato salsa or "drunken" salsa when serving.

GRASSHOPPER TACOS

Serves 4 as an appetizer

—12 oz (350 g) grasshoppers
—1 cup (250 ml) guacamole (see recipe 7, page 297)
—9 oz(250 g) refried black beans
—5 oz (150 g) Oaxaca cheese, shredded
—Limes, for serving
—8–12 4⅓-inch (11 cm) corn tortillas
—Hot salsas (see recipes 26 or 27, pages 306–307; or recipes 14, 15, 18, 29, or 30, pages 301–307)
—Sea salt

Various preparations
In Mexico, grasshoppers (*chapulines*) are sold prepped and ready to eat, so it's important to find the freshest ones, ensuring that they are of tested provenance and quality.

One way of preparing grasshopper tacos is to spread a thick base of guacamole, then sprinkle the grasshoppers on the guacamole. Top with the salsa of your choice.

Simpler tacos can be made with just the grasshoppers, a few drops of lime, salt, and some salsa—great with a shot of mezcal!

You can also spread a base of refried beans, add the grasshoppers, and a good spoonful of "drunken" salsa.

Yet another variation consists in preparing the taco with a corn tortilla, some shredded Oaxaca cheese, and a healthy serving of grasshoppers, then heat everything up on a griddle. (Though this taco is more like a quesadilla.) Accompany with arbol chile salsa.

CHICATANA ANTS

THE BEST

Casa Oaxaca

104-A CONSTITUCIÓN, CENTRO, OAXACA

Alejandro Ruíz, the top chef in contemporary Oaxacan cuisine, replaced the tortilla with slices of jicama to offer tacos with *huitlacoche*, string cheese, and grasshopper salsa.

El Cardenal

23 PALMA, CENTRO HISTÓRICO, MEXICO CITY

The menu of the capital's top restaurant specializing in Mexican food includes insects, depending on the season: white maguey worms from June to July, then *chinicuiles* (moth larvae) from August to the start of October.

El Gran León de Oro

21 MERCADERES, SAN JOSÉ INSURGENTES, MEXICO CITY

The modern building in no way takes away from the cantina feel. The ant larvae tacos (prepared with butter, chiles, and epazote) are served in ceramic bowls.

La No. 20

10 ANDRÉS BELLO, POLANCO, MEXICO CITY

Now the most elegant cantina in Polanco, it still offers its traditional dishes alongside its most refined fare, which includes ant larvae and maguey worms.

Los Danzantes

12 JARDÍN CENTENARIO, COYOACÁN, MEXICO CITY

At its now famous annual "Bug Festival," you can enjoy ant larvae and maguey worms on tacos along with a shot of the house mezcal.

Benito Juárez Market

BETWEEN FLORES MAGÓN, LAS CASAS, ALDAMA, AND 20 DE NOVIEMBRE, CENTRO, OAXACA

Here tourists mix with locals, all clamoring to enjoy Oaxacan cuisine. Don't miss out on the grasshoppers with lime, either in tacos or on their own.

Cuautla Market

36 FRANCISCO MENDOZA PALMA, COL. GABRIEL TEPEPA, CUAUTLA, MORELOS

Here you'll find women seated on the floor in the halls offering tacos with *jumiles*. Savor the insects live in a tortilla garnished with *nopales* and salsa.

Paxia

47 AVENIDA DE LA PAZ, SAN ÁNGEL, MEXICO CITY

The owner and chef, Daniel Ovadía, uses *chinicuiles* creatively, putting them in tacos with a mortar-ground Oaxacan pasilla chile salsa, criollo avocado, radish, and *papaloquelite* oil.

Restaurante Chon

160 REGINA, CENTRO HISTÓRICO, MEXICO CITY

This restaurant near La Merced market draws the culinary faithful to taste its *jumiles*, ant larvae, maguey worms, grasshoppers, and other delectable items of pre-Hispanic haute cuisine.

Santiago de Anaya

SANTIAGO DE ANAYA, HIDALGO (BETWEEN PACHUCA AND IXMIQUILPAN)

For three decades now, this town has held its "Culinary Festival of the Valle del Mezquital" before Holy Week, offering ant larvae and maguey worms, among other delights.

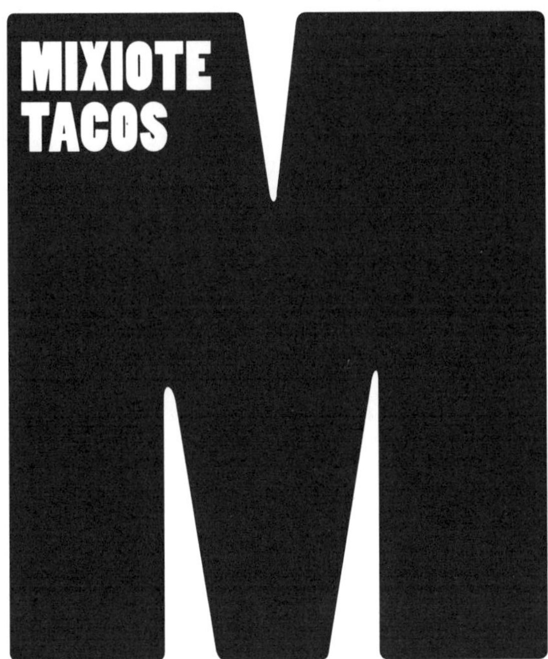

***Mixiote* is a dish that is intimately linked to lamb *barbacoa* for a number of reasons: the first is that this specialty can be cooked in the same oven pit as *barbacoa*. What's more, the best-known *mixiotes* are the ones made with lamb, and the maguey plant is closely involved in both processes. Finally, *mixiote*, rather than being a particular dish, is more of a way to prepare food. As we'll see, this method of cooking can be used with nearly any ingredient and, of course, *mixiotes* make great tacos too—perhaps that's why they're so popular in street markets and stalls, where whole families sit down to savor this delight.**

TIE A YELLOW RIBBON 'ROUND THAT OLE MAGUEY

This food has pre-Hispanic roots that run deep in popular tradition and, when prepared well, is a delicacy worthy of haute cuisine. Though *mixiote* goes unmentioned in the annals of chroniclers during the Conquest and colonial times, its name comes from the Aztec *mixiotl*, meaning "skin," referring to the outside skin of the thick maguey leaf. Though this dish can be prepared in a *barbacoa* oven pit, it can also be made in a pot or water bath on the stove-top or, of course, in the pressure cooker used for tamales. These days, the shortage of maguey skin has led to the emergence of various substitutes, the most common being a special paper made for *mixiote* and sold as such. It retains all the properties of the original product, being waterproof, and comes in square-foot-sized pieces, the ideal size for a good serving of meat. While the paper doesn't alter the taste of the meat wrapped inside, it doesn't flavor it either, and it is worth noting that the maguey leaf-skin wrap does impart an aroma. Greaseproof paper can be used, as well as butcher's paper, aluminum paper, and, naturally, plastic wrap or bags for cooking. It's important to note that natural *mixiote*, a raw material sourced from maguey and used to make the leaf-skin wrap, is now on the endangered species list because demand outstrips production (bear in mind that a maguey plant takes over eight years to reach maturity, before it can be used). In fact, there's even a form of pillaging that goes on, with thieves making off with the skins—and even the leaves themselves—to use them in *mixiote* production. As a result, it's more and more difficult to find this product in its orthodox, original form—but given the threat to the plants and their lengthy growing time, perhaps it is better to use alternatives for a while. These tacos are usually accompanied with red salsàs made with the chiles found in *adobo*: guajillo, pasilla, or morita chiles. They can also be served with onions in habanero or manzano chile marinades, which makes for a

TYPICAL IN HIDALGO, QUERÉTARO, GUANAJUATO, TLAXCALA, PUEBLA, MEXICO CITY

MADE WITH LAMB, CHICKEN, PORK, RABBIT

COOKED IN A BARBACOA OVEN OR IN A TAMALE POT

LITTLE TORTILLAS WITH LARD

Little tortillas with lard,
For mommy, who's always glad.
Little tortillas with bran,
For daddy, who's an angry man.
Little tortillas with maize,
For mommy, who's always pleased.
Little tortillas with ham,
For daddy, who's always mad!

TRADITIONAL
This traditional clap-along song is sung to children on their mother's knee.

delectable contrast with the *mixiote* (see recipes 4, 6, 18, 20, 21, 25, and 29, pages 296–307). The salsas served with *mixiote* tacos should be spicy and have a side of onion, radishes, oregano, lime, and salt. While another fine accompaniment is a classic *nopal* salad, better still is to enjoy *mixiote* served in a tortilla with its broth serving as the only salsa: the broth requires so much preparation in and of itself that it has a flavor all its own, one that chiles tend to cover. One thing's for sure, though: nothing goes better with *mixiote* than a liter jug of good white pulque—the traditional pre-Hispanic alcoholic beverage made from maguey (see page 104)—and a green chile to nibble on.

MIXIOTE WITHOUT ACHIOTE!

In modern versions of *mixiote*, it is not just the wrapping that has changed: there is also an infinite variety of fillings to accompany the dish, beginning with the salsas (among them achiote, *piloncillo* [brown loaf sugar], chocolate, guajillo or chipotle chiles), adding the condiments (Mexican pepperleaf or *hoja santa*, avocado leaf, cloves, black pepper, or allspice), and lastly the principal ingredient (frog, *axolotl* or Mexican salamander, fish, shrimp, ant larvae, olives, or *nopales*). It might be said that this dish is still in a state of evolution, because it still has surprises left in store for the taco connoisseur. It's interesting to imagine what could be done using modern sous-vide cooking techniques if they were applied to *mixiote* tacos, since the idea is pretty much the same: the principle of cooking ingredients in their own juices.

Everything here is natural. We still use the ancient *mixiote* recipe.

We make our *adobo* with nothing but guajillo and ancho chiles, cilantro, black pepper, and, above all, the secret house recipe. The *mixiote* is the skin that comes off the maguey leaf, and it's used to wrap up meat (lamb, chicken, rabbit, venison, or any other type of meat). The ones here are natural: today there are artificial substitutes and plastic wrap, but we stick with the traditional recipe because it really changes the flavor. When you use a real maguey leaf, the *mixiote* has a different flavor—the artificial stuff leaves a plastic taste. The freshness of the meat counts for a lot too. We use fresh meat here and we just use lamb. We don't use any artificial stuff or frozen meat. I think that's what's kept us where we are in the market, with our customers and the sales we've got. There's the cleanliness, the hygiene standards: it's how we do everything here. We

"IF THE MIXIOTE IS MADE WITH MAGUEY LEAVES, IT HAS A DIFFERENT FLAVOR."

make it with lamb and chicken during the Easter period; but in the normal run of things, customers order rabbit or, when there's nothing else, pork. Pork's not as good, though: the food loses the *mixiote* taste because of the fat content. The best-tasting *mixiote* is definitely the lamb one. Before, *mixiote* was made in the oven, like *barbacoa*, but wood's too pricey today: a bundle of wood costs about 500 pesos, while gas is about half that, so that's how we do it, by steaming it. We use green and red salsas, *nopales*, red onion with habanero chiles, radish, cucumber, pineapple, and limes. Finely chopped onion and cilantro are in there too. I've been working here for fifteen years, but the business has been in the family for more than forty—it's a tradition. We're from Tulancingo, Hidalgo.

Abel Castelán
EXQUISITOS TACOS DE MIXIOTES STAND IN PLAZA GIORDANO BRUNO, CORNER OF LONDRES AND ROMA, COL. JUÁREZ, MEXICO CITY

THE
AZTEC
WORD
MIXIOTL
REFERS TO
THE SKIN OF
THE
MAGUEY LEAF,
USED TO WRAP UP
THE
MEAT.

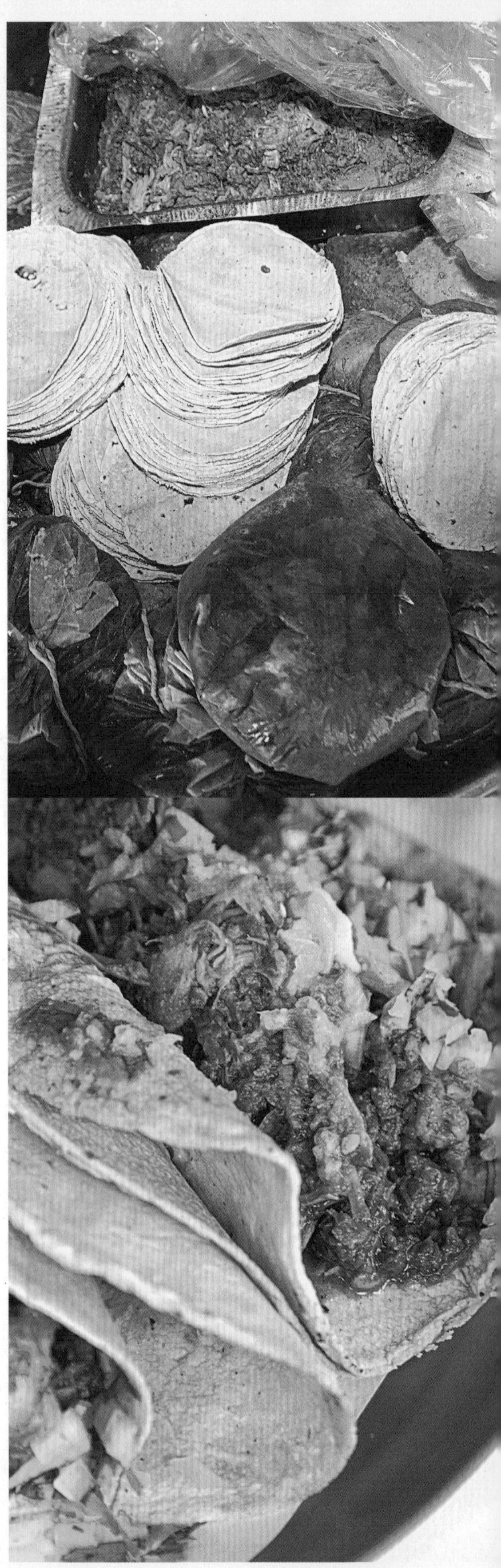

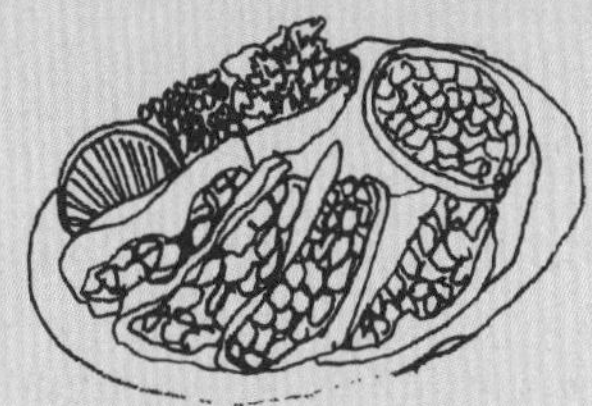

PORK MIXIOTE TACOS

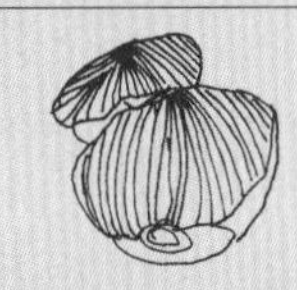

MIXIOTE

Serves 4

—2¼ lb (1 kg) pork leg, cut into 1-inch (2.5 cm) cubes, rinsed, and patted dry
—1 cup (250 ml) *adobo* (see next recipe)
—9 oz (250 g) *nopales,* spines removed, sliced into strips
—Sea salt
—1 clove garlic
—A pinch of baking soda
—2 avocado leaves

1. Combine the meat and the marinade in a large bowl. Cover and refrigerate overnight.
2. Bring a large pot of salted water to a boil. Add the *nopales*, garlic, and baking soda, and boil for 5 minutes. Rinse and set aside.
3. Prepare the *mixiotes*: Place a serving of marinated meat, some *nopales*, and a piece of avocado leaf on a piece of aluminum foil. Tightly wrap the foil around the food to seal it inside.
4. Place the closed packets together in a pressure cooker with 3½ cups (870 ml) water. Lock on the lid, bring to pressure, and cook on low heat for 1 hour.
5. Remove the packets and transfer to a large plate. Carefully unwrap the aluminum foil so that your guests can prepare their tacos by adding the garnish and salsa of their choice.

ADOBO

MAKES 1½ CUPS (350 ML)

—2 dried sweet guajillo chiles
—2–3½ oz (50–100 g) achiote
—1 cup (250 ml) fresh orange juice or white pulque
—2 cloves garlic
—½ medium onion
—1 tablespoon dried oregano
—2 whole cloves
—6 whole black peppercorns
—Sea salt

1. Set a large griddle over high heat. Roast chiles on the griddle, without burning them, 3–5 minutes. Once cooked, remove the veins and seeds and set aside.
2. Dissolve the achiote tablet in the juice or pulque.
3. Process all the remaining ingredients, dissolved achiote and chiles in a blender until smooth, then strain into a bowl. Set aside until ready to marinate the meat.

FISH MIXIOTE TACOS

Serves 4

—2 ¼ lb (1 kg) dogfish fillets, cut into strips
—1 cup (250 ml) *adobo* (from previous recipe)
—4 leaves of Mexican pepperleaf (*hoja santa*)
—9 oz (250 g) carrots, cut into sticks
—4 oz (120g) green peas
—3½ oz (100 g) green pepper, thinly sliced
—1 medium onion, sliced into rings
—Sea salt

1. Marinate the fish in the *adobo* in a medium bowl for at least 3 hours; keep refrigerated.
2. Prepare the *mixiotes*: On a piece of aluminum foil or in *mixiotes* wrap, place a leaf, a serving of marinated fish, some carrot sticks, some peas, some green pepper, some onion, and salt. Wrap the food up tightly to seal.

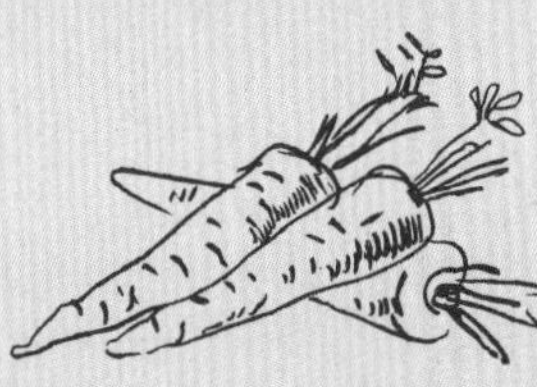

3. Place the closed packages together in a steamer basket, set in a pot with simmering water on the bottom. Steam, covered, for 30 minutes.
4. Divide *mixiotes* packages among plates. Carefully open the packets and use the contents as taco filling.

VEGETARIAN MIXIOTE TACOS

Serves 4

—7 oz (200 g) panela cheese, diced
—5 oz (150 g) mushrooms, cleaned and quartered
—1 medium carrot, sliced
—1 medium zucchini, diced
—1 medium onion, cut into rings
—4 jalapeño chiles, seeded, deveined, and cut into strips
—1 cup (250 ml) *adobo* (from previous recipe)
—4 sprigs epazote

1. Mix the cheese into the other ingredients (except the epazote) in a large bowl. Divide the mixture between four pieces of aluminum foil. Place a sprig of epazote on each.
2. Tightly wrap the ingredients into sealed packages. Steam in a steamer basket over a pot with simmering water on the bottom for 30–45 minutes.
3. Divide packages among plates. Carefully open the packets and use the contents as taco filling.

THE BEST

El Rey del Mixiote
COL. SAN MANUEL, PUEBLA
6103 RÍO MAYO
Here *mixiote* tacos are on sale individually or by the dozen in a meal deal that includes the indispensable tortillas, salsa, *charro* beans, lamb broth, and even spaghetti.

Enrique
4061 INSURGENTES SUR, TLALPAN, MEXICO CITY
This place is found at the exit for Cuernavaca, which lends a suitably provincial feel to your mutton—or chicken—*mixiote*.

La Gruta
KM 22.6 ECATEPEC-PIRÁMIDES, TEOTIHUACÁN, STATE OF MEXICO
As well as its juicy lamb and rabbit *mixiote*, there's the imposing plus of enjoying your meal next to the pyramids of Teotihuacán.

Las Delicias
1027 INSURGENTES SUR AV., COL. CIUDAD DE LOS DEPORTES, MEXICO CITY
This restaurant with a lively family atmosphere is near the big bullfighting ring, Plaza de Toros México. They offer lamb *mixiote* and all the salsas you could want.

Los Virreyes
32 PLAZA VIRREINAL, TEPOTZOTLÁN, STATE OF MEXICO
One of the most traditional restaurants in the area, it has colonial decor and an attractive panoramic view. It serves a succulent lamb *mixiote*.

Mixiotes Castelán
CORNER OF LONDRES AND BRUSELAS, COL. JUÁREZ, MEXICO CITY
At this renowned street stand tucked away in Plaza Giordano Bruno, the owners take the liberty of setting up shop only on Wednesdays, Saturdays, and Sundays.

Restaurante Espartacos
115 CARRETERA FEDERAL, COL. EMILIANO ZAPATA, CHALCO, STATE OF MEXICO
Here women prepare tortillas on the comal to accompany the many offerings available in this family restaurant, including lamb and chicken *mixiote*.

Restaurante La Posada
911 16 DE SEPTIEMBRE, CENTRO, APIZACO, TLAXCALA
Tlaxcala is also a pulque-producing region, and the *mixiote* prepared in the restaurant of this Apizaco hotel is cooked in real maguey-leaf skin.

Restaurante Mary Cristy
11 HIDALGO, CENTRO, PACHUQUILLA, HIDALGO
Near the Pachuca-Tulancingo highway, this place offers meal deals with *mixiote*, *barbacoa* broth, and rice.

Restaurante Nortesur
302 IGNACIO COMONFORT, COL. SAN ANA, TOLUCA, STATE OF MEXICO
Its extensive menu includes an interesting variety of boneless rib-*mixiote* served with green tomato mortar-ground salsa alongside avocado with tomato, onion, and fresh chile salsa.

DEL INAPAM
foil

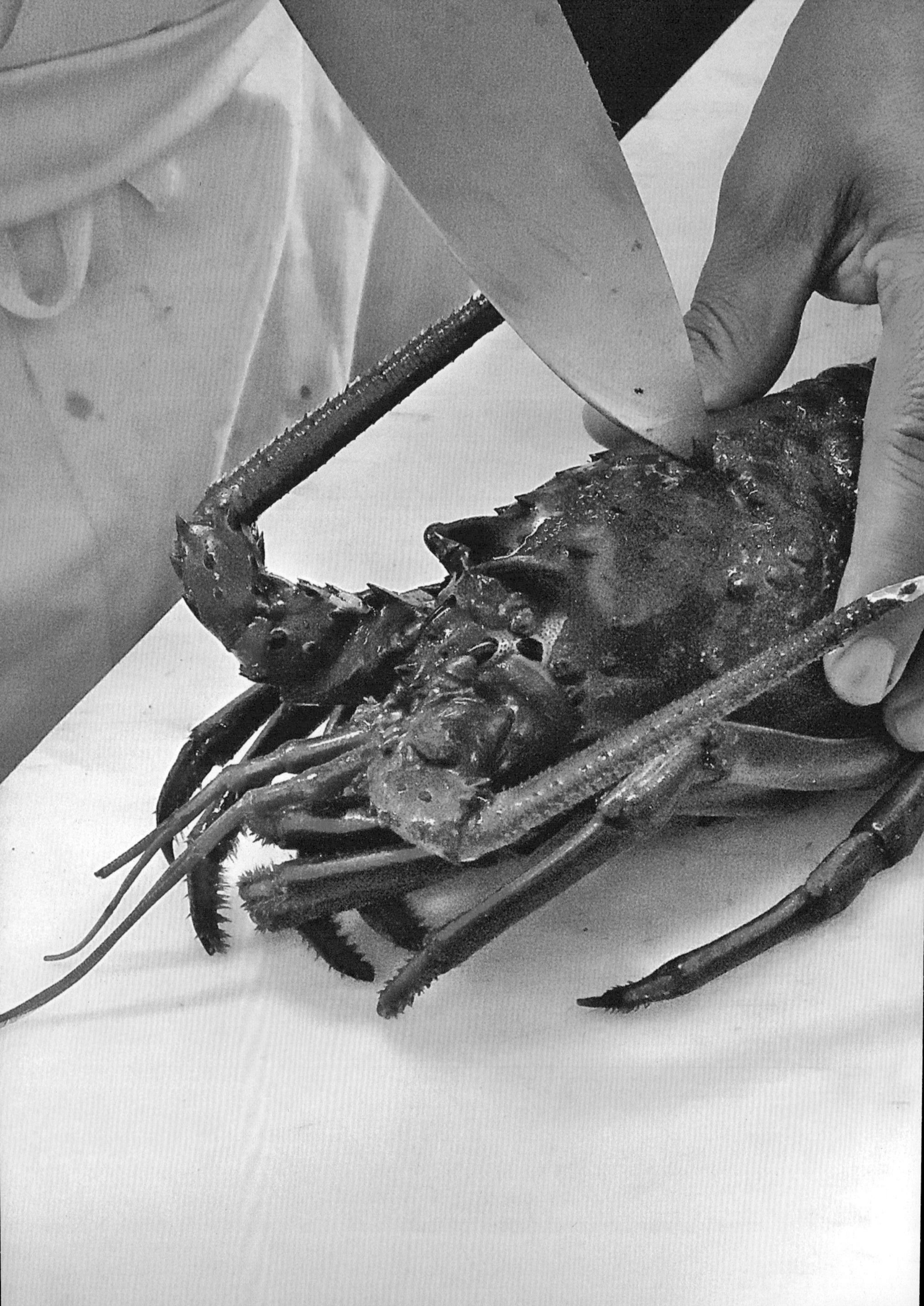

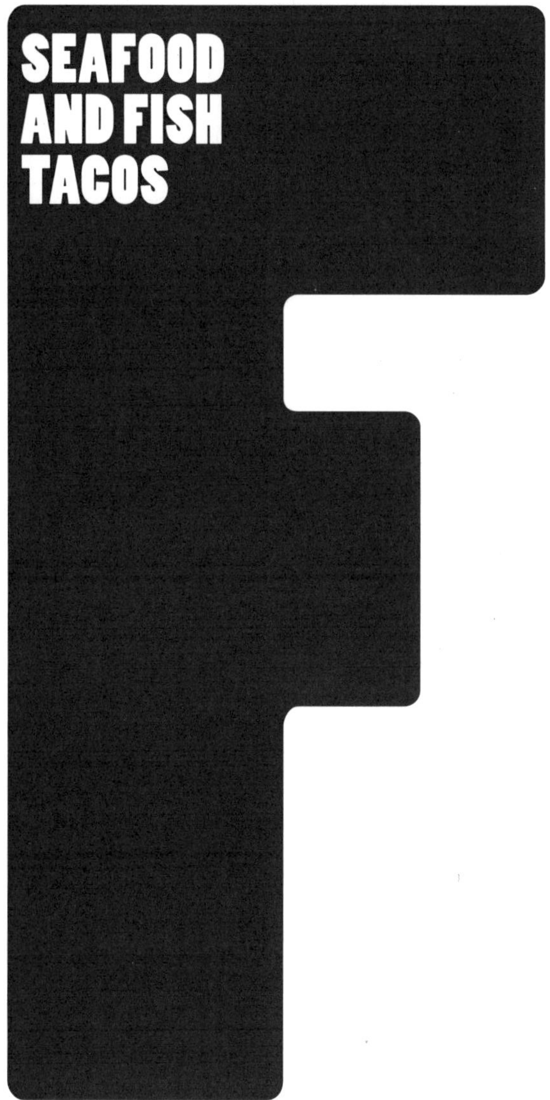

SEAFOOD AND FISH TACOS

Fish tacos are the proof that contemporary Mexican cooking is in a state of flux. Up till a few years ago, it was unusual to find fish tacos outside coastal regions, but it seems that their ship has come in, so to speak... not only because of their great popularity but also because they have experienced fusion with other world cuisines. Fresh tortillas have, naturally, been enjoyed as an accompaniment for fish and sea food, but less commonly as a way to make tacos. Now, though, fish tacos come in all shapes and sizes: *flautas*, *al pastor*, griddled, charcoal-grilled, and even in basket tacos. They're just versatile that way: the most popular recipes from the coasts have made their way inland, where they enjoy an unqualified success.

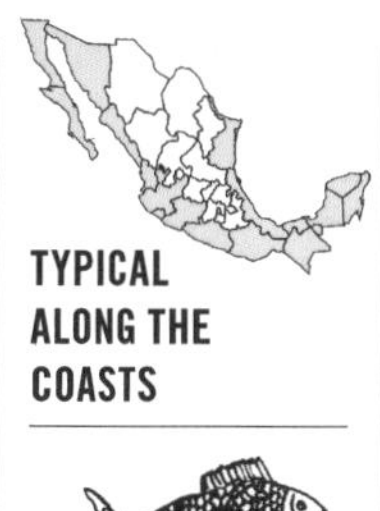

TYPICAL ALONG THE COASTS

MADE WITH FISH, OCTOPUS, SHRIMP, CRAB

COOKED ON THE GRILL, ON THE GRIDDLE, IN A BARBACOA OVEN PIT, IN A SKILLET, OR IN A POT

OF TAPESCOS AND TAMEMES

The big trouble with seafood has always been how to keep it from going bad. Wood-smoking can prove an effective means to preserve fish and seafood, and there's a pre-Hispanic instrument, the *tapexco*, or *tapesco*, made just for that purpose. It consists of a low table or bench made of sticks and leaves. A fire is lit below it, and the meat is left to smoke on top. In Tabasco, the *tapexco* is used to prepare the famous *tapesco* oysters, a typical regional treat. Legend has it that the Aztec kings had fresh fish brought to their table by runners who relayed fish all the way from the coast. In fact, the story refers to *tamemes*, professional carriers, who transported all kinds of goods in pre-Hispanic Mesoamerica, since beasts of burden were unknown at the time. The carriers used a *mecapal*, a leather or fiber strap that transferred the weight of the load from the carrier's back to his head. The *mecapal* is still used in Mexican markets today, but the fleet-footed carriers of fresh fish from the coast are a thing of the past. It should be noted that freshwater fish were also a staple for the inhabitants of Tenochtitlán, along with birds, frogs, and other edibles drawn from the lake. As for the preparation of fish, the ancient Mexicans wrapped fish in maize leaves (or banana or maguey leaves) and gently heated it to dry it out for future meals. This is how seared fish, *mex tlapique*, is prepared and eaten today, reheating the

> "Sleepless, gazing through the window into the neon night, [...] Belascoarán confirms what he had though: there is no hate. Just an enormous, infinite feeling of love for the mutant city in which he lived and which lived him, in which he dreamt and which dreamt him. A will to love that, instead of being defined by rage, possession, or sex, shifted towards tenderness. It must be the protests, the golden light of the Zócalo, the bookstands, the *carnitas* tacos, the rivers of profound solidarity, the friends in the garage in front that waved to him as he went by. Perhaps it was that marvelous winter moon. Perhaps. Héctor sat on the couch to have a smoke. He spent the night smoking and listening to the noises from the street. Without knowing why, the face of Héctor Monteverde's lame dog came to mind. At dawn he was asleep."
>
> **PACO IGNACIO.**
> Taibo II and Subcomandante Marcos.
> *Muertos Incómodos.*
> Mexico: Joaquín Mortiz, 2005.

meat in the same natural wrapping or rehydrating it in a sauce. Another ancient preparation is *salazón*, a process that consists of drying the meat with salt in the heat of the sun. This practice is used mostly on the northwest coast of Mexico, where they make *machaca*—shredded dried beef—and use the same method for lobster and manta ray. As for marinated fish, it should be mentioned that in the early colonial period, fish was prepared in the traditional European style, with oil and vinegar, but these recipes were soon enriched with the addition of local ingredients including tomatoes and chiles, ideal complements for this kind of food. These foods were stored in little barrels called *cuñetes*. The artisanal *cuñete* business later evolved into the fish-canning industry that makes the ever-present cans of tuna and sardines, which in turn has led to the popularity of sardine and tuna tacos (see page 173).

A THOUSAND AND ONE COOKING TALES

In Sonora and Sinaloa, tacos and a diverse range of other *antojitos* are made from smoked tuna and marlin: *carnitas*-style tacos, *flautas*, seafood salads and *salpicón* on soft tacos. Roasting seafood, over the coals is surely the oldest way to prepare it, and among other foods cooked over the griddle, we find *pescado zarandeado* from the coast of Nayarit (this specialty is grilled over mangrove wood to infuse the fish with its aroma), Guerrero-style grilled fish prepared along Mexico's Pacific coast in the center of the country (left to soak in an *adobo* of chile salsa before roasting), and the *tikin-xik* fish from the Yucatán peninsula (doused in *mojo* or achiote marinade while over the coals). When it comes down to it, anything from out of the sea can be thrown on a hot griddle. Yet another way to cook fish comes from out of the *barbacoa* oven pits—for example, fish *birria* in the west of Mexico. However, any kind of oven can be used to prepare Mexican-style seafood, eaten on fried or soft tortillas with a chile salsa. Traditionally, the famous *charales* or silversides, as well as battered fish sticks and fish quesadillas, are fried in sizzling oil, and are perfect examples of great tacos to enjoy with salad, salsa, and lime. Traditional Mexican cuisine offers a wide range of classic recipes cooked up in pots that can also be prepared with fish. These dishes, like any other, can also be eaten as tacos (see page 173).

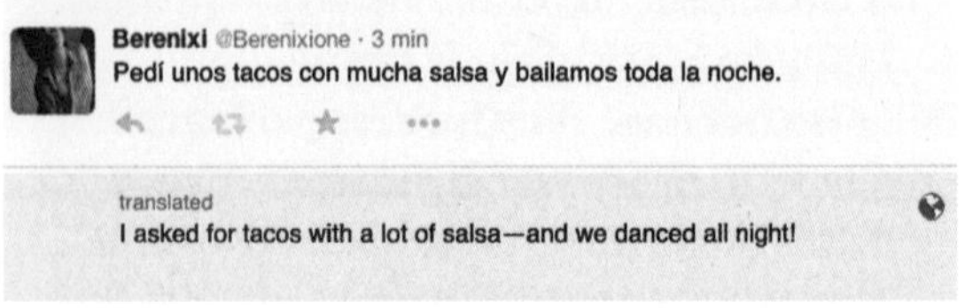

Berenixi @Berenixione · 3 min
Pedí unos tacos con mucha salsa y bailamos toda la noche.
translated
I asked for tacos with a lot of salsa—and we danced all night!

The salsas and garnishes eaten with seafood are more or less those used in other tacos, with the exception that these tacos, like most anything with fish and seafood, can also be accompanied with mayonnaise. What's more, the mayonnaise can be mixed with chipotles, cilantro, or sour cream (which makes it "mayocream") to add a special touch. The same goes for avocado, which can bring its special texture and taste to dishes in different ways, spread as a base on fried tortillas or served as a side garnish in other dishes—but wherever it is, it's always a welcome sight.

SEAFOOD SNACKS

The most common way to snack on seafood in Mexico is on a *tostada*—a crispy fried tortilla, traditionally the ideal bearer for seafood on its short trip from plate to mouth. This is how the long lineup of seafood cocktails and salads is dealt with, including *escabeche* and ceviche, without going overboard, of course. Seafood dishes have also included quesadillas (served with fresh or fried tortillas) since time immemorial. Among the most famous fillings, we find crab, shrimp, and fish, all of which are first prepared "Mexican style," that is with tomato, onion, and chiles—all of them indispensable ingredients (see page 249). Another well-known alternative is *flautas*, deep-fried tacos with all kinds of fish fillings (see page 227). With fish, the challenge is to keep this vital, oceanic treat fresh for as long as possible after it's taken out of the water. *Escabeche* is a pickled fish recipe in which the fish finishes cooking in a spicy, garlicky, vinegar-based marinade. It is best enjoyed with a cold beer, and is particularly popular during the warm spring months before the rains come. Ceviche has been eaten on the beaches of Mexico since the arrival of limes, a fruit that came over with the Spanish; and its preparation consists of cooking the fish in the acidic juice. Perhaps the most famous way to prepare it is "Acapulco style": the fish is marinated beforehand in lime juice to "cook" it, then complemented by tomato, onion, and fresh chiles—a spectacular combination. But any ceviche also goes perfectly with fried corn tortillas or tortilla chips. Along the same lines, we have cocktails garnished with raw or lightly cooked seafood like shrimp or crab.

"Cuñete.
In order to transport fish from one place to another before it decomposes, it is parboiled and prepared in a variety of manners, then placed with oil in small barrels, or *cuñetes* [...] The seasoned oil in which the fish is marinated is called *escabeche*."

Nuevo Cocinero Mejicano en Forma de Diccionario, page 237, s.v. cuñete.

IN

JAPAN

A PERSON
CONSUMES ON
AVERAGE
159
POUNDS
OF
FISH PER YEAR.
IN

MEXICO

THE FIGURE IS
22
POUNDS.

In the beginning, I used to do up a little frying pan's worth of food for myself to eat...

...and the fried fish smelled good. I lived in an old car I'd bought for twenty-five dollars. Soon, people from the beach started ordering food. I set up a little stand and sold the whole fish, fried and with tortillas, for five pesos. And I did well. I started selling fish in 1963. And today I'm 97 years old. I came here from Padilla, Tamaulipas. Back then people didn't eat fish like they do now. Today, everyone knows fish tacos, and people come from everywhere to eat them, from boats and from over the border. The first problem was the fish bones. The famous fish round here, like mackerel and flounder, are difficult to clean without leaving bones in them. A man they called "*El Bachigualato*" thought of using a type of shark, it was called the "little angel," for tacos in the early sixties. Shortly afterwards, I started to compete with him: I set up a little stand and three secondhand kids' tables and chairs, and I started selling fish near the market. This was back when a dozen fresh live lobsters cost three dollars at the port, and an order sold for a dollar. I used to prep the angel sharks for sale in central Mexico. I bought the fish at thirty pennies for five kilos. At the time people thought that shark meat was gross but, when you fried it and put it in a taco, nobody knew the difference, so I sold a lot to tourists from Tijuana and from southern California. It was my idea to batter the fish with flour, like my mother used to in Tamaulipas, so it wouldn't come apart in the frying pan. I invented the recipe to batter the fish that we use today. The trick is to dust the fish with flour, then coat it with a mixture of egg, milk, baking powder, and—the special touch that gives it more flavor—pork lard. I served it with sides of cabbage or lettuce and a salsa made from green tomato, onion, chile, and sometimes people add mayonnaise. It's easy to make them, but if you want to taste the real thing, Ensenada's the only place.

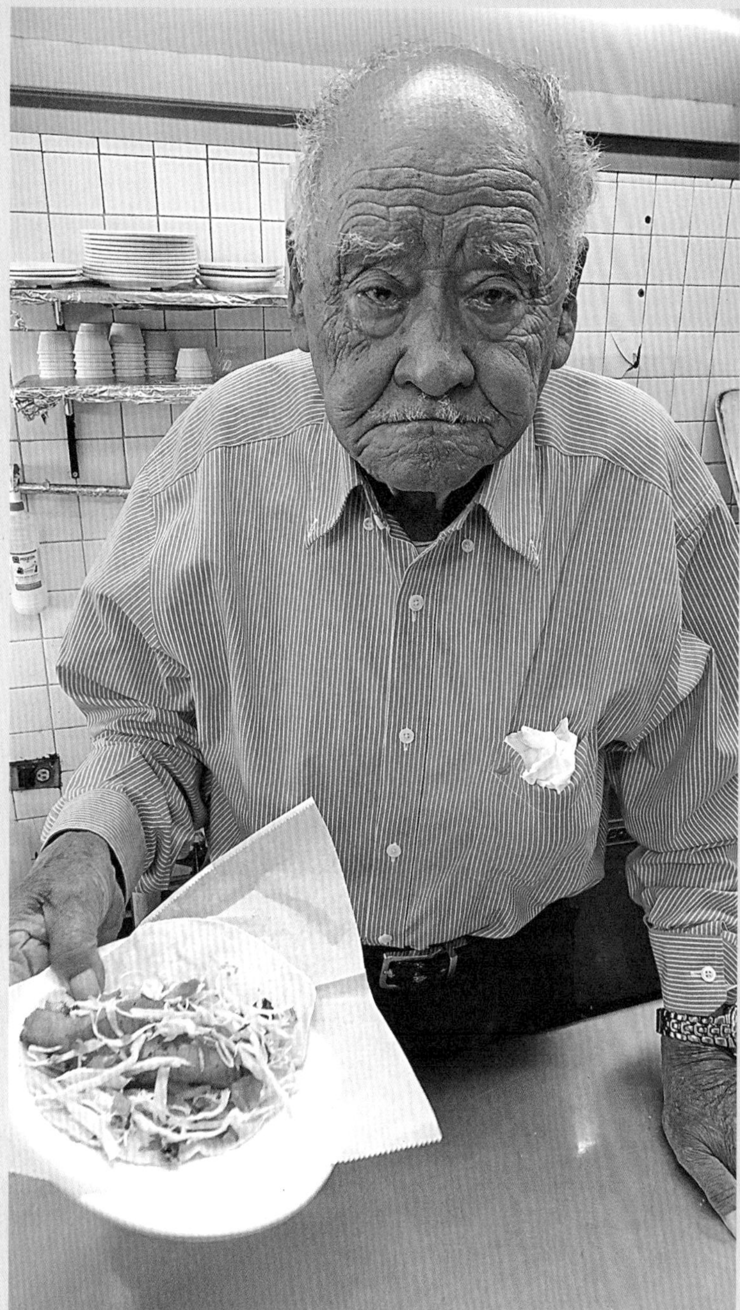

Zeferino Mancillas Fortuna
OWNER OF PLAYA AZUL RESTAURANT
113 RIVEROLL, ENSENADA
BAJA CALIFORNIA

50
PERCENT
OF ALL
FISH
CONSUMED
IN
MEXICO
EACH YEAR
IS EATEN DURING
LENT.

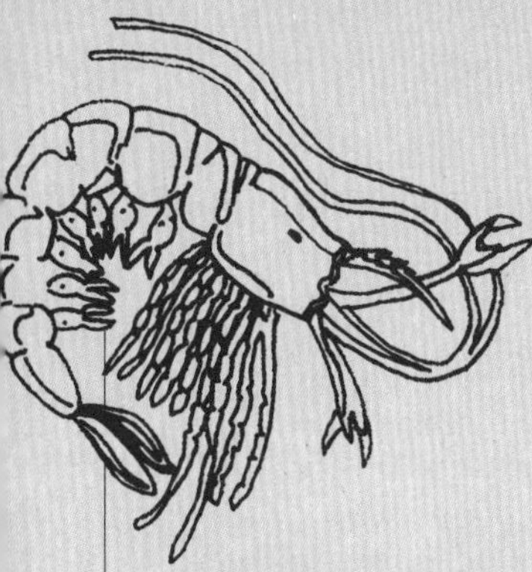

MEXICAN -STYLE SHRIMP TACOS

Serves 2

—2 tablespoons corn oil
—½ medium onion, finely chopped
—2 green serrano chiles (or to taste), seeded and thinly sliced
—2 medium tomatoes, peeled and finely chopped
—9 oz (250) g cocktail (or fresh) shrimp, peeled and cleaned
—3 sprigs cilantro
—Sea salt
—8 4⅓-inch (11 cm) corn tortillas

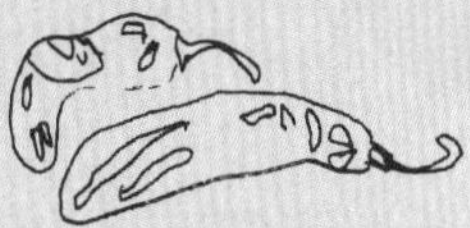

1. Heat the oil in a skillet over medium heat. Add the onion and fry for 2 minutes (do not let it brown).
2. Add the chiles and cook for a few seconds. Add the tomatoes, and cook for 3 minutes.
3. Add the shrimp, then cook for 1 minute, until the shrimp are just opaque and pink.
4. Add cilantro and salt to taste. Remove from heat and serve hot in the tortillas.

NORTHERN MEXICO-STYLE FRIED FISH TACOS

Serves 4

For the fish tacos:
—2¼ lb (1 kg) white fish fillet, cut into strips
—Sea salt
—1 cup (120 g) wheat flour
—Fish batter (see recipe at right)
—1 cup (250 ml) corn oil or lard
—8 4⅓-inch (11 cm) corn tortillas
—Shredded cabbage, to garnish
—Mayocream, to garnish (see next recipe)
—Lime halves and Mexican salsa (see recipes 1 and 18, page 296 and 302), for serving

For the spicy dressing (if desired):
—2 medium avocados, pitted and chopped
—2 green serrano chiles, halved and seeded
—3–5 tablespoons sour cream
—Sea salt

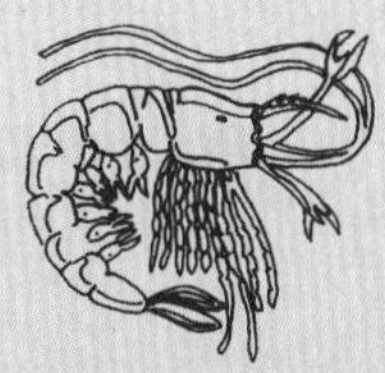

1. Cut the fish into strips, season with salt, then dredge in flour in a shallow bowl or plate, shaking off excess. Heat the oil or lard in a deep skillet.
2. Dip the fish in the batter, then fry in the skillet until golden, about 1–2 minutes per side. Place the finished fish on a paper towel to absorb the grease.
3. Prepare the tacos by placing a piece of fish in a tortilla with shredded cabbage on top. Garnish with mayocream, and serve with lime halves and Mexican salsa.
4. If desired, make a spicy dressing to accompany the tacos: blend the avocados, green chiles, sour cream, and salt in a blender until smooth.

MAYOCREAM

MAKES A GENEROUS 1 CUP (250 ML)

—½ teaspoon yellow mustard
—3 tablespoons mayonnaise
—1 cup (250 ml) sour cream
—Milk, sour cream, or corn oil (if necessary)
—Sea salt and freshly ground white pepper

Stir all the ingredients together in a small bowl until you have a smooth spread the consistency of regular mayonnaise. (If the mixture is too thick, you can add some milk, sour cream, or oil.) Season to taste and serve.

FISH BATTER

MAKES 1½ CUPS (350 ML)

—1 cup (125 g) all-purpose flour
—Sea salt and freshly ground black pepper
—1 large egg
—1 12-oz (350 ml) bottle of beer

1. Combine the flour, salt, and pepper on a large plate.
2. Stir in the egg and a little beer. Gently whisk the ingredients together, adding beer as needed until the mixture thickens to the consistency of pancake batter.

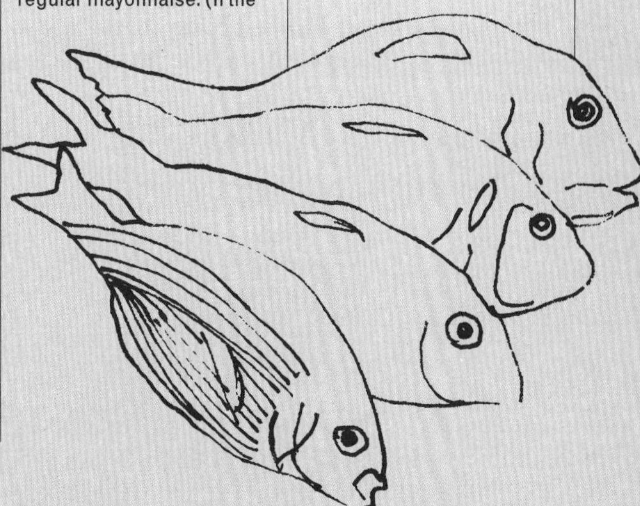

THE BEST

Boca del Río
42 RIBERA DE SAN COSME, COL. SAN RAFAEL, MEXICO CITY
One of the most traditional restaurants in Mexico City, it started as a street stand in the infamous Tepito district in 1941, and is known for its *Tacos al Patrón*, with shrimp, chipotle chile, and avocado.

Contramar
200 DURANGO, COL. ROMA, MEXICO CITY
One of the busiest seafood restaurants in Mexico City, the menu includes fish *carnitas* tacos, with the same characteristic flavor but without the stigma of pork meat.

El Pescadito
PASEO NEGRUMO, COL. DESARROLLO URBANO TRES RÍOS, CULIACÁN, SINALOA
The location in front of the government offices makes it a well-known reference point for locals, who crave their shrimp or breaded fish tacos. They even serve marlin tacos, a variety of swordfish that's a delicacy along the Pacific Coast.

El Porvenir
1403 HIDALGO (OPPOSITE THE CEMETERY) TAMPICO
Tampico's most traditional cantina, famous for its stewed seafood tacos (crab *salpicón*, fried roe, Mexican-style octopus, etc.) and their homemade cheese tortillas, also known as *asaderas*.

Entretanto
97 JUAN SALVADOR AGRAZ, SANTA FE, MEXICO CITY
Their cutting-edge Mexican fusion cuisine menu includes breaded shrimp tacos with *chamoy* sauce, served on thinly sliced jicama tortillas.

Los Arcos
CORNER OF XICOTENCATL AND LAGO CUITZEO, COL. LAS QUINTAS, CULIACÁN
Though there are more than twenty subsidiaries around the country (and one in San Diego, California), the original Los Arcos is located in Culiacán. Their grated shrimp tacos are so famous they're even copyrighted.

Pablo el Erizo
6 FERNANDO MONTES DE OCA, COL. CONDESA, MEXICO CITY
They not only brag about their Ensenada-style tacos (with shrimp and fish) but also about their Rosarito-style lobster, deep-fried and served with flour tortillas, rice, beans, and salsa.

Rosarito
ROSARITO, BAJA CALIFORNIA
On the coastal road between Tijuana and Ensenada lies this little village; its name is a synonym for lobster tacos on flour tortillas, with rice, beans, and salsa. Any of the many restaurants located here is guaranteed goodness.

Tacos El Fénix
CORNER OF 6TH STREET AND ESPINOZA, CENTRO, ENSENADA, BAJA CALIFORNIA
The local inhabitants of Ensenada recognize the quality of the fish and shrimp tacos served here. Their special appeal lies in the secret family recipe used for seasoning the coating.

Tacos Marco Antonio
RAYÓN (BETWEEN 3RD AND 4TH STREETS), COL. OBRERA, ENSENADA, BAJA CALIFORNIA
They offer dried and spiced yellow spin tuna and *caguatún* tacos, a local, tuna-based version of the *caguamanta* (a traditional manta ray stew from Sonora state).

RUTA DE
EVACUACION
Corona

EL BORREGO VIUDO
AL PASTOR
SUADERO
LONGANIZA
SESOS
LENGUA
TEPACHE
REFRESCOS
GRACIAS POR SU PREFERENCIA
RICOS TACOS DE
CABEZA
1969-2007
M.S.S.
Taqueria

Recent decades have witnessed the rise of a food of very humble origins: we've seen *suadero* move from shantytowns to the smartest avenues. Indeed, *suadero* is no longer a marginal curiosity—its privileged place in the world of street tacos is widely recognized. *Suadero* is made out of beef or pork, but it also includes offal and cold cuts, finely seasoned with cilantro, onion, and chiles. In this combination, the only true pre-Hispanic ingredients are the tortilla and the chiles, making it clear that Mexican cuisine is enriched and enhanced by its encounter with the old world.

A CHILANGO SPECIALTY

There's no doubt *suadero* comes from Mexico City, but no written account or testimony to its exact time or place of origin can be found. However, it seems logical that if fried pork is a delicacy, someone would eventually do the same with beef. The obscure origins of *suadero* tacos define their character, as their true flavor comes from the wisdom of the *vox populi* and they reflect the appetites of a whole culture. Fat and corn are always a great combination—even more so if you add a real spicy salsa. We're getting hungry just thinking about it!

SUADERO HAS MANY NAMES

Suadero or *fritanga* tacos are made from the most diverse beef cuts, including *suadero* and tripe (beef offal), as well as pork *longaniza. Suadero* is a beef cut from the lower parts of the cow, and it is known by many different names in different places: skirt, chest, *sobrebarriga*, *dorada*, *matambre*, *fresada*, flank steak, forequarter flank, *os blanc*, *nach-brust*, *petto sottile*, or, as the butcher would say: "the muscles we use for abdominal exercises." This cut left the back door of the kitchen and landed in the most popular dishes around the world, where it developed into many different recipes. It is a thin muscle intermingled with a lot of fat that requires long cooking hours in order to reach its characteristic softness and great flavor. Even though each cow yields just one portion of *suadero*, it is not an expensive cut; but its scarcity requires that it be mixed with other cuts, such as ribs, shoulders, and sirloin. Many people, both locals and foreigners, have yet to taste *suadero* tacos, though as a meat it is commonly found in different dishes and stews. The secret of *suadero* tacos lies in the special cooking technique: a convex-concave comal must be employed, a unique instrument unknown outside of Mexico. This comal allows for two simultaneous usages—it's a griddle and a deep-fryer at the same time! The meat

TYPICAL IN MEXICO CITY

MADE WITH BEEF AND PORK

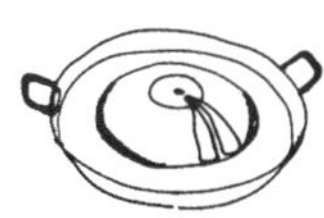

COOKED IN A CONVEX-CONCAVE COMAL

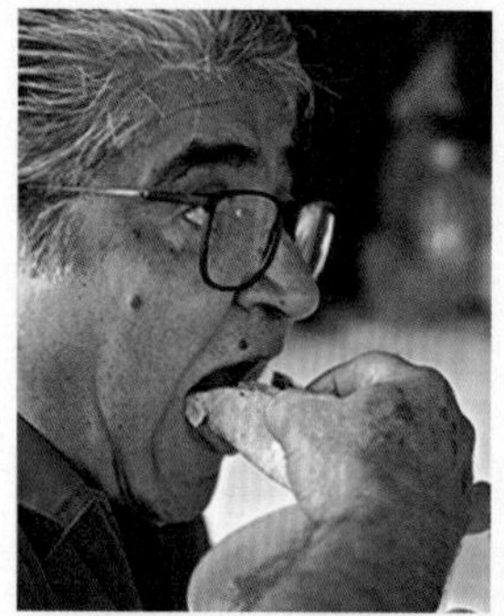

is simmered in oil on the concave side of the comal—a practice known as *confit* in other dishes—and it results in a meat that is crunchy on the outside and juicy on the inside. That's the reason why these tacos are also known as "*fritanga*"—a fry-up. All the meat and the sausages must be cooked in oil so that their own fat comes out, and since both pork sausage and beef are naturally fatty, this patient preparation brings out all of their virtues. Some people just use salt to season the meat, while others use milk and even sodas; in the end, the secret stays with the chef. The convex side of the artifact is where the tacos are finished up to perfection. When you place your order, the taco maker rescues a portion of meat from the sea of oil, and places it on the concave side of the comal, where the high temperatures take charge, help to release the oil and allow the meat to acquire its perfect, golden finish. Next, the meat is chopped on a thick chopping board and served over small tortillas with onion, cilantro, and hot salsa, with limes on the side. You can find *suadero* tacos at any time of the day, but they're more common at nighttime, when it's hard to see what's on your taco. However, for those who like to eat standing up by the side of a hot comal, there is just one important garnish: the salsa, above all red salsa. Of course, there are many choices in life, for example, raw green salsa, avocado salsa, or onion with manzano or habanero chiles. Many establishments also offer a variety of fresh garnishes, such as sliced cucumbers, radish, or *papaloquelites*. The convex-concave comal is also used to cook *nopales* (after being boiled to remove their natural slime), potatoes, slow-cooked green onions, or anything else that springs from the imagination of the taco makers.

NOT JUST ONE

When we talk about *suadero* tacos we're really talking about three different kinds of meat: *suadero* itself, tripe, and *longaniza*. Another classic version are the *campechano* tacos, where the first two ingredients shake hands. When we say tripe, we simply mean beef intestines, both small and large, which must be very clean. In some places you also find *machitos*, a special preparation of sausages artistically tied together, first boiled in broth and then deep-fried until golden. *Machitos* can also be made from lamb tripe. *Longaniza* is a kind of pork sausage stuffed with chiles and spices and cured for a relatively long period of time. Different varieties have different proportions of fat, spices, and meat. In the case of beef *longaniza*, the small intestine is cleaned up and stuffed with a special paste made out of a range of different entrails, lean meat, and fat from the same animal, ground together with spices, chiles, and salt, and cured the same way as pork sausage. Many people prefer the pork version because of the particular flavor contributed by the lard. Nowadays, the majority of the taco places that sell *suadero* also serve other beef cuts; beefsteaks are grilled on the convex section of the comal and seasoned with the fat from the mixture. Sometimes you can also find pork *cecina* or *carne enchilada* tacos in these same places. These are tacos made with thin pork steaks that have been marinated or seasoned, and are cooked to order on the convex part of the comal.

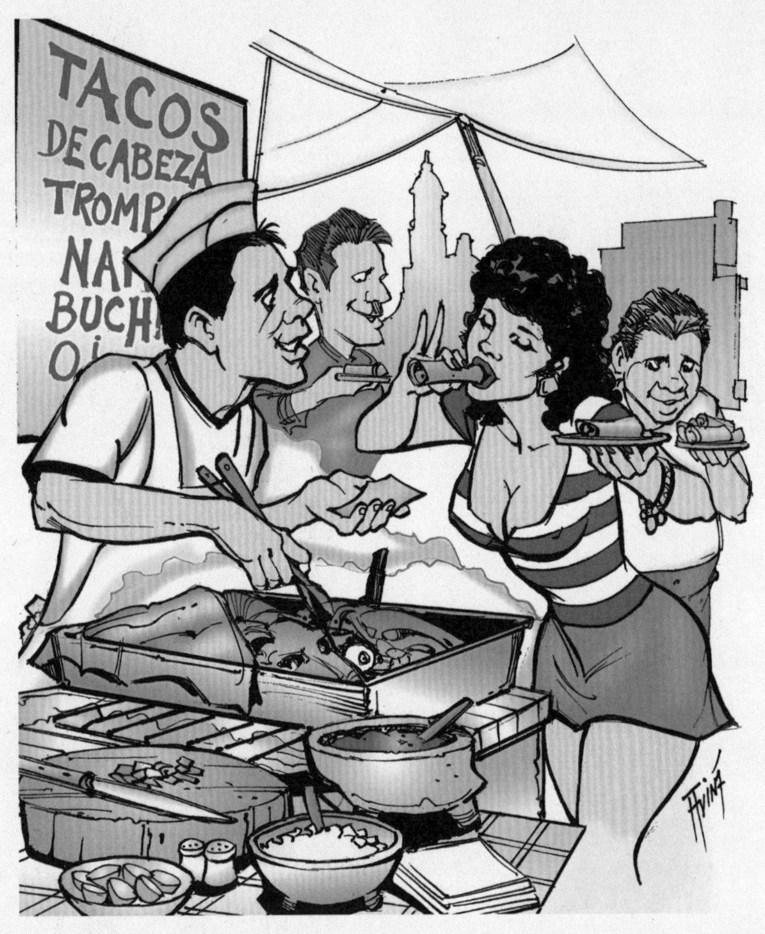

"AQUÍ NOMÁS, ECHÁNDOME UN TACO DE OJO."

"I'm just enjoying an eyeball taco."

Meaning you're taking pleasure
from looking at something you cannot touch.

SUADERO TACOS ARE THE ONLY TACOS TO HAVE BEEN INVENTED IN MEXICO CITY

(AS FAR AS WE KNOW).

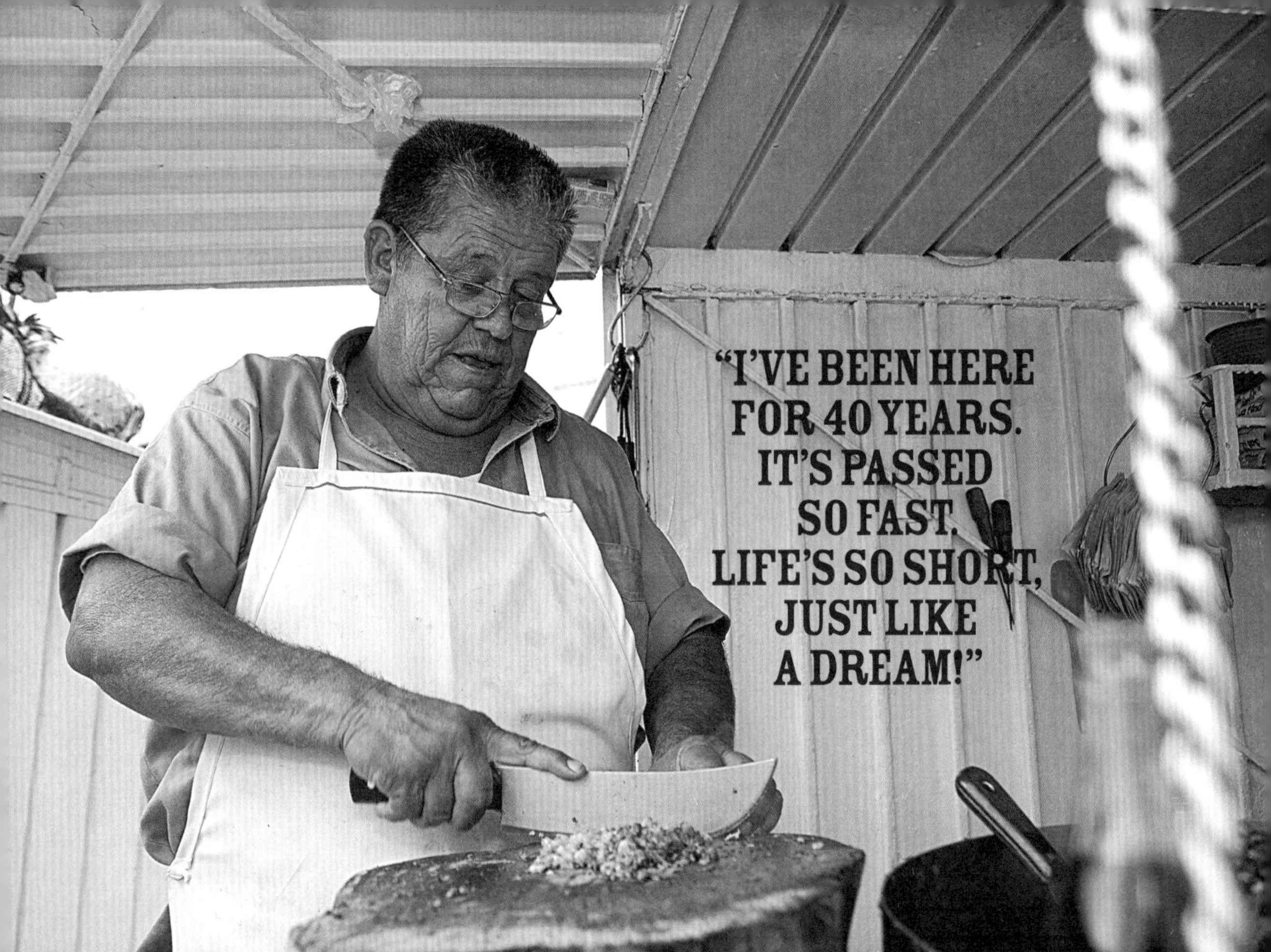
"I'VE BEEN HERE
FOR 40 YEARS.
IT'S PASSED
SO FAST.
LIFE'S SO SHORT,
JUST LIKE
A DREAM!"

The authentic *suadero* comes from the brisket.

However, it's not a lot of meat and it's tough as leather. That's why we end up adding ribs or any other cut. Here we use chuck, which is a kind of rib, but as long as it's beef, really any meat can be used for making *suadero* tacos. The cooking time is what's important; the preparation needs the right amount of heat to get its flavor. Making *suadero* requires patience: it takes at least 2½ hours, depending on the texture of the meat. Some people boil it beforehand, but not us. It goes raw right into the comal with the rest of the ingredients, oil, and seasonings. Then it's like any other food, it demands a special touch: low heat, turn it up a little, not too much, whatever it takes so that the result is soft and tasty. Then we season it and move it to one side, remove the excess fat, and serve it up: a golden meat without any fat. Fat is our enemy. I taught myself fifty years ago, in Tacubaya. I would go there regularly to eat my tacos, and one time, at a taco place called "La Espuma de Oro," close to the Tacuba traffic circle, they asked me if I wanted to help sell the drinks. That's how I began to teach myself how to do it right. Later on I had other jobs, but I soon realized they were not my path. I started selling tacos here when I got married. It's been forty years so far here in Ixtapaluca: life goes by too fast. You look back and you say: life's so short, just like a dream! We Mexicans love tacos. Some people eat just three tacos, but I've seen clients eat fourteen or fifteen. They're good, for all tastes. In this job you don't really need much if you know how to do it, a comal, a burner, a roof, a good little salsa, good flavor, good hygiene, and to know how to cook it. It's the preparation that's really important.

Martín Alcalá González
OWNER AND TACO MAKER, TACOS DE CABEZA, TRIPA Y SUADERO
KM 27.5, MEXICO-PUEBLA FEDERAL HIGHWAY (BY THE FIRE STATION)
IXTAPALUCA, STATE OF MEXICO

IN THE EARLY '80S, THE SINGER TACO OCKERSE —KNOWN AS TACO— MADE IT TO THE BILLBOARD HOT 100. HE THOUGHT HE HAD THE SPECIAL SAUCE.

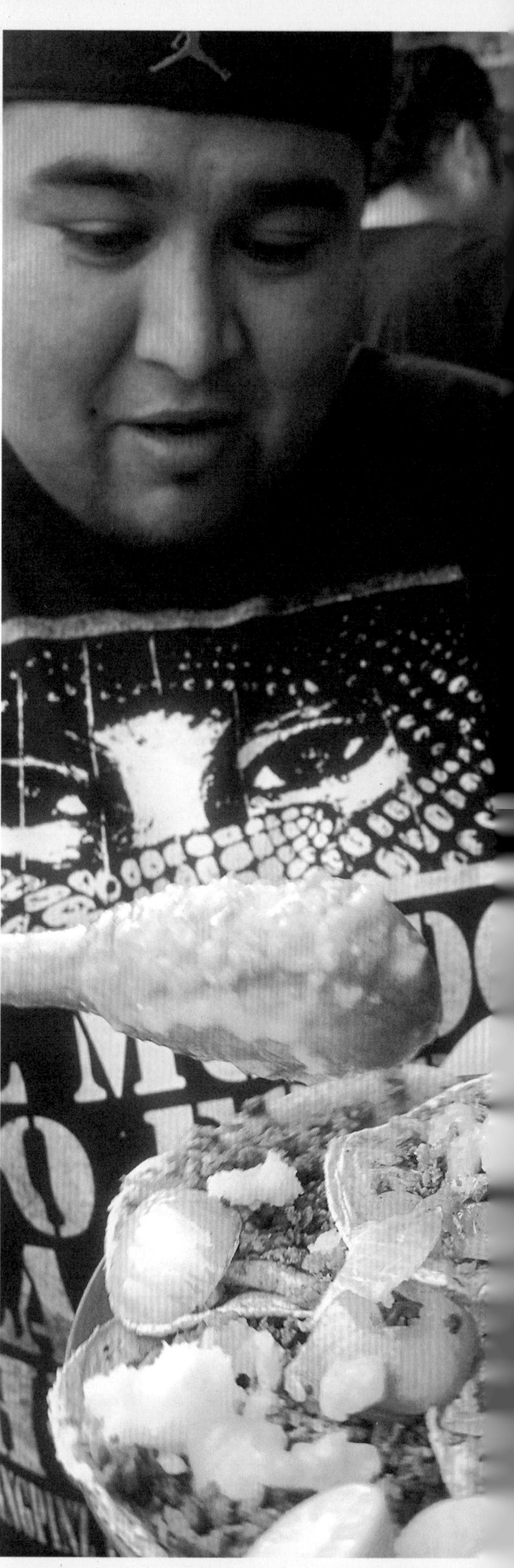

SUADERO TACOS WITH CHEESE AND EPAZOTE

Serves 4

—1 lb (450 g) *suadero* or skirt steak
—¼ medium onion
—1 clove garlic
—1 bay leaf
—Sea salt
—2 tablespoons corn oil
—7 oz (200 g) Chihuahua cheese, grated
—5 or 6 leaves epazote, thinly chopped
—Salsa (see recipes 7, 11, 12, 13, 15, 16, or 30, pages 297–307), for serving

1. Place the meat in a large pot and cover with water. Add the onion, garlic, bay leaf, and salt. Bring the water to a boil, cover, and reduce heat to medium for 1½ hours or until the meat is tender (40 minutes in a pressure cooker).
2. Remove from heat; let the meat cool in its own broth, then transfer the meat to a cutting board and dice; discard the broth.
3. Heat the oil in a large pan over medium heat. Add the meat and fry until crispy, about 3–5 minutes.
4. When the meat looks ready, lower the heat and add the grated cheese and epazote. Cover the pan and cook until the cheese melts.
5. Take the covered pan to the table. Uncover the pan and use a spatula to serve the meat from the bottom, with the melted cheese on top. Serve with salsa.

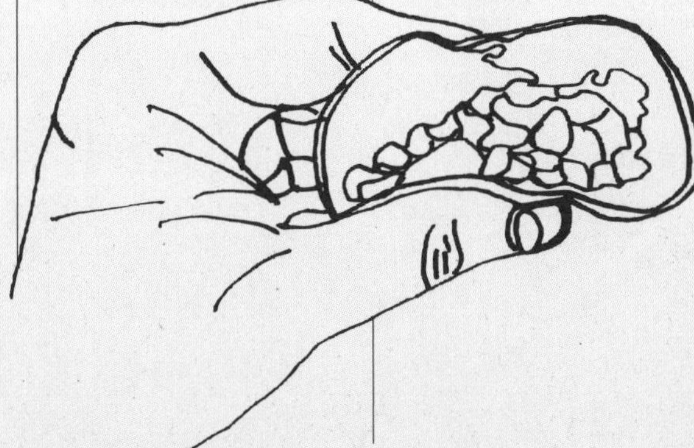

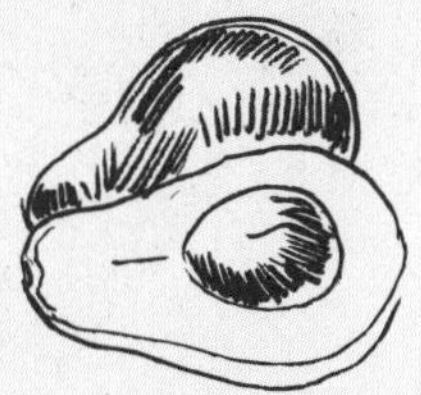

TACOS CAMPECHANOS WITH LONGANIZA AND SUADERO

Serves 6

—1 lb (450 g) *suadero* or skirt steak
—¼ medium onion
—1 clove garlic
—1 bay leaf
—Sea salt
—⅔ cup (150 ml) corn oil
—9 oz (250 g) *longaniza*, chopped
—6–12 4⅓-inch (11 cm) corn tortillas, for serving
—Chopped onion, finely chopped cilantro, lime wedges, chopped cucumber, radishes, and salsas (see recipes 7, 11, 12, 13, and 16, pages 297–302), for garnish

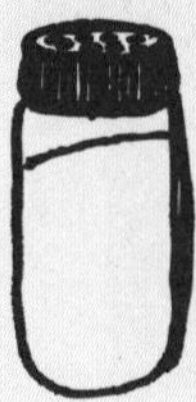

1. Place the *suadero* in a large pot and add enough water to cover.
2. Add the onion, garlic, bay leaf, and salt, and bring to a boil. Reduce heat to medium-low and cook for 1½ hours or until the meat is tender (40 minutes in a pressure cooker).
3. Let the meat cool in its own broth, then transfer to a cutting board and dice.
4. Heat 2 tablespoons oil in a large pan over low heat. Add the sausage and fry until it releases all its fat and turns crispy, about 3–5 minutes. Remove the sausages from heat and finely chop. If there's too much fat on the pan, strain it.
5. Return the pan to medium and brown with 2 tablespoons of oil for 3–5 minutes. When the meat is ready, add the sausage and cook for 1 minute.
6. Dip the tortillas in the remaining oil and heat up on the griddle until crisp.
7. Make your tacos with a little meat and sausage, and serve with the garnishes.

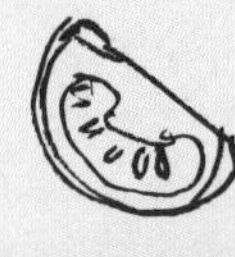

TRIPE TACOS

Serves 4

—8 lb (3.5 kg) tripe (cow's small intestine; you can buy raw at the butcher)
—1 medium onion
—1 clove garlic
—2 bay leaves
—Sea salt
—4¼ cups (1 liter) corn oil

1. Cut the tripe into 8-inch-long pieces, then clean it thoroughly inside and outside with plenty of water.
2. Add the tripe to a large pot with enough water to cover, along with onion, garlic, bay leaves, and salt. Bring to a simmer and cook 1 hour or until tender.
3. Strain the tripe and discard the water and vegetables.
4. Heat the oil in a large skillet over low heat. Add the tripe and cook until golden brown (this can take up to an hour).
5. Raise the heat to medium-high just before serving so the tripe gets really crispy. Transfer the meat to a cutting board and chop before preparing the tacos.

THE BEST

El Paisa de la Escandón

CORNER OF JOSÉ MARTÍ AND GRAL. FRANCISCO MURGUÍA, COL. ESCANDÓN, MEXICO CITY

Between the Condesa and Tacubaya neighborhoods lies this taco stand, famous for its *suadero* and its unusual orange-hued salsa.

El Pastorcito

4503 LORENZO BOTURINI, COL. 24 DE ABRIL, MEXICO CITY

Mostly visited by Mexico City's night owls, it's known for the tacos *al pastor* that give it its name, and also for the *suadero* tacos.

El Rey del Suadero

206 HORACIO, COL. POLANCO, MEXICO CITY

Upmarket Polanco might appear too fancy for a taco place that specializes in not-so-glam *suadero*, but its loyal clientele don't seem to care.

El Tinacal

17 PAFNUNCIO PADILLA, CIUDAD SATÉLITE, STATE OF MEXICO

A very successful *pulquería* offering "milk-calf tripe": grilled and golden and served with different salsas and a tasty house guacamole.

El Torito

83-A ISABEL LA CATÓLICA, CENTRO HISTÓRICO, MEXICO CITY

Their very spicy red salsa enhances the flavor of the tripe tacos prepared here, griddled on a comal before being served.

La Insurgenta

952 INSURGENTES SUR, COL. DEL VALLE, MEXICO CITY

This fancy cantina has a menu that offers *suadero* tacos as well as *chinchulines* (Argentine-style tripe) with pan-fried chiles.

La Lupe

45 AVENIDA DE LA PAZ, SAN ÁNGEL, MEXICO CITY

A concept restaurant that reproduces all the classic aspects of a cantina—including a menu with "low-class" food, such as *suadero* tacos—for a wealthy clientele.

La Tapatía

20 AZTECAS, COL. TEPITO, MEXICO CITY

Nestled for over half a century in the famously rough neighborhood of Tepito, behind the Granaditas market, this place may be identified by its tacos made of tripe and other entrails.

Tacos Álvaro Obregón

90 ÁLVARO OBREGÓN, COL. ROMA, MEXICO CITY

The swift service, long opening hours, and *suadero* tacos made this place a landmark long before the Roma neighborhood became fashionable among young and trendy night owls.

Tacos Charly

201 SAN FERNANDO (CORNER OF FUENTES), COL. TORIELLO GUERRA, MEXICO CITY

Found along the road linking Insurgentes and Tlalpan avenues, this taco stand for insomniacs is famous for its *suadero* and its arbol chile salsa.

RICOS TACOS

Eating deep-fried tacos, also known as *flautas* if they're long enough, requires special skills. You must be able to pick up the salsa, keep the sour cream under control, and avoid spilling the lettuce. The most skilled diners even learn how to keep their hands clean in the process. But it's a skill acquired through frequent practice, and deep-fried tacos are a favorite in many households, as they can be stuffed with different kinds of shredded meat, *barbacoa*, and potatoes, among other ingredients. They can also be found at special occasions, diners, street stands, and specialist restaurants. They are even prepared with high-quality ingredients in elegant restaurants, making them an haute cuisine dish. Deep-fried tacos are a contrast between fried and fresh, tart and fatty, and cold and hot. It's all about the game of oppositions, resulting in a dish that brings pleasure to any palate.

TYPICAL THROUGHOUT MEXICO

MADE WITH BEEF, LAMB, CHICKEN, POTATOES, BEANS, CHEESE

COOKED IN A SKILLET

TRADITIONAL FROM EAST TO WEST

It's easy to imagine that their usual name, *flautas* (flutes), comes from their characteristic cylindrical shape, but this is no more than a wild guess. However, we do know for sure that, as a fried dish, their origin can be traced back to colonial times, when olive oil and pork lard first arrived in the Americas. These tacos are very traditional all over Mexico, and each region or household uses its particular ingredients and techniques. They are often eaten as the main meal at lunchtime, though traditionally they are an evening snack. Elsewhere, they can be found on sale at any time of the day, but not usually late at night.

WE'RE CRISPY!

Deep-fried tacos are basically a rolled tortilla that's been stuffed with something, then deep-fried in plenty of oil or lard. The dryness of the fried tortilla is balanced out with the fresh sides it's served with: salsas, salads, sour cream, and cheese are not just optional, but also an essential part of the experience. These tacos are very easy to make, but the secret lies in using fresh tortillas, because they're elastic and flexible. Once filled and rolled, they must be covered with a tea towel and allowed to rest for a while, so they keep their shape during the frying process. Toothpicks are also commonly used to stop them unrolling. The salsas and sides are spooned onto the tacos right as they're being served. With the exception of *codzitos*, a Yucatán specialty that is stuffed only with thin air, all deep-fried tacos come with some kind of filling: shredded beef, chicken or lamb *barbacoa*-style or just boiled; potatoes, beans, cheese, or *requesón*, by themselves or with condiments; and a great variety of home-made preparations, including picadillo, sliced poblano chiles, or fish and seafood. In fact, in every corner of the country a different version of deep-fried tacos is to be found, distinguished by a small detail, a local touch: they are in fact the quintessence of Mexican gastronomy. A few of these different styles are described below.

HOME-STYLE DEEP-FRIED TACOS

These tacos are made from round tortillas fried in oil, and are served in portions of three tacos per plate. They can be stuffed with chicken, shredded beef, picadillo, potatoes, potatoes and chorizo, beans, cheese, and a variety of home-made stews. You can serve them with green or red salsa (either cooked or raw), lettuce, sliced tomatoes, onion, avocado or guacamole, sour cream, and grated white cheese. Sometimes they're also served with a side of refried beans.

BANQUET-STYLE DEEP-FRIED TACOS

This may be the most distinguished and celebrated presentation of deep-fried tacos. For special occasions, people prepare large quantities of the specialty, artistically displayed on large platters as appetizers at parties and family gatherings. They're made with regular tortillas, filled with chicken or cheese, and cut in half, as you should be able to eat them standing up without the need for plates or cutlery. They should be attractively arranged on platters, accompanied with raw red or green salsa, salads, sour cream, and grated white cheese. Pickled chiles or *escabeche* (see recipe 31, page 308) are a good match, too. It's also common to see them served along with other small snacks or miniature *antojitos* on the same dish, like quesadillas or *chalupas* (see page 275).

FLAUTAS

Flautas are another popular version of deep-fried tacos; they're made from a special large oblong-shaped tortilla known as a *memela*. Their thin, elongated shape resembles the musical instrument whose name it shares. They must be very tight and fried in oil. The three main versions of *flautas* are: diner-style, street-stand-style, and creamy. Diner-style *flautas* are very common in Mexico City. They're stuffed with cheese or *barbacoa* (see page 101) and served with red or green salsa, onion, sliced tomatoes, avocado, cheese, and sour cream. Meanwhile, it's common to find street stands selling *flautas* at town fairs and traditional festivities around the country. These street-stand *flautas* are similar to the first version, but much larger, fried in

> “Instead of answering, I got up, paid with a ten-peso bill, and walked out without even waiting for the change or saying good-bye. I saw death everywhere: in the little pieces of animal about to become sandwiches and tacos, along with the onions, tomatoes, lettuce, cheese, cream, beans, guacamole, jalapeño peppers. Live animals like the trees they had just finished pruning on Insurgentes. [...] It's one of Rosales's bluffs, an idiotic joke, he has always been a jerk. He wanted to get his revenge because I saw him starving to death with his little box of chewing gum and me with my tennis racket, my white suit, my Perry Mason in English, my reservations at the Plaza. I don't care if Jim opens the door: I don't care if I make a fool of myself. Even though everyone is going to laugh at me, I want to see Mariana."
>
> **JOSÉ EMILIO PACHECO.**
> *Battles in the Desert & Other Stories,* Trans. Katherine Silver. New York: New Directions, 1987.

pork lard, and served one by one. They're stuffed with the same ingredients, and served with lettuce, onion, sliced tomatoes, avocado, cheese, and sour cream. They're also good with pasilla chile sauce and just a mix of onion and cilantro. Finally, we have the famous creamy *flautas*. That's precisely what people mean by the expression "You add a lot of sour cream to your tacos," because, as everyone knows, the presence of sour cream adds class to any taco. They're also served in portions of three or on larger platters, and filled with lamb *barbacoa*, shredded chicken or beef, mashed potatoes, asadero cheese, or refried beans. In addition to the usual grated cheese and sour cream, these *flautas* swim in a pool of cooked green salsa, cooked red ancho chile salsa, or cooked red salsa, or even with two different salsas at once. Bathing them in *mole* and serving with onion rings is another classic combination. Because every version has its own particular characteristics and ingredients, we've detailed them in the following sections. But the element that's common to all of them is the salsa, which cannot be missed and gives each possibility its unique flavor. Sour cream is also present in most varieties, as well as the lettuce, onion, and avocado. Or it can be cabbage and cilantro... these seem like details, but that's where the character of the taco lies.

FROM SONORA TO YUCATÁN...

Many parts of the country claim their own version of deep-fried tacos. Every one of these varieties has a special something that makes them delicious and unique.

CHIMICHANGAS

Chimichangas are one of the most important dishes in Sonora's cuisine, typically eaten in the late afternoon. They are made from flour tortillas and they're closed at the ends, which gives them that special touch. Fried flour tortillas are actually delicious, though somewhat fatty. That's why they're usually balanced by crisp cabbage, sliced tomatoes, onion, and a red salsa that's a perfect match.

CODZITOS

These Yucatán-style deep-fried tacos, known

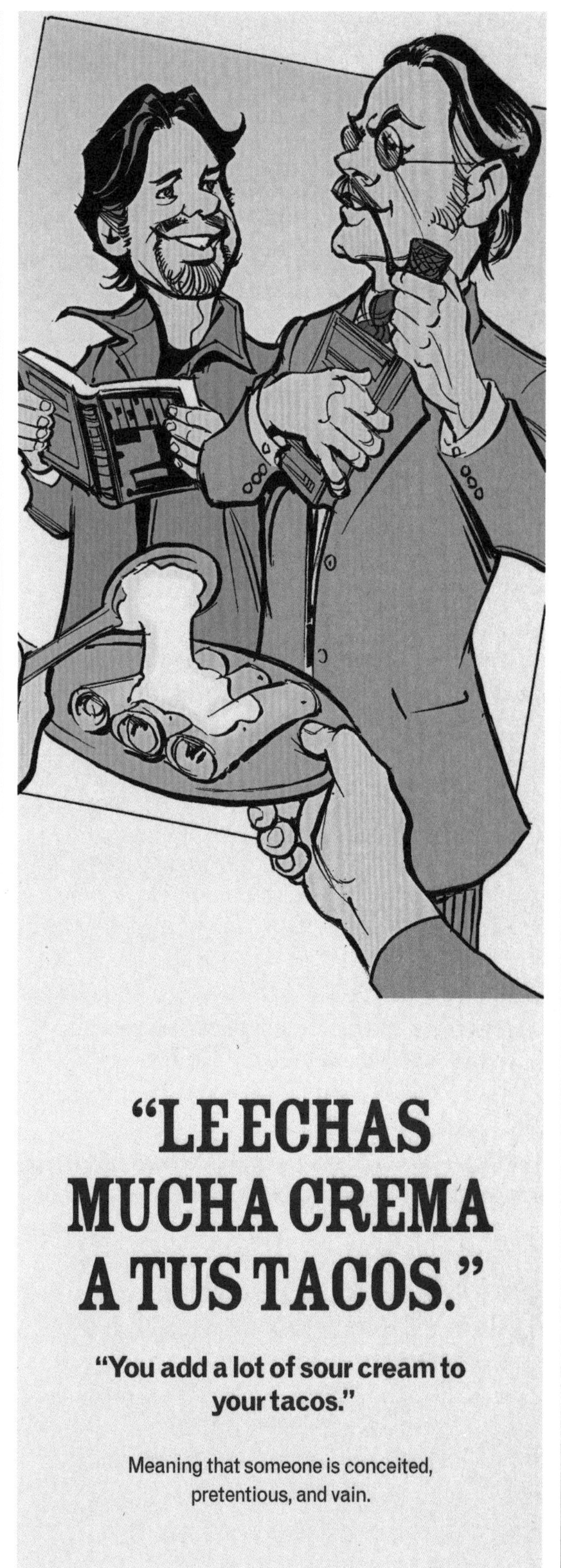

"LE ECHAS MUCHA CREMA A TUS TACOS."

"You add a lot of sour cream to your tacos."

Meaning that someone is conceited, pretentious, and vain.

as *codzitos*, are made from small, round corn tortillas that are fried in pork lard and served in portions of three; they're the perfect companion for soups and broths. They do not have any filling at all, but you can top them with cooked tomato and habanero salsa, grated white cheese, and, sometimes, with chopped hard-boiled eggs.

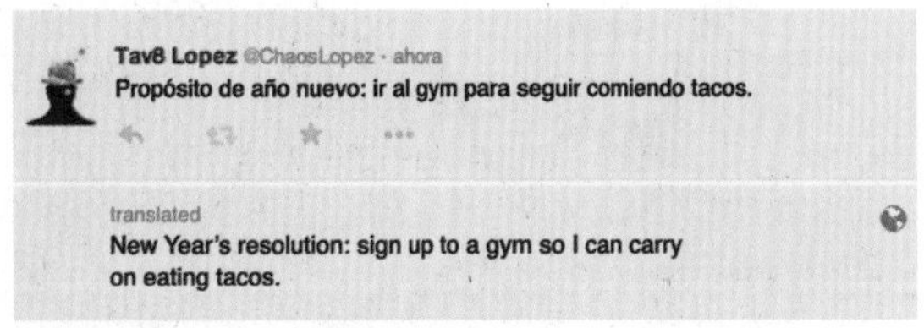

DEEP-FRIED TACOS MORELOS-STYLE

These are also made from small, round corn tortillas, fried in pork lard, and served in trios. In their home in the state of Morelos, they are typically eaten with a hearty serving of *pozole* soup. They're stuffed with chicken, mashed potato, or *requesón*, and garnished with a side of cooked red tomato salsa, sour cream, and grated white cheese.

DEEP-FRIED TACOS SAN LUIS POTOSÍ–STYLE

The principal characteristic of these tacos is that they're made from small, round, red tortillas (to achieve the red color, the dough is stained with chipotle and guajillo chiles), which are folded in half like a quesadilla and stuffed with potatoes. They're initially fried in pork lard, and then reheated on a charcoal grill just before serving. Red salsa, made from chiltepin or piquin chiles (also known as *chiles de monte* or wild chiles in Mexico), lettuce, tomato, onion, and pickled pork rinds are their usual companions.

DEEP-FRIED TACOS SINALOA-STYLE

Just like most versions of deep-fried tacos, they're made from round tortillas, fried in oil, and served in trios, but they're filled with marlin, tuna, or shrimp *machaca*, cooked with onion and tomatoes. They can be served with cooked red tomato salsa, mayonnaise, sour cream, or a homemade preparation of "mayocream" (see page 213). The classic garnishes or accompaniments include cabbage, avocado, and cucumbers. There's also a delicious regional dish that consists of a helping of these deep-fried tacos filled with marlin, served inside a bowl of fish or shrimp broth.

DEEP-FRIED TACOS GRINGO-STYLE

These are the taco shells that are commonly found in the United States. A round tortilla is deep-fried with the help of a mold to give it the traditional U-shape, and then it's filled with ground beef, grilled pork, or chili con carne, and garnished with cooked red tomato salsa, lettuce, sliced tomatoes, onion, sour cream, and grated cheese (such as cheddar or Monterrey Jack).

REQUESÓN CHEESE TACOS

These plain tacos, originally from Michoacán, may not have the fame and splendor of pork *carnitas*—the state's most renowned taco export—but they are absolutely delicious nonetheless, especially as a dinner option. *Requesón* is a dairy product with a coarse and crumbly texture—not unlike ricotta—that really comes into its own when heated, as for this recipe. It is a very simple style of deep-fried taco, and is ideally served with an onion salsa with manzano chile (see recipe 6, page 297). The resulting contrast between flavors and temperatures is just perfect.

BEACH TACOS

A corn tortilla folded over any ingredient, deep-fried in plenty of oil, and pierced with a toothpick so that it holds its shape: that's the *taco playero* or beach taco. They are also known as fried quesadillas, and you can find fish, shredded beef, and mashed potato versions, among other options.

CHUCHULUCOS

Tightly rolled, small tacos, sometimes sliced up to be served in bite-size pieces like canapés on a platter. They are typically made with chicken, shredded beef, or mashed potato.

Our secret lies in the quality, intensity, taste, and quantity.

And above all, in the cost-benefit analysis! We also take care of the atmosphere, cleanliness, and good service. We prepare our food in front of our customers so they can see what they're paying for. Our special *flauta* is made from beef—that's the one people prefer, but we also have other combinations, like the ones with mashed potato, chicken, or cheese. Our contribution to the world of *flautas* is in how they are presented. The classic *flauta* is served over a bed of sour cream, with red salsa on one side and green salsa on the other, like the colors of the Mexican flag. We make everything ourselves, it's an artisanal labor, from shredding the meat and cheese; we ensure a perfect cut, so you won't bite into any large pieces of meat. The broth is essential for a perfect pairing, that's how we call it —though it's not wine and cheese— but there's a perfect pairing between the *flauta* and the broth. A liquid and a solid, two different flavors that combine perfectly in your mouth. We give a cup of broth for free with all of our dishes; that's our trademark. Actually, our clients won't buy the *flautas* if we run out of broth. People who work close by come to us early in the morning for a cup of broth, especially if they are hungover! We have all kinds of clients, from the poorest to the richest, people from the garages, market vendors, and actors and people working at Televisa. Especially on weekends, since we're right under a theater, as you can see... Here at our stand, which has been here for twenty-three years, we sell about 500 orders a day (with three *flautas* each), every day of the year. In the restaurant, we sell around 300 orders, and close to 200 at our stand in Plaza Insurgentes. We know when the Attorney General wants *flautas*, because he sends his secretary with a silver tray. Sometimes they call ahead of time, "We want thirty-two *flautas*," the number that fits on the tray. "Only with meat, and a lot of salsa on the side." They always take their broth too, they can't be doing without that.

"THE CLASSIC FLAUTA IS SERVED WITH CREAM, AND RED AND GREEN SALSAS: THE SAME COLORS AS THE MEXICAN FLAG."

Elías Torres Cortés
OWNER AND CHEF, FLAUTOMANÍA
CENTRO CULTURAL TELMEX
19 CUAUHTÉMOC, COL. ROMA, MEXICO CITY

The meat is shredded...

FLAUTAS

FROM THE MARKET

They're fried...

And garnished with lettuce, cheese, and sour cream...

Tortillas are stuffed and rolled...

Laid out on the dish...

Enjoy!

BANQUET OF CHICKEN TACOS

Serves 4

—$2\frac{1}{4}$ lb (1 kg) boneless and skinless chicken breast
—2 bay leaves
—3 black peppercorns
—Sea salt
—16 $4\frac{1}{3}$-inch (11 cm) corn tortillas
—2 cups (500 ml) corn oil
—Lettuce leaves
—Sour cream, green salsa (see recipe 3, page 296), Cotija cheese, sliced onion, radish, and pickled chiles (see recipe 31, page 308), for serving

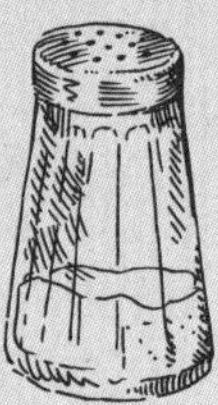

1. Bring a pot of water to a boil. Add the chicken breast, bay leaves, peppercorns, and salt, and bring to a boil, decrease the heat to low, and simmer for 1 hour.
2. Strain the chicken and let cool on a plate, covered, until cold. Shred the chicken and set aside.
3. Warm the tortillas in a skillet, then stuff each with 2 tablespoons of the shredded chicken and put them on a plate. Cover the tacos with a tea towel and let settle for an hour.
4. Heat the oil in a deep skillet. Add the tacos and fry 3–4 tacos at a time until they're golden brown, about $1\frac{1}{2}$ minutes on each side. Transfer the finished tacos to a plate lined with paper towels to soak up the excess oil.
5. Spread lettuce leaves around the edges of a large tray. Cover the bottom of the tray with some of the remaining lettuce, finely chopped.

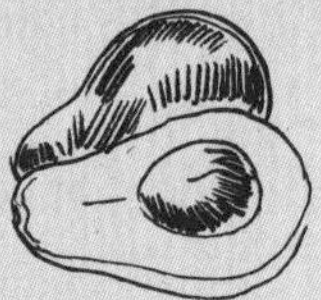

6. Cut the tacos in half and place on top of the lettuce, making two layers of tacos. Decorate with streaks of sour cream.
7. Use a spoon to add green salsa on top of each of the tacos. Shred or grate some Cotija cheese and spread it all over the tray.
8. Scatter sliced onion, radish, and the rest of the chopped lettuce as the final decoration. Serve with pickled chiles.

CHIMICHANGAS

Serves 4

—1 cup (250 ml) plus 3 tablespoons corn oil
—$\frac{1}{2}$ medium onion, chopped
—1 medium tomato, peeled and diced
—1 chipotle chile in vinegar, seeded, deveined, and finely chopped
—9 oz (250 g) refried black beans (see page 139)
—Sea salt
—5 oz (150 g) grated Chihuahua cheese
—12 $4\frac{1}{3}$-inch (11 cm) corn tortillas
—Finely chopped cabbage, sliced tomatoes, sliced onion, sliced avocado, sour cream, roasted red salsa (see recipe 11, page 300), for garnish

1. Heat 3 tablespoons of oil in a large skillet. Add the onion and fry lightly for 1 minute. Add the tomato and cook for 1 minute. Add the chile and cook for 1 minute. Add the beans and a pinch of salt; cook over low heat for 3–5 minutes. Remove the skillet from heat and spoon the mixture onto a tray until cool. Add the grated cheese and stir to combine.
2. Slightly heat the tortillas until they're flexible enough to fold.
3. Add 1 tablespoon of beans and cheese to each tortilla. Fold up the ends and then roll the tortillas as if closing a package. (You can use a toothpick to secure)
4. Heat the remaining oil in a deep skillet. Once hot, add the tacos and fry until golden brown, about $1\frac{1}{2}$ minutes on each side. Transfer to a plate lined with paper towels.
5. Garnish the tacos with the chopped vegetables, avocado, sour cream, and salsa, and serve.

REQUESÓN TACOS

Serves 4

—3 epazotle leaves, chopped
—9 oz (250 g) fresh *requesón* cheese
—Sea salt
—12 $4\frac{1}{3}$-inch (11 cm) fresh corn tortillas
—3 tablespoons corn oil
—Chopped cilantro and manzano chile onion salsa (see recipe 6, page 297), for garnish

1. Mix the epazotle and cheese together in a small bowl. Season to taste with salt.
2. Add a spoonful of the mix to each tortilla, spreading it along the surface. Then, roll your tacos tightly.
3. Heat the oil in a deep skillet. Once hot, fry the tacos until golden brown, about 1 minute on each side.
4. Remove the tacos to a plate lined with paper towels. Serve immediately, garnished with the cilantro and salsa.

THE BEST

Cenaduría Chayito
2407 TENIENTE AZUETA,
CENTRO, MAZATLÁN
Half a century of being a local favorite guarantees the quality of the deep-fried tacos (and the grilled beef tacos) from this spot in the center of Mazatlán.

El Rey de las Ahogadas
360 COYOACÁN,
COL. DEL VALLE,
MEXICO CITY
Stunning presentation of chicken, potato, beans, or beef *flautas*, served in a deep dish with onion and green tomato broth, like enchiladas.

El Socio
202 AL ARROYO,
COL. PRADOS VALLARTA,
ZAPOPAN, JALISCO
Their "house" ground beef filling has a special bacon flavor; served with a special hot tomato salsa and an arbol chile salsa.

La Casa de Toño
439 CUAUHTÉMOC,
COL. NARVARTE,
MEXICO CITY
Their beef, chicken, and potato *flautas*—along with their *pozole* and other goodies—create long lines that stop the traffic in front of the Plaza Delta mall.

La Flautería
87-A NUEVO LEÓN (CORNER OF CADEREYTA), COL. CONDESA,
MEXICO CITY
You can choose from potatoes, chicken, *barbacoa*, cheese, and beans with cheese, in addition to a delicious broth with rice, chickpeas, and shredded chicken or giblets.

La Valentina
393 MASARYK,
COL. POLANCO,
MEXICO CITY
The menu boasts a dish of deep-fried tacos based on the original recipe by the grandmother of Diego Rivera, baptized with the name "Frida's Mexican Tacos."

Piccolos
1526 FIDEL VELÁZQUEZ, COL. ATEMAJAC, GUADALAJARA
Their huge (16-inch) *flautas* are filled with pepper slices, *requesón*, beans, beef, picadillo, chicken, stewed tongue, brains, or pork rinds inside a thin, crispy tortilla.

Porfirio's
214 MASARYK,
COL. POLANCO,
MEXICO CITY
Mexican cuisine with all of Polanco's glamour; the menu includes a dish of Veracruz-style deep-fried tacos made with crab.

Pujol
254 FRANCISCO PETRARCA,
COL. POLANCO,
MEXICO CITY
Chef Enrique Olvera's renowned restaurant has an avocado *flauta* on its menu, served with a cilantro emulsion and grated chipotle mayonnaise.

Tacos Don Chuy
ZARAGOZA, BETWEEN RUPERTO MARTÍNEZ AND ARAMBERRI,
CENTRO, MONTERREY
Known for their red corn tortillas filled with potato and garnished with lettuce, green tomato slices, pork skin, and piquin chile salsa.

INGREDIENTES

PART
3

MEET THE FAMILY

ENCHILADAS

There are certain dishes you have to taste at least once in your life to be able to understand them. Maybe that's the case with enchiladas; there's a universe of possibilities hidden behind this simple dish. Every state of Mexico has its own version of enchiladas, though even then the official recipes are a source of frequent debate. They have a close relationship with tacos; the main difference (but not the only one) is that enchiladas are bathed in large amounts of salsa, meaning you need a knife and fork to eat them. Also, you can make enchiladas by either rolling the tortillas closed or folding them in half.

FROM PULQUERÍAS TO FANCY RESTAURANTS

This recipe is as old as its ingredients and, if tortillas are as ancient as chile salsas, we may come to the conclusion that enchiladas can be traced back to Quetzalcoatl's time. No one should be in any doubt that the *tortilla-salsa* or *tortilla-chile* pairings are so inspired, they must have a mythological origin. Some might say we're reaching hasty conclusions, and some argue that enchiladas are a Baroque invention that emerged from the culinary creativity found in convents during colonial times. Whatever the true story, there's no doubt about the fact that the Mexican diet experienced a dramatic transformation during the Conquest, when cooking oil was introduced, and indeed the traditional recipe for enchiladas states the tortillas must be fried in oil. It is also true that both the ingredients and uses of chile salsas changed dramatically with this historical turning point. However, most salsas are good for making enchiladas, be they simple or the complex. Enchiladas, in the end, are a popular dish that's easy to make, a fast fallback in any kitchen, and a perfect side for special dinners. Their relatively straightforward preparation has given rise to timeless popular phrases and sayings like: "*Esto no es enchílame otra*"—"this ain't like making enchiladas," or, roughly, "this is no piece of cake." It is worth bearing in mind that enchiladas were the classic accompaniment to a jug of pulque for the longest time, and were frequently offered in bars specializing in the fermented cactus drink. Now, however, they have become the main attraction in restaurants, diners, snack bars, and other eateries, where each region displays its particular flavors and recipes with pride.

TYPICAL THROUGHOUT MEXICO

MADE WITH CHEESE, CHICKEN, BEEF

COOKED IN CERAMIC POTS OR A SKILLET

THE REAL ENCHILADA

Enchiladas are basically a plate of fried tortillas in a chile-based sauce, but this is something achieved in three possible ways: the tortilla is first fried in plenty of oil and then dipped in the chile salsa; the tortilla is first dipped in the salsa and then fried; or the tortilla is fried directly in an oily salsa or lard with chile. Once the tortillas are fried and soaked in chile, there are also many different options when it comes to fillings, salsas, and garnishes. Not all enchiladas need a filling, but the fillings can range from cheeses, to vegetables, to all kinds of meat. Nowadays, chicken enchiladas are the most common. The three main styles of presenting enchiladas are described below.

ENCHILADAS WITH JUST A LITTLE SALSA

For this preparation, it could be said that enchiladas are served "dry." The tortillas are just dipped in the salsa or lard with chiles, filled, and finally decorated with garnishes or seasonings. This is the style of traditional enchiladas from the state of Querétaro, which are stuffed with sliced onions and melted cheese, and topped with lettuce and grated white cheese. Similar to these, the enchiladas from San Luis Potosí are also served with a garnish of fried carrots and potatoes.

ENCHILADAS WITH SALSA ONLY

When enchiladas are served as an accompaniment for another dish, they do not need to be stuffed with anything. In these cases, tortillas are fried, dipped in salsa, and served on the side of the main dish, topped only with a little cheese. This is how some classic dishes are finished off, like Tampico-style steak, where it is common to find the enchiladas folded in four to form a triangle, in order to take up less room on the plate.

STUFFED ENCHILADAS WITH A LOT OF SALSA

This is the most celebrated style of enchiladas, the method behind enchiladas with *mole* poblano, green salsa, or red salsa, among many other versions. The tortillas are well-dressed in salsa before being stuffed with some kind of shredded meat, cheese, or any other desired filling. There are also many different options when it comes to decorating them; the most common garnishes for soaked enchiladas consist of shredded cheese, onion slices, and sour cream. The sour cream and cheese alleviate the spiciness of the salsas, and onions add freshness to every bite. That's precisely the case of enchiladas with mole or ancho chile sauce, where onions are considered absolutely essential. For these reasons these three ingredients can be found together in a dish of enchiladas, but also on their own: sour cream, shredded cheese, and onion. Diced carrots and potatoes are another popular garnish for enchiladas, and can be boiled or fried: they're the special touch of the traditional enchiladas from San Luis Potosí, as well as those from Querétaro. Thinly sliced romaine lettuce is also a great companion. Finally, refried beans and rice are sometimes served on the side, which may seem a bit over-the-top, but is definitely a combination guaranteed to satisfy the hungriest among us!

> "We walked into an elegant restaurant and asked for *enchiladas potosinas.* Gustavo ordered four enchiladas, but the waitress understood he wanted four servings. So there we were looking at four pounds of enchiladas. Gustavo got angry. He said, "Dammit," and later, "I'm not going to tip the waitress." There were three wealthy families in the restaurant, and a lady who was so good-looking it gave us a headache. Later on we left, each with two pounds of enchiladas in our bellies, and facing a difficult choice: the church or the movies."
>
> **GUILLERMO SHERIDAN.**
> "Tardes de Ocio Potosinas,"
> In *Frontera Norte y otros.* Mexico:
> Fondo de Cultura Económica, 1988.

VARIETY IS THE SPICE OF LIFE

Enchiladas allow for endless variety and elaboration: a subtle change to the dish can transform it altogether, making every recipe a unique and delicious experience. In the group of "dry" enchiladas we find: red enchiladas from Aguascalientes (in white corn tortillas, fried in lard, dipped in a tomato and ancho chile salsa, stuffed with cheese and chopped onion, and served with fresh sour cream and fried potatoes); traditional enchiladas from Nuevo León (with red corn tortillas, stuffed with cheese and chopped onion, and served with fried potatoes, pan-fried chiles, and salsas); miners' enchiladas from Guanajuato (stuffed with aged cheese and guajillo chile salsa; garnished with fried carrot and potato, lettuce, onion, fresh sour cream, and slices of chiles in vinegar); traditional enchiladas from Querétaro (fried in plenty of oil, dipped in an ancho chile salsa, with a filling of carrots and potatoes, and served with sliced lettuce, sour cream, and shredded cheese); and enchiladas from San Luis Potosí (in red corn tortillas, filled with aged cheese or a mixture of onion, tomato, chiles, and cheese, garnished with lettuce and served with fried potatoes and salsas). Meanwhile, enchiladas bathed in plenty of salsa also have many variations across the country. To start off with there are the unique enchiladas made with pulque, a dish from the state of Hidalgo. For this recipe, a special salsa is made from ancho and pasilla chiles and plenty of pulque in the place of broth or water. They can have a chicken filling or no filling at all, but they're always bathed in the salsa and garnished with shredded cheese and onion rings. Then there are the renowned enchiladas with *mole* poblano and with *mole oaxaqueño*, from the states of Puebla and Oaxaca, respectively; the traditional enchiladas from Quintana Roo, made with a peanut sauce; traditional enchiladas from Coahuila, served with strained yogurt or *jocoque*; traditional enchiladas from Colima, with ground pork and vegetables, olives, almonds, and raisins, bathed in a sweet *mole* sauce; traditional peanut enchiladas from

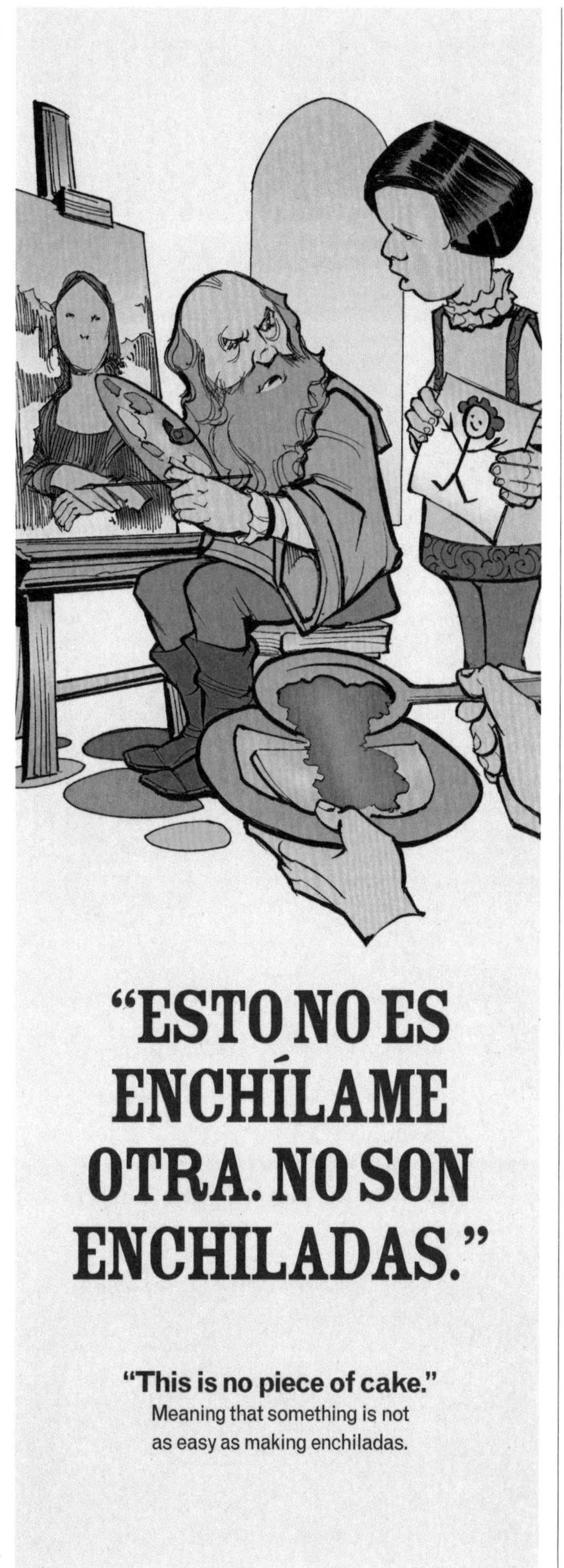
"ESTO NO ES
ENCHÍLAME
OTRA. NO SON
ENCHILADAS."
"This is no piece of cake."
Meaning that something is not
as easy as making enchiladas.

MORE THAN 2,000 ENCHILADAS

Alejandro Kuri—owner and chef of La Casa de las Enchiladas (110/A Tokio, Col. Juárez, Mexico City)—has developed a different approach to enchiladas in his restaurant. Here, you can create your very own enchilada by choosing the kind of tortilla, your filling, your salsa, and your garnishes. More than 2,000 combinations are possible: you can choose from blue, white, or green tortillas, tortillas made with chile, all-purpose flour, whole wheat... filled with chicken, turkey, pork, shrimp, skirt steak, *cecina*, chicken and potato, mushroom, vegetables, cheese... very hot or very mild salsa... garnished with white or red onion, white or black sesame seeds, cilantro, shredded or melted cheese, and so on.

Durango; and the delicious *papadzules* from the Yucatán Peninsula, stuffed with hard-boiled eggs and dipped in a sauce of pumpkin seeds. "Swiss" enchiladas are another category all their own, where the last step consists in baking or grilling the enchiladas to gently melt a final layer of cheese over the tortillas. The cheeses used for this purpose are Chihuahua, manchego, or asadero. They can be made with red or green salsa, mild or spicy, sweet or hot, depending on individual taste. *Entomatadas* are prepared with a tomato salsa without any chile, a subtle but significant difference. This is how *entomatadas* from Sonora are made, using red corn tortillas, as are those from the north of the country generally (further south the usual white corn tortillas are used). *Enfrijoladas* substitute a thick bean soup for the chile salsa, and have a garnish of cheese and fresh sour cream. They can also be baked to melt a final layer of cheese, and they're typically stuffed with chicken or cheese, although there are always other possibilities. Veracruz-style eggs, for example, consist of *enfrijoladas* with a filling of Mexican-style scrambled eggs, garnished with slices of poblano chile and fried chorizo.

PASEADAS

To prepare *paseadas*, the tortilla is fried, dipped in the salsa, folded over, and then fried again until it is golden brown on both sides. They're served with onion and cheese. This snack, a close relative of enchiladas, is a great companion for meat dishes from San Luis Potosí, Querétaro, and Guanajuato.

DOBLADAS

This traditional dish from Chiapas—and also to be found in Guatemala, Honduras, and El Salvador—is very similar to enchiladas. A tortilla is first folded and fried in oil, then filled with beef, chicken, cheese, beans, or potatoes. In Guatemala, *dobladas* with a filling of *loroco* (an aromatic flower used in a number of dishes and known in Mexico as *quelite*) are a popular favorite.

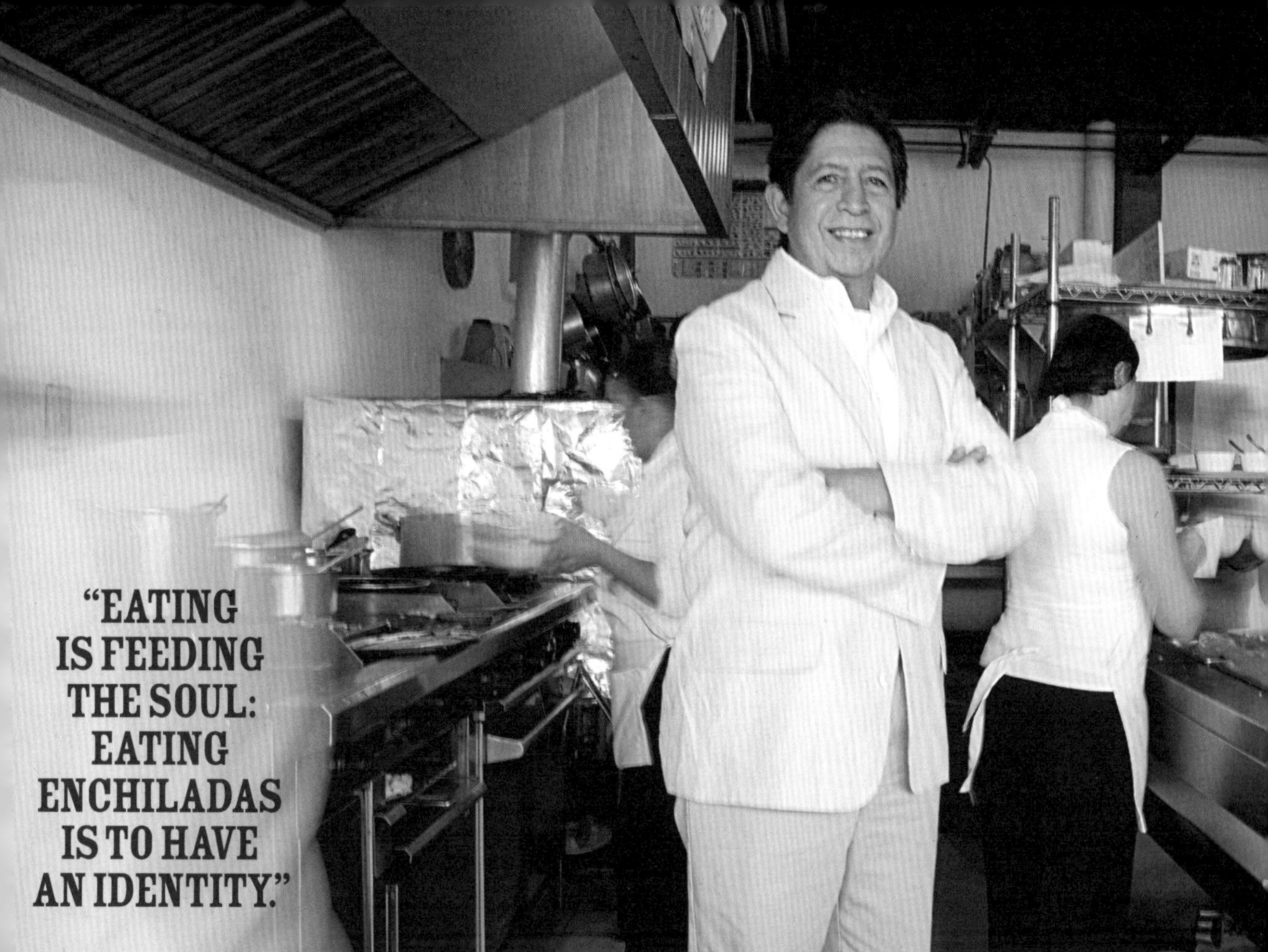

"EATING IS FEEDING THE SOUL: EATING ENCHILADAS IS TO HAVE AN IDENTITY."

We have close to twenty different kinds of enchiladas in our restaurant, but we change them every year.

We like to innovate. Take, for example, the chicken used for the filling: some people just boil the chicken, but we broil it with chiles and other seasonings, and we even use the remaining liquid to make the salsa. It's delicious! In 2010 in Iztapalapa we won a Guinness World Record for creating the largest enchilada in the world. We did everything in fifteen days: organization, the creation of special machinery, burners... everything! It weighed more than 1,000 pounds, and over 400 people participated in the whole process. Also in 2010, we were among the ten finalists in the competition of recipes for Mexico's bicentenary of independence celebrations, with a dish of Commemorative Enchiladas, filled with shrimp *esquites*, garnished with corn salsa and beans seasoned with fish *minilla*. On top of that, we also organize the Enchilada Street Fair every September, in the plaza at the center of Iztapalapa. Our main goal is to rescue the cultural legacy from our ancestors. We would really like enchiladas to become the national dish; they're very emblematic of Mexican cuisine, and they bring together the main ingredients of our nutrition—maize, chiles, and beans. The whole enchilada! For our tenth year, we're holding an exhibit about maize and the *milpas*—the maize fields—because a lot of people don't know that Mexico gave maize to the rest of the world, or how nutritional the *nixtamal* dough is. We love how, after visiting the fair, people feel proudly Mexican when they eat their enchiladas. It's also some kind of spiritual nurturing. Eating tacos or enchiladas really means having an identity.

Jaime Ortega
ORGANIZER OF THE ENCHILADA STREET FAIR AND OWNER OF DON JIMMY'S RESTAURANT
PLAZA TULYEHUALCO,
STANDS #46 AND #47
1577 TLÁHUAC, IZTAPALAPA,
MEXICO CITY

IN
SEPTEMBER,
IN THE BOROUGH
OF
IZTAPALAPA
IN MEXICO CITY,
THE
ENCHILADA
STREET FAIR
OFFERS
MORE THAN
20 DIFFERENT
RECIPES.

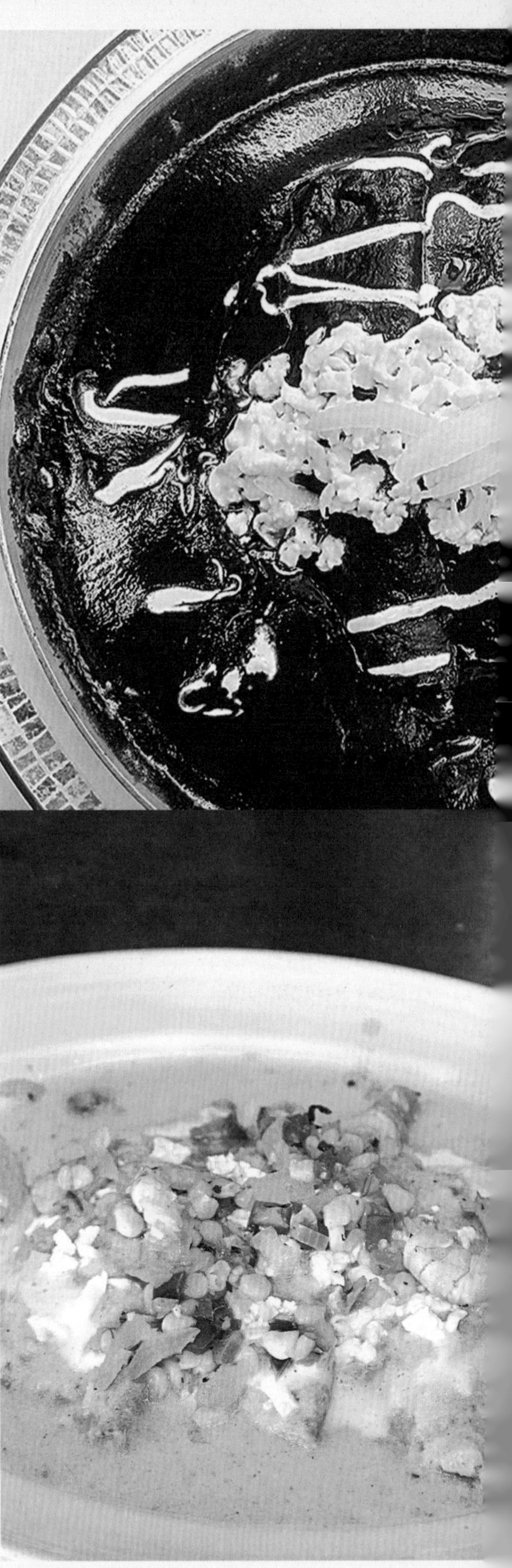

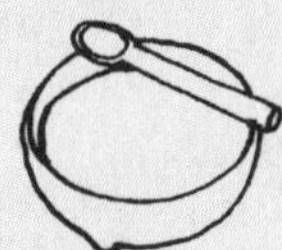

GREEN ENCHILADAS

Serves 4

—1 lb (450 g) boneless and skinless chicken breast
—1 medium onion, plus extra sliced for garnish
—1 clove garlic
—2 bay leaves
—3 black peppercorns
—Sea salt
—1 cup (250 ml) corn oil
—12 4⅓-inch (11 cm) corn tortillas
—6 cups (1.5 liters) roasted green salsa (see recipe 12, page 300)
—1 cup (250 ml) fresh sour cream, for garnish
—9 oz (250 g) Cotija or Chiapas cheese, for garnish

1. Bring a large pot of water to a boil. Add the chicken breast, onion, garlic, bay leaves, peppercorns, and salt. Reduce heat to medium-low cover, and cook for about 1 hour.
2. Drain the water and transfer the chicken to a cutting board. Once it has cooled completely, shred the chicken and set aside.
3. Heat the oil in a large skillet. Add the tortillas and fry one by one until just shiny, without letting them brown or go rigid. Set aside.
4. Simmer the salsa in a casserole over low heat for 3–5 minutes. Add water to thin it if necessary.
5. Dip the fried tortillas in the hot salsa for a few seconds until coated completely, and then transfer them to a serving dish.
6. Place a small portion of the shredded chicken breast on top of the dipped tortillas. Fold or roll the tortillas around the chicken as filling. Once all the tortillas are stuffed, cover the finished enchiladas with the rest of the hot salsa.
7. Add sour cream, sliced onion, and shredded cheese on top. Serve immediately.

SIDE ENCHILADAS

Serves 4 as a side dish

—1 cup (250 ml) corn oil
—12 4⅓-inch (11 cm) corn tortillas
—6 cups (1.5 liters) ancho chile salsa (see recipe 17, page 302)
—½ cup (120 ml) sour cream
—3½ oz (100 g) Cotija or Chiapas cheese
—½ onion, cut into rings

1. Heat the oil in a deep skillet. Add the tortillas and cook in the oil until just crispy.
2. Dip the fried tortillas in the salsa to coat, and place them on a dish, folded in half, without any filling.
3. When all of the tortillas are on the dish, add the rest of the salsa, sour cream, grated cheese, and onion, and serve immediately.

ENFRIJOLADAS

Serves 4

—6 large eggs
—1 cup (250 ml) corn oil
—12 4⅓-inch (11 cm) corn tortillas
—6 cups (1.5 liters) bean salsa (beans blended in their own broth)
—½ cup (120 ml) sour cream
—3½ oz (100 g) Cotija or Chiapas cheese
—½ medium onion, cut into rings
—Mexican-style salsa (see recipe 1, page 296), for serving

1. Beat the eggs together in a small bowl, then cook them in a hot skillet until they are completely cooked to your liking, about 4–5 minutes. Remove from heat and set aside.

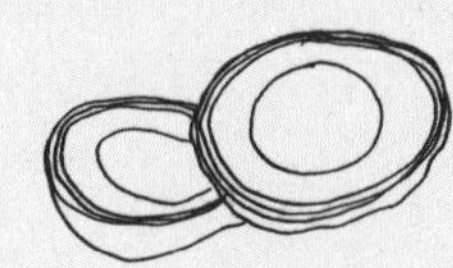

2. Heat the oil in a deep skillet. Add the tortillas and cook in the oil just until shiny and pliable.
3. Heat the bean salsa in a small pot over medium heat until very hot. Set aside.
4. Dip the tortillas in the salsa, fill them with scrambled eggs, and place them on a dish, folded in half.
5. Pour the rest of the salsa over the tortillas, and garnish with sour cream, cheese, and onions. Serve with a big bowl of Mexican-style salsa.

QUERETARO-STYLE ENCHILADAS

Serves 4

—1 cup (250 ml) corn oil
—9 oz (250 g) diced carrots
—9 oz (250 g) diced potatoes

—2 cups (500 ml) roasted guajillo chile salsa (see recipe 21, page 303)
—12 4⅓-inch (11 cm) corn tortillas
—2 cups thinly sliced lettuce, for garnish
—1 medium onion, cut into rings, for garnish
—9 oz (250 g) grated panela cheese, for garnish
—½ cup (120 ml) fresh sour cream, for garnish

1. Heat the oil in a deep skillet. Add the carrots and potatoes and fry until crisp, 4–5 minutes. Set aside.
2. Heat the salsa in a skillet until thickened. Dip the tortillas in the salsa to coat.
3. Reheat the oil in a deep skillet. Add the tortillas and cook in the oil until just crispy. Place each finished tortilla on a serving dish and fill with carrots and potatoes, then fold in half.
4. Add some more salsa over the enchiladas and garnish with lettuce, onions, cheese, and sour cream. Serve in portions of three enchiladas as a side to grilled beef or fried chicken.

THE BEST

Azul Condesa
68 NUEVO LEÓN, COL. CONDESA, MEXICO CITY
Their hibiscus flower enchiladas with chipotle chile salsa are among the most famous dishes created by the chef and owner of this restaurant, Ricardo Muñoz Zurita, a serious aficionado of Mexican gastronomy.

Casa Merlos
80 VICTORIANO ZEPEDA, COL. OBSERVATORIO, MEXICO CITY
The best restaurant specializing in Puebla's traditional cuisine in Mexico City is located right behind the National Observatory. They are only open from 1:00–6:00 p.m., Thursday–Sunday, which tells us something about the quality of their *mole* enchiladas.

Ciudad Tinto
159 DAKOTA, COL. NÁPOLES, MEXICO CITY
Behind Mexico City's World Trade Center lies this restaurant and wine cellar, with surprisingly good enchiladas with *mole*, chipotle, and peanut sauce, filled with a mixture of chicken and *requesón cheese*.

El Biche Pobre
600 CALZADA DE LA REPÚBLICA, JALATLACO, OAXACA
For locals, Oaxacan *entomatadas* are more popular than enchiladas with *mole*, with the rich and spicy sauce happily replaced with tomatoes, onion, cheese, and parsley.

El Rincón Huasteco
232 CUAUHTÉMOC, COL. LA MODERNA, SAN LUIS POTOSÍ
This culinary landmark of the state capital offers the classic *enchiladas potosinas*, and many other exquisite varieties, including a sesame-based sauce and a sauce made from *piloncillo* (brown loaf sugar).

Gran Café de la Parroquia
34 VALENTÍN GOMEZ FARÍAS, VERACRUZ
Almost as famous as its traditional *lechero* coffee and cream pastries, the *enfrijoladas* served with onion and cheese at La Parroquia—an establishment now over 200 years old—are a true culinary heritage of the port of Veracruz.

La Casita
3912, 16 DE SEPTIEMBRE, COL. HUEXOTITLA, PUEBLA
Three decades of experience, more than a hundred specialty dishes (with particular attention to *moles* and stews), and support from the locals—all contribute to the quality of the *mole* enchiladas from La Casita.

La Coronita
208 DÍAZ ORDAZ, CENTRO, OAXACA
The quality of the *mole* enchiladas served at this more than sixty-year-old hotel restaurant is backed up by the support from the demanding palates of its local patrons.

Náos
425 PALMAS, COL. LOMAS DE CHAPULTEPEC, MEXICO CITY
Gourmet enchiladas in the style of chef Mónica Patiño, stuffed with shredded turkey and flooded in Oaxacan *mole*, with a topping of pickled onions and slices of *cuaresmeño* chile.

Sanborns de los Azulejos
4 MADERO, CENTRO HISTÓRICO, MEXICO CITY
Countless generations have sat in front of the meandering bar of this colonial building covered with blue *talavera* tiles, just to taste their renowned "Swiss" enchiladas.

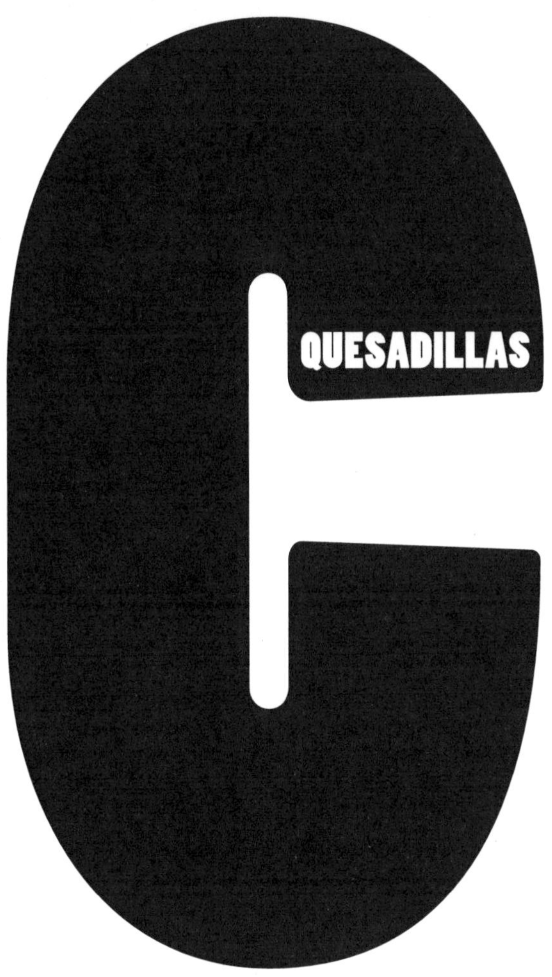

Cheese quesadillas are already a cosmopolitan dish; there's nothing easier and more delicious than placing two slices of cheese inside a tortilla. But it gets confusing if we talk about cheeseless quesadillas. It's a round contradiction—or a semicircular one, at the very least. Calling them empanadas is equally absurd, because they're not made from bread, but it's an illustrative term. Some people just can't get their heads round the fact that these cheeseless empanadas are called quesadillas. But that's their name, so what can we do?

THE FLAVOR OF NOSTALGIA

Colonial chroniclers mention quesadillas in a great number of texts; today, you find them at quesadilla stands in marketplaces, easily identified by their big comales surrounded with the colorful bowls that hold the fillings. They're typical of regions of Mexico where indigenous traditions remain alive and strong. Two different arts come together in this specialty. The first one derives from the virtues of the *nixtamal* dough itself, and the different ways of making it. The second has to do with the diverse preparations that make up the fillings, which represent the many regional delicacies that preserve classic Mexican flavors.

TYPICAL THROUGHOUT MEXICO

MADE WITH MEAT, VEGETABLES, AND CHEESE

COOKED ON A COMAL, SKILLET, OR CASSEROLE

MUCH MORE THAN A TACO FOLDED IN HALF

Basically, quesadillas consist of a disk of masa (*nixtamalized* maize dough), on top of which some kind of filling or preparation is added—with or without cheese. The disk is immediately closed over itself, making it something very similar, but not identical, to an empanada. There are two different ways of making quesadillas: with cooked tortillas or with raw dough. As you might imagine, the resulting flavor is completely different. Raw dough quesadillas can be filled with a huge variety of ingredients, which in turn may also be raw or prepared, and the stuffed quesadilla is then either fried in plenty of oil or griddled on a comal until it's well-cooked inside and out. On the other hand, premade tortillas or *memelas* must be fresh or at least hot to make good quesadillas, which are stuffed with the selected ingredient and then griddled on a comal on both sides. They are very close relatives of tacos. The list of ingredients and preparations used to make quesadillas can be very long, but cheese definitely tops the list. The preferred types are asadero, farmer's cheese, Oaxaca cheese, and panela cheese; and these combine well with slices of green chiles (such as serrano or jalapeño), epazote leaves, mushrooms, oyster mushrooms, or seasonal wild mushrooms, *huitlacoche*, squash blossom, chicken *tinga*, chorizo and potato, pork rinds, brains, and many, many more.

DIFFERENT OUTSIDE AND INSIDE

MOLOTES

These are fried quesadillas made from raw dough. The main difference is that the corn masa is mixed with all-purpose wheat flour, which makes them lighter. Sometimes mashed potatoes are added, and the *molotes* are formed from the resulting dough before frying them. There's a traditional recipe from Veracruz in which the dough is mixed with all-purpose flour and mashed banana, and then the quesadillas are filled with black beans. Versions of *molotes* are prepared in many Mexican states, all with different kinds of fillings.

DEEP-FRIED QUESADILLAS

A tortilla is filled with an ingredient and sealed with the help of a toothpick, then fried in plenty of oil until it's golden and crispy. The typical fillings for this style of quesadilla are pork brains, fish, or potato. Another name for them is "beach tacos" (see page 227).

SINCRONIZADAS

Perhaps the croque-monsieur of the Mexican culinary universe, the classic *sincronizadas* have ham and cheese inside a pair of flour tortillas, garnished with guacamole. However, just adding some cheese and any other ingredient between two tortillas and heating them together over a comal can make a *sincronizada.* Either flour or corn tortillas can be used to prepare *sincronizadas,* along with any of the above-mentioned cheeses, and the cheese is typically combined with ham, pork leg, turkey, chorizo, beefsteak, pork chops, grasshoppers, mushrooms—essentially, whatever filling you prefer.

EMPALMES

In shape, these are very similar to *sincronizadas*, but in essence they are very different. *Empalmes* are a typical dish from the north of Mexico: two corn tortillas are filled with refried beans. These beans must be cooked with a good dose of pig lard, made either Sonora-style, with dried chiles that give them a characteristic red tint, or Nuevo León–style, with a generous spoonful of richly flavored, chile-laden dripping from a hog roast (this substance is curiously called *veneno,* or "poison"). In addition to the beans, the tortillas can be filled with any other ingredient you like: grilled beef, chorizo, cheese, a few slices of meat from that hog roast, picadillo. The idea is that the tortillas absorb the lard and turn golden when cooked, but not completely toasted. Freshly made, hot *empalmes* are a truly local snack with more than a few high points (and calories to match).

VAMPIRO

This variety can be easily described: it's a quesadilla made from a flour tortilla and any other ingredient. They possibly come from the surroundings of the beautiful beaches of Mazatlán, Sinaloa, though their success has taken them beyond the border. Today you find *vampiros* made with grilled beef, chorizo, or chicken breast, and their preferred garnish is guacamole.

THE BEST COMPANY

Quesadillas are served with a diverse range of spicy salsas. Red salsas are perfect for cheese quesadillas, but as the saying goes, "different strokes for different folks." Deep-fried quesadillas, as well as quesadillas prepared on the griddle or comal, are usually served with salsas, fresh sour cream, grated white cheese, finely sliced lettuce, onion, and slices of avocado, depending on the region and personal taste. *Sincronizadas* and *empalmes*, on the other hand, are served with many different kinds of chile salsa or pickled chiles, whether pickled alone or with carrot, cauliflower, and onion, a preparation known as *escabeche* (see recipe 31, page 308).

"[...] thereupon he undertook to secure all which was necessary of food, turkey pasties, meat stewed with maize, turkey stewed with maize [...]."

Sahagún. *Florentine Codex,* Book 9: The Merchants, sixth chapter.

BESIDES TORTILLA DOUGH, OTHER

PRODUCTS

SUCH AS PAPER, CARDBOARD, TOOTHPASTE, SWEETENERS, AND CANDY CAN ALSO BE MADE FROM

MAIZE.

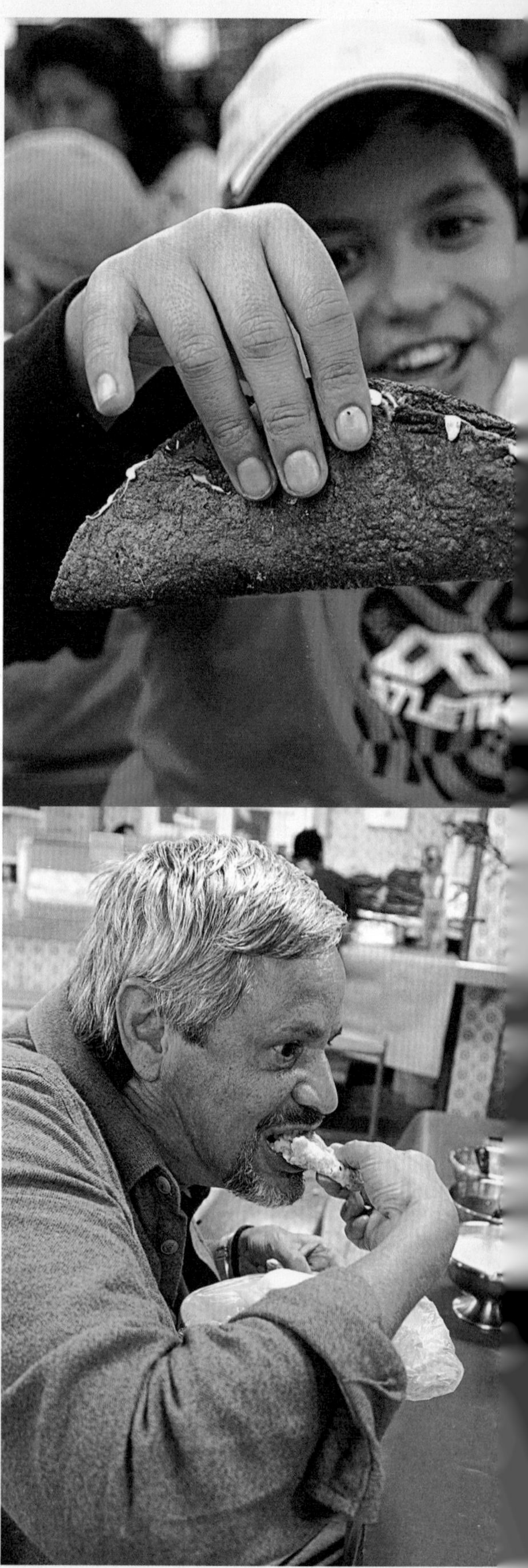

We make our quesadillas with love. I think that's the reason why they're the best. Everything's delicious, right?

Here we have different dishes you can enjoy, with plenty of variety and great quality. We have quesadillas with chicken, pork rinds, *huitlacoche*, cheese, mushrooms, beef, brains, picadillo, potatoes with cheese, and squash blossom with cheese. You can have them deep-fried or griddled; it's up to you. The owner brings the fillings early every morning and we prepare them here. We also make the tortillas from scratch, and that enhances the flavor; they're fresh and tender. All kinds of people come here: foreigners, workers, and passersby who are just enjoying a day in the plaza. We've been in the business for twenty-five years.

It started as a street stand, on that corner right in front of the bakery, with little charcoal stoves under a tarpaulin. Later on they were able to rent this space in the market, and here we are. But I think the food still tastes the same.

"HERE, WE PREPARE THE TYPICAL QUESADILLA, BUT BETTER THAN ELSEWHERE."

How many quesadillas do we sell in a day? Whoa! I have no idea! I have never counted—but they're a lot. Fried quesadillas are everyone's favorites. They're tastier, but I think they make you fat. Among the fillings, pork rinds, beef, and chicken sell best. But really, everything sells. These are just typical quesadillas. We don't do anything different to them, but they're still better than in other places. I don't know why, but a lot of people come here to make movies. It might be because people talk about us, I don't know. Once, they made a movie about José José. Well, a part of the movie. They've also been here making TV shows. The chef Oropeza was here once, for the show *Venga la alegría*; he did an interview with my boss. A lot of TV shows come here. And that's all I can say. Our days here are quite normal.

Rosario Ramírez
COOK AT QUESADILLAS LAS DIETÉTICAS COYOACÁN FOOD MARKET, STAND #10, HIGUERA, NEAR CORNER WITH CABALLO CALCO, COL. DEL CARMEN, COYOACÁN, MEXICO CITY

A COMPETITION FOR THE LARGEST QUESADILLA IN THE WORLD IS HELD EACH YEAR IN ÍMURIS, SONORA, KNOWN AS

"THE QUESADILLA CAPITAL."

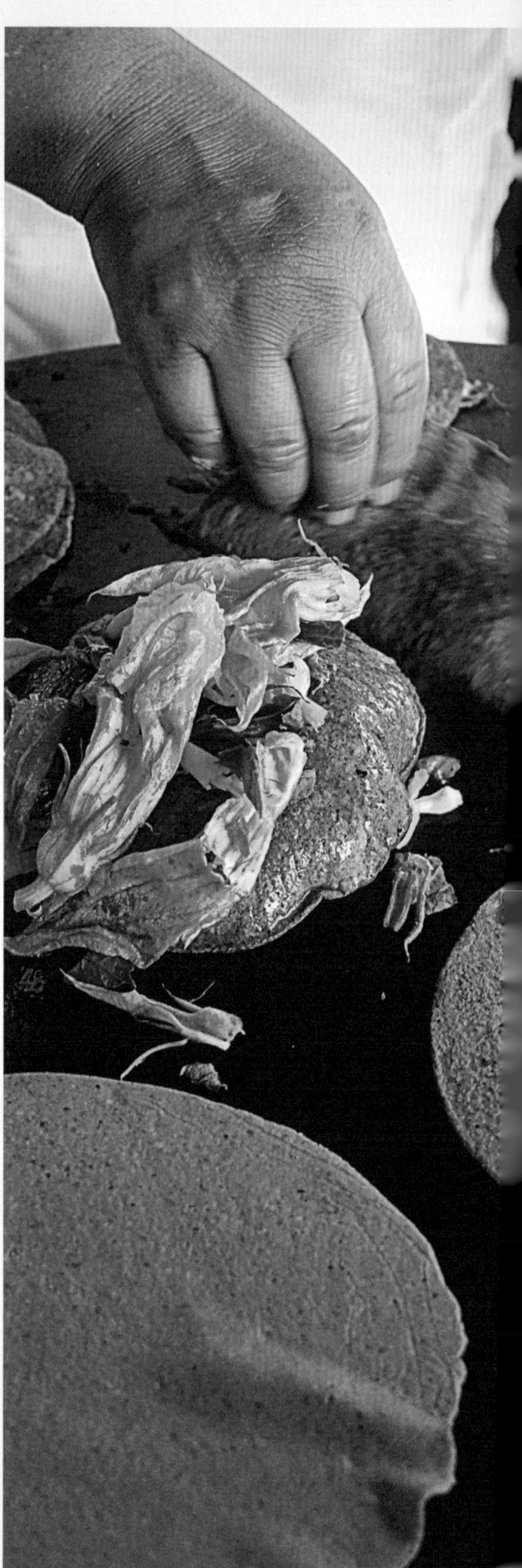

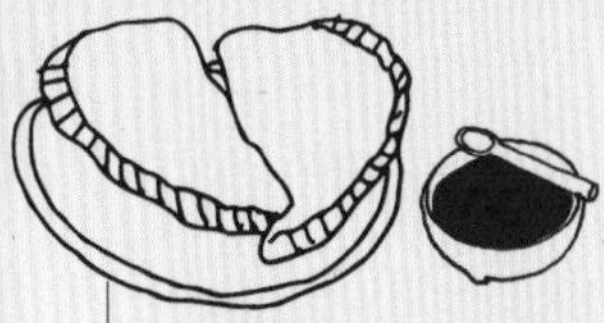

MOLOTES DOUGH

Serves 10

(Makes enough dough for 20–30 tortillas)

—1 lb 5 oz (600 g) corn masa
—¼ cup (30 g) all-purpose flour
—1 tablespoon lard
—Pinch of sea salt

1. Mix all the ingredients together in a large bowl and knead together with moistened hands until you have a uniform mass. If the dough seems dry, add water.
2. Divide the dough into 16 equal-sized pieces and roll into small balls.
3. Make the tortillas using a tortilla press and a thin sheet of plastic. Set aside until ready to stuff.

CHEESE

(Makes enough to fill 4 molotes)

—5 oz (150 g) grated cheese (asadero, Sierra, panela, or Oaxaca)
—Leaves from 1 sprig of epazote
—2 cups (500 ml) corn oil

1. Stuff the tortillas with a spoonful of grated cheese and a few leaves of epazote, and fold to close.
2. Heat the oil in a deep skillet, then fry the *molotes* on each side for 2 or 3 minutes. Drain over a piece of absorbent paper, then enjoy right away while hot.

SQUASH BLOSSOM

(Makes enough filling for 4 molotes)

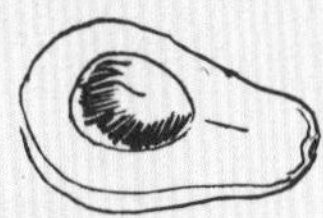

—5 oz (150 g) squash blossoms
—2 tablespoons corn oil
—4 oz (120 g) onion, finely chopped
—1 clove garlic, finely chopped
—1 medium poblano chile, peeled, seeded, and diced
—1 medium tomato, peeled and chopped
—1 tablespoon epazote finely chopped
—Sea salt

1. Remove the pistils and stems from the squash blossoms, then chop.
2. Heat the oil in a medium pot over medium heat. Add the onion and garlic and fry for 1–2 minutes. Add the pepper and tomato, and cook for 2 minutes.
3. Finally, add the blossoms, epazote, and salt, mix together, and cook until the excess liquid evaporates.

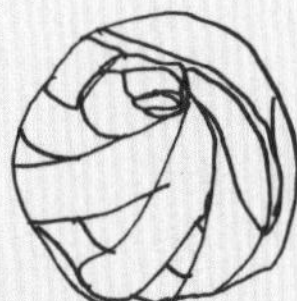

CHICKEN TINGA

Serves 10

—2 tablespoons corn oil
—2 dried chipotle chiles
—9 oz (250 g) sliced onion
—1 medium tomato, peeled and diced
—1 whole clove
—Pinch of ground cumin
—Pinch of dried oregano
—Freshly ground black pepper
—2 bay leaves
—9 oz (250 g) skinned and shredded chicken breast
—Sea salt
—Guacamole, sour cream, and salsa (see recipes 1, 7, 11, and 12, pages 296–300), for serving

1. Heat the oil in a skillet over medium heat. Add the chiles and fry slightly, about 1–2 minutes. Add the onion and sweat over low heat until it turns translucent.
2. Add the tomato and clove, cumin, oregano, pepper, and bay leaves. Simmer until the color changes, about 3–5 minutes.
3. Add the chicken, salt, and ½ cup water, and bring to a simmer. Cook until the sauce thickens, about 3 minutes. Discard the chiles and bay leaves. (For extra spice, slice the chiles and return to the preparation.) Serve with guacamole, sour cream, and salsa.

CHORIZO AND POTATOES

Serves 10

—1 lb 5 oz (600 g) potatoes, peeled and diced
—Sea salt
—2 tablespoons corn oil
—5 oz pork chorizo (150 g), peeled and diced

1. Bring a large pot of water to a boil. Add the potatoes and salt and boil until very tender, about 10 minutes. Drain and mash the potatoes with a fork in a large bowl.
2. Heat the oil in a deep skillet. Add the sausage and cook until brown, about 3–5 minutes. Add the potatoes to the skillet and mix well. Season to taste with salt and serve.

THE BEST

El Pipos
105 COSTERA MIGUEL ALEMÁN, FRAC. COSTA AZUL, ACAPULCO
The business began in the 1950s under the initiative of a creative fisherman, and it's still frequented by locals and tourists for, among other reasons, their dogfish quesadillas.

Fonda del Refugio
166 LIVERPOOL, ZONA ROSA, MEXICO CITY
These quesadillas have spectacular flavor (enhanced by a special raw green salsa), and are served in a colorful display of tissue paper.

Izote
513 MASARYK, COL. POLANCO, MEXICO CITY
Traditional Mexican food is elevated to the rank of gourmet cuisine by the intervention of chef Patricia Quintana, who offers squash blossom and *huitlacoche* quesadillas prepared on the traditional comal.

La Bipo
155 MALINTZIN, COYOACÁN, MEXICO CITY
This classic Coyoacán cantina and diner has Northern-style *chimichangas* (deep-fried quesadillas) on its menu.

La Fuente de la Juventud
CORNER OF 2ND AVENUE AND 7TH STREET, COL. SAN PEDRO DE LOS PINOS, MEXICO CITY
Operating for more than half a century from inside the San Pedro de los Pinos market, La Fuente is famous for its seafood, and offers delicious fish quesadillas as appetizers.

La No. 20
ANDRÉS BELLO, COL. POLANCO, MEXICO CITY
The menu of this flashy cantina, nestled in Polanco's hotel district, includes soft conch crab, *dobladitas*, served on flour tortillas with jalapeño salsa.

Los Colorines
13 TEPOZTECO, TEPOZTLÁN, MORELOS
This restaurant located on the street that takes you to the Tepozteco pyramid offers a wide variety of quesadillas. They named their place after a seasonal flower, which is also the filling of one of their most interesting quesadillas.

Piélago
263 SAN JERÓNIMO, TIZAPÁN, MEXICO CITY
Located inside Plaza Escenaria, Piélago offers a menu with a Mediterranean touch that includes trios of turkey and octopus quesadillas.

Safari
200 CHOPOS (CORNER OF JIMÉNEZ CANTÚ), CUAUTITLÁN IZCALLI, STATE OF MEXICO
Their charcoal-grilled tacos are almost as famous as their *quesafaris*: quesadillas filled with *cecina*, pork chops, *al pastor*, beefsteak, skirt steak, and even vegetables.

Villa María
704 HOMERO, COL. POLANCO, MEXICO CITY
Even though this place is pretty tourist-oriented, they offer really good snacks: *huitlacoche*, epazote, cheese, and squash blossom *dobladas*, for example.

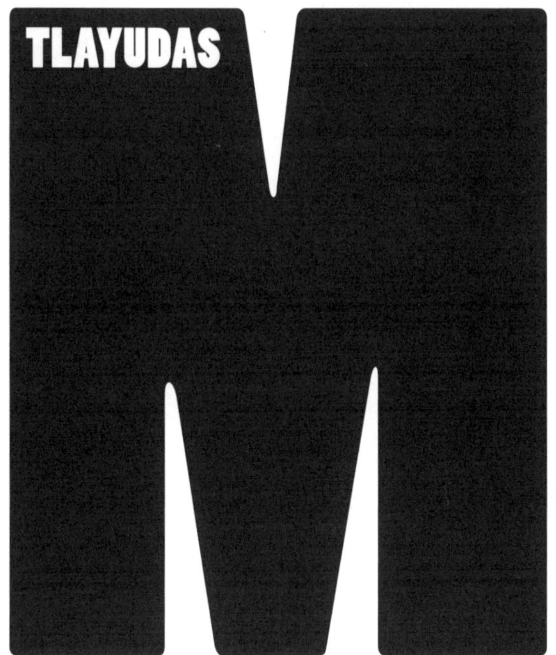

Many things in Oaxaca are unique: places, buildings, people, monuments, streets, landscapes . . . the state's diversity is almost infinite. The same is true with its food: it's diverse, delicious, and different than anywhere else in Mexico, both because of its singularities and because of its character. The existence of seven different kinds of *mole* is a proof of their search for the perfect detail and the exquisite accent. But Oaxaca has yet another surprise for us, a rare specialty beyond compare: the *tlayuda*. You can find them at any time of day in markets and restaurants, but they're really a nighttime dish. It's a real spectacle when, all along Libres street in the capital of Oaxaca, people come together to enjoy *tlayudas* from sunset till sunrise, close to the heat of the comales from the street stands that feed night owls and pleasure seekers before they head home.

AS UNIQUE AS OAXACA ITSELF

Everything in Oaxaca is drenched in history, and *tlayudas* are no exception. This traditional artisan product is like an X-ray of Mexico's past, since it can only be found in the Central Valley of the state of Oaxaca. You won't come across *tlayudas* anywhere else, with the exception of Oaxacan restaurants, where they're a very popular item. A *tlayuda*, in essence, is the name given to a large tortilla, which ranges from 10 inches to 16 inches in diameter. However, they are cooked to a very different finish to the usual tortilla, since *tlayudas* must be hard and slightly crispy, but not like a *tostada*. They must maintain a certain rigidity, but be flexible enough to fold in half once reheated. There's no single method to prepare this dish, but ancient traditions survive in its creation: the homemade corn masa, the use of a volcanic stone *metate* to grind the dough, shaping by hand, charcoal grilling—and 100 percent female labor throughout the whole process. These elements speak of the considerable antiquity of this tortilla, recalling an ancient tradition that has been preserved into the present. The ingredients used in its preparation combine pre-Hispanic elements like *nixtamal* dough, beans, chiles, and tomatoes with components from other cultures, like pork lard, dairy products, and beef, among many other possibilities yet to be invented. All in all, the *tlayuda* is the very distillation of authentic Mexican cuisine.

TYPICAL IN OAXACA

MADE WITH BEEF, BEANS, VEGETABLES

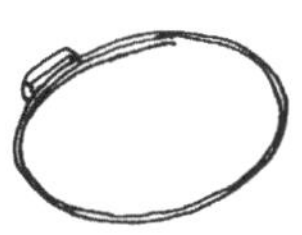

COOKED ON A COMAL

SIZE... DOES MATTER

Even when the term *tlayuda* refers only to this special kind of corn tortilla, the *tlayuda* with its topping is a distant cousin of the tacos that

Angélica begins grilling the meat.

She spreads the beans.

EL TULE TLAYUDAS

Shredded cheese goes on top...

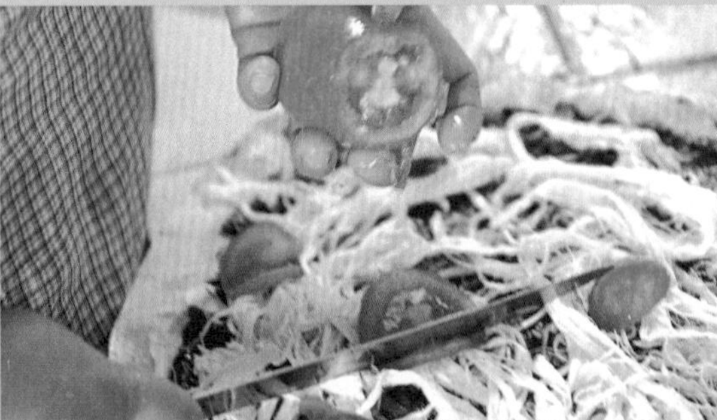

Tomato is added...

And the avocado...

TA-DA! One tlayuda!

we have observed throughout this book. It all starts when the *tlayuda* is heated over a comal, a grill, or directly over charcoal embers, spread with a layer of lard, and sprinkled with crumbs of pork cracklings. The other ingredients are then added in the following order: beans, shredded Oaxaca cheese, thin slices of white cabbage, sliced tomatoes, onion, avocado, sour cream, and salsa. At this point, it's possible to say we have a prepared *tlayuda*. If you still need more to it, you can also add some kind of meat. The most typical is *tasajo de Oaxaca*, a regional beef jerky of special quality and one of the outstanding traditional products of the region. But you can also add chorizo, spicy pork *cecina*, shredded chicken, beef steak, or pork chops. Some people even add fish. Small pieces of the final ingredient are scattered over the *tlayuda* and then, it's decision time… to fold or not to fold. It's normal to eat *tlayuda* folded, where the ingredients blend in a delicious mixture; but you can also choose to eat it unfolded, over a large plate. Some people even use a knife and fork. Both choices are equally valid. There are several salsas perfect for seasoned *tlayuda*. The first options are the typical green or red salsas used in any taco (see recipes 11, 12, 13, and 15, pages 300–301), but other salsas with a slightly different taste are also suitable, like those made from ancho or pasilla chiles (see recipes 17 and 18, page 302). In addition to these, a special salsa that includes maguey worms in the ingredients is also a great choice (see recipe 22, page 303). There is no doubt, however, that a shot of mezcal with red maguey worm salt is the ideal companion for Oaxacan *tlayuda*.

IT'S ALL ABOUT THE STYLE

It's difficult to talk about different varieties of *tlayuda*, since they're a true regional specialty dish. The only possible variations are found in the size of the tortilla (they're either big, or even bigger). Some of the ingredients may be switched around, as we have seen, with beef jerky or vegetarian versions, for example, but that's about it. The rest is a matter of style—to each their own.

"SI PARA COMER TASAJO HAY QUE SOBARSE EL LOMO CHINGUE A SU MADRE EL TRABAJO, MEJOR NO COMO."

"If you must sweat to eat jerky, I'd rather stay hungry!"

Meaning it's better to be lazy and eat whatever's available than working hard to be able to consume expensive food.

A WOMAN
FROM OAXACA
CAN MAKE
UP TO

400

TLAYUDAS

PER DAY.

A WHOLE VILLAGE CAN
MAKE AROUND

3,000

TLAYUDAS
IN A SINGLE DAY.

Here we sell *barbacoa*, chicken tacos, black *mole*, *tlayudas*, quesadillas...

I wake up early and come here to prepare the *mole*, the salsas, the casserole, the broth. The owner goes to the main market and buys everything: chocolate, vegetables. Everything is prepared fresh here: we make quesadillas, *memelas*, lamb *barbacoa*, chicken broth, *mole*, *coloradito*, *entomatadas*, enchiladas, all of that, stuffed chiles, *tlayudas* . . . And everything sells! We work from nine in the morning to nine or nine thirty at night during vacation time. On regular days, we close at seven. We prepare everything while we're waiting for our clients. Laura here makes the quesadillas, empanadas, *memelas*, the grilled steaks. I make *barbacoa* tacos, *mole*, *coloradito*, *enfrijoladas*, *enmoladas*, and *tlayudas*. And there's Teresa, the owner. Others do the dishes, sweep, and wait tables. *Tlayudas* are a favorite among the customers. We make them with a large tortilla, griddled in a special way so it gets like this. Then I spread the lard; that's the first thing that goes on the *tlayuda*. Then I spread the beans and add the greens—a mix of cabbage and cilantro. On top of that goes the stringy cheese; then the tomatoes and avocado; and lastly, the grilled meat. Then, it's all toasted, and it's ready to eat! We serve it like this, but if you want it folded, we'll fold it for you. I'm from Miahuatlán, three hours away from El Tule, in the Sierra Azul, towards Puerto Escondido. I came to Oaxaca looking for work, and I landed here. My family is in Miahuatlán; I see them once every five or six months, sometimes once a year. I can't go more often because of work. I had a job back there, but I wanted to leave. I'm 25 years old and single. My plans? Well . . . maybe to open my own stand, somewhere else. In Oaxaca, maybe in Miahuatlán, but not in El Tule. I live in El Tule. But not under the big tule tree! What are you talking about? I live close to the tree, but not under it!

Angélica Reyes
COOK AT ANTOJITOS JUANITA FOOD MARKET IN THE VILLAGE OF EL TULE, OAXACA CENTRAL VALLEY

ARTIST ENRIQUE RAMOS WON A **RIPLEY** RECOGNITION FOR HIS **GIANT TLAYUDA,** WHICH MEASURED **10 FEET** ACROSS AND WEIGHED **265 POUNDS.**

TLAYUDAS WITH BLACK MOLE SAUCE

Serves 4

—12 oz (350 g) black *mole* from Oaxaca
—2 tablespoons lard, plus more as needed
—9 oz (250 g) black refried beans (see page 139)
—4 8-inch (20 cm) *tlayudas* or 10 corn tortillas
—1 cup chicken breast (cooked and shredded)
—1 small onion, sliced for garnish

1. Heat the *mole* in a skillet until hot and thick. Set aside.
2. Melt a spoonful of lard in a small skillet over medium heat. Add the refried beans and heat while stirring, adding more lard if necessary to make an even and tasty paste.
3. Toast the *tlayudas* (or tortillas) on a comal, and transfer each to a large plate.
4. On top of each *tlayudas*, add a layer of lard, then spread the refried beans, the *mole,* and finally the shredded chicken. Garnish with onion.

HOMEMADE TLAYUDA STYLE TASAJO TACOS

Serves 4

—9 oz (250 g) black refried beans (see page 139)
—2 tablespoons lard
—4 8-inch (20 cm) *tlayudas* or 10 corn tortillas
—1 lb 2 oz (500 g) *cecina* or *tasajo* from Oaxaca, cut into small strips
—9 oz (250 g) Oaxaca cheese, shredded
—½ medium lettuce or cabbage, finely chopped
—5 or 6 medium tomatoes, sliced
—½ medium onion, sliced
—Sour cream and salsa (see recipes 11, 13, 14 and 15, pages 300–301), for garnish

1. Heat the refried beans in a skillet, adding a 1 tablespoon of lard and stirring to make a smooth paste.
2. Heat the *tlayudas* (or tortillas) on a comal or griddle, until they are gently browned but still flexible. Transfer each tortilla to a large plate.
3. Heat a small skillet, then add the *cecina* and cook with the remaining lard until warmed through.
4. Spread some refried beans over each tortilla, and top with the *cecina*. Garnish with the shredded cheese, lettuce or cabbage, tomato, onion, and sour cream and salsa to taste. Eat folded or open-faced.

TLAYUDAS WITH CEVICHE

Serves 4

—1 cup (250 ml) fresh lime juice
—2 teaspoons sea salt, plus more as needed
—1 teaspoon dried oregano
—1 lb (450 g) cubed sea bass
—4 oz (120 g) chopped cilantro
—4 tablespoons chopped mint
—1 clove garlic, sliced
—1 fresh arbol chile, seeded, deveined, and chopped
—4 oz (120 g) cubed onion
—3 tablespoons olive oil
—4 *tlayudas*
—9 oz (250 g) black refried beans (see page 139)
—1 ripe avocado, sliced

1. In a bowl, mix ½ cup lime juice, salt, and oregano. Add the fish and let soak for 1 hour.
2. Pulse the cilantro, mint, garlic, and chile together in a blender to make a smooth dressing.
3. Drain the fish from the lime juice and place in a clean bowl. Pour the dressing over the fish. Add the onion, olive oil, and the remaining lime juice. Add salt to taste and let sit for a half hour.
4. Place each *tlayudas* on a large plate. Spread the beans over each *tlayudas*, add the ceviche, and decorate with slices of avocado.

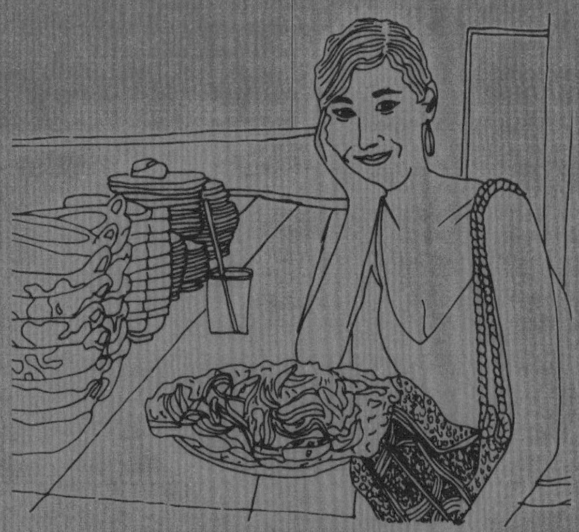

THE BEST

Barro Negro
222 HAMBURGO,
ZONA ROSA, MEXICO CITY
Even though they boast about their menu of "contemporary Oaxacan cuisine," they still serve great traditional *tlayudas* with *tasajo* or chorizo.

Café Bar del Jardín
10 PORTAL DE FLORES,
CENTRO HISTÓRICO,
OAXACA
Located in the porticos opposite Oaxaca's main square. Their *tlayudas* are praised by those in the know because they have preserved the real local flavor without making concessions to tourism.

Corazón de Maguey
PLAZA JARDÍN, 9-A CENTENARIO,
COYOACÁN, MEXICO CITY
In this temple of Oaxacan gastronomy, nestled in the center of Coyoacán, you can worship the gods of mezcal and other delicacies, including *tasajo tlayudas*.

Doña Lula
7109 REVOLUCIÓN,
COL. GUADALUPE INN,
MEXICO CITY
One of the most famed Oaxacan restaurants in Mexico City, it offers the classic *tlayudas*, with their obligatory "preparation" of lard and beans, and with *tasajo*.

El Milenario Restaurante
4 GUERRERO, SANTA MARÍA
DEL TULE, OAXACA
Under the shadow of the enormous tule tree on the outskirts of Oaxaca city, this traditional restaurant is geared towards tourists, but deservedly famous for its great flavor.

La Guelaguetza
241 ANDALUCÍA,
COL. ALAMOS,
MEXICO CITY
Another of those hidden places in seldom-visited areas of the city, La Guelaguetza is worth visiting because the cooks stick to the authentic taste of traditional *antojitos*.

La Oaxaqueña
18 LIBERTAD, SAN SIMÓN
TICUMÁN, MEXICO CITY
This cult restaurant for Mexico City–based lovers of food from Oaxaca is located in the busy surroundings of the Portales market.

La Tlayudería
155 TONALÁ, COL. ROMA,
MEXICO CITY
This traditional Oaxacan dish, and all of its toppings, quickly found a soft spot in the palate of both locals and visitors in the capital's Roma neighborhood.

Taquería Mayra
PRIMERA ORIENTE, SECTOR
REFORMA, PUERTO ESCONDIDO,
OAXACA
This Puerto Escondido restaurant is worth a visit both for the *tlayudas* and other inland dishes, and their fish and seafood specialties.

Terranova
116 PORTAL BENITO JUÁREZ,
CENTRO, OAXACA
Under the arches to one side of Oaxaca's cathedral, locals and tourists alike enjoy the *tlayudas* and other specialties from the state's Central Valleys that are served here.

WOOD FIRED KID MEAT TACOS
AL PASTOR CHARCOAL-GRILLED MEAT WITH FLOUR TORTILLAS AND CHILE PIQUÍN OR CHILE DE MONTE SALSA.
LAGUNERO TACOS (SEE P. 176)
MACHACA WITH EGGS TACOS (SEE P. 176)
WOOD FIRED KID MEAT TACOS
AL PASTOR CHARCOAL-GRILLED MEAT WITH FLOUR TORTILLAS AND MOLCAJETE SALSA.
FRIED KID TACOS KID BLOOD FRIED WITH GARLIC, ONION, AND CHILIES OVER FLOUR TORTILLAS.
GRILLED PORK TACOS WITH COLORADO CHILI PORK MEAT IN A PASILLA OR MULATO CHILI, GARLIC, ONION, CUMIN, AND TOMATO MARINADE.
BEEF BARBACOA TACOS (SEE P. 106)
MARROW TACOS (SEE P. 174)
SKIRT STEAK TACOS (SEE P. 72)
CHICHARRON DE MONTEMORELOS TACOS (SEE P. 150)
SONORA
SMOKED MARLIN TACOS (SEE P. 208)
CHIVICHANGAS (SEE P. 229)
GRILLED BEEF TACOS (SEE P. 250)
BURRITOS (SEE P. 177)
ENTOMATADAS (SEE P. 242)
CHIHUAHUA
BURRITOS (SEE P. 177)
CASSEROLE BARBACOA TACOS LIKE BEEF BARBACOA TACOS, BUT WITH GOAT OR LAMB MEAT COOKED IN A PRESSURE COOKER. (SEE P. 177)
COAHUILA
NUEVO LEÓN
BAJA CALIFORNIA
BAJA CALIFORNIA SUR
LOBSTER TACOS WITH BEANS LOBSTER FILLETS (FRIED, BOILED, OR GRILLED) OVER RICE AND REFRIED BEANS, WITH FLOUR TORTILLAS AND RED SALSA OR CHIPOTLE AND MAYONNAISE.
LOBSTER MACHACA OR MANTA RAY TACOS THE MEAT IS COOKED MEXICAN-STYLE, WITH ONION, TOMATO, AND GREEN CHILIES.
SMOKED MARLIN TACOS PREPARED LIKE A COCKTAIL, OR MEXICAN-STYLE. IN BOTH CASES, THE TYPICAL GARNISH IS CABBAGE AND MAYONNAISE OR MAYO-CREAM.
SINALOA
ZACATECAS
CHILORIO TACOS (SEE P. 154)
MULLET MACHACA TACOS PREPARED WITH ONION, TOMATO, AND GREEN CHILIES.
GOVERNOR TACOS FISH OR SEAFOOD COOKED WITH BACON, TOMATO, ONION, GREEN CHILIES, AND MELTED CHEESE.
SMOKED MARLIN TACOS
DEEP-FRIED TACOS WITH SHREDDED MEAT IN BROTH
SHRIMP CRACKLING TACOS FRIED BATTERED SHRIMP WITH CABBAGE, MAYONNAISE, AND RED SALSA.
NAYARIT
ZARANDEADO FISH TACOS (SEE P. 208)
BIRRIA TACOS (SEE P. 113)
JALISCO
DURANGO
CALDILLO DURANGUEÑO TACOS BEEF IN A GARLIC, ONION, TOMATO, AND ANCHO OR MULATO CHILI MARINADE.
OLD LADY TACOS GOAT MEAT FRIED IN LARD.
CASSEROLE BARBACOA BEEF TACOS (SEE P. 106)
BIRRIA TACOS (SEE P. 213)
TACOS WITH CHARALES (SEE P. 208)
COACHALA OR CUACHALA TACOS PORK AND CHICKEN MEAT IN A PASILLA CHILI SAUCE, THICKENED WITH A BALL OF NIXTAMAL.
MICHOACAN
GUERRERO
CARNITAS TACOS (SEE P. 193)
COTTAGE CHEESE TACOS (SEE P. 23
PEPENA TACOS (SEE P. 196)
TACOS WITH CHARALES (SEE P. 20
WHITE FISH TACOS
APORREADILLO TACOS CHOPPED AND FRIED BEEF CECINA, WITH ONION, GREEN CHILIES, TOMATO, AND SCRAMBLED EGGS.
COLIMA
BRAIN TACOS (SEE P. 123)
CHILAYO TACOS WITH PULLED PORK, NOPALES, AND PURSLANE, COOKED IN A GREEN AND RED TOMATO SALSA.

TACOGRAPHY

The gastronomical map of Mexico is so vast that only the most exquisite tacos have made the grade to be considered typical of a region or state. Even if the list may be endless, here we present the tacos that proudly represent the flavor of the different regions of the country.

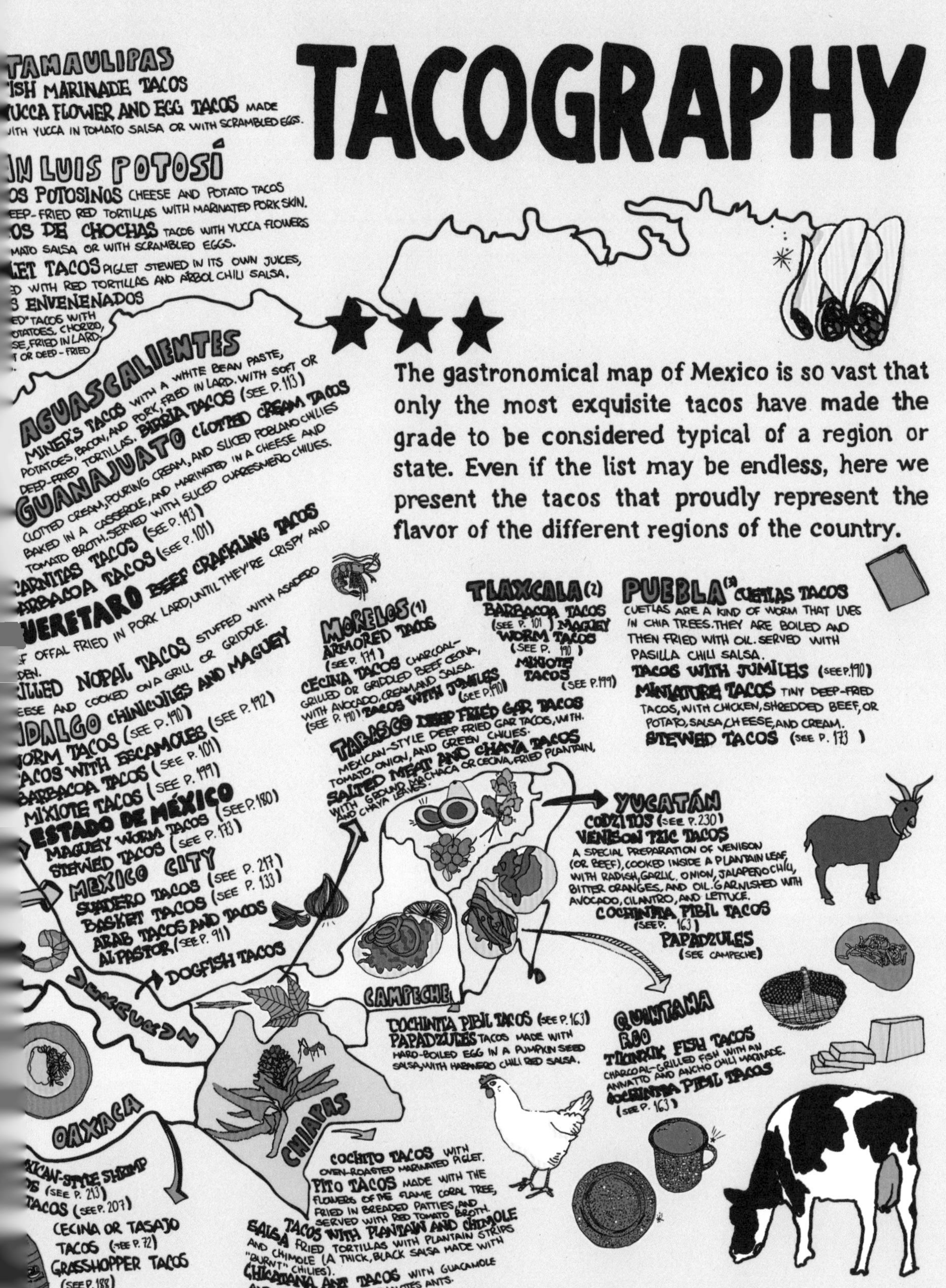

TAMAULIPAS
ISH MARINADE TACOS
UCCA FLOWER AND EGG TACOS MADE
ITH YUCCA IN TOMATO SALSA OR WITH SCRAMBLED EGGS.
N LUIS POTOSÍ
OS POTOSINOS CHEESE AND POTATO TACOS
EEP-FRIED RED TORTILLAS WITH MARINATED PORK SKIN.
OS DE CHOCHAS TACOS WITH YUCCA FLOWERS
MATO SALSA OR WITH SCRAMBLED EGGS.
LET TACOS PIGLET STEWED IN ITS OWN JUICES,
D WITH RED TORTILLAS AND ÁRBOL CHILI SALSA.
S ENVENENADOS
ED" TACOS WITH
OTATOES, CHORIZO,
SE, FRIED IN LARD,
T OR DEEP-FRIED
AGUASCALIENTES
MINER'S TACOS WITH A WHITE BEAN PASTE, POTATOES, BACON, AND PORK, FRIED IN LARD, WITH SOFT OR DEEP-FRIED TORTILLAS. BIRRIA TACOS (SEE P. 113)
GUANAJUATO CLOTTED CREAM TACOS
CLOTTED CREAM, POURING CREAM, AND SLICED POBLANO CHILIES BAKED IN A CASSEROLE, AND MARINATED IN A CHEESE AND TOMATO BROTH. SERVED WITH SLICED CUARESMEÑO CHILIES.
CARNITAS TACOS (SEE P. 143)
BARBACOA TACOS (SEE P. 101)
QUERÉTARO BEEF CRACKLING TACOS
F OFFAL FRIED IN PORK LARD, UNTIL THEY'RE CRISPY AND
DEN.
RILLED NOPAL TACOS STUFFED WITH ASADERO
EESE AND COOKED ON A GRILL OR GRIDDLE.
IDALGO CHINICUILES AND MAGUEY
WORM TACOS (SEE P. 190)
TACOS WITH ESCAMOLES (SEE P. 192)
BARBACOA TACOS (SEE P. 101)
MIXIOTE TACOS (SEE P. 199)
ESTADO DE MÉXICO
MAGUEY WORM TACOS (SEE P. 180)
STEWED TACOS (SEE P. 173)
MEXICO CITY
SUADERO TACOS (SEE P. 217)
BASKET TACOS (SEE P. 133)
ARAB TACOS AND TACOS AL PASTOR (SEE P. 91)
DOGFISH TACOS
MORELOS (1)
ARMORED TACOS
(SEE P. 174)
CECINA TACOS CHARCOAL-GRILLED OR GRIDDLED BEEF CECINA, WITH AVOCADO, CREAM AND SALSA.
(SEE P. 190) TACOS WITH JUMILES (SEE P. 190)
TLAXCALA (2)
BARBACOA TACOS
(SEE P. 101) MAGUEY
WORM TACOS
(SEE P. 190)
MIXIOTE
TACOS
(SEE P. 199)
PUEBLA (3) CUETLAS TACOS
CUETLAS ARE A KIND OF WORM THAT LIVES IN CHIA TREES. THEY ARE BOILED AND THEN FRIED WITH OIL. SERVED WITH PASILLA CHILI SALSA.
TACOS WITH JUMILES (SEE P. 190)
MINIATURE TACOS TINY DEEP-FRIED TACOS, WITH CHICKEN, SHREDDED BEEF, OR POTATO, SALSA, CHEESE, AND CREAM.
STEWED TACOS (SEE P. 173)
TABASCO DEEP FRIED GAR TACOS
MEXICAN-STYLE DEEP FRIED GAR TACOS, WITH TOMATO, ONION, AND GREEN CHILIES.
SALTED MEAT AND CHAYA TACOS
WITH GROUND MACHACA OR CECINA, FRIED PLANTAIN, AND CHAYA LEAVES.
YUCATÁN
CODZITOS (SEE P. 230)
VENISON TZIC TACOS
A SPECIAL PREPARATION OF VENISON (OR BEEF), COOKED INSIDE A PLANTAIN LEAF WITH RADISH, GARLIC, ONION, JALAPEÑO CHILI, BITTER ORANGES, AND OIL. GARNISHED WITH AVOCADO, CILANTRO, AND LETTUCE.
COCHINITA PIBIL TACOS
(SEE P. 163)
PAPADZULES
(SEE CAMPECHE)
VERACRUZ
CAMPECHE
COCHINITA PIBIL TACOS (SEE P. 163)
PAPADZULES TACOS MADE WITH HARD-BOILED EGG IN A PUMPKIN SEED SALSA, WITH HABANERO CHILI RED SALSA.
QUINTANA ROO
TIKINXIK FISH TACOS
CHARCOAL-GRILLED FISH WITH AN ANNATTO AND ANCHO CHILI MARINADE.
COCHINITA PIBIL TACOS
(SEE P. 163)
OAXACA
CHIAPAS
ICAN-STYLE SHRIMP
OS (SEE P. 213)
TACOS (SEE P. 207)
CECINA OR TASAJO
TACOS (SEE P. 72)
GRASSHOPPER TACOS
(SEE P. 188)
COCHITO TACOS WITH OVEN-ROASTED MARINATED PIGLET.
PITO TACOS MADE WITH THE FLOWERS OF THE FLAME CORAL TREE, FRIED IN BREADED PATTIES, AND SERVED WITH RED TOMATO BROTH.
TACOS WITH PLANTAIN AND CHIMOLE
SALSA FRIED TORTILLAS WITH PLANTAIN STRIPS AND CHIMOLE (A THICK, BLACK SALSA MADE WITH "BURNT" CHILIES).
CHICATANA ANT TACOS WITH GUACAMOLE AND GRIDDLED ATTA CEPHALOTES ANTS.

APPENDIX

SPICE IT UP

VITAMIN T

Mexicans often say "Vitamin T" is what keeps them going. A wide array of traditional delicacies fall under this curious concept. Their main ingredient is, of course, the *nixtamal* dough, and most of their names start with the letter "T": tacos, tamales, *tlayudas*, *tlacoyos*, *tortas*...

Also known as *antojitos mexicanos* or Mexican appetizers, these foods are sold in markets, plazas, street fairs, all kinds of sidewalk stands, and indeed restaurants. It's not entirely crazy to say they're the very soul of Mexican kitchens.

Some of these dishes emerged in very remote ancient times and are present-day versions of the diverse forms of bread known in Mexico before the Conquest.

Many other ingredients were added to these ancient traditions with the arrival of the Spaniards, such as wheat-based flour and pork lard, in addition to meats and seasonings, thus vastly increasing not only the number, but also the diversity of these *antojitos*.

What is not in question is that, despite their apparent simplicity, the world of *antojitos* offers a rich panoply of culinary pleasures.

Beyond the tacos, quesadillas, *tlayudas*, *flautas* and enchiladas described in detail in this book, there are countless other offspring of that fertile ball of *nixtamal* dough. It is the source of all the *antojitos*. Their common origin lies in patting that ball of masa between the palms, until a disk is formed. It is then worked in various different ways in order to make tortillas or any of the other so-called "fruits of the comal."

THE CHILDREN OF THE TORTILLA:

REGULAR TORTILLAS

Small tortillas dipped in lard and pressed into a mold before being deep-fried, creating a cup shape resembling the traditional boat that inspires its name. They are served with a few strips of shredded meat, salsa, and raw onion, and are typical of the state of Puebla.

GARNACHAS. A tortilla dipped in lard, topped with shredded meat, onion, salsa, and cheese. Typical of Oaxaca and Veracruz states. The "Orizaba-style" version has an additional special ingredient: small cubes of boiled potatoes.

PANUCHOS. Tortillas fried in lard until they puff up, allowing the two layers of the tortilla to be separated. This pouch is then filled with a thin layer of refried beans. Once this delicate operation is complete, they're topped with a variety of preparations (usually meat or poultry) and garnished with salad, tomatoes, avocado, marinated red onions, and habanero chile salsa. This is a specialty of the states of Campeche, Quintana Roo, and Yucatán.

PASEADAS. The tortilla is fried, dipped in salsa, folded, and then fried again until it's brown on both sides. *Paseadas* are served with onion and a bit of cheese. A close relative of enchiladas, they are a common companion for meat dishes in the states of Querétaro, Guanajuato, and San Luis Potosí.

PICADAS AND PELLIZCADAS. In order to better absorb a layer of pork lard and salt, fresh, griddled tortillas are pinched or pierced on one side. Sometimes they are dipped in salsa as well. Since all that is needed for this variant is fresh tortillas, they are eaten throughout Mexico, but it can be said they're typical of Veracruz, Puebla, State of Mexico, Morelos, Hidalgo, and Oaxaca.

SALBUTES. Tortillas fried in lard, with a spread of refried beans, and topped with *cochinita pibil*, marinated turkey, or any other preparation. They're garnished with marinated red onion and habanero chile salsa. This is a delicacy typical of Campeche and the Yucatán Peninsula.

SOPITOS. These are *antojitos* made from tiny fried tortillas, either hard and crunchy or soft and light. They are typically topped with picadillo and dipped in a very light tomato sauce. They are finished off with aged cheese, sliced lettuce, and lime juice. They are a classic from the state of Colima.

THICK TORTILLAS

BOCOLES. They're similar in shape to *gorditas* (see below). The difference lies in the incorporation of pork lard into the corn masa. They're griddled over the comal, sliced open, and stuffed with a wide range of ingredients and garnishes. As a typical dish from the Huasteca region, they are to be found in Veracruz, San Luis Potosí, and Tamaulipas. The classical fillings are also traditional preparations from this region.

CHAMBERGOS. A lighter kind of *gordita*, where the corn masa is mixed with all-purpose flour and even eggs. They're usually sprinkled with sugar on top and served for dessert. A typical specialty from San Luis Potosí.

GORDITAS. This *antojito* comprises a small, but rather thicker, tortilla (about a quarter- to a half-inch thick). It can be griddled on a comal or fried in lard. Once cooked, it is split open and stuffed with a wide array of fillings. You can find many versions of *gorditas*, and the quality of the dough has a decisive impact on the final result: there are very soft ones, made from fine and delicate corn masa; in other cases, the dough is mixed with a touch of all-purpose flour to make them lighter; and *gorditas* are also sometimes made with corn grits, giving them a slightly rougher texture. The size of the *gorditas* can also vary, and the different fillings produce very diverse results. There are many possibilities for the toppings, which range from salsa only, to lettuce, cabbage, shredded cheese, or *requesón*. They're easy to find all over Mexico, but they're considered a specialty of the central and northern regions of the country, from the Bajío to the U.S. border.

GORDITAS WITH PORK RINDS. In this version, the raw dough is mixed with pressed pork rinds before being cooked on a comal. It can also be mixed with other ingredients, like beans, *requesón*, or different cheeses. They are often served with a garnish of lettuce, onion, and a topping of grated cheese. The combination of maize and pork is one found throughout Mexico. In that sense, *gorditas* with pork rinds are omnipresent: they're everywhere!

DIFFERENT-SHAPED TORTILLAS

CAZUELITAS. Small dough balls are pressed in the middle with the fingers to form the shape of a tiny bowl or *cazuela*—hence their name. These are fried in lard until they're golden, and then stuffed with pulled pork, salsa, onion, and chipotle chiles, though they can hold all kinds of fillings. Think of them as close relatives of the tostadas. The most famous ones, *cazuelitas* de Chilapa, are from the state of Guerrero.

HUARACHES. A large *memela*, or oval-shaped tortilla, with the following ingredients: lard, beans, salsa, cheese, onion. They are topped with beefsteak, ribs, chorizo, or chicken. They are most commonly found in Mexico City and the surrounding area.

ITACATE. Halfway between a *gordita* and a quesadilla, this typical snack from the picturesque village of Tepoztlán in the state of Morelos is distinguished by its unusual triangular shape. They are stuffed with any of the traditional ingredients for quesadillas, sour cream, and grated white cheese.

MEMELAS. This is the traditional oval tortilla that dates back to pre-Hispanic times. Once it's heated on a comal, the simplest preparation involves a layer of lard, onion, and salsa. Sometimes a little cheese is added to round it off. Since this oval version of the tortilla is very ancient, it's commonly found all over the country, especially from the central Bajío right down to Central America, always fresh and crackling on the comal.

PENEQUES. These consist of a small stuffed tortilla, folded and cooked on a comal. They're similar to *tlacoyos* (see below), but somewhat more delicate. They must be stuffed—with cheese or *requesón*—then coated with beaten egg, and finally fried, the same way as stuffed chiles or *tortita* patties are coated and fried. They're served bathed in tomato broth or green salsa. You can find them raw (to be cooked at home) in markets all over Mexico City.

SOPES. This snack consists of a thick *nixtamal* dough tortilla with a raised edge to prevent its multiple toppings and salsas from sliding off. They come in multiple sizes and shapes, round or oval; they can be fried or griddled on the comal, or griddled and then fried. Garnishes must start with a layer of lard and refried beans, followed by a great variety of possible toppings, including chicken, chorizo, bone marrow, potato, poblano chile slices… finishing with the salsa, onion, cheese, and sometimes, with lettuce and sour cream too. Most likely, wherever there is corn masa and a hot comal, someone will eventually end up making *sopes*.

TECOCOS. Similar to *tlacoyos* in their shape, but filled with cheese and ancho chile. Specific to the state of Hidalgo.

TLACOYOS. An oval-shaped snack made from raw corn masa, usually stuffed with beans, *requesón*, pork rinds, or lima beans, and cooked on the comal. *Tlacoyos* are eaten with a chile salsa, and in some places they're also topped with onion, cheese, and cilantro. You can find this ancient dish in the central region of Mexico: Morelos, State of Mexico, Guerrero, Oaxaca, Puebla, Hidalgo, and Mexico City.

STALE TORTILLAS

If left uncovered, tortillas quickly harden once they have cooled, and they do not regain their suppleness properly if they are reheated. If you still want to use them, the best option is to let them dry properly for a couple of days, and then fry them in plenty of oil or lard. It is surprising how something tough and unappetizing quickly turns into something crunchy and tasty again.

TOSTADAS. These are simply tortillas fried until they turn golden brown. Yet they provide a vehicle for an endless range of new culinary possibilities. There are different kinds of *tostadas*: you can make them frying stale or fresh tortillas, frying raw corn masa, or using the fat-free, baked dough version. Then there are *tostadas* made from red maize dough. In short, the possibilities are endless. A typical *tostadas* has a base layer of refried beans and is topped with different kinds of meat, and garnished with lettuce, tomato, avocado, onion, cheese, sour cream, and salsa. They can be made with chicken, potato, picadillo, *tinga*, or pig's trotters. Another version of *tostadas* has a first layer of guacamole, topped with a variety of seafood. *Tostadas* can also be served at the center of any table as a substitute for bread. Every region of the country has its own way of preparing *tostadas*, making for an enormous range of choices.

TOTOPOS. Stale tortillas are cut into triangles and allowed to fully dry out. They're fried and served as decoration over refried beans, or as appetizers at the center of the table, along with different salsas. Some would say that *totopos* are characteristic of Mexico City, but now they have crossed borders and are known all around the world as nachos.

CHILAQUILES. Freshly fried *totopos* are bathed in plenty of salsa and served with onion, cheese, and sour cream. They can be topped with

MUY PICANTE

different kinds of meat, and even eggs. They can be prepared in many ways, and in Mexico are a very common breakfast choice.

TAMALES

We cannot talk about *nixtamal* without mentioning tamales. Basically, tamales consist of a dish where the corn masa is kneaded with lard and pieces of meat or another ingredient are added. A portion is then wrapped in corn husks or a banana tree leaf, and finally boiled or steamed. Some tamales can be cooked in a *barbacoa* oven. Anything edible can end up inside a tamale, and if you're curious about a particular ingredient, there's a high probability that the tamale you're looking for already exists somewhere in Mexico. The differences lie in the ingredients, wrappings, fillings, sizes, and way of cooking them. These are some of the most celebrated versions.

BARBONES. Typical of Sinaloa, they get their name from the shrimp antennas or "beards" that stick out from the edge of the tamale.

BORRACHO. These are made with pork ear and jalapeño chiles, pork leg, or chicken. They're larger than regular tamales and come from Nuevo León and Tamaulipas.

CHAMITLES. Sweet corn tamales from Veracruz. They may be stuffed with shredded coconut, cheese, or raisins.

CHANCHAMITOS. Originally from Tabasco, these tamales are wrapped in a banana leaf and stuffed with pork marinated in achiote.

CORUNDAS. These are from Michoacán and have many diverse fillings. Triangular in shape, they're wrapped with the green leaves of the maize plant, rather than the corncob husks.

DZOTOBICHAY. Originally from the Yucatán Peninsula. The masa is mixed with chaya leaf and a paste made with pumpkin seeds. The main ingredient is hard-boiled eggs, and they're wrapped in banana leaves.

ENCUERADOS. These are regular tamales but removed from their wrapping and fried in lard before serving. Typical of Mexico City.

ESTABINGUIS. Originally from Oaxaca. The dough is mixed with pork rinds. They're wrapped in corn husks, and have a dried shrimp *mole* filling.

MUCBIPOLLOS. A traditional tamale from Yucatán, usually cooked in an oven—traditionally a *barbacoa* pit. They're more like a type of cake than regular tamales, because they do not have any wrapping at all.

NACATAMALES. Even though they're more typical of Honduras and Nicaragua, this style of tamale can also be found in Mexico. They're wrapped in banana leaf, and stuffed with pork, olives, raisins, almonds, bay leaves, and more.

NEJOS. These tamales from Morelos, Guerrero, and Michoacán are made with plain dough and wrapped in the leaf of the maize plant. The corn masa is made with wood ashes instead of lime. They're usually served with green *mole*.

NIXCOCOS. Originally from Sinaloa. Their typical red tint comes from the brazilwood used as seasoning. They're wrapped in the husk of the corncob, and their most common fillings are zucchini or *quelites*.

BEFORE
THE CONQUEST,
TAMALES
WERE KEPT
SOFT
AND
TENDER
AFTER COOKING
USING FAT
FROM
FISH
AND
WATERFOWL.

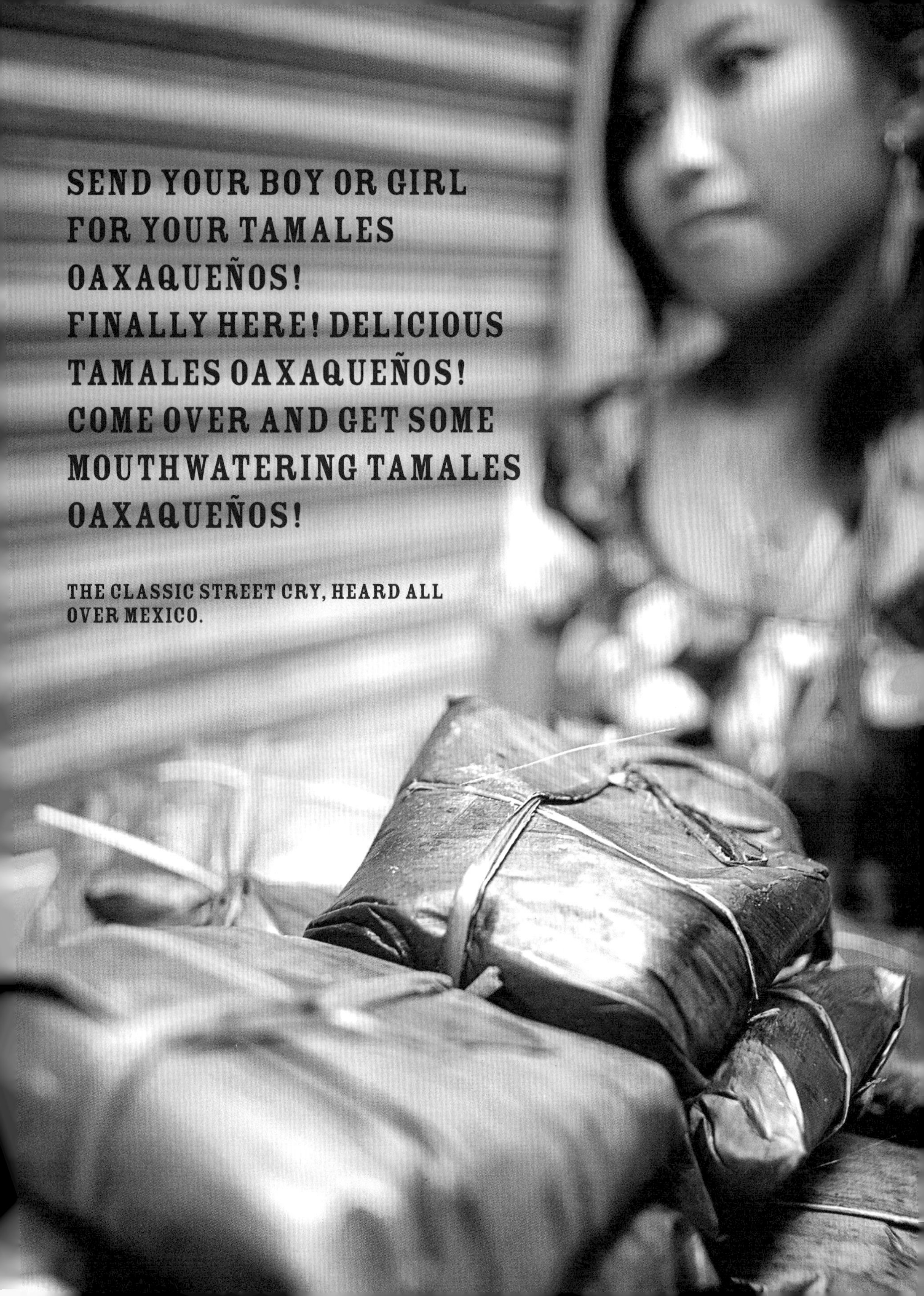

SEND YOUR BOY OR GIRL FOR YOUR TAMALES OAXAQUEÑOS! FINALLY HERE! DELICIOUS TAMALES OAXAQUEÑOS! COME OVER AND GET SOME MOUTHWATERING TAMALES OAXAQUEÑOS!

THE CLASSIC STREET CRY, HEARD ALL OVER MEXICO.

PADZITOS. From Chiapas. They're made with beans or peas. Sweet versions are also to be found.

PIBIPOLLOS. Huge tamales wrapped in banana leaf, with a filling of chicken or pork, seasoned with achiote. Typical of Campeche and Yucatán.

THE TAUTOLOGICAL TAMALE SANDWICH

A very popular, if singular, combination from Mexico City consists of placing a tamale inside a bread roll. This is a perfect example of what might be called "eating bread with bread." The tamale sandwich, which is nicknamed a "*guajolota*" or turkey, is a common breakfast usually sold from bicycle baskets around the city. Though it is undoubtedly a calorific bomb, some people swear by the tamale sandwich as the best way to start the working day.

PINTOS. From Veracruz, they're wrapped in the husk of the corncob and filled with string beans, green chiles, and cilantro.

PULACLES. Common in Puebla and Veracruz, they're usually made with beans, pumpkin seeds, cilantro, chiles, *hoja santa* (Mexican pepperleaf), and more.

TAMALES DE BOLA. They're made with pork meat and are originally from Chiapas. Their name refers to their circular shape, and similar preparations can be found all over Mexico.

TAMALES DE CAMBRAY. They're from Chiapas and have almond *mole* inside.

TAMALES DE CENIZA. Common in many parts of Mexico. Their name—"ash tamales"—refers to the gray color that results from mixing the *nixtamal* dough with black beans.

TAMALES DE GÜEMES. Typical of Baja California; made with pork, olives, and raisins.

TAMALES DE LA BUFA. Made with pork seasoned with ancho chiles; typical of Zacatecas state.

TAMALES DE LIBRO. Black bean tamales prepared without lard and wrapped in corncob husks. They can be either sweet or savory. Originally from Veracruz.

TAMALES DE MUERTO. Found in the Bajío region, they're made with black, blue, or purple corn, with an ancho chile seasoning.

TAMALES DE PATA DE MULA. Literally "mule leg tamales," these hail from Colima. Made with beans—no mule involved—and wrapped in maize leaf.

UCHEPOS. Corn tamales from Michoacán.

UNGUIS. Sweet tamales with cinnamon and anise, from Hidalgo.

XOCOS. Triangular tamales with a black dough, from Veracruz. They can be sweet or savory.

ZACAHUILES. Casserole tamales cooked in an underground oven; they can be stuffed with pork or poultry. Typical of Hidalgo and San Luis Potosí.

In addition to this long list of tamales, many other versions are made with beans, like the *cuitones* and *tamales de capita* (with epazote) from Veracruz; *nolochis*, *pitaúles*, and *toro pinto* tamales from Chiapas; and *vaporcitos de Ticul*, from Yucatán. *Mimiles* from Veracruz and *pictes* from Chiapas are also made with sweet corn.

ATOLE

Another of the many products made from *nixtamalized* maize is the famous *atole* drink. Tradition mandates that tamales and *atole* be eaten together. The process of making *atole* consists of diluting and cooking the maize dough in boiling water. It really is a simple process, and there are *atoles* for every taste: sweet, savory, sour, or spicy. Some have a pre-Hispanic aura, while others are reminiscent of colonial kitchens in monasteries. It's a matter of style that depends on context and location. From white *atole* we move onto *atole champurrado*, prepared with chocolate, and then we have *atole granío*, *atole de citún*, and *atole de puzcúa*. Other *atole* drinks have ancient names, like *xocoatolli*, *chacuatole*, *chacualole*, *cuatole*, *chilatol*, *xole*, and *atol*. You can also find *atole* drinks with milk, strawberry, vanilla, and chocolate. Today we can find *atole* prepared with corn flour, corn grits, wheat flour, and even rice. To simplify things, instant *atole* (plain cornstarch in a packet) was invented.

WHEAT VS. NIXTAMAL

Wheat has contributed many dishes to the infinite world of Mexican *antojitos*: the compound sandwich (*torta compuesta*), the drowned sandwich (*torta ahogada*), *cemitas*, *pambazos*, *pastes* (a descendant of the Cornish pasty, brought over by English miners working in Hidalgo), puff pastry, and *chilindrinas*, just to mention a few. The story goes that Juan Garrido, a black Portuguese who arrived with the Conquistadors, brought with him three grains of wheat—supposedly, the origin of all the wheat we have in the Americas. This charming myth attempts to bring a romantic legacy to a clash of cultures: the war between bread and tortillas. The reader is welcome to visit a bakery anywhere in Mexico at six in the afternoon to get an idea of how the story ends. Because in Mexico, you might find different types of bread for breakfast, maybe at lunchtime . . . but for the afternoon snack, bread is a must-have item. Mostly sweet breads come in an enormous variety of shapes, with names to match. Sandwiches in Mexico are no exception to the trend followed all over the world: it just seems natural and logical to place whatever ingredients are available between two pieces of bread or in a bun. But that's all grist for another mill.

SO YOU'VE GOT THE SPECIAL SAUCE?

"*¿No que muy salsa?*" is a Mexican saying, used to question an excessive display of "manliness" from someone who's been acting like a blowhard, since the level of spiciness of a really hot salsa can only be handled by the toughest constitutions, or by the thickest-skinned among us, or by "real Mexicans." Regardless of this, the important thing is that without a doubt, salsa is the true soul of the taco. Chiles and tomatoes are its basic elements: these two ingredients, plus an infinite variety of seasonings and mixtures, add that fiery spice to any meal.

Even though chile salsas are an archetypical trait of Mexican cuisine, we find they incorporate spices from all around the world, including cilantro, onion, garlic, cumin, pepper, cloves, and cinnamon. They can be quick and simple dishes, or highly complex mixtures requiring a detailed and laborious preparation. Many are served directly to guests at the table, so that diners are free to use as much or as little as they desire; others are used in the kitchen to season special dishes with their power and aroma.

We can distinguish three main groups of chile salsas: raw salsas, cooked salsas (in which all the ingredients have been cooked beforehand), and mixed salsas. We could divide this last group into three additional categories: emulsions, pickles, and marinades, all of which, beyond the simple distinction of raw vs. cooked, require patience and knowledge to embark on their lengthy preparation.

Obviously these divisions are not written in stone. One of the key characteristics of Mexican cuisine is its versatility, which means it is always adapting to circumstances without losing its essence. From the simplest combinations to the most baroquely complex salsas, each recipe has its raison d'être and brings together centuries of accumulated knowledge.

There can be no doubt: salsas are the very soul of tacos, the soul of *antojitos*, and even the soul of Mexican haute cuisine. They leave their mark on everything they touch, and bring every dish to life with their zest and vitality.

OH SO MEXICAN

The discovery of chiles by Europeans was the fruit of their encounter with the American continent. Christopher Columbus crossed the ocean in search of gold and spices, and his voyage was vindicated when he took these spicy fruits back home with him, where they found immediate success. This marked the beginning of a precarious transatlantic trade in chiles.

The Conquest of Mexico, however, led to a huge transformation. The Aztec Empire already had in place a large-scale and very complex system of production, storage, and distribution of chiles within its territory. Indeed, chiles were used as one of the principal forms of paying tribute within the Empire. Their techniques for storage and transportation of chiles, as well as the great number of varieties of chiles available, led to a rapid increase in the level of trade, which by the seventeenth century acquired a vast reach. Spain became the hub for distribution of this new kind of "pepper" throughout the Mediterranean, and from there, chiles were soon to be found all over the world.

> **"[...] THERE IS ALSO PLENTY OF *AJÍ*, WHICH IS THEIR PEPPER, WHICH IS MORE VALUABLE THAN BLACK PEPPER, AND ALL THE PEOPLE EAT NOTHING ELSE, IT BEING VERY WHOLESOME; ONE COULD FILL FIFTY CARAVELS A YEAR WITH IT IN HISPANIOLA."**
>
> CHRISTOPHER COLUMBUS. *THE FOUR VOYAGES OF COLUMBUS*, TRANS. CECIL JANE. NEW YORK: DOVER, 1988.

The plant's own generous nature allowed each country to adopt the species best suited to their tastes, cultivating and adapting them to their own cuisine. It is also a fact that chiles (unlike black pepper, which needs very specific conditions to thrive) can easily grow in almost any soil and any warm climate. All the chiles of the world come from America, no matter how they're called: capsicum, paprika, cayenne, *malagueta*, *ají*, *piripiri*, peperoncino, and bell peppers too—they're all chiles!

Mexico remains one of the largest

"[...] THEIR STAFF OF LIFE WAS THE CHILE. THUS DID THEY EAT: THE TORTILLAS CAME FROM A POTTERY GRIDDLE; THEY DIPPED THEM IN THE CHILE; THEY SIMPLY BROUGHT THEM TOGETHER."

SAHAGÚN. *FLORENTINE CODEX*, BOOK 10: THE PEOPLE, TWENTY-NINTH CHAPTER, THE TOTONAQUE.

consumers of chiles in the world, but many other countries have incorporated chiles into their national cuisine: Hungary is famous for its use of paprika, Spain uses smoked pimiento, and many Asian countries are crazy for chiles. The cuisines of India, Thailand, Malaysia, and Szechuan (China), for example, are famed for their extensive use of countless varieties of chile. What is remarkable is that they entered the kitchens of these countries only after the discovery of the American continent.

Tomatoes have been used in Mesoamerica and the Caribbean since time immemorial; there's no archeological record of when and how they were first consumed. Indeed, the word "tomato" comes from the Aztec word *xitómatl*. Tomatoes and chiles also share a family history. They're both species of the Solanaceae family, with the difference that tomatoes belong to the genus *Solanum*. There are thousands of different varieties of tomatoes, but the most common commercial types are given names based on their shape and size: globe, plum, cherry, beefsteak, grape, etc. These can also be found in many different colors—yellow, orange, even purple. In addition to the best-known types of tomato, other varieties are still being grown in many parts of Mexico, and are known as "criollo" tomatoes, with shapes, colors, flavors and aromas to amaze the eye and palate alike. However, these are principally regional products, because their colors and shapes are not homogenous enough to meet the requirements for large-scale commerce. This means it's only possible to find them seasonally, in occasional stands in traditional markets, or deep in the countryside. It's a shame that even in Mexico, land of origin of this magical fruit, this huge diversity of tomatoes is not better known or enjoyed.

In Mexican Spanish—just as in English—two different fruits (or are they vegetables?) go by the name of tomato: *jitomate* (red tomato), with its characteristic sweet flavor, and *miltomate* or simply *tomate* (green tomato or tomatillo), with a pleasurable tartness of flavor. Although their similar appearance has led to them receiving the same name, there are particular recipes and uses for each one of them.

1,001 CHILES

Chiles are also fruits. They belong to the Solanaceae family within the plant kingdom, and their genus is Capsicum, which groups together all kinds of chiles. There are more than forty different species, and even each one of them has varieties of its own. As a result, there are hundreds of different kinds of chiles.

"THE CHILE SELLER [IS] EITHER... A WORKER OF THE FIELDS, OR A RETAILER. HE SELLS MILD RED CHILES, BROAD CHILES, HOT GREEN CHILES, YELLOW CHILES [...] HE SELLS WATER CHILES, CONCHILLI; HE SELLS SMOKED CHILES, SMALL CHILES, TREE CHILES, THIN CHILES, THOSE LIKE BEETLES. HE SELLS HOT CHILES, THE EARLY VARIETY, THE HOLLOW-BASED KIND. HE SELLS GREEN CHILES, SHARP-POINTED RED CHILES, A LATE VARIETY [...]."

SAHAGÚN. *FLORENTINE CODEX*, BOOK 10: THE PEOPLE, EIGHTEENTH CHAPTER, THE CHILE SELLER.

Some chiles are sweet, some chiles are hot; some are used as garnishes, and some represent the main ingredient at the table. Their nutritional value is exemplary, and their taste, well, need we say more?

C. annuum is native to Mexico. Some of its varieties are known and produced all over the world. Below we present a list of the most popular manifestations of this celebrated species: Serrano chile, also known as green chile.

Jalapeño or *cuaresmeño* chile, which, once it's dried and smoked, becomes the chipotle chile. Mora and morita chiles, a variety of small jalapeño chile that is dried in ovens. Arbol chile, used fresh or dried. Poblano chile, also called ancho or mulato when it's dried. Chilaca chile; called pasilla in its dried version. Mirasol chile, which can have many different shapes. Once dried, it goes by the names of guajillo, *puya*, *cascabel*, or *catarino*. Sweet chiles, and all kinds of chiles, like bell peppers, piquillos, gernika peppers, *padrón* peppers, *ñoras*, and paprika... Within this same species we also find chiles that belong to the aviculare variety, known because birds are the ones who help in their reproduction. The very tiny and very hot chiles belong to this group: *piquín*, *chiltepín*, chile *de monte*, chile *parado*, *pico de pájaro*, *amomo*...

The species C. chinense comes from the jungles on the slopes of the western Andes mountain range in South America, with the habanero chile—one of the hottest in the world—included within its varieties. This chile came to Mexico through Cuba, as its name suggests. It left the Amazon during the Spanish Conquest, and came back to America as a treasure in the hands of black slaves, once it had adapted to the African palate. Habanero chile is mostly used in Caribbean and Central American countries, and it's also the preferred variety in the Yucatán Peninsula. Some Mexicans believe that it's native to this region, but this is a mistake.

The species C. pubescens also comes from South America. Manzano chile was widely welcomed in Mexico as recently as the early twentieth century. It is also known as ciruelo, *perón*, *canario*, *cera*, *caballo*, *chilcapo*, and *chamburato*, among other names. It's the Mexican version of the famous Peruvian *rocoto* chile, which also takes on other names and varieties in its country of origin.

THE BLENDER OR THE STONE

In Mexico, many different tools are used in the preparation of salsas, from the modern blender to the ancient *molcajete*, a pre-Hispanic stone mortar and pestle. If you choose to use a *molcajete* to make your salsa, it's going to take a lot longer than using the electric blender (but of course, according to Mexican grandmothers, the results are infinitely better when you use the stone mortar). When using the mortar, always begin with the salt, followed by the dry ingredients in the recipe. You can chop the ingredients with a knife beforehand to save time and work. It's even easier to grind ingredients that have been roasted in advance. The secret of this archaic instrument is patience, but the final result compensates for the effort. It's also possible to use different kinds of mortars, made from less porous stones or other materials; however, none is as good as the *molcajete* when it comes to grinding chiles, tomatoes, and onions.

Another item of pre-Hispanic technology that has made its way to the present day is the *metate*. Learning to use it properly is another challenge. It's employed to grind different kinds of foods, and in the case of salsas, it is used for crushing ingredients like pumpkin seeds and peanuts. It comes in handy when making *moles*, *pipianes*, and *adobos*.

However, we must not underestimate the value of the electric blender. The feats of the contemporary Mexican kitchen depend on the correct functioning of this appliance.

COOKING WITH CHILES, TOMATOES, AND ONIONS

Caution is required when handling chiles in your kitchen, because they can be really hot. You must be especially careful with your face and your eyes. Some people resort to using plastic bags or rubber gloves to handle them, but this is probably only necessary if you have sensitive skin or are using large amounts of chiles. An important piece of advice, though: wash your hands thoroughly once you've finished cooking with them!

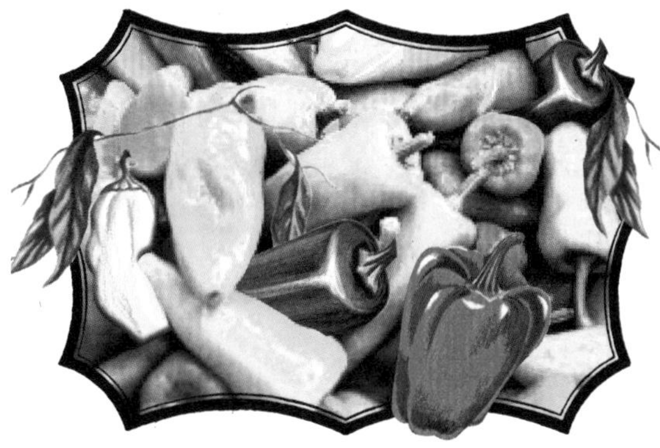

1. FRESH CHILES

DESEEDING AND DEVEINING THE CHILES

You must remove the seeds and veins (the white membranes inside the fruit) from the chiles if you don't want them hot, or too hot. You can do this by slicing them in half lengthways, and then again in quarters. This makes it easier to access the interior of the chiles and remove the veins with a knife. Another way is to open the chile from the stem and use the knife to take out the seeds and veins without damaging the shape of the fruit. If you want them even milder, you can let the deseeded and deveined chiles sit for an hour in a bowl of water with salt and a few drops of vinegar, then drain and wash them right before cooking.

PEELING THE CHILES

Some recipes require that you peel or remove the skin of the chiles; this can be done with all kinds of green chiles. One of the procedures is to roast and char them on the comal or directly over a flame. (Be sure to rotate the chiles regularly as they roast, so that the heat reaches the whole fruit.) The skin of the chile should turn brown, with small blisters indicating that the skin is peeling off. It is important not to burn them completely, however, or they'll turn sour. Once roasted, chiles are removed from the heat and placed inside a plastic bag or moistened towel for 15 minutes, so that they can "sweat." Finally, the chiles are cleaned up by removing the skin and all of its seeds, which can be done with the help of a kitchen towel or under running water. However, if you need to peel a large amount of chiles, the easiest way is to fry them, one by one, in plenty of oil. The procedure is basically the same, but faster, because hot oil reaches the whole surface of the skin at the same time.

2. DRIED CHILES

CLEANING AND DESEEDING THE CHILES

Sometimes dried chiles are a bit dirty when they reach your kitchen. You can use a moistened kitchen towel to clean them, if that's the case. When removing the seeds, you can make a cut on one of the sides if you're cooking them whole. But if you're grinding them, seeds and veins must be removed from the top, around the stem. It helps to soak them in water beforehand.

ROASTING THE CHILES

Many recipes ask that you "awaken" the flavor and aroma of the chiles by roasting them in advance. You can roast them on a comal or directly over the flame until roasted and fragrant. The heat must be evenly distributed over the surface of the chiles, and you should be careful not to burn them, or they'll get sour. Seeds are easily removed from roasted chiles.

REHYDRATING THE CHILES

In other recipes, dried chiles should be rehydrated before being used, sometimes even after roasting them. It is amazing to observe how this process brings new life into the chiles. It's all about soaking them in a bowl with enough water to cover them completely, plus adding some salt and a few drops of vinegar. This water is used afterwards in some recipes, but not always. Seeds can easily be removed after rehydrating the chiles.

FRYING THE CHILES

Chiles can be fried for the same reasons they're usually roasted, and if you're serving a dish with a side of dried chiles, frying them is the best way to prepare them. Even when the procedure is different, both have similar results. You must be careful not to burn them, because they will turn sour. The seeds are also easily removed from fried chiles.

3. TOMATOES AND ONIONS

Almost every recipe that includes red tomatoes in its ingredients requires that you peel them in advance, unless it's a salad or you puree them in a blender. If you don't remove the skin, it will appear in pieces again in your salsas and dishes, and they won't look as good. Peeling raw red tomatoes is very simple. First, you place them in boiling water for a minute or so, and then remove them when the water starts to return to a boil. Once they're cold again, the skin is easy to remove and the fruit will still be plump and fresh.

To peel roasted red tomatoes, you have to roast them carefully over a comal on every side without letting them burn. Remove the roasted tomatoes from the comal and let them cool off for a couple of minutes. It's easy to peel them using a knife, but best to do it on a plate to keep the juice from going everywhere.

Green tomatoes (tomatillos) are different. It's good to know that this particular fruit comes with a natural, leaf-like enclosure, with a slightly sticky sap around the tomato. Sometimes this has been removed before they are put on sale. You must wash them thoroughly under running water. Their skin can be peeled off using the same techniques as with red tomatoes.

NEUTRALIZING THE ONIONS

Some people find the flavor of raw onions disagreeable or too persistent in the mouth. Neutralizing this flavor is not difficult at all. Just cut the onion in slices and soak them in plenty of water with salt and a few drops of lime juice for half an hour. Drain the water, and they're ready!

IT BURNS!

Chiles can be seriously hot, and when they are, they really burn! Several methods are used to alleviate the burn from a hot chile. The most used technique is to put salt on your tongue. Others prefer to drink something very cold. Both procedures do work, but it has been scientifically proven that the chemistry of dairy products acts to neutralize the uncomfortable burn of the chiles. It is advisable to eat cheese or sour cream with your salsas, and luckily, they're both quite common in Mexican dishes. This suggests that this is precisely their role as an ingredient: to extinguish the fire. Or, if you prefer, you can drink a glass of cold milk with your tacos.

36 SUPER SALSAS COOKBOOK

1 MEXICAN-STYLE SALSA

MAKES 1 CUP (250 ML)

—½ medium onion, cubed
—2 medium tomatoes, diced
—3 green serrano chiles, seeded and finely chopped
—3 sprigs cilantro, roughly chopped
—Sea salt and fresh lime juice or apple cider vinegar

1. If you want to neutralize the onion after chopping, place it in a strainer under running water or let it soak in water for a couple of minutes, then drain and place in a medium bowl.
2. Mix the vegetables, chiles, and cilantro in the bowl, and season with salt and lime juice or vinegar to taste. Serve immediately.

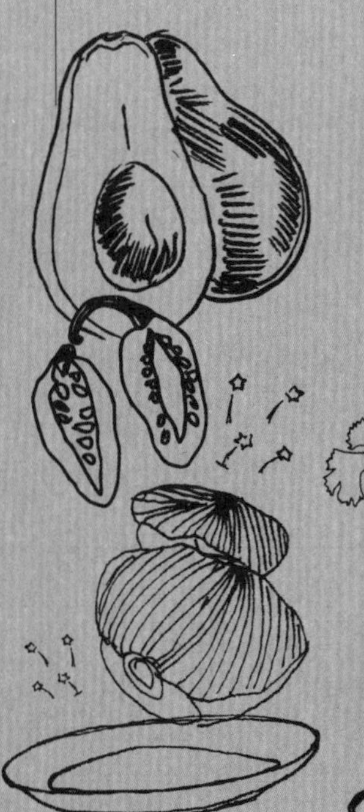

2 MEXICAN-STYLE RAW RED SALSA

MAKES 1 CUP (250 ML)

—2 large tomatoes, quartered
—½ medium onion, quartered
—1 sprig cilantro, roughly chopped
—6 roughly chopped green serrano chiles
—Sea salt

Process all the ingredients in the blender, adding a little water and salt as needed, until you have a coarse salsa. Serve immediately.

Variation
Once all the ingredients are blended, add a little additional chopped onion and cilantro leaves for extra texture. The juice of half a lime may also be added.

3 RAW GREEN SALSA

MAKES 1 CUP (250 ML)

—4 roughly chopped green serrano chiles
—6 large tomatillos, husked and quartered
—½ medium onion, quartered
—1 sprig cilantro

Grind all the ingredients in the blender, adding a little water and salt as needed, until you have a smooth salsa. Serve immediately.

Variation
1. Once all the ingredients are blended, add a little extra chopped onion, cilantro leaves, and two mint leaves. Blend again and serve.
2. Add the juice of half a lime.
3. Add cubes of avocado to the salsa just before serving.

4 HABANERO CHILE ONION SALSA

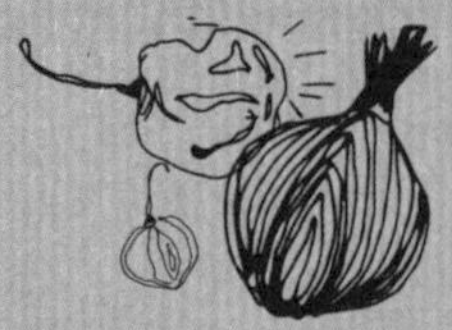

MAKES 1 CUP (250 ML)

—2 habanero chiles
—1 medium red onion, halved and cut into small cubes
—Juice from 4 limes
—Coarse salt

1. Devein and seed half of the chiles. Cut the chiles into thin slices.
2. Mix the chiles and onion together in a bowl with the lime juice and plenty of salt. Let sit for 30 minutes to marinate, and eat on the same day.

5 YUCATÁN-STYLE HABANERO CHILE SALSA

MAKES 1 CUP (250 ML)

—2 habanero chiles
—1 medium red onion, finely chopped
—¼ medium green or red cabbage, finely chopped
—2 medium radishes, finely chopped
—Juice from 2 limes
—Sea salt

1. Devein and seed one of the chiles. Slice the chiles.
2. If desired, you can neutralize the onion in advance using a strainer under running water or soaking it for a couple of minutes.
3. Mix the vegetables in a bowl with the lime juice and salt. Let sit for 30 minutes to marinate, then eat on the same day.

6 MANZANO CHILE ONION SALSA

MAKES 1 CUP (250 ML)

—2 habanero chiles, deseeded and sliced
—1 medium white or yellow onion, halved and thinly sliced
—4 medium limes, cut into wedges
—Coarse salt

Place the chiles and onion in a nonreactive bowl, squeeze the limes over the top, scatter with coarse salt, and mix well. Serve the same day.

7 GUACAMOLE

MAKES 1 CUP (250 ML)

—2 medium ripe avocados
—1 large tomato, cubed
—2 green serrano chiles, finely sliced (seeded if you prefer it milder)
—½ medium onion, chopped

—3 sprigs cilantro, finely chopped
—Sea salt
—Juice from ½ lime

1. Peel the avocadoes and mash the pulp with a fork in a large bowl until you make an even paste.
2. Mix the vegetables and herbs in a bowl and season to taste with salt and lime juice. Serve immediately. (To prevent your guacamole from turning black, leave the pits of the avocado inside the mixture.)

8 RAW MOLCAJETE-STYLE TACO SALSA

MAKES 1 CUP (250 ML)

—1 large tomato, quartered
—2 medium tomatillos, husked and quartered
—2 green serrano chiles, chopped
—2 fresh arbol chiles, chopped
—½ medium onion, quartered
—1 clove garlic
—3 sprigs cilantro, chopped
—Sea salt

Manually grind all the ingredients with a *molcajete* or stone mortar and pestle into a rough salsa, adding water and salt as needed. Serve immediately.

Variation
Once the salsa is ready, add additional chopped onion and whole cilantro leaves. Add the juice of ½ lime.

HOLY GUACAMOLE

Even if the Oxford English Dictionary defines "guacamole" (from the Aztec *ahuacamulli*) as "A dish of mashed avocado mixed with chopped onion, tomatoes, chiles, and seasoning," in reality, it's much more complex. In fact, we really need to come up with new words to clearly express the many variations and characteristics of guacamole, just as the Inuit are reputed to have many different words for snow. All Mexicans are experts on the subject, and many foreigners, too, are prepared to fight to the death to defend their version. It therefore might not only be a risky endeavor to try to probe deeper into the subject, but also a paradoxically fruitless one, as it is a dish impossible to fully encompass or describe. Very spicy, or without chiles; diced, or in liquid form; with cilantro, with oregano, or with mint; with oil, with milk, with sour cream—or with cheese!; with red or green tomatoes; well-blended, or in bite-sized chunks... To fully comprehend the wealth of guacamole varieties, we must approach the matter carefully, beginning with the avocado itself. Avocado is the fruit of a tree native to the Americas, which belongs to the genus Persea americana mill, of which there are three principal varieties or families: Mexican, Guatemalan, and Caribbean. These also vary in color, texture, size of the pit, etc., but the principal differences lie (ask an expert!) in the flavor that each one of the varieties brings to the table. But in the end, all of them are good for guacamole.

If you already have an avocado, you will also need:

THE CLASSIC INGREDIENTS:

1. Green chiles

The mix of chiles and avocado is an ancient combination. In fact, we can translate the Aztec word *ahucamulli* as avocado salsa—or *mulli* (*mole* sauce)—which suggests the presence of chiles in the mix. The preferred choices are serrano, jalapeño, or *cuaresmeño* chiles; but you can use any kind of green (meaning freshly harvested) chiles. There's no right amount of chiles for a guacamole, it all depends on your taste. Some people chop them in large chunks, to make them visible, and also to make it possible to remove them if necessary. Others chop them finely, or you can grind the chiles before adding them to the mix. It's also possible to achieve a milder taste by removing the veins and/or seeds before chopping the chiles.

2. Onion

The Spanish conquistadors brought this plant to America, and it makes a regular appearance in guacamole, whether roughly and thickly chopped or perfectly ground in the blender or *molcajete*.

3. Cilantro

This herb arrived in the Spanish caravels, but blended in perfectly in Mexican kitchens—so much so that many would swear it's native to the country. You can grind it, chop it finely or roughly, or scatter the whole leaves over the guacamole almost as a garnish.

4. Tomatoes

The magical combination of tomato and avocado leads us to suppose that this delightful mix is also an ancient tradition. You can use red tomatoes, but local varieties (which come in many different colors) are also often found in guacamole, and it is also made with the green tomato or tomatillo as well.

ADDITIONAL INGREDIENTS:

1. Lime juice and vinegar

There's still a sharp dispute about whether these two ingredients belong in a guacamole or not. There are those who believe that a few drops of lime juice, on top of enhancing the flavor, also prevent the avocado turning black. Others argue that the flavor of lime takes over all the others, distorting the guacamole's real taste. Using vinegar is far less common, but it has the same tartness and antioxidant virtues.

2. Herbs

Papaloquelite, mint, epazote, marjoram, oregano; each one on its own. You must learn their flavors and effects to really get a hold of how to employ them in guacamole. They're used in very specific cases, for guacamoles that are meant to be enjoyed with particular foods.

3. Other chiles

The same jalapeño, *cuaresmeño*, or serrano chiles can be used even if they're fully ripe and have turned yellow or red. You can also used dried chiles, like piquin, or chiltepin chiles (also known as chile *de monte*), or arbol chile, even if it's not the ideal nor the usual choice. Jalapeños in vinegar, canned chipotles, or commercial hot sauce are only used in extreme cases and exotic variations, when you have no other option, in areas near the U.S. border, or, now, by creative foreigners.

4. Garlic

Raw garlic adds a bitter taste and a special hotness to the preparation, as well as deepening the aroma. It is not one of the typical ingredients, but its use is no capital sin either. However, the flavor of roasted or fried garlic is too intense to be part of an orthodox guacamole.

5. Oil

Even when many natural fats are present in avocados, adding olive or vegetable oil to a guacamole is perfectly respectable. They're used as much for their flavor as to increase the volume of the mix, and to make its texture even smoother. The use of other oils, like peanut or sesame, is not recommended. Some people substitute the oil with mayonnaise, adding a little extra flavor to the guacamole.

6. Dairy products

These are the few dairy products that are occasionally added to guacamole: sour cream, to soften the flavor of the avocados; milk, to make the mix more liquid; cheese, as a garnish; or aged cheese (like Cotija or *chincho*) to add a contrasting kick.

7. Fruits and vegetables

Although it may seem hard to believe, there are people who add very curious ingredients to their guacamole: diced mango, pineapple, or *nopales*. Guacamole is also frequently served as a dip for other raw vegetables, like carrots, cucumbers, or celery.

What else can we say that won't raise people's hackles? You'll find guacamole in three main consistencies or presentations: liquefied, as a salsa; ground and thick, as a paste; and chopped or diced, like a salad. Truth is that, when it comes to guacamole, no one ever gets the last word.

COOKED SALSAS

9 EASY RED SALSA WITH ARBOL CHILE

MAKES 1 CUP (250 ML)

—6 dried red arbol chiles
—2 medium tomatoes
—2 cloves garlic
—½ medium onion
—Sea salt and apple cider vinegar

1. Grind the vegetables in a blender, adding water as needed, until you have a loose salsa.
2. Add salt and a few drops of vinegar to taste.

Variation
Once the salsa is ready, add roughly chopped onion and whole fresh cilantro leaves.

10 GROUND GREEN SALSA WITH PIQUIN OR CHILTEPIN CHILES

MAKES 1/3 CUP (75 ML)

—2 tablespoons green serrano chiles
—Sea salt and apple cider vinegar

Manually grind the chiles in a *molcajete* (or grind them very briefly in the blender) with just a little water until you have a coarse salsa. Pour into a bowl and add vinegar and salt to taste.

11 COOKED RED SALSA

MAKES ½–1 CUP (125–250 ML)

—6 green serrano chiles
—½ medium onion
—1 clove garlic
—2 medium tomatoes
—2 sprigs cilantro
—Corn oil

1. Grind all the ingredients in a blender, adding water as needed, until you have a loose salsa. (You can roast or fry the chiles, onion, garlic, and tomatoes, or you can use them raw.)
2. Heat the sauce in a skillet with a little corn oil over medium heat until it thickens and changes color. (You can also boil and sieve the salsa to make it thinner.)
3. Refrigerate for up to 1 week.

Variation
Once you remove the salsa from the heat, add chopped onion and cilantro.

12 COOKED GREEN SALSA

MAKES ½–1 CUP (125–250 ML)

—8 medium tomatillos, husks removed
—½ medium onion
—1 clove garlic
—1 sprig cilantro
—1 sprig epazote
—8 green serrano chiles
—Sea salt
—Corn oil

1. Boil the vegetables and herbs in a stockpot with 2 cups of water and a pinch of salt for 5 minutes. Remove from heat and let cool slightly.
2. Remove the epazote and grind the boiled vegetables in a blender, with 1 cup of cooking water, until smooth.
3. Pour the salsa in a skillet and fry with a little corn oil until it thickens. Season to taste with salt and remove from heat.
4. Refrigerate for up to 1 week.

Variation
Once you remove the salsa from the heat, add chopped onion and cilantro leaves.

13 COOKED TACO SALSA

MAKES ½–1 CUP (125–250 ML)

—2 large tomatoes
—3 medium tomatillos, husks removed
—2 green serrano chiles
—3 dried arbol chiles
—½ medium onion
—1 clove garlic
—3 sprigs cilantro
—½ tablespoon ground cumin
—½ tablespoon dried oregano
—Sea salt
—Corn oil

1. Grind the vegetables and herbs in a blender, adding water and salt until smooth.
2. Using a little oil, cook the sauce over a medium heat in a skillet until thickened. (You can also boil and sieve the salsa to make it thinner.)
3. Refrigerate for up to 1 week.

Variation
Once you remove the salsa from the heat, add

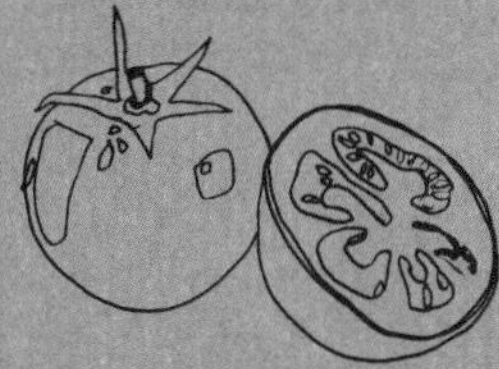

additional chopped onion and cilantro leaves.

14 SALSA RANCHERA

MAKES 1–1 ½ CUPS (250–350 ML)

—10 *cuaresmeño* or serrano chiles (red or green)
—2 large tomatoes, peeled
—Olive oil
—1 medium onion, sliced into strips
—1 clove garlic, finely chopped
—1 cup (250 ml) chicken broth
—1 tablespoon dried oregano
—Sea salt and freshly ground black pepper
—¼ lb (100 g) *panela* cheese, diced

1. Remove the veins from the chiles and cut them into strips. Soak in a bowl of salted water for 1 hour.
2. Chop the tomatoes very finely, until you have a smooth paste. Set aside.

3. Heat a little olive oil in a skillet. Add the onion and cook over medium heat, about 1 minute until transparent. Add the garlic and cook for another 1 minute.
4. Drain and add the chiles to the skillet. Stir-fry the mix for 1 minute, but do not let the vegetables brown.
5. Add the tomato and cook for 1 minute. When the salsa starts to lose its liquid, add the broth, oregano, and season to taste with salt and pepper.
6. Raise the heat to medium-high and let the salsa boil until it thickens. Finally, add the cheese and serve.

Variations
1. Omit the cheese.
2. Omit the tomatoes.

15 RED ARBOL CHILE SALSA

MAKES ½–1 CUP (125–250 ML)

—6 arbol chiles
—Corn oil
—1 medium tomato
—1 clove garlic
—¼ medium onion
—Sea salt and apple vinegar

1. Roast the chiles on a comal, or fry in a little oil.
2. Grind everything in a blender, adding water as needed, until you have a loose salsa.
3. Cook the salsa in a skillet with a little oil for 3–5 minutes, or until it thickens.
4. Add salt and a few drops of vinegar to taste, and serve.

Variation
Once the salsa is ready, add additional chopped onion and fresh cilantro leaves.

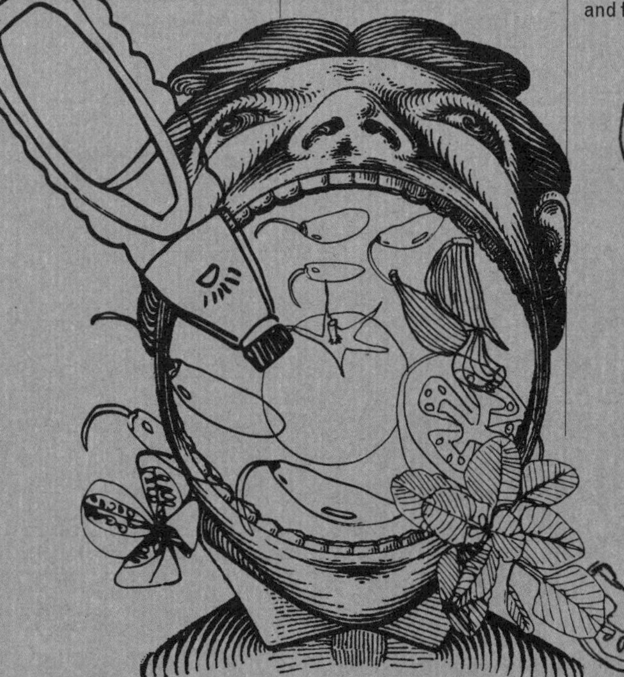

16 ROASTED CHIPOTLE CHILE SALSA

MAKES ½–1 CUP (125–250 ML)

—2 dried chipotle chiles
—Balsamic vinegar
—1 medium tomato
—2 cloves garlic
—¼ medium onion
—2 sprigs cilantro
—1 bay leaf
—2 mint leaves
—2 epazote leaves
—½ tablespoon fresh marjoram leaves
—Sea salt

1. Roast the chiles on a comal; then soak in warm water with a few drops of vinegar for 30 minutes. Drain the chiles and grind with the tomato, garlic, onion, and cilantro in a blender with a little water until the salsa is loose.
2. Fry the salsa in a skillet with a little oil over a low heat for about 3–5 minutes, until thickened.
3. Finely chop the bay leaf, mint, epazote, and marjoram. Add the fresh leaves to the salsa with salt to taste. Cook for 5 minutes in the skillet, and serve immediately.

17 ANCHO CHILE SALSA

MAKES ½–1 CUP (125–250 ML)

—4 large dried ancho chiles
—2 dried arbol chiles
—2 medium tomatoes
—½ medium onion
—1 clove garlic
—½ tablespoon ground cumin
—Corn oil
—Sea salt and apple cider vinegar

1. Roast all the chiles on a comal for 3–5 minutes, being careful not to burn them.
2. Add the chiles to a pot with the tomatoes, onion, garlic, cumin, and 1 cup (250 ml) water, and boil for 5 minutes.
3. Grind all the ingredients in a blender or with a mortar and pestle until you have a loose salsa. Strain the salsa through a fine sieve, and cook in a little oil in a skillet until it is a smooth, thick sauce. Add a few drops of vinegar, salt, and water as needed, and cook for 5 minutes, until the salsa has thickened.

18 PASILLA CHILE DEVILED SALSA

MAKES 1–1½ CUPS (250–350 ML)

—2 tablespoons corn oil
—15 pasilla chiles
—10 cloves garlic (about 2 heads)
—1 medium onion
—2 bay leaves
—1 sprig thyme
—1 sprig marjoram
—5 whole black peppercorns
—3 whole cloves
—2 cups (500 ml) apple cider or white wine vinegar
—1 cup (250 ml) olive oil

1. Roast or fry the chiles for 2–3 minutes, without letting them turn bitter.
2. Cook the chiles, garlic, onion, bay leaves, thyme, marjoram, pepper, cloves, and vinegar in a medium pot for 20 minutes over high heat.
3. Remove the salsa from heat and let cool slightly, then grind everything in a blender until you have a loose salsa.
4. Strain through a sieve (add water to make it easier), and pour the strained salsa back into the used pot. Bring back to high heat and cook again until it thickens, about 2 minutes.
5. Remove the salsa from heat and let cool slightly, then grind the salsa in the blender once more, pouring in the olive oil as you puree the salsa until smooth.
6. Let cool, uncovered; pour the resulting salsa in jars. Cover and chill. (The flavor improves over time.)

19 PEANUT SALSA

MAKES ½–1 CUP (125–250 ML)

—Olive oil
—4 dried ancho chiles
—2 dried pasilla chiles
—1 arbol chile
—4 oz (100 g) unsalted peanuts
—2 cloves garlic
—Sea salt
—1 cup (250 ml) chicken broth (if needed)

1. Heat a few inches of olive oil in a deep skillet. Add all the chiles and fry for a few minutes, but do not allow them to burn.
2. Strain the chiles, then add to a bowl with 1 cup (250 ml) hot water. Set aside and

soak for 20 minutes. Peel the skin from the chiles.
3. Fry the peanuts in the used frying oil for just a few seconds, until they change color. Remove from heat.
4. Process the chiles, soaking water, garlic, and fried peanuts in a blender until the salsa is smooth.
5. Transfer the pureed salsa to the skillet with the frying oil and bring to high heat, adding salt to taste, until slightly thickened. (If the salsa is too thick, thin it with the chicken broth.)
6. Pour the salsa into a glass jar, seal, and refrigerate. Store for up to 2 weeks.

20 MORITA CHILE SALSA

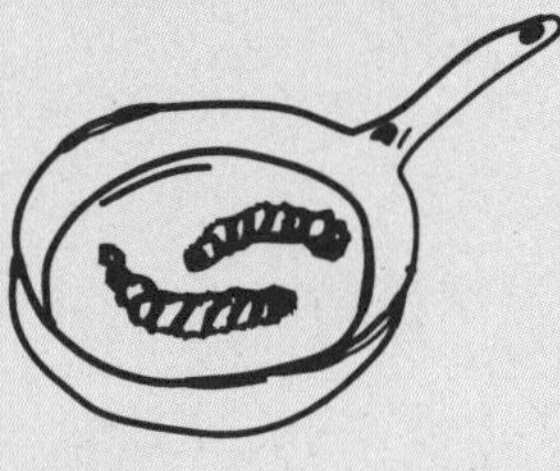

MAKES ½–1 CUP (120–150 ML)

—10 dried morita chiles
—2 medium tomatoes
—2 medium tomatillos
—½ medium onion
—1 clove garlic
—½ tablespoon ground cumin
—2 sprigs cilantro
—3 epazote leaves
—1 tablespoon dried oregano
—2 tablespoons corn oil
—1 tablespoon brown sugar
—Sea salt and apple cider vinegar

1. Roast chiles in a comal or fry the chiles for 2–3 minutes and remove the seeds.
2. Add the chiles, tomatoes, tomatillos, onion, garlic, cumin, cilantro, epazote, and oregano to a large skillet and boil for 5 minutes with 1 cup (250 ml) of water.
3. Remove the cilantro and the epazote and grind together the cooked ingredients in a blender until you have a smooth salsa.
4. Fry the salsa with a little oil in a skillet, add the sugar and salt and vinegar to taste. Cook for 5 minutes, until it thickens. Serve immediately.

Variation
Add small pieces of pork cracklings to change the flavor and texture.

21 COOKED GUAJILLO CHILE SALSA

MAKES 1–1½ CUPS (250–350 ML)

—3 hot dried guajillo chiles
—6 sweet dried guajillo chiles
—3 medium tomatoes
—½ medium onion
—1 clove garlic
—Corn oil
—3 epazote leaves, finely chopped
—Sea salt and apple cider vinegar

1. Roast chiles in a comal or fry all the chiles for 2–3 minutes and remove the seeds.
2. Boil the chiles, tomatoes, onion, garlic, and 1 cup (250 ml) water in a pot for 5 minutes over medium heat.

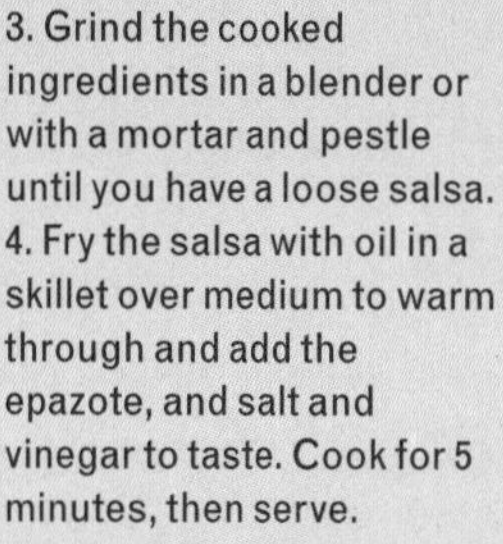

3. Grind the cooked ingredients in a blender or with a mortar and pestle until you have a loose salsa.
4. Fry the salsa with oil in a skillet over medium to warm through and add the epazote, and salt and vinegar to taste. Cook for 5 minutes, then serve.

22 GUAJILLO CHILE AND MAGUEY WORM SALSA

MAKES 1–1½ CUPS (250–350 ML)

—1 tablespoon corn oil
—4 oz (100 g) white maguey worms
—3 cups (750 ml) roasted guajillo chile salsa (see previous recipe)

1. Heat the oil in a large skillet. Add the worms and fry until brown over a medium-low heat, for about 7–10 minutes. Drain on a paper towel.
2. Grind the fried worms and the cooled salsa. Serve the salsa the same day.

GIVE IT MORE SALSA!

MIXED SALSAS

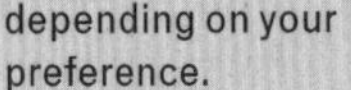

23 SAUTÉED MEXICAN-STYLE SALSA

MAKES 1–1½ CUPS (250–350 ML)

—¼ cup (50 ml) corn oil
—½ medium onion, chopped
—2 chopped green serrano chiles
—2 medium tomatoes, peeled and chopped
—Sea salt
—3 sprigs cilantro, chopped

1. Heat the oil in a large skillet. Add the onion and fry over low heat for 2–3 minutes; do not let it brown.
2. Add the chiles and fry for a few seconds. Add the tomatoes and cook to taste, either almost raw or until they are soft, depending on your preference.
3. Finish by adding the salt and cilantro. Remove from heat and eat while the salsa is still hot.

24 HAND-GROUND ROASTED TACO SALSA

MAKES 1–1½ CUPS (250–350 ML)

—1 large tomato
—2 medium tomatillos
—2 green serrano chiles
—3 dried arbol chiles
—½ medium onion
—1 clove garlic
—½ tablespoon ground cumin
—Sea salt
—3 sprigs cilantro
—Juice from ½ lime

1. Separately roast the tomato, tomatillos, chiles, onion, and garlic on a comal over low heat for 2–3 minutes each.
2. Grind all the ingredients by hand on the *molcajete*, starting with the cumin and the salt. Add the rest of the ingredients in the following order: chiles, garlic, cilantro, onion, and finally the tomatoes.
3. Season with a few drops of lime juice to taste, and serve.

25 GUAJILLO CHILE SALSA

MAKES 1–1½ CUPS (250–350 ML)

—2 hot dried guajillo chiles
—6 sweet dried guajillo chiles
—2 medium tomatoes
—2 cloves garlic
—Sea salt

1. Roast the chiles on a comal without burning them.
2. Soak the chiles in ½ cup (125 ml) fresh water for 30 minutes.
3. Grind all the ingredients, including the soaking water, in a blender until you have a smooth sauce. Season to taste with salt, and serve immediately.

26 DRUNKEN SALSA I

MAKES 1–1½ CUPS (250–350 ML)

—6 dried ancho chiles
—1 dried pasilla chile
—2 tablespoons corn oil
—¼ cup (50 ml) white pulque (or red or white wine or dark beer)
—1 clove garlic
—¼ cup (50 ml) fresh orange juice
—2 oz (50 g) aged cheese, grated
—Sea salt
—½ medium onion, sliced, for garnish

1. Roast in a comal or fry the chiles in the oil (do not burn) for 3–5 minutes over a low heat until crispy and remove the seeds.
2. Grind the chiles, pulque, garlic, and orange juice in a blender or mortar and pestle until you have a smooth salsa.
3. Pour the salsa into a bowl and add the cheese and salt to taste. Garnish with slices of onion and serve.

27 DRUNKEN SALSA II

MAKES 1–1½ CUPS (250–350 ML)

—4 dried ancho chiles
—4 dried pasilla chiles
—2 tablespoons corn oil
—1 cup (250 ml) white pulque, red or white wine, or dark beer
—6 medium tomatillos
—2 medium tomatoes
—1 clove garlic
—Sea salt
—¼ cup (50 ml) fresh orange juice
—½ medium onion, chopped
—2 oz (50 g) aged cheese, grated

1. Roast in a comal or fry the chiles in the oil (do not burn them) for 3–5 minutes over a low heat and remove the seeds. Soak the seedless chiles in the pulque in a small bowl for 20 minutes.
2. Grind the tomatillos, tomatoes, and the garlic in a mortar and pestle. Add the chiles and pulque and grind together for just a few seconds.
3. Pour the salsa in a bowl and add salt as needed. Add the orange juice and cheese. Serve immediately.

28 MOLCAJETE-STYLE BLACK SALSA

MAKES 1–1½ CUPS (250–350 ML)

3 dried arbol chiles
2 dried chipotle chiles
1 dried guajillo chile
2 medium tomatoes
½ medium onion
2 cloves garlic
2 sprigs cilantro, chopped
Sea salt

1. Roast and toast the chiles, tomatoes, onions, and garlic on a comal, without burning them.
2. Grind the salt and the garlic together using a *molcajete*. Add the chiles and grind, then chop the roasted onion and grind it into the mixture.
3. Remove the skin from the roasted tomatoes and chop, then grind into the salsa withthe cilantro. Add water and salt as needed. Serve immediately.

29 PASILLA CHILE "FLIES" SALSA

MAKES 1–1½ CUPS (250–350 ML)

—2 tablespoons corn oil
—3 large dried pasilla chiles
—½ medium onion, finely chopped
—2 tablespoons good-quality vinegar
—Sea salt
—¼ lb (100 g) hard cheese, grated

1. Heat the oil in a large skillet. Add the chiles and fry over a low heat for 2–3 minutes without letting them turn bitter. Seeds and chop the chiles, and place in a bowl with the onion.
2. Add the vinegar, salt to taste, and mix together.
3. Add the cheese on top and serve immediately.

30 EMULSIFIED GARLIC SALSA

MAKES 1–1½ CUPS (250–350 ML)

—1 cup (250 ml) vegetable oil
—2 heads garlic, cloves peeled and finely chopped
—Sea salt
—15 dried arbol chiles, chopped
—2 dried guajillo chiles, chopped
—½ cup (125 ml) red wine vinegar
—Olive oil

1. Heat the vegetable oil in a skillet. Add the garlic and cook on low heat with a pinch of salt until it browns, about 2–3 minutes.
2. Add the chiles and cook until they're golden brown. Add the vinegar, and cook for 2 minutes. Remove from heat and allow to cool, uncovered.
3. Once the mixture is cold, add a glug of olive oil, mix together, and transfer the salsa to a jar with a lid. Store refrigerated for up to 2 weeks.

PICKLED SALSAS

31 CHILES IN VINEGAR (ESCABECHE)

MAKES 2–3 ¾ CUPS (500–950 ML)

—Olive oil
—1 garlic bulb, cloves peeled and separated
—4 medium carrots, peeled and sliced
—1 lb 2 oz (500 g) jalapeño chiles
—20 green onions, roots and green leaves trimmed
—2 cups (500 ml) red or white wine vinegar
—5 bay leaves
—1 sprig marjoram
—1 sprig thyme
—1 tablespoon dried oregano
—5 black peppercorns
—Sea salt

1. Heat 2 tablespoons oil in a large saucepan. Add the garlic and the carrots and fry for 2 minutes. Add and stir-fry the chiles and the onions for another 2 minutes in the hot oil.
2. Add the vinegar and enough water to cover all the ingredients, and add the bay leaves, herbs, pepper, and salt to taste.
3. Return the liquid to a boil, stir with a wooden spoon, and let cook for 7 minutes. Remove from heat. (The ingredients must be well cooked but still fresh.)
4. Cover the pot and let cool for 15 minutes. Transfer to a glass jar and cover tightly. Cool before serving. Store, refrigerated, for up to 20 days.

Variations
1. Add cauliflower, mushrooms, or zucchini.
2. Cut the chiles in slices or rings before cooking them. This style is known as "*rajas* in vinegar."

32 PICKLED CHIPOTLES

MAKES 2–3 CUPS (500–750 ML)

—15 dried chipotle chiles
—2 cups (500 ml) red or white wine vinegar, plus more for soaking chiles
—2 tablespoon corn or vegetable oil
—1 bulb garlic, cloves separated and peeled
—1 medium onion, sliced
—4 medium carrots, peeled and sliced
—1 tablespoon brown sugar
—2 whole cloves
—1 bunch of mixed herbs (bay leaves, marjoram, thyme), tied together
—1 allspice berry
—Sea salt

1. The night before preparing the salsa, cover the chiles in warm water in a glass bowl with a few drops of vinegar. Let soak overnight.
2. Heat the oil in a deep skillet. Add the garlic and cook for 1 minute. Add the onions and carrots and cook them until they become translucent, about 1 minute.
3. Add the chiles and their soaking water to the skillet. Add the vinegar and enough water to cover all the ingredients. Add the sugar, cloves, herbs, allspice, and salt. Stir with a wooden spoon when it starts to boil.

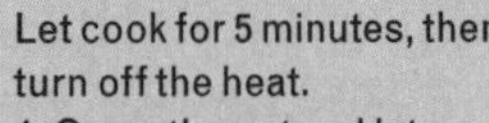

Let cook for 5 minutes, then turn off the heat.
4. Cover the pot and let cool for 15 minutes. Transfer the pickles in a glass jar and cover tightly.
5. Cool before serving. Store, refrigerated, for up to 3 weeks.

Variation
You can pickle other vegetables, such as cauliflower or mushrooms, with this recipe.

MARINADES AND SAUCES

33 ANNATTO MARINADE

MAKES 2–3 CUPS (500–750 ML)

—1 dried sweet guajillo chile
—2 tablespoons corn oil
—½ cup (125 ml) chopped onion
—2 cloves garlic
—1 tablespoon achiote paste
—1 tablespoon sugar
—3 black peppercorns
—1 tablespoon dried oregano
—2 whole cloves
—½ tablespoon ground cumin
—½ tablespoon ground cinnamon
—1 pinch ground anise
—½ tablespoon dried oregano
—1 allspice berry
—1 cup (250 ml) fresh orange juice
—Sea salt and apple cider vinegar

1. Roast in a comal or fry the chiles in the oil over low heat for 2–3 minutes until crispy without letting them turn bitter. Remove the seeds.
2. Grind the chiles, onion, garlic, sugar, and spices together in a blender until well-combined.
3. Add the orange juice, salt, and a few drops of vinegar to the blender, and pulse to combine.
4. Use this seasoning to marinade meats before cooking.

34 ANCHO CHILE MARINADE

MAKES 1 CUP (250 ML)

—3 large dried ancho chiles
—1 dried guajillo chile
—1 dried pasilla chile
—1 cup (250 ml) fresh orange juice
—1 medium tomato
—½ medium onion
—2 cloves garlic
—½ tablespoon ground cumin
—3 bay leaves
—1 pinch ground anise
—1 whole clove
—½ teaspoon fresh marjoram
—1 pinch ground cinnamon
—2 tablespoons corn or vegetable oil
—Sea salt and apple cider vinegar

1. Roast or fry the chiles without letting them turn bitter. Remove the seeds.
2. Transfer the chiles to a pot and add the orange juice, tomato, onion, garlic, cumin, bay leaves, anise, clove, marjoram, and cinnamon. Bring to a boil and cook for 5 minutes.
3. Let the liquid cool slightly, then transfer to the blender and grind to a smooth mixture.
4. Strain the mixture of any residual solids and then add it to a clean skillet with a little oil. Heat the sauce with salt, a few drops of vinegar, and water as needed, cooking for 5 minutes over a medium heat until it thickens.

35 TACOS GONZÁLEZ-STYLE SALSA

(López y Vizcaínas, Centro, D.F.)

MAKES 1–1½ CUPS (250–350 ML)

—Coarse salt
—2 cloves garlic
—2 habanero chiles
—2 jalapeño chiles
—3 medium tomatoes
—1 medium onion, cut into chunks

1. Grind the salt and garlic to a paste using a *molcajete*. Add the habanero chiles and grind into the mixture.
2. Roast the jalapeños and tomatoes on the comal.
3. Cut the tomatoes and grind them at the *molcajete*. Slice the chiles and add them to the *molcajete*.
4. Add the onion to the *molcajete*, and grind everything together once more. Season to taste with salt.

36 PICO DE GALLO

MAKES 1–1½ CUPS (250–350 ML)

—1 medium jicama, diced ¼-inch
—2 medium tomatoes, cubed
—1 medium onion, chopped
—2 jalapeño chiles, deveined and finely chopped
—1 green serrano chile, finely chopped
—1 small sprig cilantro, chopped
—1 oz (30 ml) fresh orange juice
—A splash of vodka
—Sea salt

Mix the vegetables, chiles, and cilantro together in a bowl. Add the orange juice, vodka, and salt to taste. Serve immediately.

PARA
INCLUYE
TORTILLAS
ORDENES DE
POLLO
MEDIO
TACO
TORTA
PESCUEZOS
SALCHICHAS
REFRESCOS
DE LATA
TORTILLAS
PAPAS

EXTINTOR
Papas!

GLOSSARY OF INGREDIENTS AND OTHER CURIOSITIES

ACHIOTE
A natural coloring and condiment, also known as annatto. *72, 163, 166, 169, 203*

AL MOJO
Fish prepared with garlic and butter. *208*

ANTOJITOS
Literally "little cravings," *antojitos* are traditional corn-based Mexican delicacies. *275–278*

BISTEC
In tacos, any piece of meat cut into thin slices. From the English "beef steak." *72, 82*

CAMPECHANO
Slang word for something improvised — used for certain kinds of tacos. *84*

CECINA
Thinly sliced, salted meat cured in a dry and well-ventilated place. *72, 83, 84, 87, 265*

CECINA ENCHILADA
A version of *cecina* made from pork, salt cured and marinated in achiote with ground chiles. *72*

CHARALES
Very small silversides that can be found fresh or dried, with or without seasoning. *208*

CHARRO BEANS
A *charro* is a Mexican cowboy, and this is a hearty dish of stewed pinto beans. *72, 77*

CHILANGO
Chilango means someone from Mexico City. *137, 217*

COA
A pre-Hispanic wooden hoe for working in the *milpa*. *36*

COMAL
Circular flat griddle traditionally made from clay, now usually from metal. *37, 81, 187, 249*

CUÑETE
Small barrel used to preserve fish. *209*

ESCABECHE
Pickled chiles, often with onion, potato, carrot, and cauliflower. *134, 209, 250, 308*

HUITLACOCHE
Huitlacoche is an edible fungus that grows on corn cobs. *249, 253, 256*

LONGANIZA
Pork sausage stuffed with chiles and spices and cured. *75, 84, 87, 217, 223*

MACHACA
Shredded dried beef. *176, 206, 208, 230, 261*

MACIZA
Lean meat. *123, 144, 146*

MECAPAL
A leather or fiber strap that transfers the weight of a load from the carrier's back to his head. *207*

MEMELAS
Long, tapered maize tortillas. *228, 249, 277*

METATE
A flat, rectangular mortar dating from pre-Hispanic times. *34–36, 40*

MEXTLAPIQUE
Seared fish that can be reheated in the same natural wrapping, or rehydrated in a sauce. *207*

MILPA
Traditional system of small fields used for growing maize, beans, and squashes. *243*

MOLE
Generic name for a thick, richly flavored sauce made with a large number of spices, seeds, nuts, and sometimes chocolate. *190*

NIXTAMAL
The process of boiling maize in lime then grinding it to make corn masa. *34–41*

NOPALES
Nopales are the edible pads of the prickly pear cactus. *181, 218*

PAPALOQUELITE
Also known as *papalo*, it is a herb used fresh in guacamole and other dishes, and tastes similar to cilantro. *84, 106, 146, 218*

PESCADO ZARANDEADO
Fish grilled over wood to infuse it with its aroma. *208*

PICADILLO
Ground beef with carrots, potatoes, peas, and tomatoes. *151, 177, 227, 276*

PICO DE GALLO
Between a salsa and a salad, this ubiquitous garnish is made with chopped tomato, onion, cilantro, and lime juice. *167, 309*

PIPIÁN
Pipián is a variety of *mole*, made with pumpkin or squash seeds. *173, 291*

POZOLE
A pre-Hispanic soup made with whole grains of maize, meat, and chiles. It had a ritual meaning. *230*

REQUESÓN
A dairy product with a coarse and crumbly texture like ricotta. *230, 233*

SALAZÓN
The process of drying meat with salt in the heat of the sun. *208*

SALPICÓN
A cold meat dish condimented with lemon, onion, and oregano and eaten with tostadas. *179, 208*

TAMEME
A person who transported goods in pre-Hispanic Mesoamerica. 207

TAPESCO
A structure made of sticks and leaves traditionally used for smoking fish and meat. *71, 207*

TASAJO
A type of beef jerky popular in the state of Oaxaca. *72, 261, 264, 265*

TORTA
A sandwich made with a bread roll. *113*

TORTA AHOGADA
A sandwich "drowned" in a red chile or tomato sauce. *285*

TOSTADA
A hard fried or baked tortilla served with the various types of taco fillings, often for cold dishes. *278*

WORMSEED
Known as epazote in Spanish, it is a herb similar in taste to cilantro. *195, 223, 233*

INDEX OF RECIPES

T

Z

INDEX OF TAQUERÍAS AND RESTAURANTS

A

B

C

D

INTERVIEWS

BERNARDO AJA *263*
ERICK ALBA *149*
MÓNICA BRAUN *157*
ALEJANDRO ESCALANTE *85, 95, 117, 127, 137, 193, 201, 221, 243*
ERICK FALCÓN *211*
SERGIO HEISINGER *75, 107, 179, 231, 253*
ISAÍAS QUIJANO *167*

PHOTOGRAPHY

BERNARDO AJA *191, 258, 260, 263, 264*
BENJAMÍN ALCÁNTARA *14–15*
GEORGINA ÁVILA *60–61*
MÓNICA BRAUN *145*
ARTURO BUITRÓN *86, 98–99, 117, 166, 234–235, 238, 246–247, 248*
DANTE BUSQUETS *10*
INÉS ECHEVARRÍA *186, 244, 318–319*
ERICK FALCÓN *206, 210, 211*
HÉCTOR GUERRERO *112, 115, 116, 118, 119–120*
DÉBORAH HOLTZ *136*
JESÚS LÓPEZ *129, 136, 252, 232, 279*
JUAN CARLOS MENA *10, 11, 279, 298*
VÍCTOR MENDIOLA *65*
GUILLERMO MERINO *19*
PABLO NAVAJAS *80, 90, 94, 110–111, 222, 279 , 310–311*
JORGE PERAZA *154, 157, 158, 160–161*
ISAÍAS QUIJANO *162, 164, 167, 170–171*
HÉCTOR RAMOS *193*
MARCEL RIUS *18, 19, 21, 75, 85, 86, 88–89, 95, 104, 105, 107, 124, 126, 127, 130–131, 132, 134, 135, 137, 138, 140–141, 148, 166, 168, 178, 179, 184–185, 194, 201, 202, 204–205, 218, 219, 220, 221, 226, 231, 232 , 242, 243, 244, 252, 253, 256–257, 266–267, 304–305, 316–317*
IVÁN SÁNCHEZ *142, 148, 149, 152–153*
PAULO VIDALES *1, 23, 94, 122, 126, 128, 216, 220, 224–225*
ADAM WISEMAN *11, 20, 36, 37, 41, 43, 44–45, 46, 47, 58, 59, 62, 63, 66, 67, 70, 74, 78–79, 96, 100, 105, 108, 150, 172, 180, 189, 191, 194, 196–197, 198, 212, 214–215, 254, 262, 274, 279, 281, 282, 283, 286, 289, 292, 293, 294*

ARCHIVE PHOTOS

FOTOTECA NACIONAL ©399205 *(35, top)*, 197955 *(35, bottom)*, 399396 *(43, top)* CONACULTA.INAH. SINAFO.FN.MÉXICO
© LATINSTOCK/*Album/Oronoz/ Album Art (Tlatelolco Market), 43*
©THE GRANGER COLLECTION/ OTHER IMAGES HISTORY OF HUASTECA CIVILIZATION *28*
AZTEC HARVEST CEREMONY *30*

LA MOLENDERA *34*
WORKS BY DIEGO RIVERA
(26, 28, 32 and 34) reproduced with the authorization of the Bank of Mexico: © 2012 Banco de México, executive trustee of the Diego Rivera & Frida Kahlo Museums Trust. 2 Cinco de Mayo, Col. Centro, Cuauhtémoc 06059, Mexico City.
© SENSACIONAL DE DISEÑO MEXICANO *33, 76*

INFOGRAPHICS

ÓSCAR REYES, BERENICE MARTÍNEZ *176*
KITZIA SÁMANO *268–269*

REPROGRAPHIC

BOB SCHALKWIJK *26*

ILLUSTRATIONS

JORGE AVIÑA *38–39, 73, 83, 93, 103, 115, 156, 165, 175, 188, 192, 200, 209, 219, 229, 241, 251, 261, 272–273*
BERENICE MARTÍNEZ *265*
ÓSCAR REYES *195*
KITZIA SÁMANO *29, 31, 35, 48, 49, 50, 51, 52, 53, 54, 55, 56, 57, 58, 59, 62, 63, 64, 65, 66, 67, 77, 87, 97, 102, 109, 119, 139, 159, 169, 181, 183, 203, 223, 233, 255, 265*

CARTOONS

JORGE AVIÑA

COLLAGES

ÓSCAR REYES and BERENICE MARTÍNEZ *275, 276, 277, 278, 280, 284, 285, 290, 291, 294*

ARTWORK

ALEC DEMPSTER *40*
IBRAHIM DOMÍNGUEZ *4–5*

SPECIAL TYPEFACES

ÓSCAR REYES

TACOS
CHINGONES
CHULETA
PECHUGA

GORDITAS
SEXYS
TACOS
PAMBAZOS
HUARACHES
QUESADILLAS
SOPES
ciel

SABEMOS QUE
LE URGE;
PERO... NO SON
ENCHILADAS

RECIPE NOTES

Butter should always be unsalted, unless otherwise specified.

Pepper is always freshly ground black pepper, unless otherwise specified.

Eggs, vegetables, and fruits are assumed to be large size, unless otherwise specified. For the UK, use medium eggs.

Milk is always whole, unless otherwise specified.

Cooking and preparation times are for guidance only, as individual ovens vary. If using a fan oven, follow the manufacturer's instructions concerning oven temperatures.

To test whether your deep-frying oil is hot enough, add a cube of stale bread. If it browns in thirty seconds, the temperature is 350–375°F / 180–190°C, about right for most frying. Exercise caution when deep frying: add the food carefully to avoid splashing, wear long sleeves, and never leave the pan unattended.

Some recipes include raw or very lightly cooked eggs. These should be avoided particularly by the elderly, infants, pregnant women, convalescents, and anyone with an impaired immune system.

ACKNOWLEDGEMENTS

The publisher would like to thank René Redzepi for bringing *Tacopedia* to our attention and Juan Carlos Mena and Déborah Holtz for creating an amazing book.

Phaidon Press Limited
Regent's Wharf
All Saints Street
London N1 9PA

Phaidon Press Inc.
65 Bleecker Street
New York, NY 10012
www.phaidon.com

First published in English 2015
Reprinted 2016

First published in Spanish by Trilce Ediciones as *La Tacopedia*

trilce.com.mx

This edition published by Phaidon Press Limited under licence from Trilce Ediciones, Carlos B. Zetina #61, Col. Escandón Mexico City, Mexico

A CIP catalogue record for this book is available from the British Library and the Library of Congress.

Conceived and originally edited by Déborah Holtz and Juan Carlos Mena
Original design: Juan Carlos Mena
Original design team: Brenda Rodriguez, Kitzia Sámano, and Óscar Reyes
Research and texts: Alejandro Escalante
The Tacography map was created by Déborah Holtz and Juan Carlos Mena

Commissioning Editor: Emily Takoudes
Project Editors: Laura Loesch-Quintin and Olga Massov
Production Controller: Amanda Mackie

Cover design by Hans Stofregen
Interior redesign by atlas.

Printed in Romania